RED CHINA'S GREEN REVOLUTION

Red China's Green Revolution

TECHNOLOGICAL INNOVATION, INSTITUTIONAL CHANGE, AND ECONOMIC DEVELOPMENT UNDER THE COMMUNE

Joshua Eisenman

Columbia University Press
New York

Columbia University Press
Publishers Since 1893
New York   Chichester, West Sussex
cup.columbia.edu
Copyright © 2018 Joshua Eisenman
All rights reserved

Library of Congress Cataloging-in-Publication Data
Names: Eisenman, Joshua, 1977- author.
Title: Red China's green revolution : technological innovation, institutional
change, and economic development under the commune / Joshua Eisenman.
Description: New York : Columbia University Press, [2018]
Identifiers: LCCN 2017054574 | ISBN 9780231186667 (hardcover and pbk. : alk. paper)
Subjects: LCSH: Green Revolution—China. | Communes (China) |
Agriculture—Economic aspects—China. | Agriculture and state—China.
Classification: LCC S471.C6 E37 2018 | DDC 338.10951—dc23 LC record
available at https://lccn.loc.gov/2017054574

ISBN 978-0231-18666-7 (hardcover)
ISBN 978-0231-18667-4 (paperback)
ISBN 978-0231-54675-1 (e-book)

Columbia University Press books are printed on permanent
and durable acid-free paper.
Printed in the United States of America

Cover design: Noah Arlow

To the memory of Richard Baum,
who taught me how to seek truth from facts.

CONTENTS

CONTENTS

LIST OF FIGURES
AND TABLES

LIST OF FIGURES AND TABLES

FOREWORD

This book offers a startling new analysis of China's most important local institution in Mao's time, the people's commune. In particular, it explores the least-well-reported years of recent Chinese history, the 1970s, when the country's so-called economic rise began. Most officials, journalists, and scholars still treat that institution and decade as simply radical and backward looking. Most of the 1970s is described misleadingly in many books as part of a basically homogeneous Cultural Revolution, before China began to prosper. The commune as an institution was indeed a failure after 1958, bringing famine and poverty to millions; so most writers presume it remained an economic and political failure until it was abolished during the few years after Deng Xiaoping became China's supremo in 1978.

To the contrary, Joshua Eisenman shows that after 1970 China's communes, production brigades, and production teams became crucial generators of rural prosperity. He uses new sources, presenting statistics to prove that rural productivity grew quickly—nationwide—in the 1970s. This achievement occurred not just in a few selected and traditionally rich regions, such as Jiangnan and Guangdong, where a few previous writers had noticed. Instead, this productivity was widespread in many parts of the country. Eisenman presents data from eight major provinces, and from China as a whole, demonstrating that rural production from the early 1970s rose rapidly per commune member, per land unit, and in total.

These findings refute the conventional, quasi-official story, which holds that before 1978 China's rural (as distinct from urban) economy was in dire straits, requiring neoliberal efficiencies to fix it. Eisenman's revisionist book offers hard data that disprove that conventional understanding. Communes, brigades, and teams bred more successful local leaders and entrepreneurs than practically anybody—including Deng Xiaoping, economists, or others—thought possible.

Maoist communes, with support from some central and local leaders, created China's green revolution. This change was supported by material elements (high-yield seeds, multi-cropping, controlled irrigation, agricultural extension, and high rates of rural saving and investment). These factors were also supported by strong communalist values. Most sources have defined China's reform as a post-1978 phenomenon—and have attributed it mainly to market efficiency. This usual periodization of the start of the economic surge begins nearly a decade too late. Change in the places where most Chinese lived—the countryside—have largely been ignored. Communalist–Maoist norms, as well as the improved agronomy that they sustained, brought more prosperity to the fields in which hundreds of millions of Chinese toiled during the late 1960s and early 1970s.

For the majority of Chinese, who tilled land, the 1970s was not a "lost decade." Intellectuals, who write history, indeed had a grim time. But Eisenman chronicles in the early 1970s a quick increase of rural electric generators, walking tractors, fertilizers, trucks, pumps, and tool shops in which to repair them. He points out that the Northern Districts Agricultural Conference, held in 1970, spread the green revolution to new areas. Agricultural extension and mechanization changed China well before 1978. This book offers extensive statistics on these concrete, situational factors of change—but it equally treats the communalist ideals and management organizations that supported these material inputs to the new agronomy, and then to rural factories.

The commune was the "church of Mao." Songs about Mao as savior of the East; dancers waving his *Little Red Book*; and posters of ardent workers, badges, and icons of the chairman demonstrated far more intense personal commitments than contemporary modern people generally muster for any cause. Such rituals are often derided in Western publications, yet a religion of this sort reduces moral hazard problems that are inherent in communitarian projects. Maoist norms shamed free-riding and flight from field labor.

Eisenman fully reports the coercive aspects of this form of organization; his treatment of commune militias is more complete than any other. Enforcement of the urban household registration system meant that Sent-Down youths or ambitious peasants could not move easily into big cities. Thus, brain drain from the countryside was discouraged. The commune was militarized at a time when China was trying to balance threats that national leaders perceived from both the Soviet Union in the north and the United States in Vietnam. Maoist enthusiasm and more responsive remuneration systems were essential to increased commune productivity.

Eisenman explores the comparative history of communes in diverse cultures, ranging far from China, to Pietists, Shakers, Owenists, *kibbutzim*, and other examples. Such organizations are not always successful in serving their members—but under some conditions, they are so. The book gives due attention also to the histories of high-modernist communes (e.g., in the Soviet Union) and to reasons for their various failures and successes. But in China during the 1970s at least, this book proves that communes, brigades, and teams brought more wealth to places that had been poor.

What made farmers work productively? Three main factors emerge from the data: Tillers need capital (including tools embodying technology). They need normative incentives to work hard rather than shirk work. They need to be organized in units that are small enough to achieve face-to-face trust but large enough to ensure that resources join their labor. These three themes unify the book and adapt its structure for comparative study of work contexts anywhere.

New insights emerge from findings about all three of these themes, notably the organizational one. Eisenman uses state-of-the-art statistical analyses to show that having many brigades per commune and many households per team usually meant higher productivity. Also, output rose when relative commune size was small. He offers explanations for these new discoveries, which all are available in this book for the first time.

His analysis is always political, even as he freely calls on theories of economics and sociology. Eisenman uses the standard economic development models of Arthur Lewis and Robert Solow to show how Chinese communes, production brigades, and teams fostered rural growth. But unlike many economists, he also shows that politics is an essential determinant of change. Available information about Chinese economic strategies comes mostly from leaders in the central government—but provinces, prefectures, counties, communes, brigades, teams, and families all have leaders and policies, too. Fairly autocratic patriarchy is a common pattern at each of these degrees of zoom.

In China, this is particularly well documented at the top of the party-state apparatus. Eisenman corroborates analyses by his former teacher Richard Baum, to whom his book is nicely dedicated, showing what happened in Chinese factional politics at "the center" in the 1970s. He is consistently clear that politics guides economic decisions.

Traditions of communal fairness exist at each size of collectivity. Unlike many social scientists, Eisenman is thoroughly sensitive to moral as well as concrete bases of change. Communes generally could make their own annual and multiyear plans, so long as they delivered taxes (usually in grain). Brigades and teams likewise had a good deal of autonomy, either because they could hide information or because Mao said their leaders should persuade ordinary members to coordinate—by forceful means, if necessary—votes for policies that they deemed appropriate to immediate local conditions. The result from communes, brigades, and teams, when they were supported by the national government and by local households, was a boost of productivity from fields, higher rural savings, more retention of profits in units that prospered, and faster mechanization leading to factories that used excess labor in agricultural slack seasons.

All of these institutions were—and in new and urbanized forms still are—the basic platforms of Chinese politics. The midsize institutions served most of the nation's people well in the 1970s and were largely privatized or abolished in the 1980s. Prices of many industrial factors soared so high by 1985 that state planning of these commodities ended. Inflation contributed to political unrest by the late 1980s, and to more centralization in later decades. In Russia after the demise of the late great USSR, a similar process occurred. In China, the process was abetted by leaders (including Deng, heads of some rural families, and others) who gained power during privatizations. This book squarely addresses the main issues of China's rise from the time it started. Those same concerns predominate in both official and academic thinking about the country in the twenty-first century, but this book revises the start of the usual story. Anyone who wants to know where China is going must read this book, if only to discover where the road began.

Lynn T. White III
Princeton and Berkeley

PROLOGUE:
CHINA'S MISSING INSTITUTION

The process by which the people built socialism under the leadership of the Party can be divided into two historical phases—one that preceded the launch of Reform and Opening-up in 1978, and a second that followed on from that event. Although the two historical phases were very different . . . we should neither negate the pre-Reform and Opening-up phase in comparison with the post-Reform and Opening-up phase, nor the converse.

—XI JINPING[1]

As a graduate student in 2000, I visited China to study why the country had abandoned its commune system and returned to household-based farming, a process officially known as "Reform and Opening-up" (*gaige kaifang*). My first stop was the National Museum of China on Tiananmen Square, to see how the institution was treated in the official history. Surprisingly, no references were made to the commune, the only trace being the tattered "secret contract" signed by the members of Xiaogang Production team in Liyuan Commune, Fengyang County, Anhui Province (figure 0.1).

According to the official account, in 1978, these courageous, starving farmers "gave birth" to China's nationwide campaign to decollectivize agriculture. In Beijing, I also met with several Chinese experts and scholars, all of whom confirmed the official account: the commune was abandoned because it was an economic failure. Moreover, they added sheepishly, because the Chinese government does not like to admit mistakes, the institution had been largely whitewashed from the official history.

Inspired by this tale of spontaneous grassroots reform, I headed straight for Xiaogang. There, I had a chance to speak with several farmers whose names and thumbprints ostensibly appeared on the document displayed in the museum. Each of them recounted their saga of starvation under the commune and their risky gambit to increase production by abandoning the collective and returning to household farming. One old farmer, himself a signatory,

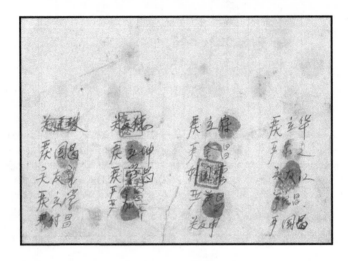

FIGURE 0.1. Xiaogang Contract No. 1, displayed at the National Museum of China as viewed in December 2000 and May 2013.

reminisced about how Anhui Provincial Party Secretary Wan Li, a staunch advocate of decollectivization, had visited the county in 1977.

This comment piqued my interest and suspicions. According to the official account, the Xiaogang farmers abandoned collective farming in 1978. What role, then, could the appearance of China's leading agricultural reformer the year *before* possibly have played in this ostensibly spontaneous, bottom-up process? This simple, unanswered question nagged at me for years. Then, in 2005, Xiaogang Village opened a museum commemorating its role in initiating decollectivization, which exhibited an enlarged image of the "secret contract" that sparked decollectivization (figure 0.2).[2] That version, which is different from the one on display in the National Museum of China, was published online by the official *People's Daily* in 2008.[3] My effort to reconcile these and other inconstancies in the Fengyang story became the impetus for this seven-year study of the commune and its abandonment.

This book was inspired by the questions that emerged from my initial fieldwork in China now nearly two decades ago: How productive was the commune system? If, after the Great Leap Forward (GLF) famine (1958–1961), the commune continued to underperform, and China's economy was closed to foreign trade, how could the country add almost 300 million people between 1962 and 1978 without experiencing another

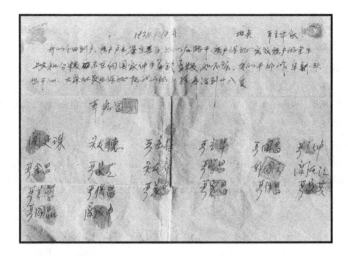

FIGURE 0.2. Xiaogang Contract No. 2, displayed at the Xiaogang Village Museum and published online by the *People's Daily* on November 11, 2008.

massive famine? But if the 1970s commune had been able to improve agricultural productivity, why was it abandoned? Did the farmers themselves or local team leaders decide to abandon the commune and, if so, how could a nationwide decollectivization process have unfolded in only a few years? Out of these questions, numerous others emerged: How did the commune—Maoist China's foremost political-economic-administrative institution—work? What happened to its members? What, if any, role did it play in creating the necessary conditions for the rapid, sustained economic growth that China enjoyed in the decades after its abandonment?

To answer these and related questions, this book tells the story of the commune—one of the largest and long-lasting high-modernist institutions in human history. Its two primary conclusions are that (1) after 1970, the commune system supported an agricultural green revolution that laid the material, technological, and educational foundations for China's emergence as an economic superpower; and (2) the system was abandoned by China's post-Mao leaders for a distinctly political reason—that is, to vanquish their rivals and consolidate their control over China.

Over five decades, a vast literature has accumulated about the Chinese countryside during the Mao era. Journalists, novelists, and scholars have examined virtually every aspect of village life. Although they disagree on many points, a broad popular consensus has emerged in keeping with the official narrative that the commune was abandoned because it failed to increase agricultural productivity. For decades, few have hesitated to judge the institution as anything other than a mistake, a misguided social experiment that placed ideological correctness over economic realities. By the turn of the millennium, this consensus had been repeated so often that it had earned the status of a traditional interpretation. This interpretation remains the only one taught in many, if not most, Chinese and Western universities, and likely is accepted by most of the readers of this book.

What is less well known is that this traditional interpretation has long been under intensive critical review by a dozen or more agricultural economists, historians, and political scientists. Some of these researchers have used local statistical records to reveal the workings and outcomes of a particular commune or its subunits; others have combined records from several localities to explain outcomes within a particular region; still others have drawn conclusions based on national-level data, interviews, and secondary sources. Yet, the explanatory power of all three approaches has been constrained by a paucity of systematic provincial- and county-level data that has prevented scholars from offering more than strongly qualified assessments of commune economic performance and its determinants and leaving important questions unresolved.

Chris Bramall and Philip Huang, for instance, two of the most sophisticated analysts of economic development under the collective system, both focus on labor productivity but come to different conclusions. Bramall argues that, through agricultural modernization, rural collectives enhanced productivity and, thus, released labor from farming, which facilitated the development of rural industry. Huang, by contrast, stresses that because of limited arable land, communes had more labor than they could productively employ in farming, so rural industry soaked up excess workers and enhanced their productivity. *But where did communes get the capital to develop rural industry?* This book provides that answer: using workpoint remuneration and other secondary mechanisms, the communes suppressed consumption and extracted the meager surpluses produced by rural labor; then they pooled and invested these resources in productive capital via the agricultural research and extension system.

This study is a comprehensive historical and social science analysis of the Chinese commune—its creation, its evolution, and its abandonment.

It applies well-established economic and social science theories to explain the national-, provincial-, and county-level data I collected between 2011 and 2016 (see appendix A). Although these data sources have been available for decades, they have remained scattered across dozens of provincial agricultural university libraries. On the basis of these hitherto neglected sources, this study contradicts many of the most important propositions in the traditional portrayal of the Chinese commune and its abandonment. It also sheds new light on how the institution functioned; how much food it produced; the essential role of Maoist ideology and the people's militia; how variations in institutional size and structure affected its productivity; the role of the agricultural research and extension system; and, finally, why and how the commune was destroyed.

KEY THEMES AND CONTRIBUTIONS OF CHINA'S GREEN REVOLUTION

For some, this may be a disturbing book to read. Many of the findings presented here and in the following chapters will force the reader to confront a radically different and wide-ranging reinterpretation of China's contemporary history and development path. The findings that emerge expose many myths that have distorted our understanding of the commune and the sources of China's economic "miracle." Following are eleven principal revisions to the traditional characterization of the Chinese commune:

1. **Agricultural productivity, life expectancy, and basic education improved substantially under the commune.** The Chinese commune evolved from an institution under which many millions starved to death in one that fed more than a billion people for two decades. According to the World Bank, the average life expectancy of a Chinese citizen increased from about forty-nine years in 1964 to about sixty-six years in 1979 (chapter 1, figure 1.6). During the 1970s, investments in agricultural capital and technology, economies of scale, diversification of the rural economy, and the intensive use of labor substantially increased agricultural productivity. The start of decollectivization coincided with historically high levels of agricultural productivity per unit land and per unit labor, life expectancy, basic literacy, and the promulgation of bookkeeping and vocational skills. Increased industrial and agricultural output under the commune can be explained using both neoclassical and classical theories of economic growth (see chapter 4).

2. **The decision to decollectivize was overwhelmingly political, and it was made by China's top leaders, not rural residents**. In December 1978, Party Chairman Hua Guofeng's "loyalist" faction lost a bitter political battle to control China to Vice-Chairman Deng Xiaoping's rival "reform" faction. The commune's fate figured prominently in this power struggle: Hua's supporters were pro-commune, whereas Deng's supporters promoted decollectivization. Hua had advocated continuing China's commune-led economic development strategy, known as the Dazhai model. In February 1978, when Hua announced his Ten-Year Plan calling for "consolidating and developing the people's communes," nobody predicted that within five years the institution would be gone.[4] Throughout 1977 and 1978, Deng and his provincial allies (including Zhao Ziyang in Sichuan and Wan Li, the Anhui party secretary who visited Xiaogang) worked to build local support for the Household Responsibility System (*baochandaohu*) and end Maoist indoctrination. These policies *intentionally* undermined the communes' ability to extract from households and eroded the Maoist ideology that bound commune members to each other and the institution. Collective property and lands were distributed to households, and localities' capacity to extract households' resources was reduced substantially. The state procurement price for agricultural products was increased for the first time in nearly a decade. By redistributing valuable capital and land, and by paying farmers more for their crops, decollectivization delivered a double consumption boost to previously deprived rural localities and won widespread political support, especially from local leaders who benefited most from the privatization of collective property. Chinese reformers, in short, eliminated the commune to consolidate their power and not because the system failed to increase agricultural productivity.

3. **The commune was not an "irrational" system created and perpetuated by brainwashed Maoists who failed to consider, or were indifferent to, economic outcomes**. The opposite was true; that is, the primary objective of the commune's creators (including Mao Zedong) was to increase rural development to improve agricultural productivity with a focus on grain and pig production. The Maoists obsession with long-run increases in agricultural production meant that they subordinated household consumption in favor of extracting more resources to invest to increase productivity. But, although an increasing percentage of household savings was extracted, after the GLF, there is no evidence that commune members were starving or too hungry to work. The workpoint remuneration system was designed to incentivize rural residents to work hard and maintain consumption levels that were just high enough to enable them to do so. Rather

than starve people, which would have reduced their productivity, the objective was to extract the maximum percentage of annual household income to support continuous investments in capital and technology to increase food production.

4. **Before China's green revolution, communes had *both* a surplus and a scarcity of labor.** During planting and harvest, communes often faced labor shortages, whereas during the slack season, there was generally a sizable surplus of labor. In practice, this meant that although farmers often had free time, they were still tied to the land during certain times of the year when they worked round the clock and sometimes even slept in the fields. During the slack season, farmers were encouraged to create cottage industries and sideline plots to meet latent market demand for basic consumer goods and vegetables, but they would be punished for working them instead of the collective fields during planting and harvesting time. Simply put, commune and brigade enterprises and factories gave farmers something to do when they didn't have fieldwork, thus making them more productive and expanding their skills beyond agriculture alone. By the mid- to late 1970s, sustained investments in agricultural modernization and population growth had left millions of farmers with little to do and less and less land to do it on. Yet they remained trapped in the countryside until decollectivization when the end of collective remuneration rendered the residency permit (*hukou*) system unenforceable. Beginning in the early mid-1980s, tens of millions of farmers began moving to urban areas—an internal migration that has continued for more than four decades. The first generation of these migrants—who acquired their basic reading, bookkeeping, and vocational skills in communes—improved the efficiency of urban industries and became a sizable contingent of the skilled workforce that fueled economic growth in the 1980s and 1990s.

5. **Private household plots, small-scale animal husbandry and cottage industries, and rural markets (collectively known as the Three Small Freedoms) were formally adopted in 1962 and practiced throughout the remainder of the commune era—including during the Cultural Revolution.** These activities were legal and conducted *openly* under the auspices of commune, brigade, and team cadres. They provided an essential consumption floor for households and were often its primary source of vegetables, eggs, meat, and cash income. Commune subunits were encouraged to support households' investments through small grants and loans, improved seed varieties, fertilizer, machines, and veterinary and stud services. Rural markets provided an outlet for excess private household production, created income for the elderly, and offered the pricing information cadres needed to make productive investments.

6. **The commune system was not collapsing economically when decollectiv-
izaition began**. This study uncovered no evidence that economic or grassroots
pressures alone would have been sufficient to bring down the commune system without direct intervention from political leaders in Beijing and provincial
capitals. The system was all any rural Chinese under the age of twenty-five had
ever known, and they presumed it would remain in perpetuity. No scholarly
or official publications before 1979 have been uncovered that predicted China
would soon decollectivize. Many former commune members interviewed for
this project claimed they were also surprised, both by the decision to decollectivize and by how quickly it was implemented.

7. **Able-bodied farmers rarely slacked or shirked collective labor. Rather, communes incentivized farmers to *overwork*, and then underpaid them**. Workpoints, regardless of how they were awarded, were the institution's primary
method of remuneration and resource extraction. After the Northern Districts
Agricultural Conference in 1970, a variety of workpoint remuneration methodologies—such as task rates, time rates, and piece rates—became permissible
and generally were decided at the team level. The value of the workpoint was
determined by each team *after* the harvest and all taxes and production and
social service costs had been deducted. Regardless of how many workpoints
were awarded to members or which method was used to disburse them, about
half of gross collective income was extracted before members were allowed to
squabble over the remainder. Because members did not know how much their
points would be worth as they were earning them, they strove to accumulate as
many as possible, which disincentivized slacking and shirking and allowed the
collective to minimize household consumption and maximize investment. In
some localities, team leaders awarded or deducted workpoints based on a member's performance; in others, the contribution of more productive workers, as
well as the harm done by loafers and free riders, was broadcast each day at team
meetings or over the village loudspeakers.

8. **Red China's green revolution was made possible by reforms to the nationwide agricultural research and extension system undertaken during the
Cultural Revolution**. China's substantially increased food production was the
result of the vastly expanded application of improved agricultural inputs (e.g.,
hybrid seed varieties, fertilizers, mechanization, and irrigation) that, when
used together, were extremely effective. The reformed agricultural research
and extension system rewarded applied, results-driven science over theoretical work. It was a vertically integrated subinstitution nested into the commune

and its subunits that responded to local needs and developed crops appropriate for local conditions. Experts were rotated on a three-year basis: the first year in the lab, the second in a particular commune, and the third traveling around a particular prefecture or province to test innovations and farming techniques on a larger scale. Despite its extraordinary success, when the commune was destroyed, so was its agricultural research and extension system.[5]

9. **The commune was the church of Mao.** Maoism was an *essential* psychological tool that cadres used to coerce households to forgo a larger portion of their income than they otherwise might have done without resorting to foot-dragging or outright protest. After the GLF, Maoism became a national religion that demanded total loyalty to the chairman and to the collective and was fanatical about increasing agricultural production. During decollectivization, China's new leaders destroyed Maoism, and with it the bonds that had united commune members to each other and the institution. Stripped of their "god" and faith, collective action problems (i.e., brain drain, adverse selection, and moral hazard) quickly spread among commune members and tore the institution apart.

10. **The people's militia was an important conduit to transmit Maoism into every rural locality, and an institutional connection between Mao and the military.** The people's militia, a semiautonomous substitution nested within the commune and its subunit the brigade, linked Maoism with the prestigious People's Liberation Army. Despite its purported tactical value to the military, Mao's reasons for establishing the militia were primarily political: to create an informational conduit accountable to him alone, through which Maoism was transmitted to the commune and local reports were transmitted back up to Mao via the military—rather than the party—bureaucracy. Militia units became an integral component and proponent of Mao's collectivist ideology under the commune and were linked by state media to the Dazhai agricultural model. Like the "guardians" in Plato's *Republic*, the militiamen's ideological commitment placed them in the distinguished position of enforcing both the commune's collectivist ethos and its external security. They conducted regular political propaganda and study sessions using the *Little Red Book* and other approved texts and often were called on to set the pace during collective work. When the commune was abandoned, the militias, whose members were paid in workpoints, were disbanded.

11. **Taken together, the relative size of the commune and its subunits were statistically significant determinants of its agricultural productivity.** The commune's structure was substantially altered after the devastating GLF famine to increase agricultural productivity. These reforms reduced its size and

introduced two levels of administrative subunits—the production brigade and
its subordinate production team. In the decade after its creation, the size of the
commune and these subunits were adjusted continuously. The empirical analysis of data covering all 117 counties in Henan Province presented in chapter 6
reveals that taken together these changes in the relative size of the commune
and its subunits were a statistically significant determinant of the temporal and
geographic variations observed in agricultural output. Commune relative size
exhibits a strong influence on the effect of team size, such that when average
commune relative size is small, smaller teams have higher agricultural output;
however, as average commune size increases, the effect is mitigated and even reversed. Large communes enhanced public goods provision, which increased the
marginal productivity of labor and reduced the importance of close monitoring
of workers. Hence, the advantage of smaller teams becomes less obvious and
having fewer, larger teams can simplify agricultural planning and the allocation
of productive factors. In this way, increased organizational efficiency at the supervisory level helped mitigate the negative effects of the free rider problem at
the working level. Simply put, the increased efficiency gains from economies of
scale in larger communes mitigated the negative effects of reduced supervision
in larger teams.

Even this summary of revisions to the traditional characterization of the
commune and its abandonment raises the question of how those who dismissed the institution as an economic failure and accepted the story of
spontaneous grassroots decollectivization could have been so wrong. The
scholars whose views are now called into question were conscientious and
diligent; they strove to portray Chinese history as it actually was. The explanation, then, does not turn on issues of personal bias. Rather, it hinges to
a large extent on the lack of available data about the commune, and the
success of the four-decades-long official campaign to downplay its productivity to justify its abolition on economic rather than political grounds.
Times have changed, however; the requisite data are now available to allow
researchers to shed light on how the commune worked and its contribution
to the country's modernization.

This study makes intuitive observations using simple data about productive inputs (e.g., fertilizer, tractors, seed varieties, and vocational training)
and agricultural outputs (i.e., grain, pigs, and edible oils). Although less
captivating than firsthand accounts, these records are vital to explaining

and judging the commune's performance and to understanding how it worked and why it was abandoned.

In considering the evidence presented in this book, readers should remember the limitations of the data and theories presented, which answer an important but narrow set of questions. Data on the amount of fertilizer, the number of tractors, or the size of commune subunits in a particular province, for instance, cannot directly measure the quality of people's lives or their relations with their neighbors. Nor is it possible to develop a meaningful index of the effects of commune life on the personality or psychology of those who lived under the institution. This does not mean these critical aspects have gone entirely ignored; much important information was gleaned from numerous discussions with Chinese agricultural experts and former commune members, as well as from press articles and scholarly works. However, detailed provincial- and county-level data on capital investment, food productivity, and institutional size and structure have long been required to place these supporting materials in their proper context. Without systematic time-series data to serve as a ballast, accounts of commune performance have tended to vary widely based on the perspective and experiences of the author or those interviewed as well as on the locality or region under examination.

Another word of caution is in order. There is no such thing as errorless data. All researchers must grapple with the nature of the errors contained in different types of data, and the biases that such errors may produce in conclusions that are based upon them. Evidence does not fall neatly into two categories—good and bad—but along a complex continuum in which there are many categories and varying degrees of reliability. This study's conclusions are based primarily on evidence from the most reliable end of the continuum: systematic data. Even when biased, systematic data were prioritized over fragmentary data, because the nature of the bias could be elucidated. The least confidence was placed in fragmentary evidence based on the unverifiable impressions of individuals whose primary aim was the defense of an ideological position. Eyewitness accounts were considered more reliable, but they exist in only a somewhat-random pattern, especially in a country as large and diverse as China. Regardless of how often they have been repeated or the objectivity of the sources, arguments based only on impressionistic, fragmentary evidence were considered less reliable than those based on systematic data. This study used fragmentary, impressionistic, and eyewitness evidence in two ways: (1) to illustrate conclusions based on systematic data, and (2) to fill gaps in areas in which it is not possible to gather systematic data, such as workpoint remuneration methods or the practices of Maoist "worship" ceremonies.

Finally, whenever possible, this book avoids the word "peasant." This decision was intentional, as the term has become a contentious catchall, an often-pejorative moniker for small rural landholders. Paul Robbins defines "peasants" as "households that make their living from the land, partly integrated into broader-scale markets and partly rooted in subsistence production, with no wage workers, dependent on family and extended kin for farm labor."[6] Such definitions, as the reader will soon discover, are an ill-fitting description of life under the commune, and thus the more accurate terms "team members," "rural residents," and "farmers" are used instead. Commune members were neither slaves nor landless "peasants"; they were members of an institution that was supposed to and, in the most basic sense did, guarantee their livelihood and take their interests into account.

ACKNOWLEDGMENTS

There are nine people without whom this book would not have been possible: Richard Baum, Ronald Rogowski, Marc Blecher, Theodore Hutors, Herman Pirchner, Wang Duanyong, Anne Thurston, Yang Feng, and my wife, Iris. Professor Baum was both a mentor and exemplar. For six years (from 2006 to 2012) under his exceptional tutelage, I studied how to interpret the machinations of the Chinese policymaking process and conduct field research in China. Ron provided essential theoretical and historical insights and introduced me to the economic theories of W. Arthur Lewis, which unlocked the relationship among the causal variables. Marc's meticulous feedback on my chapters, continuous intellectual and moral support, and limitless knowledge of the political economy of rural China were indispensable. Ted was instrumental, not only in teaching me the Chinese language, but also in encouraging me to continue my research despite some initial setbacks. Herman supplied the guidance and support I needed to keep mind and body together throughout the lengthy research and writing process. Duanyong deserves special thanks for his unparalleled efforts, thoughtful critiques, generous dedication of time, and insights into rural development in Henan. Professor Thurston's course on grassroots China at Johns Hopkins SAIS, particularly our class trip to meet the members of Xiaogang Production team in Liyuan Commune, Fengyang County, Anhui, proved the inspiration behind this project. I am grateful to Yang Feng for helping make the statistical model in chapter 6 a reality. Most important, day in and day out, Iris' support and encouragement were the emotional bedrock that sustained me.

Several other people deserve special recognition. My mother-in-law Sun Guihua's first-hand accounts of life in Weihai, Shandong, in the 1960s and 1970s opened my eyes to the hardships of austerity under the commune. Lynn T. White III provided me with essential mentorship and expert comments on my chapters and I am most grateful for his excellent foreword. Richard Lowery offered critical advice and suggestions to ensure that I correctly applied and specified the Solow–Swan economic model, while Thomas Palley lent essential support on the classical framework. Eric Schwartz skillfully shepherded the manuscript through the publication process at Columbia University Press. I am grateful to both anonymous reviewers for their valuable comments and support for the book. I would also like to express my gratitude to the numerous Chinese academics and former commune members that shared their insights and hospitality with me during my fieldwork. I am grateful to the dozens of librarians and graduate students at China's agricultural universities who helped me navigate their institutions and archives.

Through countless correspondences, professors Edward McCord, Li Huaiyin, Dorothy Solinger, David Zweig, Harry Harding, Michael O. Moore, Jonathan Unger, Edward Friedman, Frederick Teiwes, Pricilla Roberts, Arne Westad, and Andrew Field were generous with their sharing of insights and research. Professors Arthur Stein, Barbara Geddes, Michael Ross, and Michael O. Moore always made time to provide their sound advice and strategies for field research and writing. Zachary Reddick contributed his excellent research and insights on China's military. Peggy Printz shared her recollections and unique pictures of Guang Li Commune in 1973. Tang Ying shared her images and recollections of rural Fujian in the 1970s. Liz Wood and Ilan Berman supplied expert editorial assistance. Li Xialin inputted the data. James Blake and Roche George helped edit the images. Gu Manhan, Luo Siyu, and Mi Siyi provided essential research and produced the high-quality graphic displays in book. I am grateful for the ongoing support and encouragement of longtime friends and mentors Jonathan Monten, Randy Schriver, Devin Stewart, Richard Harrison, Jeff

M. Smith, William Inboden, Rana Inboden, Jamie Galbraith, Jeremi Suri, Catherine Weaver, David Eaton, Josh Busby, Joseph Brown, Jack Marr, and Sifu Aaron Vyvial.

I would also like to recognize several institutions for their financial support for my fieldwork in China: the University of Texas at Austin, LBJ School of Public Affairs; the American Foreign Policy Council; the Clements Center for National Security; the Strauss Center for International Security and Law; the UCLA Political Science Department; the UCLA Center for International Business Education and Research; New York University–Shanghai; and the Carnegie Council for Ethics in International Affairs.

Finally, this book stands on the shoulders of two groups of people I will never meet. The tens of thousands of men and women who diligently recorded, collected, and published the data presented; and the economic theorists W. Arthur Lewis, Robert Solow, and Trevor Swan, whose models I used to explain it.

Austin, Texas
January 1, 2018

RED CHINA'S GREEN REVOLUTION

Chapter One

INTRODUCTION

Assessing Commune Productivity

Many experts and most laymen, Chinese and non-Chinese alike, trace China's sustained economic growth to the expansion of rural markets and material incentives beginning in 1979. The contentions that under the People's Commune (from here on, the commune), excessive planning and an overly egalitarian collective remuneration system reduced agricultural productivity are well accepted. Conventional wisdom suggests that market-based incentives and investments in productive capital and technology initiated during decollectivization produced a V-shaped economic recovery. Economic collapse was narrowly avoided by life-saving rural reforms, known as the Household Responsibility System (HRS, or *baochan daohu* in Chinese). HRS reintroduced household-based farming, which revived the rural economy after the commune's failure.[1]

But was the commune an economic failure? Was the commune, as the conventional view suggests, unable to provide sufficient material incentives for rural workers, leading them to slack off or shirk their collective responsibilities? A lesser-known view suggests that the opposite is true. The commune, proponents of this alternate view maintain, helped modernize Chinese agriculture, increased its productivity, and laid the groundwork for the mass urbanization and industrialization that occurred after decollectivization.[2]

After presenting these two divergent assessments of commune economic performance, this chapter uses national-level data to evaluate which one is more accurate. Production data for grain, pigs, and edible oils, included in the "Data Presentation" section and provided along with provincial-level data in appendix A, reveal that claims that the commune failed to increase food production are largely erroneous. Considered together, these data show that after 1970, communes generated substantial increases in aggregate food production, as well as productivity per unit land and per unit labor. These trends are particularly evident in grain and pig production, which compare favorably with levels of production and life expectancy in other large agricultural countries (i.e., India, the Soviet Union, and the United States).

Simply put, the Chinese commune was *not* an economic failure remedied by decollectivization. During the 1970s, the commune was able to support a larger, longer-living population on a diminishing amount of arable land and to overcome high capital depreciation rates.

BOOK STRUCTURE

The chapters that follow tell the tale of the commune—why it was created, how it was transformed over the course of two decades, and how it was ultimately destroyed. They identify the three sources of commune productivity—super-optimal investment, Maoism, and organizational structure and size—and explain why and how the institution was abandoned during decollectivization.

Chapter 2 examines the origins of collective agriculture and its evolution until 1970. I argue that the commune had four distinct, yet interrelated, phases: the Great Leap Forward (GLF) Commune (1958–1961), the Rightist Commune (1962–1964), the Leftist Commune (1965–1969), and the Green Revolution Commune (1970–1979). Each of these phases was distinguished by its size, mandate, remuneration system, and strategy to promote agricultural modernization. Each also built on its predecessor, creating an institutional inertia that predisposed the commune to retain policies rarely associated with communism, including household sideline plots, cottage enterprises, and rural markets (collectively known as the Three Small Freedoms).

In chapter 3, I argue that after 1970, policies that increased household savings rates kick-started a virtuous cycle of investment that produced sustained growth in agricultural output. Using previously unexploited national- and provincial-level data, I identify three economic challenges China faced after the GLF famine—rising rates of population growth, shrinking arable land, and high capital depreciation rates—and explain the policies implemented through the commune to alleviate them. Capital investments and technological innovations made via the agricultural research and extension system increased output per unit land and labor, and freed farmers first to move into the light industrial and service sectors of the rural economy, and later to urban areas after decollectivization.

In chapter 4, I use neoclassical and classical economic growth models to identify the transitional dynamics of growth under the commune. These models clarify the patterns of productivity for each phase of the commune identified in chapters 2 and 3, and explain the relationships among relevant economic variables (i.e., technological progress, savings rates, capital investment and depreciation, and labor input) and agriculture output. This chapter demonstrates how the commune used coercive measures to increase agricultural output by underwriting super-optimal investment— that is, the extraction and investment of household resources at levels beyond what families would have saved (as opposed to consumed) had they been given the choice. The commune's workpoint remuneration system and, to a lesser extent, redistributive policies and rural credit cooperatives helped to conceal the gradual increases in household savings rates that funded agricultural modernization.

In chapter 5, I use collective action theories to explain the importance of Maoism, the commune's pervasive collective ideology. The commune's collectivist ethos had five interlocking aspects: Maoism's religiosity, the people's militia, self-reliance, social pressure, and collective remuneration. Together, these elements constituted the institution's essential political backbone, which allowed it to maintain higher household savings rates than members normally would have tolerated without fleeing, resisting, or resorting to slacking or shirking. Maoism helped the institution to overcome the collective action problems inherent to all rural communes—namely, brain drain, adverse selection, and moral hazard. Once extracted from households, resources were channeled into productive investments via the commune-based agricultural research and extension system described in chapter 3.

In chapter 6, I draw on organizational theories to explain how changes to the size and structure of the commune and its subunits improved its productivity. After the devastating GLF famine, the commune was substantially altered. Its size was reduced and two levels of administrative subunits were introduced: the production brigade and the production team. Exploiting two decades of detailed county-level data from Henan Province, and examining both cross-sectional and over-time variation, I find a consistent nonlinear relationship between the size of communes and their subunits and agricultural productivity. Smaller communes with smaller teams were most productive, but as commune size increased, the effect of team size was mitigated and eventually reversed such that large communes with large teams were more productive than large communes with small teams.

In chapter 7, I present a top-down political explanation for commune abandonment. This account challenges the contentions that households abandoned the commune and that it was dismantled because it was unproductive. The campaign to abandon the commune began quietly in 1977, was accelerated in 1979, and culminated in the system's nationwide elimination by 1983. Unified by a desire to solidify its tenuous grip on power, Deng Xiaoping and his fellow reformers set out to boost rural household incomes and end Maoism. These interrelated policy goals challenged the commune's mandate to extract household savings to underwrite investment, eliminated its collectivist ideology, and sowed discord among the institution and its subunits. Without its economic, political, and structural supports, the commune collapsed. During decollectivization, collective property and lands were distributed and the state procurement price for agricultural products was increased for the first time in nearly a decade. This distribution delivered a double consumption boost to previously deprived rural localities and won widespread political support, especially from local leaders who benefited most from the privatization of collective property.

Finally, in chapter 8, I provide a synopsis of the book and review its conclusions. I summarize the institutional changes that took place under the commune; the three sources of commune productivity examined in chapters 4, 5, and 6; and the top-down, political explanation for decollectivization offered in chapter 7.

Appendix A presents national- and provincial-level production data during the commune era for grain, pigs, and edible oil. Appendix B includes the supplemental materials for the statistical analysis conducted in chapter 6.

Appendix C is a compilation of the nine essential official policy documents on the commune, most of which have not previously been translated into English. It is divided into three sections: commune creation, commune governance, and decollectivization.

HISTORICAL OVERVIEW: THE PEOPLE'S COMMUNE

Beginning in 1958, for more than two decades the commune was rural China's foremost economic and political institution and the lowest level of full-time, state-supported government.[3] At their peak size in 1980, communes held about 811 million members, representing 82 percent of all Chinese, or 1 out of every 5.5 people on earth. Between 1970 and 1983, the average commune included twelve production brigades, ninety production teams, three thousand households, and about fourteen thousand people. These averages disguise substantial regional disparities in commune size, and after 1961, regardless of size, all Chinese communes shared the same three-tiered administrative structure and were coercive institutions—that is, *members could not leave without permission.*

The household formed a fourth subunit under the commune and controlled the rural private sector. Households supplemented their collective income with private income generated from their often home-adjacent sideline plots (*ziliudi*) and cottage enterprises; they would either consume these crops and handicrafts or sell them to the collective or to other households at the local market (*ganji*). Households had the basic facilities and supplies (i.e., a small courtyard or pen and food scraps) and the experience necessary to raise a few chickens or a pig or two. They did not compete directly with the collective, but instead worked with and received material support from their teams to ensure that any resources left over from collective production would not be wasted.[4]

During the Anti-Rightist Campaign, from mid-1957 until the GLF began in late 1958, between 550,000 and 800,000 educated members of Chinese society were branded as Rightists and publically denounced.[5] Over the next two years, the GLF's infamous red-over-expert policies further demoralized China's already scarce human capital. The GLF's failure resulted in the loss of between 15 and 30 million lives, as well as the construction of vast quantities of poor-quality physical capital and infrastructure, which either depreciated quickly or collapsed.

After the GLF calamity, in 1962, the Communist Party of China (CPC) Central Committee officially promulgated the Regulations on the Rural People's Communes (i.e., the *Sixty Articles on Agriculture*), which remained the institution's primary working directive for two decades (see appendix C). These regulations reintroduced income incentives, private sideline plots, and free markets, and scaled back the size and mandate of communes. Public services such as collective dining and childcare were returned to household control. Throughout the 1960s, quickly depreciating rural capital stocks, population growth, and a steady decrease in arable land inhibited China's ability to generate substantial increases in agricultural output per unit of land and per unit of labor. The effects of these severe economic challenges and China's policy responses are detailed in chapters 2 and 3, and their transitional dynamics are elucidated using economic growth models in chapter 4.

In 1969, Premier Zhou Enlai was placed in charge of agriculture, and provincial-level meetings were held to pull together the lessons of the commune's first decade. That year, a number of provinces—including Gansu, Inner Mongolia, Anhui, Shandong, Hunan, and Guangdong—held conferences on the topic.[6] After a preparatory session in June 1970, Zhou's agricultural policy review culminated in the Northern Districts Agricultural Conference (*beifang diqu nongye huiyi*, or NDAC) held at Dazhai Commune in Xiyang County, Shanxi Province, and in Beijing from August 25 to October 5. Under the slogan "Learn from Dazhai," the conference reiterated support for the *Sixty Articles* and launched a nationwide rural reform agenda designed to improve commune economic performance. These reforms called for increased investment in grain production, rural capital construction, pig production, and fertilizer, and for "[investment] in agricultural machinery so that 50 percent of the land would be farmed mechanically."[7]

In October 1970, China's draft constitution reemphasized the team as the commune's basic accounting unit (i.e., the level at which household remuneration took place) and guaranteed access to household sideline plots. In November and December, provinces including Shanxi, Yunnan, Guangxi, and Hunan held agricultural work conferences to disseminate these policies, which were published in the State Council's NDAC report in December 1970. The following year, the CPC Central Committee transmitted to each county its directive on Distribution in the People's Communes, which protected incentive-based remuneration and household sideline plots (see appendix C). Under the slogan "Grasp the revolution, improve production," at least a half-dozen radical provincial leaders were replaced with proponents of agricultural policies that prioritized productivity.[8]

After 1970, the commune's institutional structure and mandate remained stable for a decade. With political control, economic management, and public security unified under a single institution, virtually no dimension stood beyond its purview. Communes and their subunits administered schools, hospitals, banks, shops, police and fire departments, telephone services, post offices, and radio broadcasting; they organized local, cultural, and sports activities; and they supported propaganda-related activities. Each administrative level was charged not only with modernizing agriculture but also with building a new Maoist political consciousness based on self-reliance and patriotism and placing the collective before individual interests—a potent combination that gave cadres nearly unlimited power over the lives of commune members.

Communes implemented population control measures, such as job allocation, the household registration (*hukou*) system, and family planning, but above all, they were tasked with improving their subunits' agricultural output with an emphasis on food productivity—particularly grain and pork. At each administrative level, the commune's planting and investment plan was risk adverse and gradualist, aiming for slow and steady increases in food output, rather than intermittent surges in production followed by stagnation. Although commune leaders were under pressure to increase yields using modern capital and techniques, they enjoyed wide autonomy in choosing their approach. Commune cadres drew up preliminary production plans and budgets that apportioned quotas and agricultural inputs to their brigades. Each brigade then conducted a similar process among its subordinate teams, which, in turn, transmitted instructions to households under their jurisdiction. County, commune, and brigade leaders developed and vetted production and investment plans at an annual gathering known as the three-level meeting (*sancenghui*).

During the 1970s, team leaders selected the workpoint remuneration methods that best incentivized workers. Households were informed of relevant agricultural modernization plans and workpoint schemes (e.g., task rates, time rates, piece rates) during team meetings and were obliged to abide by them. During mandatory assemblies, leaders transmitted Mao's vision of selfless collectivism via propaganda materials, songs, dances, ceremonies, and dramatic reenactments. Cadres were encouraged to take local conditions into account; were warned to avoid waste and overconsumption; and were rewarded, above all, for delivering steady, long-run increases in food grain and pig production.

WAS THE COMMUNE PRODUCTIVE?

The Conventional View: Poor Performance

This section summarizes the conventional view, which identifies the commune as an impediment to economic development and productivity—one that was unable to capitalize the rural economy, promote technical innovation, or increase agricultural output. Official accounts and many prominent researchers juxtapose the commune's economic shortcomings with the subsequent successful introduction of markets and incentives under HRS, which, they argue, brought China's unproductive rural economy to life. In the next section, I compare this view with a prominent alternative perspective that contends that after more than a decade of adjustments, the commune ultimately was effective in modernizing agriculture and steadily increasing food production during the 1970s.

Explanations for commune economic failure, of course, have dissimilarities. Researchers disagree with each other and the official narrative about countless details. The meaning and relative significance of policy statements, publications, and meetings are always subject to the researcher's interpretation and explanation. Despite these variations, the essence of the metanarrative on commune failure appears consistent: the lack of incentives in Chinese communes caused collective action problems (e.g., shirking and slacking) that retarded development and reduced productivity. Members simply lacked the motivation to work hard or monitor each other's work. As a result, a moral hazard problem developed whereby free riders neglected their collective duties, dragging down commune productivity while still reaping nearly the same rewards as actual contributors thanks to the institution's overly egalitarian remuneration system. Over time, lackluster collective production led initially hard-working members to also begin shirking collective work and focusing on more profitable private sideline ventures.

Poor commune productivity caused rural Chinese families to go hungry, which only served to further reduce agricultural output. Sometimes rural workers would show up for collective work exhausted, sometimes they worked slowly to conserve energy, and sometimes they did not show up at all. As a result, tensions emerged between the increasingly unproductive collective and its dynamic private households. Despite a strong desire among rural residents to return to market-based household farming, explains John K. Fairbank, "highhanded but ignorant cadre intervened destructively," stifling their pleas.[9] Kenneth Lieberthal writes that the economy was entirely government administered, and "market forces and personal incentives played virtually no role in the system." He observes:

The highest priority was developing heavy industry for defense (and prestige reasons) and maximizing urban employment, with no noticeable attention to issues of efficiency or to effective use of capital. The result was lackluster economic growth, with nearly all real gains stemming from bringing more resources to bear rather than from improvements in productivity based on technological and systems. There were no private property rights and virtually no private property at all (with the exception of peasant housing). There was almost no international trade, as Mao had pursued a policy of autarky.[10]

Officially, between 1966 and 1976, extreme leftist policies that "disregarded the low productivity of the countryside" unleashed "ten years of turmoil [that] caused serious damage in the rural economy."[11] A 1985 government publication described economic stagnation under the commune's "feudal-fascist regime" and claimed that "commune members were forbidden to engage in sideline production [and] private plots were eradicated, seriously damaging normal economic life in the countryside."[12] Fairbank and Merle Goldman agree that "in the 1970s the Cultural Revolution spread its coercion into the countryside, where, for example, peasants were required to abandon all sideline occupations such as raising pigs, chickens, and ducks in order to 'cut off the tail of capitalism.' For many peasants this meant starvation."[13] According to Carl Riskin, "state dictated cropping plans" and "caps on team income" created a "weakening of work incentives and a palsy of creative effort," such that "collective agriculture in many places turned passive and uninspired."[14] Kate Xiao Zhou explains economic stagnation under the commune:

Farmers . . . were left with little or no incentive to increase or even maintain collective productivity. Not only did the state set family autonomy aside, but it put people who were good at politics, but not necessarily at farming, in charge of farming. Cadres organized farming on a commune, brigade, and team basis, regardless of the implications for productivity. They gave farmers no individual incentives to work hard to increase the level of productivity.[15]

Then, according to the widely accepted official account, in 1978, eighteen brave households from Xiaogang Production Team, Yangang Brigade, Liyuan Commune in Fengyang County, Anhui, "risked their lives to sign a secret agreement to divide communally owned farmland into individual pieces called household contracts, thus inadvertently lighting the torch for China's rural revolution."[16] Xiaogang native He Hongguang describes wretched poverty and a scarcity of agricultural capital under the commune:

By the end of 1977, the Commune members had nothing left. Nearly everyone in the village had become a beggar. The doors of 11 households were made of sorghum stalks: some were so poor that they had to borrow bowls from other families when their relatives came to visit. The village was so poor that it only had three huts, one cow, one harrow, and one plough.[17]

In the *People's Daily*, Yan Junchang, Xiaogang's team leader and one of the eighteen signatories, explained how a combination of hunger and Maoist politics reduced productivity and prompted villagers to abandon the collective:

Villagers tended collective fields in exchange for "workpoints" that could be redeemed for food. But we had no strength and enthusiasm to work in collective fields due to hunger. We even didn't have time because we were always being organized by governmental work teams who taught us politics. It was then that I began to consider contracting land into individual households.[18]

Extrapolating from the Fengyang story, Anne Thurston explains why malnourished farmers across China continued laboring under the commune for two decades despite its poor economic performance:

One of the great mysteries of rural China during the Maoist era is why the peasants, who provided the major support for the communist revolution, did not rebel, or even fight back, when the revolution first betrayed and then began devouring them. The answer from Fengyang in famine seems obvious. Starving people do not rebel. To the extent they move at all, it is to search for food.[19]

According to the *People's Daily*, the introduction of HRS increased Xiao-gang's food grain output from 15,000 kilograms (kg) in 1978 to 90,000 kg in 1979.[20] In recognition of these extraordinary productivity increases, Xiaogang's households received powerful public support from Anhui Party Secretary Wan Li and other top leaders, including Sichuan Party Secretary Zhao Ziyang and Propaganda Chief Hu Yaobang. According to Tony Saich, Deng Xiaoping "remained agnostic" about decollectivization until 1981.[21] In his memoirs, Zhao—a principal proponent of decollectivization—describes the success of the Rural Household Land Contract (RHLC) system, also known as the HRS:

The transformation of the nationwide system of three-tiered ownership of people's communes into the RHLC schemes was a major policy change and a profound revolution. It took less than three years to accomplish this smoothly. I believe it was the healthiest major policy shift in our nation's history. As the implementation of the RHLC scheme expanded, *starting from the grassroots and spreading upward*, its superiority as a system became increasingly obvious.[22] (Italics added for emphasis)

The similarity between Zhao's account and that of Saich, who also stresses the upward spread of "grassroots" economic reforms, is notable:

In 1979 poor farmers were beginning to abandon the collective structures and grassroots experimentation took place in contracting output to the household. Gradually this practice spread throughout other areas of rural China. As late as 1981 Deng remained agnostic as to whether this was a good thing. As practice at the grass roots radicalized, the centre could do nothing but stand by and make policy pronouncements to try and catch up with reality. In this initial stage of reform it is clear that *the central authorities were being led by developments at the grass roots level*.[23] (Italics added for emphasis)

Not all agree, however, that farmers themselves began the movement to abandon the commune. Ezra Vogel explains that when officials gave "peasants a choice between collective or household farming, they overwhelmingly chose the household."[24] In contrast to this view, Jonathan Unger claims localities were "channeled" from communes into HRS "irrespective of the types of crops grown or the level of local economic development." According to Unger, "Contrary to repeated claims of the Chinese news media and top political leaders alike . . . very few villages were offered any choice."[25]

Despite disagreements on the origins of HRS, there is broad agreement that it increased productivity more than the commune. According to Fei Hsiao-tung, it was only after "land was contracted to the peasant households for independent management [that the rural economy] overcame the ill effects of the commune system, which had constrained the productive forces."[26] Fairbank agrees that systemic changes that "moved responsibility down to the individual farm family provided a great incentive." He writes:

The earlier Maoist system had used moral exhortation as an incentive, had demanded grain production only, and had banned sideline production and incipient "capitalism"—a triumph of blueprint ideology over reality. This change of system now made a big difference. Now the whole community could join in planning to maximize production and income. The result was a massive increase in both, a triumph for Deng's reforms. This was due to new motives of personal profit.[27]

Again, it is noteworthy how close this narrative of commune failure remedied by HRS hews to the official position as elucidated by then-Communist Party Chairman Hu Yaobang at a speech celebrating the sixtieth anniversary of the party's founding on July 1, 1981:

Now that liquidation of the long prevalent "Left" deviationist guiding ideology is under way, our socialist economic and cultural construction has been shifted to a course of development. With the implementation of the Party's policies, the introduction of the system of production responsibilities and the development of a diversified economy, an excellent situation has developed in the vast rural areas in particular, a dynamic and progressive situation seldom seen since the founding of the People's Republic.[28]

According to the official story and to many prominent researchers, substantial increases in rural agricultural and industrial productivity were observed only *after* decollectivization began in 1979. Zhou has described this process as "spontaneous, unorganized, leaderless, nonideological, and apolitical."[29] Draft animals, tools, and equipment were divided among households, which contracted the land, farmed it as they liked, and sold their crops at local free markets. The commune's economic failure, according to the official account promulgated in 1981, prompted Chinese families to forsake it in favor of "various forms of production responsibility whereby remuneration is determined by farm output," and "sideline occupations and diverse undertakings," which caused "grain output in the last two years to reach an all-time high" and "improved the living standards of the people."[30] According to Huang Yasheng, by 1985, rural China became a "socialist market economy" that introduced incentives and markets, resulting in the emergence of "10 million *completely and manifestly* private [italics in the original]" local businesses known as town and village enterprises.[31]

This narrative, often referred to as Reform and Opening Up, has been the conventional interpretation in both academic and policy circles for four decades.[32] In the 1980s, positive assessments of economic growth during the Mao era became politically charged—so much so that an American academic who had visited China in the 1970s risked being branded a Maoist and denied a visa.[33] It was worse in China, where Deng's emergence heralded a purge of party "ultra-leftists" whose rural policies had, according to one official account, "scorned all economic laws and denied the law of value."[34] In Henan alone, more than 1 million Maoists were detained and some four thousand were given prison sentences after closed-door trials.[35] Under these conditions, few defended the austerity, self-sacrifice, and investment-first policies pursued under the commune. Instead, consumption was king and to get rich was "glorious."[36] "By the 1990s," Chris Bramall has observed, "the academic consensus was that the Maoist commitment to rural development had been more notional than real."[37]

The Alternative View: China's Green Revolution[38]

Some researchers have offered a lesser-known alternative evaluation of rural economic performance during the 1970s and the commune's legacy.

They argue that the commune did modernize Chinese agriculture and increase food output and that China's improved agricultural productivity came from the vastly expanded application and improvements in agricultural inputs and techniques. Sigrid Schmalzer observes that both modern and traditional techniques "coexisted as strategies for increasing production in Mao-era China."[39] Speaking directly to the quality of these investments and their consequences for agricultural output, John Wong observes: "There can be no doubt that over the long run such labor intensive works of the communes as land improvements, flood control and water management, have borne fruit."[40]

According to Lynn T. White III, during the 1970s, agricultural advances in mechanization, seeds, and fertilizer freed up surplus rural labor and increased factor mobility.[41] White explains that agricultural modernization quietly changed China's political structure by capitalizing rural areas and increasing food production, which freed up labor; supported rural industry; and, ultimately, altered local political networks and organizational structures.[42] Bramall agrees, asserting that

[t]he conventional wisdom . . . ignores the evidence pointing to trend acceleration in the growth of agricultural production in that decade [the 1970s] driven by the trinity of irrigation, chemical fertilizer inputs, and the growing availability of new high yielding crop varieties . . . Maoist attempts to expand the irrigation network were very real, and brought lasting benefits. All this continues to distinguish Maoism from the strategies adopted across most of the developing world.[43]

Barry Naughton also recognizes that communes "were able to push agricultural production up to qualitatively higher levels" and that "green revolution technologies were pioneered by the West, but Chinese scientists, working independently, created parallel achievements and, in one or two areas, made independent breakthroughs that surpassed what was done in the West."[44] Enhanced food security helped improve average life expectancy in China from thirty-two years in 1949 to sixty-five in 1978—compared with fifty-one in India, fifty-two in Indonesia, forty-nine in Pakistan, and forty-seven in Bangladesh.[45] According to Louis Putterman:

The commune system played a major role both in the delivery of healthcare, and in the distribution of basic foodstuffs to the population, none of whom, despite their massive pressure on a meager base of land, suffered the landlessness and associated deprivation faced by tens of millions of rural dwellers in China's otherwise similar populous Asian neighbors.[46]

These researchers' contributions are vestiges of an academic literature that originated after the U.S.-China rapprochement, when Sino-American agricultural exchanges resumed for the first time since 1949. Western agricultural experts were again permitted to visit select Chinese agricultural regions—albeit under close supervision—and were allowed to observe the extensive capital investments made under the commune system. They noted reforms in China's agricultural research and extension system, and they documented (as best as they could, using the limited data available) increases in food output, investments in agricultural capital, and technological advancements in seed varieties and agricultural chemicals.

The firsthand observations of scientists and agricultural experts from the United States and European countries as well as the data and interviews they collected provided valuable insights about Chinese agriculture in the 1970s.[47] This literature contrasts with many academic works on 1970s China, which analyze either leadership politics or the sometimes-violent and disruptive urban political campaigns.[48] Instead, those studying China's agricultural sector in the 1970s and early 1980s were most interested in two closely related topics essential to evaluating commune economic performance: (1) measuring agricultural output, and (2) analyzing variations in agricultural policies and inputs and measuring their effects on agricultural output.

From August to September 1974, a plant studies delegation that included George Sprague, professor of agronomy at the University of Illinois–Urbana, spent a month visiting twenty agricultural research institutions and universities and seven communes in Jilin, Beijing, Guangdong, Shanghai, and Shaanxi. After returning, the group published a report for the National Academy of Sciences.[49] Sprague summarized the report in an article in *Science* magazine published in May 1975:

The current ability of the Chinese people to produce enough food for over 800 million people on 11 percent of their total available land is an impressive accomplishment. This has been achieved, in large part, through the expansion and intensification of traditional practices. Water control practice—irrigation, drainage, and land leveling—now include nearly 40 percent of the cultivated area. The intensity of cropping has been greatly increased. China has probably the world's most efficient system for the utilization of human and animal wastes and of crop residues. The development of "backyard" fertilizer plants and the utilization of hybrid corn and *kaoliang* (sorghum) are new elements contributing to agricultural progress.[50]

From August to September 1976, the National Academy of Sciences and the American Society of Agricultural Engineers (ASAE) hosted a reciprocal visit from the Chinese Society for Agricultural Mechanization (CSAM). CSAM Vice President Xiang Nan (who later became Vice Minister of Agriculture from 1979 to 1981) led the fifteen-member Chinese delegation, which visited American colleges, U.S. Department of Agriculture research stations, farm equipment manufacturers, and farms in ten states.[51] In 1978, CSAM invited Merle Esmay, a professor of agricultural engineering at Michigan State University, and fourteen other ASAE delegates to visit China. From August to September 1979, these American experts traveled to Jilin, Heilongjiang, Beijing, Henan, Jiangsu, Zhejiang, Shanghai, and Guangdong and documented the various investments in agricultural capital and technology made under the commune.[52]

Bruce Stone, a researcher at the International Food Policy Research Institute, has traced the causes of changes in China's agricultural output in the 1970s and 1980s. He has broken down China's green revolution by inputs, first analyzing each one's contribution to agricultural productivity and then examining their combined effects. Using this approach, Stone identifies three inputs that—when used together—were largely responsible for the rapid increases in China's agricultural output: "improved water control, abundant supplies of fertilizers, and high-yielding seed varieties responsive to these inputs."[53] He observes that the use of any one or two of these three inputs produced some yield growth, but returns were best when they were applied together in appropriate quantities.[54] Stone and Anthony Tang have found that in the 1970s China pursued an agricultural policy that was committed to the technical transformation of agriculture and included improved capital quality as "a major plank." Despite "the paucity of hard data and the controversial nature of the political system," they conclude that food grain output grew rapidly between 1972 and 1975—a conclusion corroborated by the data presented in figures 1.1–1.3 and appendix A.[55]

Between 1974 and 1978, Benedict Stavis published four essential works on the politics of China's green revolution.[56] Although his analysis spans numerous agricultural inputs, Stavis concludes that mechanization's linkage with human capital development and income distribution gave it the greatest political and social influence.[57] He explains the relationship between the CPC's desire to develop the "worker-peasant alliance" as its political base and the commune's mandate to modernize agricultural production. Stavis also highlights the importance of the research and extension system to provide feedback to agricultural scientists about the performance of new varieties and inputs under diverse local conditions.

Stavis' 1978 book, *The Politics of Agricultural Mechanization in China*, published on the eve of decollectivization, explains the relationship between Maoist politics and China's rural development scheme.[58] He examines the commune's institutional structure and agricultural extension system and their contribution to China's capital and technological development.[59] Stavis argues that agricultural mechanization not only increased output but also caused the expansion of localized rural industry, diversified the rural economy, and reduced rural–urban income inequality.[60] He observes with foresight that, "as in Taiwan and Japan," investments in agricultural mechanization had displaced many rural workers who were "considering migrating to urban areas in search of industrial employment."[61]

Over the years, numerous other scholars have documented the wide-reaching investments in agricultural capital and technological advancements in seed varieties and agricultural chemicals made in the 1970s.[62] These academic studies, which are cited throughout this volume, suggest extensive local variation in remuneration and investment strategies. Yet, they also reveal a surprising degree of consistency across time and geographic space regarding six important aspects: (1) the commune's three-tiered administrative structure, (2) the prominence and pervasiveness of Mao's collectivist ideology, (3) an emphasis on land (rather than labor) productivity, (4) the prioritization of grain and pork production, (5) the use of workpoints to distribute collective income, and (6) the inviolability of household private plots (*ziliudi*) after 1962.[63]

THEORY TESTING

Simply put, the conventional view asserts that the commune did not improve agricultural productivity, whereas the alternate view suggests that it did. In the conventional view, commune failure is attributed to flawed policies, which inhibited agricultural modernization and exacerbated collective action problems that "smothered the masses' initiative for production."[64] Conversely, those who suggest the commune was productive argue precisely the opposite—that is, that institutional and policy changes *contributed* to agricultural modernization, thus improving agricultural productivity.

"It is a capital mistake to theorize before one has data," writes Sir Arthur Conan Doyle speaking as the fictional detective Sherlock Holmes: "Insensibly one begins to twist facts to suit theories, instead of theories to suit facts."[65] Indeed, the biggest weakness of the two aforementioned theories is that both lack reliable national, provincial, and county-level data that can be replicated and used to convincingly prove or disprove the validity of their claims. Claims that commune productivity was poor often are based on anecdotal accounts, personal observations, and elite interviews in the post-commune period. Despite extensive efforts to gather data, in some cases, those who argue the commune was productive also lack the appropriate data to make definitive conclusions beyond the national or a particular locality.[66] This chapter and those that follow fill this gap using newly recovered national-, provincial-, and county-level data. They reveal that the commune substantially increased food output, elucidate the sources of this agricultural productivity growth, and explain why, despite its productivity, the institution was ultimately dismantled.

Case Selection

This study is based primarily on archival research and interviews with former commune members conducted in China between 2011 and 2016. These research trips uncovered a trove of heretofore-unexploited agricultural data on the national, provincial, and county levels, covering the commune era from 1958 to 1979. National productivity data are available in this chapter and data for *all* provinces that had communes are included in appendix A. Data on commune productivity, population growth, physical and human capital, technological innovation, and institutional structure are presented alongside other evidence, including official policy statements, the existing academic literature, and eyewitness and expert accounts. In chapters 4, 5, and 6, respectively, I interpret data with the use of economic, collective action, and organizational theories to identify causal relationships and examine the effects of capital investment and technological innovation, collectivist politics, and the commune's organizational structure on agricultural productivity. In chapter 6, for instance, I use data from Henan's 117 counties to conduct a statistical analysis to determine how changes in the size of the commune and its subunits affected agricultural productivity.

To explain trends across as much of China as possible, I selected provinces based on their relative population size and geographic location. I visited China's ten most populous provinces and obtained data on agricultural inputs and commune structure from four of them: Henan, Jiangsu, Hubei, and Zhejiang.[67] China is a big country, so to examine the effects of institutional change across grain types (i.e., rice, wheat, corn and sorghum), climates, and topographies, I successfully obtained data from two major northern agricultural provinces (Jilin and Liaoning) and sought data from two southern provinces (Guangdong and Jiangxi). Although my efforts in Guangdong proved to be ill fated, I fortuitously found data from Hunan at a small Shanghai bookstore.

To determine whether agricultural production improved under the commune, and to explain as much about collective agriculture as possible, I collected data on *grain*, *pig*, and *edible oils* production.[68] These three products were controlled by the commune and its subunits, and they were the primary sources of calories for rural residents. Families often owned a pig or two. This production, however, was tied to the collective via veterinary and stud services, through loans, and in other ways that allowed it to be accounted for. Vegetables and fruits, by contrast, were generally grown on household sideline plots, making them nearly impossible to accurately quantify during the commune era.

Data Assessment

National-level data on agricultural productivity covering the entire commune era (1958–1979) are presented in figure 1.1 and are available in appendix A along with provincial-level data. Figure 1.2 reveals that the productivity of land increased during the 1970s, and figure 1.3 shows that labor productivity improved as well, albeit at a slower rate. Between 1970 and 1979, China's production of grain, pigs, and edible oils increased by an annual average of 4.77 percent, 6.61 percent, and 6.75 percent, respectively. Within the decade, China's grain production rose by more than 120 million metric tons, reaching 332 million metric tons total, and the country added 148 million pigs, bringing the total to 320 million pigs. Edible oil production, which was not prioritized until after 1977, showed impressive increases thereafter.[69]

Figures 1.4–1.6 place China in comparative perspective alongside other large agricultural countries (i.e., India, the Soviet Union, and the United States). After 1962, China's grain production exceeded that of India and the USSR, and despite its comparatively meager base of arable land, increased apace with the United States.[70] Under the commune, China's pig production far exceeded all three of these countries, although Chinese pigs, which primarily were fed on household scraps, were about half the size of their U.S. counterparts.[71] According to the World Bank, these and other improvements in agricultural productivity meant that a Chinese person born in 1970 lived an average of 14.4 years longer than someone born in 1964 (figure 1.6).

But can these data be trusted? Pre-1979 China generally is considered to be a "black box" whose statistics are either unavailable or unreliable.[72] Indeed, it is prudent to be cautious and to recall that 1970s rural China had a closed economic and political system. Rural economic data were passed up from teams to brigades, to communes, to counties, to prefectures, to provincial authorities, and finally, to Beijing. Therefore, before examining the data, we must first question its accuracy.[73] After an extensive examination, I have concluded that there are six reasons to believe that these data reflect genuine improvements in agricultural productivity.

First, although grain output was infamously overreported during the GLF, after the famine, grain data accuracy was greatly improved. One reason for this improvement is that the legacy of famine and excessive extraction during the GLF prompted a party-wide rebuke of official exaggeration. As part of the Socialist Education Movement begun in 1965, Jonathan Spence notes that rural cadres explicitly were ordered to "clean up" their "accounting procedures" regarding "granary supplies."[74]

Second, these data include the GLF failure, which is represented by substantial declines in agricultural production at both the national and provincial levels (see appendix A). If the GLF, the commune's catastrophe, is reported, it is reasonable to assume that these data represent officials' best approximations regarding actual production.

Third, these data correspond with eyewitness accounts chronicled in the literature and statements by elderly former commune members who I interviewed during my fieldwork. After 1971, as noted previously, China began to allow Western agricultural experts to visit select rural areas. Although often dismissed as the fruits of a Potemkin village, the reports of foreign experts on China's agricultural performance are corroborated by the official data and supporting evidence presented in chapter 3 and appendix A.

Fourth, it is likely that official data systematically *underreported* increases in agricultural output during the 1970s. To reduce their tax bills and keep more resources under their auspices, commune cadres intentionally underestimated collective productivity. The same was true of subordinate brigades and teams, which manipulated data to reflect incremental productivity increases.[75] Fairbank and Goldman observe that team leaders used a "hundred ruses to deceive brigade cadres," which included "falsifying accounts, keeping two sets of books, underreporting, padding expenses, delivering grain after dark to keep it unrecorded, holding back quantities of grain by leaving the fields ungleaned, keeping new fields hidden from the brigade inspectors."[76] Informants reveal that households also regularly underreported their private sideline production to team leaders. Bramall concludes that official agricultural data for the 1970s "systematically understate" production levels, suggesting that the commune was *more* productive than the official data suggest.[77]

Fifth, provincial-level data reveal that productivity improvements occurred in the 1970s across a variety of geographic regions, crop types, and weather conditions. Obtaining data on agricultural inputs and production from numerous provinces across China helped mitigate the chances of systematic manipulation, poor-quality workmanship, or collusion among statistical bureaus.

The sixth and perhaps most convincing reason to believe that the commune successfully increased food production, at least apace with population growth, is that China—a closed agricultural economy that preached the virtues of "self-reliance"—added about 158 million people during the 1970s, and yet no large-scale famine was reported. This is strong evidence that the commune was able, at a minimum, to feed the rapidly growing population on less and less arable land.

Data Presentation

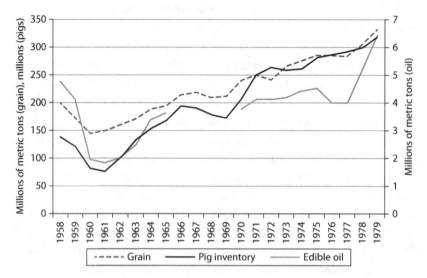

FIGURE 1.1. Total agricultural production: grain, edible oil, and pigs.
Source: Agricultural Economic Statistics 1949-1983 [Nongye jingji ziliao, 1949-1983] (Beijing: Ministry of Agriculture Planning Bureau, 1983), 143, 195, 225.

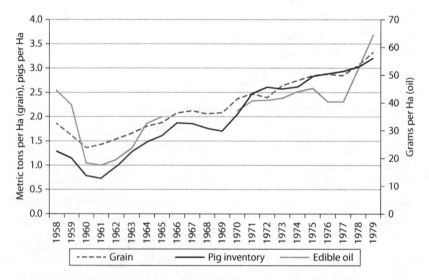

FIGURE 1.2. Agricultural production per unit land: grain, edible oil, and pigs.
Source: Agricultural Economic Statistics, 120, 143, 195, 225.

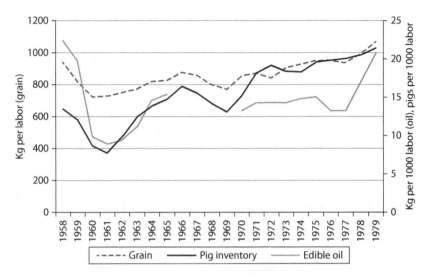

FIGURE 1.3. Agricultural production per unit labor: grain, edible oil, and pigs.
Source: Agricultural Economic Statistics, 46, 143, 195, 225.

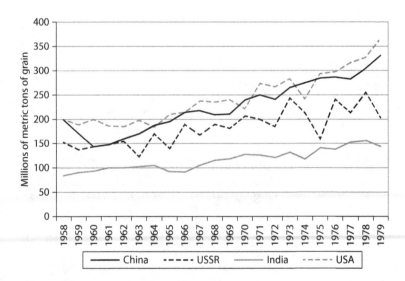

FIGURE 1.4. National comparison of grain production.
Source: Thirty Years Since the Founding of the People's Republic of China: Agricultural Statistics of Henan Province, 1949-1979 [Jianguo sanshinian: henansheng nongye tongji ziliao, 1949-1979] (Zhengzhou: Statistical Bureau of Henan Province, 1981), 410; Agricultural Economic Statistics, 143.

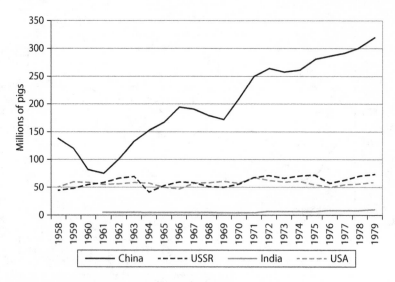

FIGURE 1.5. National comparison of pig inventory.
Source: Thirty Years: Agricultural Statistics, 421; Agricultural Economic Statistics, 225.

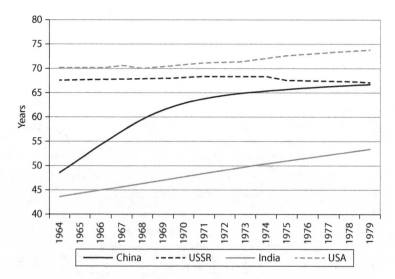

FIGURE 1.6. National comparison of life expectancy at birth.
Source: World Bank, World Development Indicators (Washington, DC: World Bank, 2015).

CONCLUSION

After observing patterns of agricultural productivity growth during the 1970s, this study applies basic insights from economic, collective action, and organizational theories to explain these trends. Following a decade of experimentation and adjustment, beginning in 1970, gradual improvements in the commune's organizational structure, remuneration methods, and agricultural research and extension system began a rural development process that substantially increased agricultural output over a sustained period and laid the foundation for continued productivity growth, urbanization, and industrialization after decollectivization.

The commune's coercive extraction of household resources financed agricultural capital accumulation and technological innovation via the research and extension system. Although this system kept rural households living in austere—often subsistence-level—conditions, it bankrolled productive investments that generated the agricultural surpluses needed to kick-start a long-run cycle of sustained investment and output growth. The commune was the fundamental institutional building block of China's investment-led rural growth strategy known as the Dazhai model.

Maoism was the commune's collectivist ethos and political backbone. It took on religious qualities that bound members to each other and to the institution. Peer pressure, group worship, venerated texts, household registration, and shared values facilitated resource extraction from productive households and helped reduce foot-dragging and shirking. These and other aspects of Maoist ideology mitigated the collective action problems inherent to all communes, thus allowing the institution to push consumption below levels that members normally would have tolerated without resorting to slacking or shirking.

After Mao's death, a reformist faction within the CPC leadership led by Vice Premier Deng Xiaoping destroyed the commune to solidify its grip on power. The reformers increased consumption levels to gain the political support they needed to unseat a rival pro-commune faction led by CPC Chairman Hua Guofeng. To achieve this, they destroyed the commune's system to extract household savings to support capital investment (i.e., the workpoint remuneration system), eliminated its administrative subunits (i.e., the commune, brigade, and team), and disavowed its cohesive collectivist ideology (i.e., Maoism)—a concurrent process known as decollectivization. Had Hua and his loyalists prevailed over Deng's reformers, however, they almost certainly would not have abandoned the commune. To the contrary, they would have used it to implement the nationwide, rural investment program detailed in Hua's Ten-Year Plan announced in February 1978.

PART I

Creating China's Green Revolution

Chapter Two

INSTITUTIONAL ORIGINS AND EVOLUTION

The contradiction between the working class and the peasant class in socialist society
is resolved by the method of collectivization and the mechanization in agriculture.

—MAO ZEDONG[1]

INTRODUCTION

This chapter examines the historic arc of rural collectivism in contemporary China before 1970. It explains the economic and political forces that created and gradually shaped the commune, and it traces changes that took place in the institution's priorities, structure, and mandate throughout the 1950s and 1960s. In so doing, it reveals how debates about agricultural modernization helped ignite the Cultural Revolution and explains how a rival institution supported by some of China's top leaders—the trust—nearly usurped the commune's control over agricultural capital and technology. These topics are examined in the context of pervasive economic challenges—rising population, falling arable land, and fast depreciating capital—that are discussed in chapter 3. This chapter recounts the first part of the commune's institutional history: *Where did it come from? Why and how was it changed over time? What role did it play in Chinese politics? Which elements of the institution continued into the 1970s, which were reformed, and which were discarded?*

From 1958, when communes were established, until decollectivization began in 1979, evolutionary changes in organizational structure, remuneration systems, and the dissemination of agricultural capital and technology reflected political changes in the top leadership that influenced every rural locality. Over time, the commune's mandate was substantially altered. Yet decisions regarding size, structure, priorities, and remuneration made throughout the first part of the institution's life span, 1958–1969, proved sticky throughout the second, 1970–1979. During the 1960s, political battles between leftists and rightists resulted in a compromise: the 1970s Green Revolution Commune. This hybrid institution combined elements of both collective and household production, economic planning and free markets, and collective and private remuneration.

Over the life of the commune, agricultural investment strategies and remuneration systems changed considerably to reflect political struggles among elite factions. In 1958 and 1959, the large Great Leap Forward (GLF) Commune instituted free-supply remuneration, ended material incentives, closed free markets, and prioritized red politics over technical know-how when making investments. To stem the GLF famine, these polices were reversed and two administrative subunits—the brigade and its subordinate, the team—were created. Private household plots, free markets, and cottage enterprises, collectively known as the Three Small Freedoms, were adopted and also remained in place until decollectivization. These and other institutional changes were made in the November 1960 "Urgent Directive on Rural Work" (i.e., the *Twelve Articles*), drafted by Zhou Enlai, and were expanded on in the "Regulations on the Rural People's Communes" (i.e., the *Sixty Articles on Agriculture*), which were drafted by Deng Xiaoping and Peng Zhen in March 1961. The *Sixty Articles* subsequently were adopted in September 1962 at the Tenth Plenum of the Eighth Communist Party of China (CPC) Central Committee in 1962 (see appendix C).

During the early 1960s, right-leaning leaders—led by Liu Shaoqi and Deng—favored a central bureaucracy that determined agricultural investments based on *profitability*. Their strategy called for large centralized trusts to facilitate the sale of agricultural equipment, seeds, and chemicals by state-owned enterprises (SOEs) to those communes that could afford them. Under Liu's direction, a dozen or more trusts were established to implement this strategy, including one trust established in 1963 to coordinate the production and sales of agricultural machines. Advocates of this centralized approach also supported shrinking the commune's size, removing agricultural modernization from its mandate, and introducing household contract farming (*baochandaohu*).

Mao and his supporters, by contrast, championed the commune as the rural institution that could introduce socialist values and boost agricultural productivity. They opposed the centralized trusts and instead supported the establishment of large semiautonomous communes, with a broad political and economic mandate. Communes, the Maoists argued, should not rely on profit-seeking state-run trusts and SOEs, but rather should own and maintain their own farm equipment, fertilizer production facilities, and crop test fields. Likewise, they believed communes should be encouraged to reinvest their profits locally with an eye toward increasing agricultural output, specifically in grain and pork production. Intracommune industry and infrastructure construction were intended to expand local production of agricultural capital and technology and to disseminate them widely. This commune-led approach to rural development, known as the Dazhai model, was an ambitious nationwide (as opposed to targeted) strategy that required high rates of household income extraction to underwrite local capital investment.

The trust, in short, challenged the commune's position as the primary institution of rural China and its ownership over the means of agricultural production. The commune stressed *local* autonomy, whereas the trust stressed *central* control; the commune prioritized *nationwide* agricultural modernization, whereas trusts prioritized development in *select* regions; the commune depended on *small-scale* local production to reduce transportation costs, whereas the trust prioritized *economies of scale* in production to generate savings.

Between 1965 and 1969, the commune experienced substantial institutional reforms. Changes were made to the workpoint remuneration system, its collectivist ideology, the agricultural research and extension system, and the ownership and control of farm machines. These reforms were completed by 1970 and were promulgated at the Northern Districts Agricultural Conference, which began in August of that year in Xiyang, Shanxi, the home of the model Dazhai brigade. What emerged was the Green Revolution Commune, which included elements of collective and private production, ample local control over workpoint remuneration methods, and an integrated three-in-one organizational structure designed to channel local resources into productive capital investments to increase grain and pig output (see chapters 3 and 4) and mitigate collective action problems (see chapter 5). After 1970, the institution not only retained the private plots, cottage industries, and rural markets that had begun in the early 1960s but also featured the collective ownership of capital and Mao's pervasive collectivist ideology.

This chapter has two sections. The first section introduces the institutional antecedents of the commune, which served as the origins of collective agriculture in contemporary China: Mutual Aid Teams (MATs; 1954–1955) and Agricultural Producer Cooperatives (APC; 1956–1957). These organizations had an economic but *not* a political mandate. The second section examines the commune's first dozen years and is subdivided by its first three phases: the GLF Commune (1958–1961), the Rightist Commune (1962–1964), and the Leftist Commune (1965–1969). The subsections examine China's agricultural modernization strategy during each one of these three phases, which are distinguished in chapter 4 using economic growth models. The average annual agricultural production growth rates during these phases are available in appendix A. It is important to note that growth rates under the Rightist Commune are amplified because that period followed directly on the heels of the GLF Commune's economic failure.

ANTECEDENT INSTITUTIONS

Mutual Aid Teams

Before 1949, the independent family farm was the dominant social and economic structure of rural China. These farms were small, averaging about 2 hectares (ha) in the north, and just over 1 ha in the south. Landlords owned nearly half of the land, which they leased to households, but they contributed little else to production. In the south, land leases were generally long, sometimes for life, whereas in the north, one-year contracts were common. As in most premodern rural societies, rents were high, generally about half of the main crop, as were interest rates, which averaged more than 30 percent a year in the 1930s. Underemployment was a serious problem, with labor in surplus most of the year but scarce during the planting and harvesting seasons. Northern peasants worked an average of 100–120 days per year, while the average southerner worked only 80–100 days per year. The local market town was the economic hub, which was connected to higher-level domestic markets.[2]

During the late 1940s and early 1950s, a land-to-the-tiller reform program was implemented in areas as they came under communist control.

The Agrarian Reform Law of 1950 revoked all land ownership, redistributed land to farmers, and branded landlords and rich peasants as class enemies before displacing, brutalizing, and sometimes killing them. Like similar programs in the Soviet Union and elsewhere, the purpose of China's land reform was to simultaneously consolidate the party's political support among poor rural farmers, wrest economic control from traditional rural elites, and initiate the destruction of "old" society and its institutions. In China, as in most agrarian societies, land ownership was closely associated with economic and political power; hence, seizing land was synonymous with seizing power. The destruction of preexisting rural institutions during land reform cleared the way for the CPC to create its own institution: the commune.[3]

In the early 1950s, land was generally distributed on a per capita basis, resulting in economic inefficiencies. Families with small children, for instance, received more land than they could manage, whereas families with older children had surplus labor. Furthermore, labor, which was abundant most of the year, continued to be scarce during planting and harvesting seasons. To alleviate these impediments, MATs consisting of about ten families each were created to facilitate labor sharing during peak demand. By 1954, 68 million families had joined MATs, which built on preexisting labor-sharing arrangements among friends, relatives, and neighbors.[4]

Land reform and MATs redistributed land and power, but they did not change ownership structures or resolve the collective action problems that continued to disincentivize households from pooling their resources to make large-scale capital and infrastructure investment. Because MATs were small, it was difficult to organize labor for infrastructure projects (e.g., irrigation works, land leveling, and terracing) or combine funds to purchase equipment (e.g., plows and waterwheels). Households continued to buy, own, and sell land and to borrow money from richer farmers. Families that lacked labor or inputs were beginning to sell their land, borrow money at high interest rates, and contract themselves out as laborers. Strong traditionalist tendencies and commercial patterns also remained—trends that, if left unredressed, threatened to gradually undo land reform.[5]

Agricultural Producer Cooperatives

The APC was an economic institution at the village or subvillage level under which households collectively managed land and productive inputs and shared costs. The premise was that larger cooperatives would reduce waste and harness surplus labor during the down season for work on capital infrastructure projects. Income was distributed based on the proportion of land and other resources each household contributed to the collective and on the labor performed that season.[6] By the end of 1955, 17 million peasant households had joined 630,000 APCs.[7] On the heels of their establishment, Mao seized the momentum and quickly expanded the size of APCs. On July 31, 1955, he proclaimed: "Throughout the Chinese countryside a new upsurge in socialist mass movement is in sight. But some of our comrades are tottering alone like a woman with bound feet. The tide of social reform in the countryside—in the shape of cooperation—has already been reached in some places. Soon it will sweep the whole country."[8]

A larger institution, Mao argued, would improve labor mobilization for local infrastructure projects and harness greater resources to purchase modern capital and inputs. It could consolidate CPC control over the countryside and prevent the rise of an independent class of rich and middle peasants. These "political considerations," explain Dwight Perkins and Shahid Yusuf, "virtually dictated eventual collectivization, although the decision was made much easier by the justification that collectivizing agriculture would yield economic benefits as well. Political objectives enjoyed primacy over economic ones."[9] Politically, the objective was to end the landlord-gentry class' domination of the rural power structure. Economically, the goal was "to stimulate the rapid recovery of agricultural production, which had been stagnant since the mid-1930s," explains Richard Baum.[10]

To achieve these goals, larger Higher-Level Producer Cooperatives (HAPC) were established in 1956. Some areas transformed directly from MATs to HAPCs. By February 1956, more than half of China's villages had opened HAPCs, and by the end of that year, 107 million farm families—more than 90 percent of China's 500 million farmers—had joined 746,000 HAPCs. The average HAPC was much larger than the APC that preceded it, with each new cooperative including one hundred to two hundred families and five hundred to one thousand people.[11]

The HAPC was usually the same size as the village, so although political leadership and economic management remained separate, for the first time, they covered the same geographic area. The cooperative administered nearly all productive inputs (e.g., land, tools, and farm animals), with the only remaining vestiges of private ownership being a few chickens or pigs and a small plot usually adjacent to the family home.[12]

HAPCs ended remuneration based on resource contribution and began to award workpoints based solely on labor contribution.[13] The number of workpoints its members earned determined each household's income, and the workpoint's value was determined after the harvest was sold and all member workpoints were added together and divided by total collective income. Each member's share (normally paid in grain or cash) was what remained after all taxes, administrative costs, input costs, advances, and welfare funds were deducted. Only production on the family's small private plot was exempt from this calculation.[14] Although the way that workpoints were awarded varied by time and place, the aforementioned method for calculating their value remained constant from 1956 until the commune's dissolution more than two decades later. The brief exception was the GLF's disastrous experiment with free-supply remuneration, which is discussed in the next section.

The HAPCs sold their output to the state and at rural markets, which remained open in 1957. Originally, the free markets established in the summer of 1956 were intended for native and subsidiary products that were not subject to state planning or purchase. After their establishment, however, these markets quickly grew to include grain and other agricultural products earmarked for government procurement. This market expansion undermined the state's power to use price controls to extract agricultural surpluses. To remedy the problem, new regulations were issued in August 1957 restricting the sale of grain, oil-bearing crops, and cotton to state purchase agencies or state-controlled grain markets.[15]

During the off-season, HAPCs supplied labor to build local infrastructure projects. Like fieldwork, workers received workpoints based on the time they spent on construction. Any increase in agricultural productivity from a project went into the institution's general fund, to be reinvested or apportioned along with all other household income based on workpoints. The HAPC successfully mobilized resources for small-scale capital investments, but it did not eliminate the difficulties associated with projects that traversed two or more cooperatives. An irrigation or road project might require labor from several HAPCs, but when only a few benefited from the project, those who gained little or nothing lacked the incentive to supply labor and materials. Leaders and members were understandably reluctant to dilute the value of their workpoints by awarding them for labor on projects that did not increase their HAPC's income.[16]

Other problems cast doubt on the sustainability of the HAPCs. Concerns were voiced on the left about the system's hierarchical organization, the clear division between manual and mental work, the aloofness and unresponsiveness of cadres, and the bureaucratization and centralization of production planning and decision-making. Leftists also criticized policies that squeezed agriculture to fund urban industrialization. Because more than 80 percent of Chinese were commune members, such a policy benefited only the minority of urbanites, and if the communes were unable to produce a surplus, it benefited no one.[17]

The economic mandate of the HAPCs soon overwhelmed its sister political institution, the township (*xiang*). The cooperative organized production, collected taxes, and distributed food and income, while the township enforced party policies, maintained the police, investigated political crimes, and handled army recruitment. But as HAPCs grew, sometimes into multivillage organizations, it became increasingly difficult for townships to provide political leadership. In 1955–1956, townships were consolidated into Big Townships (*da xiang*), which were larger than the HAPCs and intended to enhance political leadership over them. In 1957, there were about 750,000 HAPCs and about 100,000 Big Townships.[18]

THE COMMUNE'S FIRST THREE PHASES

Phase 1: The Great Leap Forward Commune (1958-1961)

Communist ideology stresses two interrelated goals, one economic and the other political: encouraging inclusive economic growth, and changing the character of social relations to promote a collectivist—as opposed to an individualist—community ethos. In a vast agricultural country like China, it is unclear which institutions can best accomplish these objectives. To design a self-sufficient, self-administered collective rural institution that could achieve these two goals, China created communes and reformed them continuously throughout the 1960s. This evolutionary process began in 1958 with the establishment of the GLF Commune.

In 1958, the HAPCs were consolidated into about 26,000 massive communes, each containing an average of about 4,500 ha of land,

24,000 people, and 5,200 households, although commune size varied substantially among provinces (see chapter 3, figures 3.3 and 3.4). William Skinner has hypothesized that because townships were the lowest level of the traditional marketing area, GLF communes generally included the cooperatives in two or three marketing areas, perhaps an intermediate market and its subordinate markets.[19] GLF communes averaged about thirty HAPCs, although some included as many as a hundred.[20]

The GLF Commune was intended to produce a revolution in agricultural capital and technology to increase food output and raise living standards. Agricultural modernization and the surpluses it was intended to generate would expand opportunities in rural industry, which, over time, would eliminate the rural–urban divide, hence solidifying the worker-peasant alliance as the CPC's political base. Mao argued that greater labor mobilization alone would be insufficient to generate these sustained increases in agricultural output. Meeting the fast-growing rural population's expanding demands without more arable land required modern agricultural capital and technology, such as fertilizers, water pumps, improved seed varieties, and farm machinery.

Mao billed the GLF Commune as the institution that could implement a nationwide rural development program. In 1956, he envisaged that mechanization would expand and diversify rural employment opportunities:

After the mechanization of agriculture there will emerge in the future various kinds of undertakings never before imagined by people, and the yields of agricultural crops will be raised several times and even scores of times the present level. The development of industrial, communications, and exchange enterprises will even be beyond the imagination of the people of the past. Likewise, there will be such developments in the fields of science, culture, education, and public health.[21]

But not everyone supported investments in agricultural capital. Opponents raised five main arguments: (1) because China's population was large and land was scarce, modernization would increase unemployment without raising yields; (2) China's massive size, mountain ranges, and east-flowing rivers would inhibit capital distribution and maintenance; (3) in many areas, topography was not conducive to tractorization; (4) mechanization required scarce resources like iron, steel, and petroleum; and (5) agricultural modernization was too expensive. In 1956, a high-level critic, Bo Yibo, warned that "with such a large reservoir of manpower in the Chinese countryside and such complicated farming systems, it is impossible to introduce mechanization. If mechanization is introduced, the problem of surplus labor power in the countryside is so acute as to defy solution."[22] Minister of Agriculture Liao Luyen similarly warned that "with the exception of those areas where land is plentiful and labor power is inadequate and also with the exception of a number of economic crop growing areas any hasty steps to achieve mechanization are unacceptable to the masses, nor will they be conducive to raising agricultural output."[23]

Despite these concerns, in October 1957, the State Technical Commission published a report that found that to cope with rapid population growth, China should prioritize agricultural modernization to increase yields. The report observed that during the harvest and planting seasons, even densely populated areas suffered labor shortages, which were exacerbated by multiple cropping systems that simultaneously harvested one crop while preparing to plant another. Improved yields thus required expanding irrigation networks and access to fertilizer, farm tools, agricultural machines, and vehicles. The successful commune, the commission argued, would use capital to free field labor to work on diverse tasks, including animal husbandry, oil processing, sugar refining, flour processing, brickmaking, pipe making, tractor repair, carpentry, iron work, and tailoring.[24]

Mao supported the GLF Commune, claiming it could quickly improve the countryside's capital-to-labor ratio. The 1958 Chengdu Conference advocated the initial deployment of agricultural capital and technology in suburban and commercial crop areas, followed by their adoption nationwide. The conference emphasized small farm machines and semimechanized farm implements, supplied by small local manufacturers.[25] In April 1959, Mao promulgated a ten-year plan to modernize China's agriculture:

The fundamental way out for agriculture lies in mechanization. Ten years will be needed to achieve this. There will be minor solutions in four years, intermediate ones in seven, and major solutions in ten. This year, next year, the year after and the year after, we will be relying mainly on improved farm tools and semi-mechanized farming implements. Every province, every district, and every county must establish farm tools research stations and concentrate a group of scientific-technological personnel and experienced carpenters and blacksmiths of the rural areas to gather together all kinds of more advanced farm tools from every province, district, and county. They should compare them, experiment with them, and improve them. New types of farm implements must be trial-produced. When they are successfully trial-produced, test them out in the fields. If they are found to be truly effective, then they can be mass-produced and widely used. When we speak of mechanization, we must also include mechanized manufacture of chemical fertilizers. It is a matter of great importance to increase chemical fertilizer production year-by-year.[26]

Three months later, at the 1959 Lushan Conference, Mao supported the creation of the Ministry of Agricultural Machinery, which opened on August 26, 1959—two days before the *People's Daily* announced the Ten-Year Plan for Agricultural Mechanization.[27] In 1960, policy statements and *People's Daily* editorials on January 13 and February 25 stressed mechanization and farm tool innovations.[28] That April, Tan Chenlin, then-deputy director of the CPC's rural work department, endorsed a three-stage agricultural mechanization plan:

1. Small-scale solution in four years (1959–63). Agriculture, livestock breeding, irrigation, and drainage. During this time, mechanization should be achieved in a preliminary way in the outskirts of big cities, market grain growing centers, the major industrial crop growing centers and the major non-staple food growing centers, while the major part of the rural area should concentrate mainly on popularizing semi-mechanization and improved implements.
2. Medium-scale solution in seven years (1964–66). By the end of seven years, mechanization should have materialized over more than half of the rural areas as a result of the gradual development of the agricultural industry and increased supply of agricultural machines.
3. Large-scale solution in ten years (1966–69). By the end of the ten years, virtually all the countryside should have mechanization and a considerable degree of rural electrification.[29]

Large-scale labor mobilization for infrastructure construction dates back to ancient times: water management projects improve crop yields, which, in turn, support more people and increase tax revenues. If village-size cooperatives could mobilize labor for small projects, the reasoning went, then pooling twenty to thirty cooperatives into a commune could build larger projects that would improve commune productivity, thus increasing the value of their workpoints and incentivizing members' participation.

The first major attempts at mass labor mobilization came in late 1957. Instead of sitting through the winter, tens of millions of farmers were organized to build dams, reservoirs, dikes, and irrigation canals. At this time, "redness"—including political zeal, enthusiasm for the collective, and class background—was prized over technical knowledge and experience, and Mao coined the phrase "take grain as the key link," which remained a cornerstone of agricultural policy until decollectivization. When Shandong Provincial Secretary Tan Qilong reported that Beiyuan Township, Lichen County was preparing to establish HAPCs, Mao said, "It is better to set up people's communes. Their advantage lies in the fact that they combine industry, agriculture, commerce, education and military affairs. This is convenient for leadership."[30] By fall 1958, communes were being established, free markets for agricultural commodities were closed, and private household plots were eliminated.[31]

The first assessments of the GLF Commune were promising. In 1958, China's reported grain harvest surpassed the United States, and party leaders were told that the country could produce as much rice as it wanted. The movement accelerated, and Mao announced that rural residents should eat five meals a day. Believing that food was abundant, party leaders raised grain procurement quotas, which commune cadres, who had inflated their grain production reports, were obligated to fulfill. Rather than upset their superiors, they lied and squeezed every grain from the hapless households under their jurisdiction. The result was an orgy of official exaggeration, while at the bottom, hundreds of millions suffered.[32]

Meanwhile, problems with the large and hastily assembled GLF communes thwarted plans to standardize and expand the application of modern inputs. GLF communes suffered from insufficient engineering know-how, scarce skilled labor, flawed techniques, poor-quality capital and inputs, a paucity of careful planning, and an emphasis on political correctness over technical expertise. The result was a large stock of useless, fast-depreciating capital, often made from poor-quality iron smelted in backyard furnaces. When the first heavy rains fell in summer 1958, many dams, canals, dikes, and reservoirs that had been quickly built the previous winter failed, inundating hundreds of thousands of acres. Within two years, more than two hundred of the five hundred largest reservoirs built in 1957–1958 were abandoned.[33] In 1962, Zhou Enlai voiced his concern about the poor condition of China's reservoirs and their associated water delivery systems: "I've been told by doctors that if a person goes without eating for a few days, no major harm will result. But if one goes without urinating for even one day, they will be poisoned. It's the same with land. How can we accumulate water and not discharge it?"[34]

During the GLF, the rapid expansion of entitlements—coupled with insufficient planning, technical skills, and oversight—created a disincentive to hard work. Between 1958 and 1960 (before the team level was created), the massive GLF communes or brigades were the basic accounting units. Because workpoints entitled members to a percentage of the entire commune's total output, if a worker was completely unproductive the value of that worker's workpoints declined by only a fraction of a percent. Too little connection existed between an individual's labor and workpoint value. Without subunits, the large commune was unable to supervise and evaluate the contribution of each of its roughly 8,500 workers.[35]

The free-supply remuneration system adopted by commune cafeterias also failed. With 50–80 percent of income distributed as "subsistence supplies" and only 20–50 percent distributed based on labor, a serious free-rider problem emerged.[36] The false sense of abundance generated by free-supply remuneration contributed to careless field management, which compounded the aforementioned problems, producing a cataclysm: between 15 million and 30 million people starved to death during the GLF famine.[37]

Despite the GLF's catastrophic failure, one of its lasting legacies was the mobilization of women in the rural workforce.[38] Carl Riskin identifies two additional contributions that outlived the movement: the nationwide system of rural communes to facilitate large-scale rural capital accumulation and technological innovation, and the proliferation of small and midsize enterprises in rural China.[39]

Phase 2: The Rightist Commune (1962-1964)

The GLF disaster prompted the Chinese government to review its agricultural policy.[40] In 1958, Mao had championed the commune as the institution that would allow China to reach communism quickly and overtake capitalist countries in terms of productivity. Before 1961, China's rural policy had prioritized transforming grassroots social relations (politics) over increasing productivity (economics). This policy altered the architecture of local power relations, but not the quantity or quality of available agricultural capital and technology. After 1961, the commune was changed to facilitate China's gradual transition from socialism (to each according to his work) to communism (to each according to his need). Economic performance was unquestionably placed at the fore, and ideology was employed to encourage productivity. A worker's industriousness and expertise became prime determinants of his or her redness.

In the early 1960s, Mao and Liu prioritized competing rural development goals. Liu, supported by Deng, Peng Zhen, and others, believed that *profitability* was essential. He argued that success in agriculture required an efficient, centralized administration; specialization and economies of scale in input (e.g., fertilizer) and machine (e.g., tractor) production; and material incentive structures for workers. Mao, by contrast, prioritized *agricultural development* and reaffirmed that the commune was the institution that could modernize rural China and spread an ethos of collectivism. Over time, Mao argued, rural industrialization under the commune would reduce the differences in capital-to-labor ratios between the agricultural and industrial sectors, urban and rural areas, and mental and manual workers, thus further solidifying the "worker-peasant alliance" as the party's political base.

The GLF famine halted Mao's Ten-Year Plan for Agricultural Mechanization and caused the commune's size and institutional mandate to be scaled back considerably. Vast quantities of poor-quality capital had been built, yet China still had little advanced agricultural technology; few world-class scientists and engineers; falling amounts of arable land; and a massive, growing pool of unskilled rural labor that still used ancient farming tools and techniques. To address these problems, new rules were promulgated between 1960 and 1962 in the *Twelve Articles* and in the *Sixty Articles on Agriculture* (see appendix C), respectively. When Deng and Peng drafted the latter document, which remained the operational guide to commune administration until decollectivization, they neglected to consult Mao. Consequently, when the draft was discussed at the March 1961 Central Committee work conference, the resentful chairman pointedly inquired: "Which emperor decided this?"[41]

These directives created and empowered the production brigade and the production team as property-owning subunits under the commune. In 1959, at the height of the crisis, the brigade level, which was about the same size as the 1957 HAPC, was created and took over accounting and remuneration from the commune level.[42] Then, in 1961, the production team, which was roughly the size of the 1955 APC, became the institution's primary accounting unit, under which the value of the workpoint was determined and income was distributed. Shrinking the size of the basic accounting unit—from the commune to the brigade and, ultimately, to the team—increased members' ability to monitor each other's performance, thereby lessening the free-rider problem.[43] Jonathan Unger describes how team-based remuneration was introduced in Chen Village in Guangdong:

Each of Chen Village's five neighborhoods was organized into a production team, and each was granted ownership and control over a fifth of the village land. This relatively small number of fifty households would be remunerated through the harvest yield from its own fields. To assure that the peasants would see a vested interest in working hard to improve their own livelihood, each of the five neighborhoods was further divided half a year later to form even smaller teams, each containing some twenty to twenty-five families.[44]

THREE FREEDOMS AND ONE GUARANTEE (SANZI YIBAO)

The primary objective of the Rightest Commune was to rapidly increase household consumption to end the GLF famine. There was substantial intraparty consensus that this required incentive-based remuneration schemes that closely linked income to work.[45] The GLF free-supply system was ended, and remuneration was again based entirely on labor contribution. Communes were permitted to experiment with ability-based work grades and various performance-based workpoint rate systems, including time, task, and piece rates.[46]

The new rules were summarized as the Three Freedoms and One Guarantee (sanzi yibao): private household sideline plots, family-run cottage industries, free markets, and household production quotas.[47] Of these measures, the latter was the most controversial and the only one that did not last beyond the early 1960s. To restore agricultural productivity in the aftermath of the GLF famine, Anhui Party Chief Zeng Xisheng applied a "designated land responsibility system," and in 1961, Beijing officially blessed household contracting.[48] Under the scheme, household income was closely tied to productivity. Each family was allotted fertilizer, seed, and a piece of land at the start of the growing season. Every plot was assigned a production quota, and after the harvest, the household would supply its crop to the team in return for a set number of workpoints. The team then would sell its crop to the state at a discount and could peddle any remainder at the local market. After covering its costs, the team distributed the remaining cash to its households based on their accumulated workpoints. Sometimes, the household could keep what it produced beyond its quota; other times, the team purchased the surplus and paid farmers a progressive workpoint bonus. Unger notes that in Chen Village, for instance, "an extra 150 pounds (of rice) over the quota would earn a family 200 extra workpoints."[49]

Private household plots were allocated on a per capita basis and were generally adjacent to the family home. According to the *Sixty Articles*, these plots were supposed to make up 5–7 percent of each commune's cultivated land. Households could plant whatever they wanted on their sideline plots, but vegetables, fruit trees, and tobacco were common. A family could also raise a limited number of pigs, chickens, ducks, and geese. The commune, brigade, or team would sell a piglet to a family on credit, provide low-cost veterinary or stud services, and be repaid when the pig was brought to market. This arrangement, which continued throughout the 1960s and 1970s, was a hybrid collective–private approach that placed both household production and rural markets under commune auspices, thus enhancing their legibility to the state.

Handicrafts, including basket weaving, embroidering, shoemaking, and tailoring, were common household sideline enterprises, as were fishing, hunting animals or snakes for food or medicine, silk production, beekeeping, and collecting firewood.[50] If an enterprise grew to include multiple households, the team could establish a cooperative. The increased output that came from sideline production and rural household enterprises was sold for cash at local free markets. As early as September 1959, at the height of the famine, Beijing reopened these markets; by 1961, China had forty thousand rural markets, and in 1962, market sales accounted for one-quarter of all rural commodity transactions.[51] Household farming expanded rapidly in 1961 and 1962, and in Yunnan, Guizhou, and Sichuan, its value exceeded collective farming.[52]

As household enterprises and rural markets expanded, tensions emerged between the private and collective sectors. In the slack season, workers' focus on private sideline plots increased output. During planting and harvest seasons, however, sideline production and cottage industries competed with the collective for scarce labor. Because the profits of the sideline enterprises went directly to the household, members began devoting more and more energy to these enterprises at the expense of collective production. To ensure that farmers prioritized the collective, cadres pressured them not to overemphasize the private sector.[53] The following account, published in 1972, reveals how local cadres pressured households and how the latter resisted:

In 1960 . . . the pernicious doctrine of the free market and material incentives were being propagated by the capitalist roaders in the Party leadership. There was a free market about 20 lis (10 km) away from the commune. I came to learn that some of our members were going to the free market and selling the produce of their private plots at exorbitant prices. They also used to take their hens and eggs for sale. The gravest situation, in this regard, arose in one of our difficult and poor brigades, namely, Yang Fang. Members would take the tobacco grown on their private plots to the free market. The normal price of such tobacco was 1.5 yuan per catty, but they would sell it at 6 yuan per catty. The same was true of chickens. If the normal price was 1 yuan, they would get on the free market about 5 yuan. Now these were dangerous tendencies. Work for the collective was ignored in favor of work on private plots. Profit was put in command. One day I went to the free market to make an investigation. My comrades, who had gone there, disappeared when they saw me. I recognized one person and I asked him: "Why are you here?" He said: "I have come to buy some things." This was not true. Then why did he lie? Because he felt that what he was doing was not right. That evening I went to this comrade's house and I asked him: "What did you buy?" He answered: "Tobacco." I asked: "Can't you grow enough on your own plot?" He did not answer. Then we organized mass meetings in the brigade. We asked, should we rely on private plots or on the collective, should we depend on 5 percent or on 95 percent? All of us cadres went to the various teams and launched a mass education campaign. Gradually, fewer and fewer people went to the free market. We mobilized the masses and started a campaign for production. People's enthusiasm was roused, and we reached a high tide in production.[54]

Under contracting, farming families with more workers or better land earned more, which allowed them to contract more land or raise more live-stock, which, in turn, further increased their income. By contrast, house-holds with young children or a weak, an old, or a sickly adult fared less well. But labor-rich households not only wanted to maximize their income but also to minimize risks, because at any time they too could face ill-ness or lose a crop as a result of drought or pestilence.[55] On the basis of interviews with Guangdong residents, Unger concludes that most farmers supported "a system of collective agriculture [that] provided a peasant with a cushion of sharing in broader economic resources than his or her family could manage on its own."[56] By 1963 and 1964, with the GLF famine a bitter memory, household contracts were designated a temporary measure and communes were instructed to return to predominantly collective systems of agricultural production and remuneration. The Three Small Freedoms, however, would remain an officially sanctioned part of the commune system until decollectivization.

THE RISE OF THE TRUST

After the GLF crisis abated, in late 1962–1963, agricultural modernization reemerged as a priority. In September 1962, the communiqué of the Tenth Plenary Session of the Eighth CPC Central Committee announced the following:

It is necessary to mobilize and concentrate the strength of the whole Party and the whole nation in an active way to give agriculture and the collective economy of the people's communes every possible material, technical and financial aid as well as aid in in the field of leadership and personnel, and to bring about the technical transformation of agriculture, stage-by-stage in a manner suited to local conditions.[57]

In October, top political leaders and agricultural experts met to discuss implementation of this directive. Participants included Zhou Enlai, Minister of Agriculture Liao, Tan Chenlin (politburo agricultural specialist), and Chairman Nie Rongzhen and Vice-Chairman Han Guang of the State Science and Technological Commission. Among them were twenty-six agricultural specialists, thirteen of whom held doctorates from American or European universities. After the meeting, 1,200 agricultural scientists and technicians gathered for a six-week conference that set priorities and outlined a national agricultural modernization agenda.[58]

In June 1963, a *People's Daily* article entitled "Exploration of a Few Problems Concerning Mechanization in Our Agriculture" identified three goals in agriculture: improving yields, guaranteeing grain production, and introducing modern agricultural equipment. To achieve these ends, the article advocated a targeted approach focused on select regions rather than one "carried out it in such an excessively scattered manner as to seem blooming everywhere. There should be concentration of forces to fight battles of annihilation, basically winning one battle before waging another."[59] At a conference of agricultural science and technology held in spring 1963, ten regions—among them Beijing, the Northeast, the Sichuan Basin, Lake Taihu near Shanghai, the Pearl River Delta in Guangzhou, and Hainan— were selected as demonstration sites.[60]

The Ministry of Agriculture was charged with building an agrotechnical extension station system from the ashes of the GLF. At least one professionally staffed extension station was created for every three or four communes to introduce new production techniques created at research institutions and agricultural universities. In fall 1961, the commune's control over the acquisition and distribution of agricultural capital was transferred to newly created and functionally independent Agricultural Machinery Stations (AMS).[61] Profit-minded SOEs administered by large monopolistic trusts supplied these AMSs, which managed machinery operation, leasing, and repair. By 1963, however, the AMS had begun to accumulate excess staff and losses, and they were told to become profitable within two years or risk facing closure. Cash rewards were given for reducing expenditures by lowering gasoline use, reducing staff, and cutting maintenance costs—a strategy that enhanced profits but not agricultural production.[62]

This agricultural strategy, which Liu and Deng supported, was predicated on centralization, gradualism, and profits. Despite Mao's opposition at the Tenth Plenum, he was unable to block the adoption of this approach, and large, centrally controlled trusts were created to disburse capital and technological inputs. The trusts centralized administration and planning in the agricultural sector and targeted investments into regions that could afford them.[63] Peng Zhen, then secretary general of the Standing Committee of the National People's Congress (NPC), explained the logic: "Use of machinery must be centralized. If ten or eight tractors are allocated to one county they cannot be well maintained. Tractors must be used in a centralized manner in counties one by one."[64] In October and December 1963, Liu promoted trusts to enhance central control over agriculture:

It is necessary to consider the trust method. Control must be exercised over manufacture as well as business management. Rather than set up truck and tractor departments, it is better to organize truck and tractor companies. The operating expenses for agricultural machines should also buy those companies. . . . In short, things must be organized and planned. Don't promote things on your own with no regard for the Center. All local undertakings must be organized, and this is what is called socialism.[65]

A dozen or more trusts were established between 1963 and 1965, each with its own monopoly. During a meeting in December 1963, Liu instructed the agricultural machinery trust to maintain tight control over agricultural modernization:

It is good to have agricultural machinery supply centers. A big trust should be formed and supply substations should be set up along railroads and highways. Don't set up stations according to administrative districts and don't put them under the direct jurisdiction of counties. Local authorities must not lay their hands on such stations. They can make suggestions, but cannot allocate money for making such stations. All agricultural machines should be under the unified management of the supply company and factories should also be under its control. Tractors, irrigation supply companies, and factories should also be under its control. Tractors, irrigation and drainage machines, and oil supply should be under the unified management of the company.[66]

Between 1963 and 1965, trusts controlled agricultural modernization. In March 1964, the China Tractor and Internal Combustion Engine Spare Parts Company was created to manage thirteen factories producing more than five thousand types of spare parts. The next month, another trust, the China Tractor and Internal Combustion Engine Industrial Company, was similarly established. It absorbed more than one hundred local enterprises and operated eight regional branches in the Northeast, Shanghai, Tianjin, and other regions. By the end of 1965, a trust in Shaanxi controlled 120 local factories and AMSs, 6 major factories, 4 schools, 10 agrotechnical research and extension stations, and about 100 stores. The trust was, in fact, a rival institution to the commune, one that—rather than operating as an autonomous, self-reliant unit—answered directly to the central bureaucracy. As Peng, who gave the report at the National Conference on Agricultural Machine Work in July 1965, explained: "When we operate a trust and have the trust take over the work of the Party, we are in fact running an industrial party."[67]

THE COMMUNE OR THE TRUST?

From 1964 to 1966, in the lead-up to the Cultural Revolution, a struggle was under way at the highest levels of the Chinese leadership between advocates of two alternative visions of socialism. Agricultural capital and technology—its manufacture, distribution, ownership, and management—played a central role in this struggle. Conflicts had emerged over which institution, the commune or the trust, would manage the production and distribution of agricultural capital and technology. These competing development strategies had been debated for years, but during the Cultural Revolution, these disagreements—previously contained within the party—exploded into every aspect of life. Although differences about which agricultural modernization strategy could best feed and employ China's growing population were not the only cause of the Cultural Revolution, they were among the most important.

Liu's strategy, which was based on the Soviet experience, was predominant before communes were established in 1958 and reemerged in the early 1960s after the GLF's failure. It stressed using agricultural surpluses to support investments in urban heavy industry.[68] As described previously, proponents favored the creation of SOEs under the auspices of centrally controlled trusts. Urban, suburban, and selected rural areas received the lion's share of investment, whereas most rural localities were excluded. This process would, Liu argued, target inputs into areas where they would have the most benefit. The central bureaucracy set production targets and decided where and how to allocate agricultural capital and technology. Success depended on a cohort of educated and honest technocrats who could identify appropriate capital and technologies and then produce and allocate them efficiently on a massive scale.

The competing strategy, advocated by the Maoists, supported the commune as rural China's primary economic and political institution. Under the slogan "self-reliance," Mao argued that communes should retain their agricultural surpluses and invest them in physical and human capital. This concept was threatened by Liu's support for a centralized and technocratic elite, which Mao feared would capture the surpluses created by agricultural modernization.[69]

The dispute between commune supporters and trust supporters was also tied to fears that agricultural modernization might exacerbate unemployment. In March 1965, Xiang Nan reiterated Bo Yibo's concerns from a decade earlier that "in areas with little land and a large population" fears that machines would displace increasingly abundant rural labor produced a "controversy over the introduction of mechanization."[70]

By the mid-1960s, some communes had the capital and technology necessary to free up enough rural labor to support rural industrialization. To study the implications of agricultural modernization on productivity and employment, two test sites were selected: Xinzhou, Hebei, and Nanhai, Guangdong. In 1965, both received electric irrigation and drainage equipment, threshers, cotton gins, diesel engines, grain-processing machines, oil presses, and tractors, and both test sites substantially increased output. Xinzhou reported a 56 percent increase in cotton output; self-sufficiency in grain production; and bumper crops in oil-bearing crops, tobacco, lotus seeds, hogs, and fish. Nanhai, despite a drought, increased rice production by 48 percent. Equally important, however, were the consequences for surplus workers, who, according to Xiang's report, were reassigned to various productivity-increasing tasks:

After mechanization was introduced, how did Xinzhou and Nanhai handle their labor power thus saved? They promptly organized their labor power for more activities of intensive farming such as plowing, hoeing, tilling, accumulating manure, selecting seeds, and preventing insect pests. Laborers were organized to go up to the mountains or down to the river—for purposes of undertaking afforestation, animal husbandry, fishing, and developing a diversified economy. They were also organized for activities of capital construction on farms such as cutting canals, building roads, building reservoirs and dams, and leveling land.[71]

Most relevant to the commune–trust dispute, Xiang reported that by themselves, capital and technology bestowed from above were insufficient for agricultural modernization to be successful. Enthusiastic and capable local leadership and planning was required at each administrative level to ensure that the units that received investments would reallocate displaced field labor into productive tasks, rather than create more idle hands.[72] In spring 1965, an inspection report on Zhouxin Commune in Guangdong agreed with the finding that insufficient planning had stoked unemployment fears among the risk-adverse farmers and prompted team leaders to resist adopting modern farming techniques:

When the production activities of basic-level production teams were unplanned there was the problem of superfluous labor power. To employ their surplus labor manpower, some production teams were willing to restore the use of the old-type water wheels for drainage and irrigation. They were not willing to use the newly built electric-operated drainage and irrigation equipment. This was a new problem, and a big problem that Zhouxin Commune had to solve urgently.[73]

Commune control over agricultural modernization was intended to facilitate increased agricultural productivity and help diversify the rural economy. Allowing local cadres to assign freed-up labor to sow new crops, including peanuts, onions, garlic, sugarcane, and bamboo, and to expand animal husbandry enhanced agricultural productivity. Commune and brigade enterprises were also encouraged to employ excess labor to manufacture farm implements, produce fertilizer, weave baskets, and make bricks (a policy response that is explained in chapter 3).

Trusts faced rising opposition in the summer of 1965. In August 1965, the National Agricultural Machinery Management Conference, although sharply divided, reinstituted commune control over agricultural modernization. It identified "collective operation" as a critical component, called for "integrating stations with communes and state-operated stations with collective-operated stations," and ordered that agricultural capital investment be financed by collective accumulation, that is, workpoints. The conference did not seem to dampen Liu's support for the trust, however, and in fall 1965, he christened another trust—the China Agricultural Machine Company.[74]

THE STRUGGLE OVER DAZHAI

In the early 1960s, Liu's vision of large, centrally controlled trusts and small, dependent rural communes gained traction among high-ranking party members including Deng. To force continued debate on this and other topics beyond Beijing and into low-level venues nationwide, Mao first sought to gain control of the Socialist Education Movement (SEM, also known as the Four Cleanups) and later launched the Cultural Revolution. The commune, Mao argued, should introduce agricultural modernization funded by high savings rates and a remuneration scheme that rewarded workers for prioritizing collective over individual interests. After 1970, this remuneration methodology, known as Dazhai workpoints, became optional, although high savings rates and agricultural modernization would remain top priorities until decollectivization.

In 1965, Mao wrestled control over the SEM away from Liu and changed it from an anticorruption campaign into a broader strategy to fund agricultural modernization via the workpoint system. The center no longer would target investment into select areas based on estimated profitability. Under the Dazhai model, the process was locally funded, decentralized to commune control, and expanded nationwide. Although data from 1966 to 1969 are unavailable, the trajectory suggests that levels of income extraction began to increase gradually at this time and continued throughout the 1970s (see chapter 4, figure 4.8).

Between 1964 and 1975, the Dazhai Brigade and its party branch secretary-cum-vice-premier, Chen Yonggui, received more official media attention than any other commune subunit or cadre. The Dazhai Brigade was located in the eponymous Dazhai Commune in Xiyang County, Shanxi Province. Before 1949, it had been a "poor and backward" mountain village, composed of about 380 peasants living in handmade caves. Its hillside lands were infertile and vulnerable to poor weather and soil erosion. After years of toil and cooperation among farmers and cadres, the brigade reported that grain output had increased from 1,125 kilograms per hectare (kg/ha) of cultivated land before 1949, to more than 6,000 kg/ha in 1964. This upsurge in grain productivity gained Dazhai the "model production unit" label, and that year, Chen served as Shanxi representative to the Third NPC.[75]

In October 1964, as Dazhai began its rise to national prominence, a central government Four Cleanups work team was dispatched to verify its production reports. The work team took control of the brigade and questioned the "unnatural phenomenon" of unity between the cadre and poor and lower-middle peasants. For two months, the team met with peasants urging them to "expose the inside story," and they subsequently accused brigade cadre of falsifying grain reports. To investigate these claims, the team spent two months interviewing households, checking the grain stores, and conducting land surveys. Following their investigation, in early December 1964, the work team reclassified Dazhai from an "advanced" unit to a "brigade with serious problems." They concluded that "there are grubs in the staff of the red banner of Dazhai. If they are not eliminated, the banner cannot be raised high."[76] But, as Baum observes, the struggle over Dazhai's reputation went far beyond the brigade itself:

Whether or not [Dazhai's] production claims in the early 1960s were fraudulent, the fact remains that in late 1964 there existed a group of higher-level Party officials who suspected them to be fraudulent, and who acted upon that suspicion by having a work team thoroughly investigate the question of agricultural acreage and output.[77]

Liu and Deng were among the "higher-level party officials" who sought to use Four Cleanups work teams to impugn Dazhai and thus prevent the spread of Mao's Dazhai model. Mao and his supporters, by contrast, maneuvered to gain control over the SEM and use it to promote their Dazhai-based conception of commune-led agricultural modernization. In this context, Mao backed Chen in his dispute with the Four Cleanups work team. After meeting with Chen on the sidelines of the NPC in mid-December 1964, Mao elevated him to the NPC Presidium and allowed him to address the delegates. According to Chen,

Chairman Mao was best able to understand us [the cadre of Dazhai], and he showed the greatest concern for us. At the crucial moment of the struggle, he received me in audience and gave me important instructions concerning work in Dazhai. To us this was the greatest encouragement, the most intimate concern, and the most powerful support.[78]

Under Liu, Mao believed that the SEM had been too centrally controlled, too detail oriented, and too focused on corruption. At the December 1964 NPC, Mao criticized its orientation and reordered its priorities at the subsequent CPC Central Committee Work Conference. Mao's instructions were clear: "We must announce what we wish to do: production, distribution, and workpoints—these are matters to which we must devote ourselves."[79] After being infused with "Dazhai Spirit," the Mao-led SEM began to promulgate a more extractive remuneration system to fund local investments in agricultural capital and technology.

Given his experience with the Dazhai Brigade, and because the Dazhai model's successful implementation would require capable, untarnished commune and brigade-level cadres, it is not surprising that Mao warned the Four Cleanups work teams against hastily accusing local leaders of corruption and ordered them to focus on only those anticorruption efforts that increased agricultural productivity: "Four Cleanups means cleaning up a few people. Where there is something unclean, clean it up; where it is clean, no cleaning up will be necessary. There must be some clean people! Where there are no lice on a person, how can you find lice?"[80]

Mao turned the SEM from an anticorruption campaign into one that promulgated the Dazhai model nationwide. On December 22, 1964, Premier Zhou praised Dazhai in his report to the NPC, called for its emulation, and summarized its successful model: placing politics in command and ideology in the lead, love for the country and the collective, and self-reliance and hard struggle.[81] The ultimate gesture of public support for Dazhai came on December 30, when Chen's picture appeared alongside Mao's on the front of the *People's Daily*. The article quoted the chairman's instruction that agriculture communes should "Learn from Dazhai," and the slogan soon swept the countryside.[82]

Phase 3: The Leftist Commune (1965–1969)

HUBEI'S MODEST PROPOSAL

The political powder keg between supporters of Mao's commune-based approach and Liu's alternative vision of a centrally administered agricultural sector controlled by trusts was ignited in January 1966 by a seemingly mundane proposal from the Hubei CPC Provincial Committee. To precipitate agricultural mechanization, the province requested permission to establish two factories to manufacture ten thousand 7-horsepower (hp) walking tractors and 20-hp riding tractors per year. Assuming that twenty-two thousand of its thirty-eight thousand production brigades could each use two tractors, Hubei leaders reasoned that widespread agricultural mechanization could be achieved in only five years.[83]

Mao approved the Hubei plan on February 19; then Liu rejected it on February 23. On March 11, Liu wrote to Mao that "the transmission of the Hubei Provincial Committee's documents should be postponed."[84] The next day, Mao sent a letter to delegates at the National Industrial and Communication Work Conference proposing (as he had in April 1959) a three-step, ten-year plan for agricultural modernization via the commune.[85] The letter criticized efforts to centralize control over agricultural modernization and instead advocated decentralization to local control:

[Agricultural modernization] must be carried out in the main by various provinces, municipalities, and regions on the basis of self-reliance, and the Center can only give assistance in the form of raw and semi-processed materials to places short of such materials. Local authorities must be given the right to manufacture some machines. It is not a good way to exercise too rigid control by placing everything under the unified control of the Center.[86]

The conference was the last time party leaders openly debated trusts. Soon afterward, against Liu's wishes, the Hubei proposals were published, first on April 4 in the *Canton Evening News*, and then again in the *People's Daily* on April 9, 1966.[87] On May 7, 1966, Mao issued a vague directive permitting communes to open small factories.[88] Then in July, on the brink of the Cultural Revolution, the CPC Central Committee convened the On-Site Conference on Agricultural Mechanization in Hubei (also known as the First National Conference on Agricultural Mechanization), which reached three conclusions affirming the Maoist line: (1) that agricultural mechanization must rely on the collective economy, (2) that it must rely on the local manufacture of machines and farm tools, and (3) that it must rely on small-size machinery. In October, these three points were published in the *People's Daily*.[89]

In retrospect, the commune's triumph over the trust seems to have been an inevitable result of Mao's political victory over Liu during the Cultural Revolution. Indeed, by late 1966, with Liu and his supporters under criticism, the trust was roundly rejected and the commune was reaffirmed. Because trusts were inspired by Soviet institutions and promulgated by "China's Khrushchev," their Maoist opponents labeled them "revisionist"— an argument made by *The People's Daily* on April 3, 1966:

In regard to production and technique, management, regulations and systems in our enterprises, shall we go our own way or copy from capitalism and revisionism? Shall we foster a collective spirit and a communist style, or cultivate bourgeois ideas?

Shall we gradually narrow down the differences between town and country, workers and peasants, and mental and physical labor or preserve and widen them?[90]

But the debate went beyond ideology. Maoists opposed trusts because they would have exacerbated the "three differences"—differences between urban and rural life, between industrial and agricultural work, and between intellectual and manual work. The commune, by contrast, promised to manufacture, distribute, and utilize agricultural capital and technology in ways that would resolve these longstanding social cleavages.

Logistical considerations also contributed to the trust's rejection. The objective of a large trust (not unlike a modern corporation) was to operate factories and warehouses at capacity while minimizing excess inventory and waste. To benefit from economies of scale in production, however, trusts required close coordination and timing to reduce transportation and storage costs. Ideally, large quantities of machines and inputs would be produced in coastal factories and transported via road or rail into the countryside. But efficient distribution would require an extensive infrastructure and logistics system, which China lacked. The inadequate transportation system would have predetermined which localities could, and which could not, receive agricultural capital and inputs. Using this approach, nationwide agricultural modernization would have first required a massive and cost-prohibitive expansion of transportation infrastructure.

Furthermore, militarily, any system that required integration and coordination over long distances was vulnerable in the event of war with the United States or the Soviet Union. The centrally controlled trusts, unlike communes, ran contrary to Mao's People's War strategy, which required a nationwide network of self-sustaining rural bases that could resist the enemy if they were cut off from the center during a conflict.

Provincial, prefectural, and county-level cadres, whose influence over agricultural development and budgetary allocations was threatened by trusts, also pushed back. Centralized production and administration, they believed, would deny most localities the positive externalities associated with modernization—that is, investments in local physical and human capital necessary for operation and repairs. They also opposed the targeted approach taken by trusts, which—even if successful—would have taken much longer to make modern agricultural inputs and technology available nationwide.

THE COMMUNE AND THE CULTURAL REVOLUTION

After the Cultural Revolution began in August 1966, China promoted commune-led agricultural modernization continuously for more than a decade. Between 1966 and 1968, the commune gradually assumed ownership and management of agricultural capital. The transfer of farm machines from the state-run AMS to the commune occurred slowly. Lacking a Central Committee directive, as late as 1968, many AMS personnel remained reluctant to transfer machines. Beginning in mid-1968, however, articles appeared in at least ten provinces praising efforts to decentralize the administration of agricultural capital, and Mao's 1958–1959 instructions on agricultural modernization were reissued. Such publications, some of which provided instructions on how to handle challenges that might arise during the transition, were unambiguous signals that the center wanted communes to take over agricultural modernization. In most cases, the transfer of agricultural capital was completed *before* the establishment of a provincial revolutionary committee, which generally occurred in 1969.[91]

The gradual transfer of agricultural capital from the AMS to the commune sharply contrasted with the hasty implementation of GLF communes a decade earlier. During the GLF, preliminary experiments had taken place in only four cooperatives outside Beijing and in Heilongjiang before they were rapidly expanded nationwide. By comparison, the 1966–1968 transfer process stressed intracommune planning and leadership rather than central directives. To ensure that agricultural capital was transferred to collective control in good condition, an evaluation team including experienced workers, cadres, and technical personnel was created to appraise each machine and farm tool one by one and to determine its appropriate price in light of its condition and current prices.[92] One official publication described the considerations during handover of agricultural equipment to commune cadres in Lankao County, Henan as follows: "Aid was given to mountain areas with consideration given to poverty-stricken communes and teams. Rational distribution of agricultural machines and implements was made with consideration given to the terrains of the communes and teams, repair force and the technical state of machines and implements."[93]

Between 1966 and 1968, the AMS were converted into three-in-one farm machinery management committees or stations. On the basis of its size and complexity, each machine or technology was matched with the appropriate subunit to achieve optimum economies of scale. Commune leaders controlled larger equipment and delegated smaller, more specialized items to their subunits. A commune, for instance, might operate a large tractor station, a multibrigade irrigation system, and a hydropower dam and its electric substations. A brigade might administer handheld tractors, smaller waterworks, and combined thresher-reaper machines to process grain or other farm products. The team could control semimechanized farm tools, a gas-powered wheelbarrow, and smaller, less complicated threshers and reapers.[94]

Three-level farm machinery management committees, which included cadre and technical personnel at the county, commune, and brigade levels, managed "scientific research" and repaired and allocated all agricultural capital within a given rural locality. Frequent team meetings, a hallmark of the commune, were used to ensure that households understood and consented to their leaders' production plans and investments, which were underwritten using collective funds procured via the workpoint system. To oversee agricultural modernization, AMS personnel, who were originally state employees, were placed under commune leadership. In one commune, former AMS personnel continued to receive their state salaries and food rations for two years. In another, they received half their compensation according to the average workpoint value of all teams, and the other half from their production team.[95] In the late 1960s, agricultural capital had been transferred to communes, yet it remained scarce relative to the large and rapidly expanding labor force.

In 1966, China had abundant rural labor and a scarcity of land and capital. To counter these trends, a nationwide plan to shift investment from heavy industry toward agricultural capital and infrastructure was announced as the Cultural Revolution began at the Eleventh Plenum of the CPC in August 1966.[96] The basic points stipulated that agricultural modernization would receive "special priority," semimechanization would be introduced as a stopgap measure, farm tools would be locally manufactured, and communes and their brigades (rather than a state bureaucracy, companies, or trusts) would own and manage all agricultural machinery. Although in 1967 and 1968 the Cultural Revolution disorder delayed the implementation of these policies in some regions, once farm machines had been transferred and the new local leadership in the form of the Revolutionary Committees was created in 1969, investment began to flow into agricultural modernization at an unprecedented rate.[97]

In 1969, with Mao's support, Premier Zhou took charge of agriculture and recommitted China to a nationwide, commune-led agricultural modernization program. The Ministry of Agriculture and its provincial and county organs were instructed to develop an ambitious nationwide scheme to maximize land productivity using agricultural capital and technology. In September and October 1969, conferences on agricultural modernization were held in a number of provinces, including Gansu, Inner Mongolia, Anhui, Shandong, Hunan, and Guangdong.[98] At these gatherings, agricultural experts and local cadre shared their experiences and were informed about the nationwide agricultural modernization program. The production team would remain the basic accounting unit (i.e., the level at which collective income was distributed), and the workpoint remuneration system could again include various task, time, and piece rates as well as other ad hoc remuneration methods. The October 1969 issue of *Red Flag* printed an article emphasizing agricultural capital investment and technical improvement: "Every county must positively set up a farm machine repairing station and manufacturing plants, establish an industrial network for serving agriculture, and contribute greater strength to speeding up the technical reform of agriculture."[99]

Radio Shanghai's November 10, 1969, broadcast proclaimed the beginning of a "new stage of realizing agricultural mechanization" and emphasized the importance of making investments in agricultural capital and technology to increase rural productivity and strengthen the worker-peasant alliance:

Today, our worker-peasant alliance has entered the new stage of realizing agricultural mechanization. Agricultural collectivization without agricultural mechanization cannot consolidate the worker-peasant alliance because it is impossible for such an alliance to rest forever on two diametrically opposed material and technical foundations. The development of agricultural production lies in mechanization. The realization of agricultural mechanization in turn will consolidate agricultural collectivization and eliminate differences between workers and peasants, towns and countryside, mental and manual labor.[100]

CONCLUSION

Each of the Green Revolution Commune's antecedent institutions—the MAT, the APC, the GLF Commune, the Rightist Commune, and the Leftist Commune—was distinguished by its size, mandate, remuneration system, and approach to agricultural modernization. Yet, from the introduction of the *Sixty Articles* in 1962 until decollectivization began in 1979, the commune retained four structural consistencies: a three-tier administrative structure, control over all local political, economic, and administrative affairs, distribution of household income (except for private household plots) as a portion of collective income, and the prioritization of grain and pork production.

The GLF Commune was an ambitious but deeply flawed and short-lived institution. After the devastating famine, the commune was redesigned to address China's most pressing concern: rising demand for food and employment caused by increasing population growth rates. Between 1962 and 1964, Liu, Deng, and other right-leaning leaders expanded remuneration to include material incentives, rural markets, household sideline plots, cottage industries, and contract farming, known as Three Freedoms and One Guarantee. Although contract farming (i.e., the one guarantee) would later be disavowed, the political inertia created by the tolerance of household sideline plots, cottage enterprises, and rural markets (i.e., the three freedoms) predisposed the institution to tolerate them until its abandonment.[101] Together, they provided an intracommune market-clearing mechanism that ensured that excess resources would not be wasted—a cardinal sin in Maoist China.[102] Furthermore, they also helped commune leaders to identify the most profitable areas for investment based on local market prices.

The Leftist Commune phase (1965–1969) introduced the Dazhai model, which extracted an increasing percentage of household savings to fund local investments in agricultural capital. Although Dazhai workpoints, which rewarded workers for placing collective above individual interests, were deemed optional after 1970, the model's commitment to investment-led growth remained. At this time, hundreds of millions of commune members were indoctrinated with Maoism, which for reasons explained in chapter 5, increased their tolerance for resource extraction. By 1969, China had transferred agricultural machines back to commune control, reformed the agricultural research and extension system, and institution-alized a remuneration system that could fund Mao's nationwide, ten-year agricultural modernization scheme.

The next chapter examines the Green Revolution Commune (1970–1979), the institution's final phase and the culmination of a decade-and-a-half of nationwide experimentation and elite political struggles. Changes made during each of the commune's three preceding phases were integrated into the 1970s commune, and many remained in effect until its dissolution. The Three Small Freedoms, for instance, remained under the Leftist Commune and coexisted, albeit sometimes uneasily, alongside Mao's virulent collec-tivist ideology.

Chapter Three

CHINA'S GREEN REVOLUTION

INTRODUCTION

This chapter examines the fourth and most productive phase of the Chinese commune: the 1970s Green Revolution Commune. It clarifies the relationship between the economic challenges that China confronted and the policies communes implemented to alleviate them. Relying primarily on previously unexploited national- and provincial-level data, it demonstrates how 1970s China—a populous developing country with increasingly scarce land resources, a rapidly rising population, and quickly depreciating capital stocks—took advantage of high returns to capital to increase food production. The following chapter then uses economic growth models to elucidate the transitional dynamics of this rural development process.

During the 1970s, to increase food production and employ surplus labor, China altered its nationwide agricultural modernization strategy known as the Dazhai model.[1] These reforms, which were adopted formally by 1,259 representatives from fourteen provinces at the Northern Districts Agricultural Conference (NDAC) from August to October 1970, were reaffirmed at the 1975 and 1976 National Conferences on Learning from Dazhai in Agriculture, and they remained national policy until decollectivization.[2] Communes implemented this rural development strategy at the local level, which kick-started a virtuous cycle of rural development that created the physical and human capital and technology that improved agricultural productivity both before and after decollectivization.[3] Figures 1.1–1.3 in chapter 1 show that during the 1970s, China experienced continuous increases in grain, pig, and, to a lesser extent, edible oil production on aggregate, per unit land, and per unit labor.

This chapter begins by summarizing how elite-level political struggles over agricultural policy in the 1960s were resolved at the NDAC. Then it introduces China's 1970s agricultural research and extension system, which implemented most of the policy responses described in the following sections.[4] This integrated network linked national- and provincial-level agricultural universities and laboratories with research teams and testing stations nested into communes and their subunits.[5] The sections that follow use national- and provincial-level data to identify the three economic challenges faced by Chinese communes in the 1970s—rising rates of population growth, falling arable land, and high capital depreciation rates—and describe the policies adopted to alleviate them.

This chapter has two primary conclusions. First, the agricultural investments and technological innovations that occurred in the 1970s were an essential driver of productivity increases both under the commune and during decollectivization. Second, the abandonment of the commune and its subunits crippled localities' ability to invest in productive agricultural capital and technology. Without communes to extract resources and invest them in agricultural modernization, collective investment in agriculture as a percentage of total collective investment in fixed assets declined from almost 40 percent in 1982 to less than 10 percent in 1988.[6] This trend can be observed in terms of agricultural investment (figure 3.1), student enrollment across all levels and vocational disciplines (figures 3.6, 3.7, and 3.8), irrigated land (figure 3.14), and machine-cultivated land (figure 3.15).

THE 1970 NORTHERN DISTRICTS AGRICULTURAL CONFERENCE

Throughout the 1960s, China's leaders were tasked with producing more food and employing more people on less arable land and doing so amid rapidly depreciating rural capital stocks. In 1970, they adopted extensive national reforms intended to improve the commune in ways that would increase population control and investment in physical and human capital and technology. This countrywide agricultural investment scheme, which

Louis Putterman has described as "rural industrialization under commune and brigade auspices," provided the rural population with the basic infrastructure, equipment, technology, and training that produced steady increases in agricultural output.[7]

Before discussing the NDAC and its outcomes, it is important to briefly review how a political consensus on increased agricultural investment via the commune emerged during the 1950s and 1960s. As discussed in the previous chapter, between 1958 and 1966, the literature generally identifies two opposing political factions: a Maoist (leftist) and a Liuist or Dengist (rightist). Writings of top economic officials Chen Yun and Deng Liqun, however, identify three *economic* policy lines among the leadership: the leftists, supporters of "overall balance," and advocates of "planned proportionate development."[8]

In the late 1960s, leftists (including Chen Boda and other ideologues) supported the commune as a vehicle to spread Mao's collectivist ideology, but they opposed the expansion of agricultural mechanization, which they believed would increase unemployment and could not improve production in mountainous or swampy areas. Modern capital and technology, they argued, would divert attention away from the heightening of socialist consciousness through class struggle, thereby opening the way for capitalistic impulses.[9]

Chinese economic planners generally agreed on the need to extract from rural households to fund capital investment—but not on *how* to best spend the money. Advocates of planned proportionate development, including top officials and cadres in the planning and heavy industrial bureaucracies, including Li Fuchun, Bo Yibo, Wang Heshou, and Huang Jing, called for extracting from agriculture to underwrite investments in heavy industry. By contrast, supporters of overall balance, including Chen Yun, Li Xiannian, Deng Zihui, and lesser officials in the Ministry of Finance, instead prescribed "a more productive and sustainable" pattern of resource allocation and argued that more resources should be directed into agriculture and light industry. As early as 1957, Chen had warned that excessive resource extraction from rural households without appropriate reinvestment in agriculture meant that "the pace of agricultural development would be slow."[10]

With support from Mao and the leftists, overall balance prevailed. The result was a hybrid approach that initiated a capital investment and agricultural modernization agenda akin to what overall balance advocates had prescribed, but did so using the commune (a leftist institution) and Maoism as its central unifying collectivist ideology. This new consensus was proclaimed at the NDAC, which opened in Xiyang, Shanxi, the home of the celebrated Dazhai Brigade, on August 25, 1970. The NDAC was a watershed for the Chinese commune; it both reaffirmed broad political support for the institution and reformed it in ways that increased its productivity.

The NDAC had three primary outcomes. First, it endorsed the commune as the primary economic and political institution of rural China. Second, it expanded the breadth of acceptable income remuneration methodologies permitted within the commune's workpoint system and endorsed household administered sideline plots. Third, it blessed the reformed agricultural research and extension system, which launched a nationwide green revolution in agriculture that expanded investments in seeds, fertilizer, electrification, and mechanization.

During a speech to more than a thousand NDAC delegates at the Great Hall of the People in Beijing, Premier Zhou Enlai "set a modernizing direction while hewing to the collective."[11] He endorsed the workpoint remuneration system and stressed the need to "increase local investment in modernizing and mechanizing agriculture."[12] Edward Friedman, Paul G. Pickowicz, and Mark Selden summarize the crux of China's post-1970 plan to fund agricultural modernization through increased household savings: "Villagers were to get rich by tightening their belts for a while, investing more, and working harder. The line evoked vague memories of the Leap. But this time, Zhou stressed the state would invest in such suitable technology as fertilizer and irrigation and would not tolerate the squandering of precious resources."[13]

According to Harry Harding, China's new agricultural modernization campaign aimed to reverse China's undersavings problem and produce "superoptimal investment generated by appeals to ideology or sheer coercion."[14] Yet, the post-1970 approach was careful to avoid overextraction of household resources, as had occurred during the GLF. In 1970 alone, more than 150 separate official Chinese press stories and radio broadcasts appeared in almost every province, stressing increased investments in agricultural capital and technology.[15] Writing in late 1970, Harding describes these articles: "The Chinese newspapers these days are full of appeals to avoid waste, to recycle industrial by-products, to work harder. But the appeals lack the sheer fanaticism of the Great Leap Forward. The demands being made on the Chinese people today are very high indeed, but they are not impossible to meet."[16]

This new agricultural modernization campaign harkened back to the GLF rhetorically, but without the harmful red-over-expert policies pursued

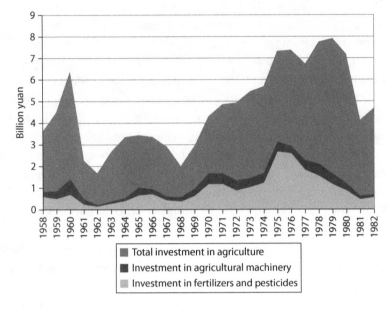

FIGURE 3.1. Investment in agriculture.
Source: Agricultural Economic Statistics 1949–1983 [Nongye jingji ziliao, 1949–1983] (Beijing: Ministry of Agriculture Planning Bureau, 1983), 302.

against agricultural specialists, engineers, and skilled peasants of "black" class backgrounds that had occurred at that time. Those policies had left skilled workers disgruntled (or worse) and produced large amounts of poor-quality capital. During the 1970s, by contrast, the status of those with agricultural and mechanical expertise was elevated; they became the backbone of China's rural economy. These highly valued teachers and technicians educated a generation of literate Chinese farmers, and they designed, created, and maintained the machines, infrastructure, and technological advancements that increased food production year after year. Figure 3.1 illustrates the rapid expansion of agricultural investment during the 1970s.

RESEARCH AND EXTENSION

The reform of the nationwide agricultural research and extension system made the agricultural productivity increases during the 1970s possible. This system included a vertically integrated network of national- and provincial-level research centers and county and commune experimentation stations that collaborated to test and disseminate productive agricultural capital and technology. Agrotechnical personnel at the county, commune, brigade, and team levels constituted a local, multitier agricultural research network that combined capital accumulation and technological innovation into a single development process. By 1976, it managed the distribution of inputs and collected feedback from 13 million members—an average of two hundred to four hundred per commune, or about two to five people in each of China's roughly 5 million production teams.[17]

Throughout the 1970s, agricultural technicians worked directly with commune-based "small teams" (*xiaozu*) to develop, test, produce, and disseminate agricultural capital, technology, seeds, and techniques on an unprecedented scale. Vertical integration improved communication and empowered local teams using a combination of experiments and demonstrations. Testing units were semiautonomous, not merely extension units that blindly implemented instructions from above as had occurred during the GLF. County units generally were smaller, and they primarily coordinated meetings and distributed information and seeds. Commune experimental stations, by contrast, were the critical link in the unified research and extension system.[18]

Beginning in the mid-1960s, China's agricultural research and extension system was expanded and decentralized in an effort to improve its responsiveness to local needs and better match crops and inputs with local conditions. In May 1964, the *People's Daily* first reported the creation of mass scientific small groups, and in February 1965, just as the movement to study Dazhai was getting under way, the National Conference on Agricultural Experiment kicked off a new "agricultural scientific experiment movement."[19] The *People's Daily* report on the conference linked this new movement with Maoist politics and proclaimed it the third of the "three revolutionary movements." "Under the party's leadership," it called for the creation of "a revolutionary movement with demonstration fields as the center, specialized science and technology teams as the backbone, and mass scientific experiment activities as the foundation."[20] A decade later, a report by the U.S. National Academy of Sciences (NAS) Plant Science Delegation praised China's "remarkable success in farm application of the accumulated knowledge of generations of peasants' experience as well as past scientific research."[21]

During the 1970s, official propaganda was published and circulated to communes across the country glorifying Huarong County, Hunan, for its model "four-level agricultural scientific experiment network." One propaganda poster from a set of six posters published in 1975. Titled "Self-Reliance; Practice Scientific Research with Diligence and Frugality," the poster extolled Huarong's ability to increase productivity using only local materials in their agricultural experiments. The poster's caption praised Jinggang Commune for establishing a "model" greenhouse in 1971, celebrated its "self-reliance and arduous struggle," and applauded "each level of the agricultural science organization [for] persistently drawing on local resources, using local methods, and improvising equipment, such that they met the needs of agricultural research and drove forward mass-based scientific farming activities."[22] The objective, as Sigrid Schmalzer explains, was to "present rural scientific experiment as humble, earthy and self-reliant— something that ordinary peasants could and should be doing."[23] Figure 3.2 is another example of propaganda created during the 1970s to promote grassroots agricultural research. Agricultural research is portrayed as something that everyone, from children to the elderly, should be contributing to.

Agrotechnical stations at the county, commune, and brigade levels constituted a locally integrated network for testing and propagating agricultural capital and technologies. Communes and brigades used the profits from their test fields or enterprises to subsidize "experiment[al] small groups" based on a "three-in-one" configuration of cadres, technicians, and experienced farmers. Group members, who received workpoints for their efforts, employed a "three-field" method for demonstration, experimentation, and seed propagation to determine which types of agricultural capital and technology worked best under local conditions.[24] They collected local productivity data and observations, disseminated techniques and inputs, sent representatives to commune meetings, tested seed varieties, and allocated land and other resources for experiments.[25] Communes and brigades controlled test plots and planting schedules and sometimes developed their own seed varieties and fertilizers.

In Jimo County, Shandong, for instance, 244 of 1,016 brigades had experimental teams to test new seeds and farming techniques in 1966. By 1972, the number of brigades with experimental teams had increased to 695, and they employed 4,043 people; by 1974, there were 851 experimental teams. By 1976, 80 percent of the communes in Jiangxi had agricultural research

FIGURE 3.2. "The Production Team's Agricultural Research Small Group," 1973. The wooden box on the floor labeled "Inoculation box" and the other scientific equipment suggest that the small group was experimenting with ways to treat plant diseases.
Source: Wenpu Jiang and Wenren Yang, "Shengchandui de keyan xiaozu," in *Nianhua* (Shandong: Shandong Renmin Chubanshe).

stations, about 60 percent of the brigades had research teams, and about 60 percent of teams had research groups.[26]

Han Dongping's recollections and research in Jimo County, Shandong, provide an example of the type of work performed by agricultural research and extension teams. He recalls that educated youth left South River Brigade to study how to cultivate and graft fruit trees. After returning to their teams, the youths formed a forestry team (*linye dui*) and planted a variety of apple, pear, and peach trees. The team planted watermelons between the fruit trees in the spring and planted peanuts in the fall. They also planted poplars, elms, pepper trees, Chinese parasols, and Chinese scholar trees to break the wind in the spring and protect against flooding in the summer. In the winter, they used twigs and tree branches to make baskets and sold them at the local free market (*ganji*) to finance their work.[27]

To improve vegetable cultivation, South River Brigade established a vegetable team led by the unit's two best vegetable farmers, and devoted

20 mu (about 1.3 hectares [ha]) to test new varieties. Previously, residents had only cabbage, turnips, and pickled mustard, and only households with irrigated sideline plots could enjoy fresh vegetables; others had to buy what they could at the rural market. The vegetable team taught members how to grow a larger variety of produce for local consumption. Meanwhile, the commune and brigade supported animal husbandry by creating sties that supplied piglets for households to raise on their private plots and sell at market.[28] Specialized *ad hoc* research and extension programs also increased output. Irrigation Management Committees responsible for water allocation within a commune, county, prefecture, or province, for instance, conducted their own research on irrigation and field tests to determine the proportions of water and chemical fertilizer that would most improve productivity.[29]

High-level officials were encouraged to participate in agricultural extension work. One prefecture-level party secretary in Guangxi, Yan Qingsheng, was admired for his close attention to agricultural production. Yan accompanied technicians to the Ministry of Agriculture to learn new techniques and helped them inspect seedlings in the greenhouse. When a farmer in Pubei County bred a new rice variety, Yan gave him a job in the Agricultural Science Institute.[30] Indeed, the connection between cultivating crops and cultivating people was well established in China since antiquity.[31] A 1971 article from Xin County, Shanxi, made the connection clear: "To cultivate sprouts you must first cultivate seeds, and to cultivate seeds you must first cultivate people."[32]

High-level agricultural research centers remained active throughout the 1970s. Top research units and agricultural universities received publications from around the world and communicated regularly with foreign agricultural institutes. Between 1973 and 1978, China received and sent about eighty delegations to these institutes to exchange information on agricultural technology. After the Sino-American rapprochement began in 1972, scientists from the United States and other nations visited at least twenty-five agricultural research institutions in China and reported that they were large and maintained substantial equipment. The Peking Institute of Genetics, for instance, conducted advanced genetic research (including pollen culture) and boasted 5 laboratories, 13 ha of experimental fields, and 375 staff and researchers, as well as numerous local trial centers. High-level institutes in other regions were comparably equipped and staffed.[33]

The 1970s system prioritized direct communications and deemphasized formal, bureaucratic channels. It rewarded applied, results-driven science over theoretical work. Agronomists were required to go beyond simply making laboratory discoveries to test, observe, modify, and propagate their innovations. Researchers spent one year in the laboratory, a second in a commune, and a third traveling around rural areas to teach and learn various techniques as well as to compare results under various local conditions. In the field, information passed directly between scientists and farmers without bureaucratic barriers. It was also shared among higher administrative levels at regular conferences organized at the county, prefectural, and provincial levels. The goal was to identify marginal improvements in capital and inputs made by farmers and technicians so they could be tested and quickly popularized.[34]

After 1970, the reformed agricultural research and extension system expanded communes' capacity to invest in productive capital and technologies. It prioritized applied science over academic research and methodology, thus deemphasizing scientific theory and placing a premium on research with practical payoffs. Although this strategy did succeed in increasing food output, the decision to take scientists out of the lab was not costless. Spending only one-third of their time in the lab and two-thirds "learning from the peasants" proved insufficient to train and motivate the next generation of agricultural scientists on cutting-edge research. Furthermore, the highly localized agricultural network created during this era suffered from a lack of uniform, systematic, and replicable experimentation processes. Experiments generally involved demonstrating techniques or testing several different methods or varieties to see which performed best under local conditions, and were not controlled tests that would have yielded more precise estimates. This lack of consistency extended to test plots, recordkeeping, and data analysis.[35]

Between 1976 and 1979, rural investments averaged 3.2 billion yuan annually, but by 1982, such investments had had fallen precipitously to 1.8 billion yuan. As Justin Yifu Lin observes, "The county-township-brigade-team research-extension system network in the collective system was very effective in promoting new technology." Nevertheless, he laments, "in the face of extraordinary success the government's investment in agricultural infrastructure, research, extension, and other activities fell from 11 percent of the government's budget to only 5 percent in 1984."[36]

By 1986, the level of state investment in agriculture had reached its lowest point since 1949 and, according to Nicolas Lardy, "can clearly be ruled out as a source of growth acceleration in agriculture since 1978."[37]

ECONOMIC CHALLENGES AND POLICY RESPONSES

Increased Rate of Population Growth

After a century of civil war and foreign invasion, the peace, unity, and optimism under the newly established People's Republic of China brought population growth. During its first five years in power (1949–1954), the Communist Party of China (CPC) encouraged procreation to strengthen the nation. Faced with the difficulties of feeding and employing tens of millions more people, however, Beijing soon reversed course.[38] To reduce population growth and disperse its negative externalities throughout the vast countryside, the CPC implemented policies designed to reduce family size and reverse the urbanization process. By forcing the growing population and workforce to remain diffused in communes and by decentralizing power and responsibility to rural cadres, Chinese leaders sought to soften the acute negative effects of population growth and prevent them from materializing in urban areas. Strict limits on labor mobility coupled with policies that relocated skilled human capital and youth from urban to rural areas were intended to transfer the skills necessary to support rural industrialization.

As shown in figure 3.3, China's population (more than 80 percent of which lived in a commune) was 830 million in 1970 and had reached 975 million by 1979.[39] In the 1970s, China's postliberation baby boom generation reached working and marrying age, pushing the number of commune workers, which was 198 million in 1960, to more than 281 million in 1970, and to 310 million in 1979.[40] Figure 3.4 shows this population surge in eight large provinces. Growing demand for food and employment remained the two primary challenges facing Chinese policymakers throughout the commune era.

China's leaders recognized that increased agricultural production and a reduction in birth rates were essential. According to a delegation of U.S. agricultural scientists who visited China in 1974, the Chinese were "making an all-out effort to reduce the population growth rate." The group noted:

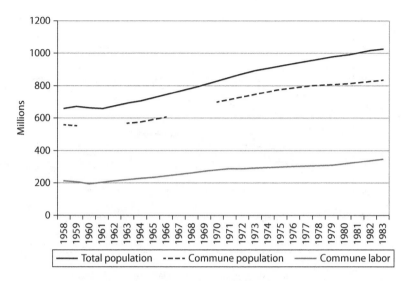

FIGURE 3.3. Population and commune labor.
Source: Agricultural Economic Statistics, 34, 46, 81.

"A population increase of no more than 2 percent per year mandates an increase in food output equivalent to 5 million tons of grain per annum just to maintain present standards of living." Without rapid reductions in population growth rates, China could anticipate "very serious food problems within a few years."[41]

POLICY RESPONSES

Population Control

Beginning in 1962, in the wake of the GLF famine, China's leaders sought to manage the negative externalities associated with excessive population growth. In a 1964 interview, Premier Zhou explained China's approach: "Our present target is to reduce population growth to below 2 percent; for the future we aim at an even lower rate."[42] Across most of China, the Cultural Revolution, which began in 1966, did not inhibit the availability of birth control paraphernalia.[43]

During the 1970s, family planning (*jihuashengyu*) was instituted in rural areas. Large numbers of urban medical personnel were detailed to communes where birth control became the responsibility of every rural clinic

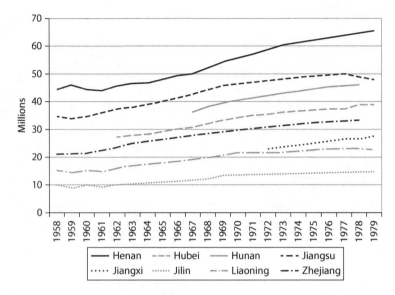

FIGURE 3.4. Commune population in selected provinces.
Sources: Thirty Years Since the Founding of the People's Republic of China: Agricultural Statistics of Henan Province, 1949-1979 [Jianguo sanshinian: henansheng nongye tongji ziliao, 1949-1979] (Zhengzhou: Statistical Bureau of Henan Province, 1981); *Agricultural Statistics of Hubei Province, 1949-1978* (Wuhan: Agricultural Bureau of Hubei Province, n.d.); *Statistics and Materials of Agricultural Mechanization in Hunan Province, 1967-1978* (Changsha: Hunan Revolutionary Committee, Administration Bureau of Agricultural Mechanics, n.d.); *Agricultural Statistics of Jiangsu Province, 1949-1975* (Nanjing: Agricultural Bureau of Jiangsu Revolutionary Committee, 1976); *Agricultural Statistics of Jiangxi Province, 1949-1979.* Nanchang: Agricultural Department of Jiangxi Province, n.d.); Agricultural Economic Statistics of Jilin Province, 1949-1985 (Changchun: Agricultural Department of Jilin Province, n.d.); Population *Statistics of Liaoning Province, 1949-1984* (Shenyang: Statistical Bureau of Liaoning Province, 1985); Statistical Bureau of Zhejiang Province, ed., *Collection of Materials on Fifty Years of Zhejiang* (Beijing: China Statistics Press, 2000).

and cadre. At the seventeenth session of the United Nations Population Commission in 1973, China's official position reflected ongoing discontinuities between Marxist ideology and existing policy: "Of all things in the world, people are the most precious. It is wrong and far from the truth to say that overpopulation is the main cause of the poverty and backwardness of developing countries."[44] The same statement, however, also pointed out that "planned population growth" policies were a natural component of China's planned economy and included various aspects of population control beyond family planning.

Labor mobility, another component of population control, was strongly disincentivized in 1970s China. Carrot-and-stick policies, including formal regulations, regular mandatory team meetings, and incentive structures, made it nearly impossible for commune members to change their residency registration (*hukou*) from "rural" to "nonrural" (i.e., urban) or even to move from one commune to another. Commune members worked locally, earned nontransferable workpoints in their teams, and were remunerated locally. These incentives appear to have been broadly successful in discouraging urban migration; between 1959 and 1976, China's official rural population fluctuated only in a narrow range (between 83.2 percent and 81.6 percent).[45]

After most barriers to labor mobility were removed in the 1980s and 1990s, the rapid pace and massive scale of China's urbanization suggest that during the 1970s tens of millions of residents had been successfully dissuaded, or coerced, to forgo urbanization. Still, footage of illegal settlements on the outskirts of Beijing can be seen in Michelangelo Antonioni's 1972 documentary *Chung Kuo*.[46] Official data on urbanization hint that some unofficial movement—referred to by Chinese officials as "blind infiltration"—did occur.[47] Figure 3.5 indicates growth in the number of large urban areas (those encompassing 1–2 million and more than 2 million residents) between 1965 and 1982. How much this increased number of urban areas was driven by

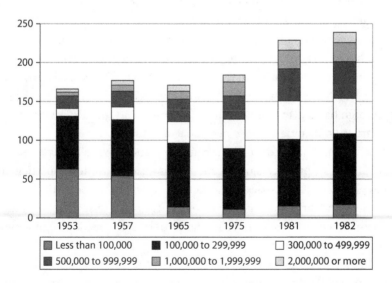

FIGURE 3.5. Number of cities by population size.
Source: Agricultural Economic Statistics, 38.

rural migration versus local population growth, expansion of a city's administrative jurisdiction, or other causal factors remains unclear.

Commune and Brigade Enterprises

In the 1970s, labor immobility and rural population growth amid a reduction in arable land left hundreds of millions of farmers underemployed.[48]
To absorb this excess manpower, Leo Orleans observes that China
emphasized agriculture "and established a network of small supportive
industries based essentially on local resources . . . Thus, the proportion
of China's rural population that is involved in non-agricultural activities is constantly increasing."[49] In 1979, Vice-Premier Wang Renzhong,
who supervised agricultural affairs, explained that the goal was to prevent an exodus of surplus rural agricultural labor to urban centers, where
"the factories could not employ so many people" and instead "utilize the
excess laborers of the 80 percent of the population that live in rural areas
in medium and small size industry."[50] By capitalizing the countryside,
commune and brigade enterprises aimed to minimize the type of mass
urbanization that produced slums and excessive inequality in many Asian
countries at the time.[51]

But commune and brigade enterprises were more than just employers.
As the rural population grew in 1970s so too did demand, which, in turn,
brought inflation in terms of both consumer and capital goods. For instance,
the average worker at the duck farm at Taiping Qiao Brigade in Luguo Qiao
Commune in Hebei had an income of 600 yuan per year, which was high
for that time, yet a sewing machine cost 180 yuan, a bicycle cost 150 yuan,
and a watch cost 80–120 yuan.[52] Most concerning for agricultural planners, high barriers to intercommune factor mobility, particularly for scarce
construction materials like cement, coal, and bricks, increased prices.[53] To
lessen demand and reduce costs, commune and brigade enterprises were
encouraged to produce small-scale light industrial products, particularly
in the "five small industries" (i.e., energy, cement, chemical fertilizers, iron
and steel, and farm machines) and were encouraged to support any industry (e.g., irrigation piping and basic farm tools) that contributed directly to
agricultural production.

"Decentralized local industries provided machinery and tools for farming and made them available to a broader segment of China's peasantry than
ever before," Harding observes.[54] Orleans agrees, "Small industries produce

an ever-increasing share of China's chemical fertilizers and cement, farm machinery and implements, generators and transformers, and, perhaps most important, spare parts, the supply of which has always presented a major obstacle to even limited mechanization of the countryside."[55]

Commune and brigade enterprises operated at different scales. Communes invested in industries that required a larger initial investment or benefited from economies of scale, whereas brigades invested in intermediate-size enterprises that required more local knowledge. Both communes and brigades increased collective income and local skill development, which, in turn, paved the way for the adoption and implementation of increasingly sophisticated technology and capital.[56] Profitable enterprises could reinvest in facilities, expand existing enterprises or create new ones, subsidize agricultural investments (e.g., irrigation systems), make loans to teams, or distribute revenues to brigade employees.

During the 1970s, the policy of "self-reliance" put commune leaders on notice that their enterprises would not receive much, if any, financial support from higher levels.[57] To underwrite their enterprises, communes developed local resources, such as coal mines and hydropower, and built or purchased vehicles to transport their products to customers. To support an initial investment, a brigade could gain financing from its commune or teams. Schemes for drawing investment from teams varied depending on local resources, cadres' priorities, and market conditions. Sometimes, the brigade combined loans or direct investments from its teams with its own funds and a loan or small grant from the commune, county, or state. Brigade enterprises might receive technical expertise, training, or loans from higher levels or neighboring brigades. Not surprisingly, the eagerness of teams to contribute depended on the benefit they envisioned they might receive. Enterprises such as brickmaking and collective pigpens, for instance, offered welcome opportunities to increase team and household income.[58]

Communes and brigades could invest in almost any light-manufacturing sector for which they had sufficient local demand and resources, from building materials to shoes.[59] Unlike agriculture modernization-related investments, however, these rural enterprises were expected to be profitable. After all input and labor costs were paid, communes and brigades kept the profits generated by their enterprises, which they could distribute or reinvest as they liked.[60] One brigade, for example, distributed 40–50 percent of the profits from its enterprises among its teams based on the number of workers that each provided. The monthly salaries of brigade enterprise workers were generally higher than those of average field laborers but were lower than those of average urban factory workers.[61] The earnings from profitable enterprises could underwrite the costs of new equipment or cover the start-up costs for another, but if an enterprise perennially depleted resources, it would be closed and its land, labor, and capital would be reallocated.[62]

State-run companies and high-level marketing units could purchase commune-made products and distribute them beyond the institution's immediate locality. Such intercommune sales and purchases generally required coordination, or at least tacit approval, from county-level authorities. A brigade orchard might supply the state and its teams and could sell any remainder at the local market, whereas a brigade machine station could charge teams for rentals and repairs. The irrigation pipe factory of Shangguan Xiantang Brigade in Yuhui County, Jiangxi Province, had a procurement officer who sold to other brigades within the commune and to at least one commune in neighboring Hunan Province, which paid via the postal service.[63]

Brigade enterprises might include animal husbandry, a dairy, a flourmill, a noodle factory, a brick or tile mill, a machine repair shop, or a small-scale fertilizer or insecticide production facility. On one end of the spectrum, Xin Tang Brigade in Tang Tang Commune had only one small brick-making facility and a repair workshop. At the other end of the spectrum, Cheng Dong Commune, near Shanghai, supported brigade enterprises that employed 3,840 of its roughly 16,000 workers in a range of activities, including the manufacture of lemon extract, bicycle spokes, and light bulbs.[64] Sui Kang Brigade, Guang Li Commune's most prosperous subunit, operated a bamboo factory, a rice mill, a peanut oil–processing facility, and a wooden tools factory. Sui Kang's one-room bamboo products factory included two bamboo-slicing machines bought from the commune's agricultural machine supply station. Two workers managed the machines, surrounded by a dozen or so others who sat on the floor, weaving and binding baskets, hats, fertilizer scoops, and baskets. The remaining bamboo leaves were then used or sold as fertilizer or fuel.[65]

Taiping Qiao Brigade opened a duck farm in 1971, which after a year had about 1,000 ducks with each female laying 190 eggs per year. The enterprise supplied ducks to teams and households at 5 yuan apiece, as well as eggs and feathers for fertilizer or down, and also produced 3–3.5 metric tons of duck manure per year. Duck experts from a neighboring commune trained seven brigade workers to run the operation in two twelve-hour shifts, which included force-feeding the birds every six hours. After the ducks were sold and the brigade took its share, workers received a portion of the profits based on their accumulated workpoints. Note, however, that the state provided 60 metric tons of duck feed per month to Taiping Qiao Brigade—a precious subsidy that few other brigades enjoyed.[66]

In 1978, notes Steven Butler, "Without question, brigade and commune industries [were] becoming a more important part of the rural economy."[67] By decade's end, each brigade had about two enterprises, and more than 80 percent of them had established at least one enterprise. Between 1971 and 1978, industrial output from commune- and brigade-level enterprises grew at an average annual rate of 30.1 percent and 17.4 percent, compared with 15.8 percent and 2.8 percent during the 1962–1971 period, respectively.[68] In Hunan, the income from commune and brigade enterprises increased at least 30 percent per year after 1970, compared with a less than 1 percent average annual increase in team income from 1974 to 1976.[69]

On average, the income derived from these enterprises accounted for about one-third of the total income of the three-level commune. These national averages, however, disguised sizable regional differences.[70] In 1976, 20 percent of total income in Hunan province's communes was earned at the commune and brigade levels; in Yantai, Shandong, in 1975, it was 35 percent; and in the Shanghai suburbs, in 1974, it was 47.7 percent (30.5 percent for the commune and 17.2 percent for the brigade).[71] The number, type, and profitability of enterprises varied widely depending on a brigade's wealth and proximity to an urban or industrial center. In 1979, commune and brigade enterprises in Jiangxi, Hunan, Shanghai, and Beijing, accounted for 24 percent, 43 percent, 65 percent, and 57 percent of total collective income, respectively.[72]

Throughout the 1970s, rural enterprises yielded an increasingly large percentage of collective income, but they generally were employing fewer workers. In Wu Gong Brigade, in Raoyang County, Hebei, enterprises employed only 105 of 1,197 workers who made rope and string, rubber, and plastics and worked in the machine repair shop.[73] In another brigade outside Shanghai, 13 percent of members produced 43 percent of commune income; in another, brigade enterprises accounted for one-sixth of total collective income.[74]

The Sent-Down Campaign

The "Up to the Mountain, Down to the Village" (*shangshan, xiaxiang*) Campaign (also known as the Sent-Down Campaign) was a program to incentivize, coerce, cajole, and reassign millions of urban residents to labor in the countryside under the slogan "Learn from the peasants." Although practiced on a limited scale before the GLF, the numbers of youths and cadres who later were forced to relocate from cities to the communes increased substantially. According to official statistics, 1.2 million urban youth were sent to the countryside between 1956 and 1966, and 12 million were sent between 1968 and 1975.[75] The Sent-Down Campaign was suspended between 1966 and 1968, but it resumed thereafter. This analysis focuses on only the latter period of the urban-rural transfer program and its implications for population mobility and labor growth.

The Sent-Down Campaign ran contrary to two widely held traditional Chinese assumptions. First, it defied the preference for urban over rural life, rooted in the realistic expectation that rural-urban inequality and income disparities would continue. Second, it countered the proposition that the purpose of education was upward mobility from manual labor to a white-collar job.

The resumption and expansion of Sent-Down transfers in 1968 and 1969 was not, as some have hypothesized, undertaken primarily to rid the cities of meddlesome Red Guard youths, although in some instances, that may have been a contributing factor. The program's principal objectives were to alleviate a glut of urban workers and deploy them to the countryside to increase rural development.[76] In 1964, before the Sent-Down Campaign was suspended, Vice-Premier Tan Zhenlin estimated that China would soon have 6 million new urban job seekers without positions—a figure that was close to the 5.4 million Chinese who were later "sent down" to rural areas between 1968 and 1970.[77] Thomas Bernstein estimates that throughout the 1970s, more than 2.2 million urban workers entered the job market each year.[78] Transfers of urban youth to the countryside fluctuated during the first half of the 1970s: approximately 700,000 were sent down in 1971, 650,000 in 1972, around 1.3 million in 1973, and about 2 million in 1974 and again in 1975. These rapid increases appear to have been primarily a response to misestimates of the number of available urban jobs, for which Vice-Premier Li Fuchun offered a self-criticism.[79]

The urban-rural transfer program was publicly promoted to send skilled labor to support agricultural modernization and rural industrialization. As early as 1964, a *China Youth Daily* editorial proclaimed: "Cultured youths with socialist consciousness are urgently needed in building a new socialist countryside."[80] The official press published numerous reports in which Sent-Down youth and cadres helped modernize agriculture, including contributions to fish farming, fertilizer and pesticide production, seed breeding and cross-fertilization, hydroelectric expansion, irrigation systems, veterinary work, tractor and agricultural machine repair, land reclamation, and the expansion of electricity.[81]

Newly arrived urbanites were charged with facilitating the dissemination of productivity-increasing vocational skills. To maximize their impact and reduce their burden on rural residents, Sent-Down urban youth were often given state subsidies and resettled on marginal land in poor and remote communes. In Jiangxi, 1,400 such youth teams were established and received 6 million yuan in 1974 and 1975 to purchase chemical fertilizer, oxen, seeds, and farm tools to improve the land.[82] By 1978, they accounted for 2–3 million of the 13 million members of the nationwide agricultural research and extension network.[83]

The Sent-Down Campaign expanded the stock of skilled and semiskilled labor and enhanced information flows into communes in three interconnected ways. First, the campaign helped spread the practical and basic math and reading skills necessary to modernize agricultural production and standardize bookkeeping. Second, it created and expanded personal networks and communication channels among rural and urban residents. Third, it acquainted urbanites, particularly agricultural specialists, with local production methods and with the hardships faced by hundreds of millions of rural residents. Although they often came at great personal cost to millions of urban youth and their families, the Sent-Down Campaign policies implemented during the 1970s helped to both disperse excess skilled urban labor and disseminate basic educational and vocational skills to a wider swath of rural population than ever before. They created countless social, economic, and political linkages among rural and urban Chinese that had never previously existed.[84]

Basic and Vocational Education

During the 1970s, basic education was expanded and, for the first time, universities were opened to millions of rural Chinese. According to official census data, the literacy rate rose from 66 percent in 1964 to 77 percent in 1982.[85] The nationwide manufacture and dissemination of agricultural capital and technology required rural residents to possess basic reading and math skills as well as some vocational training. As Han observes, widespread agricultural modernization required the commensurate expansion of relevant skills among rural residents:

There was a direct link between educational expansion and rural economic development. The large number of rural youth with the special training from joint village middle schools and commune high schools helped farmers improve the economic situation in the village. Unlike their illiterate predecessors the newly educated young farmers had the conceptual tools to modernize production.[86]

The official policy during the 1970s deemphasized elite education and prioritized disseminating basic and vocational education to the masses. During the 1970s, growing numbers of rural youths received practical education designed to help improve agricultural output. The commune served as an institutional conduit whereby basic skills and agricultural techniques were disseminated and personal networks were expanded. The stated goal was to develop the "new socialist man": a versatile, selfless, and loyal "red expert" knowledgeable about the best agricultural techniques and able to increase his or her unit's production.[87] Figure 3.6 shows that the number of teacher and secondary training schools and their student bodies expanded rapidly during the 1970s, but then stagnated during decollectivization. Figures 3.7 and 3.8 reveal similar trends existed in enrollment at the elementary, middle, and high school levels as well as among students in vocational educational programs.

Local self-reliance was stressed under the commune, especially after the Soviet invasion scare of 1969–1971.[88] Each commune was ordered to become a self-sufficient unit that could sustain itself if cut off from the center during a conflict. To achieve this goal, investment in practical education was expanded and an emphasis was placed on basic literacy, accounting, and occupational skills (e.g., tractor and machine repair).

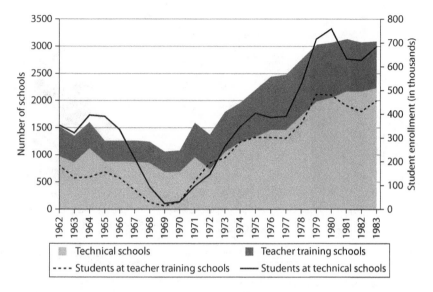

FIGURE 3.6. Technical and teacher training.
Source: Planning and Financial Bureau of the Ministry of Education, *Achievement of Education in China, 1949–1983* (Beijing: People's Education Press, 1984), 20–23.

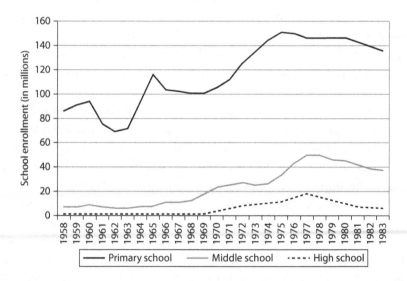

FIGURE 3.7. Primary, middle, and high school student enrollment.
Source: Planning and Financial Bureau of the Ministry of Education, *Achievement of Education in China*, 22–23.

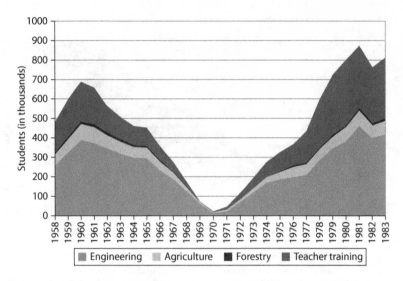

FIGURE 3.8. Students in secondary vocational training.
Source: Planning and Financial Bureau of the Ministry of Education, Achievement of Education in China, 54.

Although Chinese boys usually received more education than girls, commune education was broadly egalitarian, allowing both sexes to attend primary and often middle school regardless of their household income level. The commune coordinated teacher transfers and rotations among its subunits, so if a brigade lacked a teacher, one could be transferred from another brigade.[89]

Before 1966, universities gave priority to local urban students and were virtually impenetrable by rural residents. As part of Cultural Revolution antielitism, however, China's educational system experienced a period of political "struggle, criticism, [and] transformation" that substantially altered the lines of responsibility for research institutes, curriculum development, and student selection. Beginning in the late 1960s and early 1970s, the "worker, peasant, soldier" (gong, nong, bing) campaign gave preference and stipends to tens of thousands of rural students. This interaction helped break down barriers to higher education that had hindered agricultural investment and the dissemination of techniques for centuries. Figure 3.8 reveals that the number of students in agriculture-related fields increased consistently throughout the 1970s.

Under the "worker, peasant, soldier" program, Peking University welcomed 2,500 new students in the fall 1970, and Zhongshan University in Guangdong admitted 540 such students.[90] After receiving practical training, most commune members returned home to implement and disseminate new techniques. Publication of theoretical scientific periodicals was curtailed, courses were shortened and made more practical, and agricultural colleges moved from urban to rural areas.[91] In 1971, the U.S. botanist Arthur Galston observed how practical scientific training took place in a "ramshackle factory" at the Department of Biology at Peking University:

Molds are grown on agricultural wastes from nearby communes and used in turn to produce antibiotics. We saw tetracycline drugs that had been produced by fermentation and were being extracted, purified, tested, and sealed in glass ampoules for sale to the Chinese government for domestic use. In the course of these operations, students receive some instruction in biology, chemistry, engineering, and economics, and, on emerging from such a program, can put their training immediately to work—at least in the specific procedures they have learned.[92]

As the 1970s progressed, however, Chinese universities gradually increased student enrollment and returned to more traditional curricula and teaching styles. Visiting again in 1972, Galston observed the reestablishment of courses in theoretical physics and a new "geology-geography-geomechanics program." He noted: "The teaching of biology, which had been devoted only to new applications for medical and agricultural techniques, is being expanded to include more traditional botany, zoology, and physiology."[93]

Decreasing Arable Land

In the 1970s, China faced two additional economic challenges that exacerbated the severity of the challenges presented by its massive and rapidly growing population: falling arable land and high rates of capital depreciation.

Despite extensive investments in land reclamation, between 1970 and 1976, arable land dropped from 101.1 million ha to 99.4 million ha.[94] Flooding, blight, and salt-related damage were partially to blame for this trend, although the expansion of commune and brigade enterprises undoubtedly also contributed. Combined with the increase in rural labor described previously, this brought a reduction in the amount of land per agricultural worker. Between 1952 and 1960, China had an average of 0.62 ha of arable land per rural worker. During the 1960s, this figure gradually declined, to an average of only 0.36 ha per farmer in 1970, falling further to slightly over 0.33 ha per rural worker by 1976—just over half of 1950s levels (see figure 3.9).

Falling arable land per unit labor was a uniform phenomenon across several large agricultural provinces during the commune era. The average commune in Hunan, Jiangsu, Jiangxi, Zhejiang, Liaoning, Henan, and Hubei had increasingly less land to farm and increasingly more labor to farm it. Figure 3.10 shows that this trend continued throughout the 1960s but slowed in the 1970s. In each province for which I have data average land per worker, like the national average, experienced a continuous decline, with Zhejiang and Jiangsu facing the most desperate situation. Only Jilin bucked the national trend and enjoyed an expansion of arable land per unit labor from 1.16 ha per unit labor in 1972 to 1.27 in 1976. Generally speaking, the northeastern provinces of Jilin and Liaoning had far more land per worker than did the central and southern Chinese provinces for which I have data.

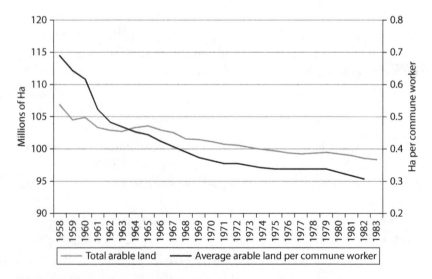

FIGURE 3.9. Total arable land and average arable land per commune worker.
Source: Agricultural Economic Statistics, 47, 120.

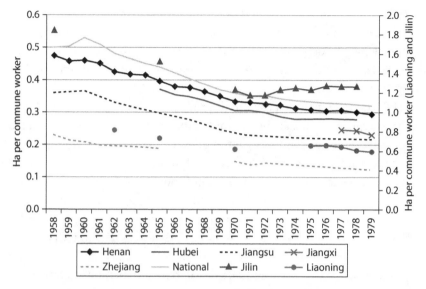

FIGURE 3.10. Arable land per commune worker in select provinces.
Sources: *Thirty Years: Agricultural Statistics of Henan Province*; *Agricultural Statistics of Hubei Province*; *Statistics and Materials of Agricultural Mechanization in Hunan Province*; *Agricultural Statistics of Jiangsu Province*; *Agricultural Statistics of Jiangxi Province*; *Agricultural Economic Statistics of Jilin Province*; *Population Statistics of Liaoning Province*; Statistical Bureau of Zhejiang Province, ed., *Collection of Materials on Fifty Years of Zhejiang*.

In response, China attempted both to increase the output of existing arable land and to reclaim as much land as possible. To achieve the former goal, the research and extension system worked to develop and disseminate agricultural technologies, including the production and application of agricultural chemicals (e.g., fertilizer and pesticide) and hybrid seed varieties. To achieve the latter goal, land reclamation investments were made to recover flooded lands, fight soil erosion, and combat blight and saltwater damage.

POLICY RESPONSES

Innovation

AGRICULTURAL INPUTS   Agricultural economist Bruce Stone argues that "improved water control, abundant supplies of fertilizers, and high-yielding seed varieties responsive to these inputs" were largely responsible for increases in China's agricultural production per unit land during the 1970s.[95] Employing one or more of these three measures produced some growth in yields, but returns were greatest when all three were correctly applied together.

Efforts to expand agricultural production through improved fertilizer application began in the mid-1950s, when 40 percent of China's cultivated land used no fertilizer at all and between 20 and 60 percent of backyard fertilizer was lost because of improper techniques. The agricultural research and extension system promoted natural fertilizers and promulgated simple, standardized, and low-cost techniques to increase fertilizer output.[96] Households, for instance, were encouraged to raise pigs to increase the availability of natural fertilizers. During a 1971 visit to the Malu People's Commune outside Shanghai, Galston observed two techniques: one that used traditional materials and methods to transform human waste into fertilizer, and another that combined composted garbage with nitrogen-fixing microorganisms.[97] The aforementioned 1975 NAS report corroborated this account and noted that natural fertilizer production reflected "China's farmers' skill and dedication" and showed "little variation" among localities.[98]

During the late 1960s and early 1970s, small-scale county- or commune-owned facilities rapidly expanded production of chemical fertilizers. Figure 3.11 shows that throughout the 1970s, fertilizer production increased rapidly. In 1973, 63 percent of total chemical fertilizer output came from small industries scattered across rural China.[99] Communes in Jimo County, Shandong, for instance, produced two types of phosphate bacteria fertilizers: one (called 5406) improved wheat yields by an average of 20 percent, and the other improved yields by 13 percent. In 1971, Jimo built a phosphate fertilizer factory, which by 1974 produced 2,576 metric tons of fertilizer, and by 1978, produced 15,543 metric tons.[100] To increase supplies, beginning in the early 1970s, China invested heavily in large-scale plants. By the early 1980s, the country had increased chemical fertilizer production faster than any other country and had become the world's largest consumer.[101]

China's agricultural scientists developed various chemical agents and biological processes to combat pestilence. As show in figure 3.12, throughout

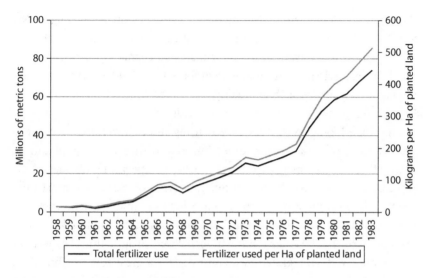

FIGURE 3.11. Total fertilizer production and use per Ha.
Source: Agricultural Economic Statistics, 120, 292.

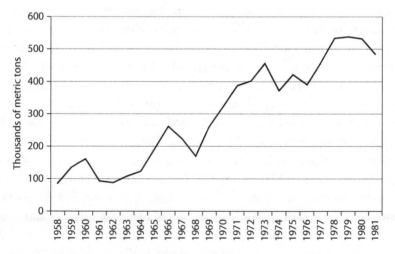

FIGURE 3.12. Total pesticide production.
Source: Agricultural Economic Statistics, 293.

the 1970s, pesticide production increased considerably. According to Ma Shichun, who headed the Insect Ecology at Peking University's Institute of Zoology in 1979, innovations in pest management achieved through investments in research and development combined with widespread local testing had four objectives: "high quality," "no environmental contamination," "low production costs," and "increased yields."[102]

One such biological technique was using insect hormones to regulate growth and sex attractants; another introduced the natural predators of destructive insects, such as red eye wasps, magpies, or ladybugs.[103] By 1970, China produced about fifty different types of pesticides, most on a small scale, with the most popular being dichlorodiphenyltrichloroethane (DDT), benzene hexachloride (BHC), and domestic products known as "666" and "Sheng."[104] After visiting in 1979, Swedish agricultural expert Per Brinck observed, "Integrated pest control plays a great role in China. . . . The new techniques made integrated pest control possible."[105]

China also conducted experiments on growth-regulating hormones. Ethrel (2-chloroethyl phosphoric acid) sprayed on rice made it ripen more quickly. Hydrolytic nucleic acids produced from molds improved root development and photosynthesis in rice. Microbiological processes were developed to control plant diseases, including rice blast and wheat scab. One organic stimulator, liquid gibberellin, increased the yield of oranges, pineapples, grapes, spinach, and other green leafy vegetables by 12 percent. Gibberellin also could break the dormancy of ginseng and potatoes and could keep vegetables fresh longer.[106] As of 1978, application of these techniques remained limited to a few test regions, but their application area was gradually expanded and laid the groundwork for future yield-increasing innovations.[107] In a 1970 study on China's research and development (R&D) for the U.S. National Science Foundation, U.S. Deputy Assistant Secretary of Defense Yuan-li Wu and Robert Sheeks note that with respect to "the distribution of new crop varieties and control of pests, a long time lag seems technically unavoidable."[108] Indeed, the lag time between testing and widespread application meant that R&D done during the 1970s often laid the foundation for productive discoveries throughout the 1980s.[109]

HIGH-YIELD SEED VARIETIES Among China's most important technological breakthroughs were new seed varieties that generated increased productivity under complex multicropping systems and in various climates and conditions. By the late 1970s, China was at the forefront of food grain research, particularly in rice, wheat, and corn seed. Chinese agronomists also developed dwarfing agents and nitrogen-fixing bacteria that helped promote multicropping while also reducing the need for chemical fertilizers.[110] "The spread of new technology," observes Scott Rozelle, "included the adoption of hybrids and the introduction of insect and disease resistant varieties."[111]

Throughout the 1970s, China continued to improve its food grain varieties to increase yields and make them more rapidly maturing, more disease resistant, and better adapted to local conditions. Wu and Sheeks conclude that exaggerated reports of the success of China's seed development programs during the GLF "would tax the credulity of even the most naive person." During the 1960s, however, initial failures prompted policy adjustments that prioritized the development of improved grain seed, making them "the major effort of Chinese R&D in agriculture" by 1970.[112]

As suggested in figure 3.13, during the 1970s, China's high-yield seed varieties (HYV) program had shown some impressive results. According to

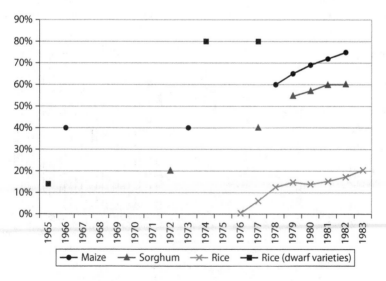

FIGURE 3.13. Percentage area sown with high-yield seed varieties.
Source: Bruce Stone, *Evolution and Diffusion of Agricultural Technology in China* (Washington, DC: International Food Policy Research Institute, 1990), 45.

Stone, "The breeding of new varieties with superior traits was very strong, and the speed with which new varieties were tested and adapted to local environments was especially rapid."[113] Decentralization allowed China to cut the development time needed for new pure strain crops from two to three years, as opposed to ten to thirty years. By 1976, two hundred units around China were studying tissue culture, and by 1978, China was a world leader in such research.[114]

Rice, southern China's most important crop, received special attention from researchers.[115] By 1977, the rapidly maturing, high-yield dwarf varieties developed in the early 1960s were grown on 80 percent of China's rice paddies (see figure 3.13). F1 hybrid rice, developed between 1964 and 1973, yielded about 15 percent more than conventional varieties, and was released and rapidly distributed in 1975 and 1976. China's creation of semi-dwarf rice occurred two years before the release of IR-8, the variety that launched the green revolution in other parts of Asia.[116] By 1986, the area planted with F1 hybrid rice had reached 8.94 million ha, about 28 percent of China's total rice-growing area. As of 1990, China remained the only country that commercially produced and distributed hybrid rice.[117]

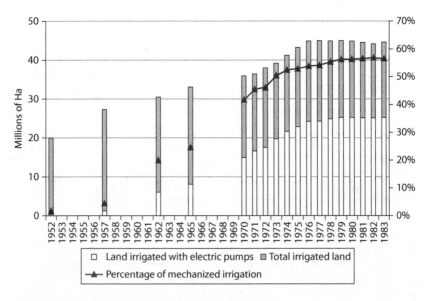

FIGURE 3.14. Irrigation infrastructure.
Source: Agricultural Economic Statistics, 291.

Seed-breeding programs also focused on wheat and corn, two staple crops in northern China. By 2007, based largely on work pioneered during the 1970s, China had created seventy-nine varieties of wheat, including new fungal-resistant strains, grown on 20 million ha.[118] HYV corn developed more slowly than rice, but over time, these varieties proved equally important. During the 1970s, Chinese researchers worked to create high-yield crossbred corn and double-crossbred corn. Like wheat, by 1978, these corn varieties were not yet in widespread use; by the late 1980s, however, hybrid corn covered 90 percent of China's corn planting area.[119] HYV sweet potatoes and sorghum also showed impressive gains in the 1970s and were "yielding as much as the best elite varieties anywhere in the world." In China's most productive areas cassava and white potato output rivaled the world's top producers.[120]

Land Reclamation

China sought to reduce the rate of arable land loss through various land reclamation techniques.[121] Official statistics and expert accounts reveal the extensive efforts and variety of techniques employed during the 1970s to increase productivity per unit of land. Throughout the decade, communes made extensive efforts to expand their arable land by reclaiming land affected by blight, waterlogging, erosion, and saltwater damage. Land reclamation was sometimes undertaken in conjunction with an irrigation system or a hydroelectric project. In 1972–1973, China began reporting national statistics on four types of land reclamation activities: plant disease and insects (i.e., blight), flood drainage, saltwater damage, and soil erosion.

Of these methods, blight treatments were used most often and were most effective. Despite these treatments, however, the problem of blight continued to grow faster than any other. In 1972, China had 71.3 million ha of blighted lands and was able to treat 50.4 million ha, or 70.6 percent. By 1976, however, the amount of blighted land had nearly doubled (to 139.4 million ha), and the amount of treated land had increased almost two and a half times to 125 million ha or about 90 percent of the total. The percentage of treated lands was lower in 1977 (80 percent), 1978 (73 percent), and 1979 (80 percent), but with the expanded application of chemical-based treatments, it increased again in the early 1980s.[122] In 1982, China experienced 175.3 million ha of blighted lands, but it was able to treat 88 percent or 154.7 million ha. In sum, despite extensive efforts to fight blight, the problem continued to spread throughout the 1970s and into the 1980s.[123]

The use of chemicals to combat blight was only partially successful, and in many cases, losses were sustained despite their application. Over time, however, the treatment does appear to have become increasingly effective. In 1972, 13.7 million metric tons of grain were produced on land reclaimed from blight, although losses after failed treatment equaled 11.1 million metric tons. By 1976, however, 15.9 million metric tons of grain could be grown on land treated for blight and losses had fallen to 8.5 million metric tons. With the exception of one year (i.e., 1978), this trend continued throughout the decade and into the early 1980s. Despite a large increase in blighted land in 1982, 21.9 million metric tons of grain were produced on land treated for blight, and losses equaled 9.2 million metric tons. In sum, although blight continued to spread, China gradually improved its ability to put blighted lands back to use.[124]

Drainage was a somewhat successful, albeit arduous, technique used to open new lands for cultivation and improve soil quality. In 1974, Qiliying Commune in Xinxiang County, Henan, drained a wetland to expand its farmland and create a fishpond. Residents made ditches on either side to drain the water, removed the top layer of soil and reed roots, and planted crops on the reclaimed fields.[125] Throughout the 1970s, flood prone lands increased slightly along with the ability of localities to reclaim these lands. In 1973, of the 22 million ha that had been flood prone or water logged, 15.6 million ha (or about 70 percent) had been reclaimed. This percentage continued to increase, and by 1976 16.7 million ha, or 75 percent, of such land had been salvaged. Between 1979 and 1982, flooded land accounted for about 23.7 million ha per year, but China managed to save about 18 million ha per year—an annual average rate of about 76 percent.[126]

Land was reclaimed from saline and alkali damage as well. In Jimo County, Shandong, and Shulu County, Hebei, for instance, a technique called "land washing" doubled grain production per unit land.[127] In 1963, about 6.7 million ha were affected—predominantly in north China, where between 10 and 20 percent of arable land was alkaline. In Hebei alone, 1.3 million ha were classified as alkaline in 1964. That year, soil specialists from China's Academy of Sciences gathered in Nanjing, Jiangsu, to discuss the problem and commission studies for the Yellow River, Huai River, and Hai River basins. Meetings continued throughout 1965, "suggesting an inability to resolve the problem within a short time," according to Wu and Sheeks.[128] Official data suggest techniques to reclaim salt-affected land proved only partially successful throughout the 1970s. In 1973, 6.8 million ha were destroyed by salt, and 3.2 million ha (or 47.8 percent) were reclaimed. This percentage steadily increased, and by 1976, 7.1 million ha of land was destroyed by salt and 4.2 million ha (or 59 percent) was reclaimed. Unlike with blight, however, the success of salt-related treatments and techniques did not continue into the early 1980s; by 1982, 7.2 million ha were destroyed by saltwater and 4.3 million ha (or 59 percent) were reclaimed.[129]

In 1973, China had 117.7 million ha of land suffering from soil erosion and had successfully treated 35.1 million ha (or 30 percent); in 1976, of the 119.2 million ha of land suffering from erosion, 42 million ha (or 35 percent) had been reclaimed. That percentage peaked in 1977 at 37 percent before dipping slightly throughout the remainder of the decade and the early 1980s. By 1982, the percentage of land successfully treated for erosion was 34 percent, with 41 million ha of 120 million ha successfully brought under the plow.[130]

By 1977, Hui County, Shanxi, and Lin County, Henan, had undertaken land reclamation by terracing the mountainsides and by filling gullies and sandy and marshy riverbeds to transform them into productive agricultural land. Dwight Perkins describes the scene: "We saw ample evidence of increasing arable land through reclamation and improvement projects in every area that we visited. In Shanxi Province, we saw badly eroded mountainous areas, with yellowish wind-deposited loess soils, being reclaimed for good arable land."[131]

As the amount of arable land fell during the 1970s, a variety of techniques were used to increase land productivity. Communes gradually improved their capacity to reclaim land affected by blight, waterlogging, erosion, and saltwater damage. Despite numerous accounts of the success of land reclamation in the Chinese press and the anecdotal accounts of Western observers, the data reveal that China continued to lose land faster than it could reclaim it. Overall, these techniques slowed—but could not stop—the decline of arable land, which continued into the 1980s (see figures 3.9 and 3.10).[132]

Increased Rate of Capital Depreciation

During 1958 and 1959, facing conditions of unlimited labor and exceedingly scarce capital, Chinese planners harnessed tens of millions of workers at subsistence wages to build large amounts of poor-quality capital.

Exaggerated reports claimed 210 million improved tools and implements were built and distributed to farmers.[133] With income extraction at peak levels and workers occupied with building farm equipment and large infrastructure projects—particularly dams and reservoirs—grain fields went untended and contributed to the GLF famine. Richard Baum explains how this occurred:

Since China was short on both investment capital and advanced technology, but long on raw, unskilled human labor, idle male laborers were conscripted from the villages to do the heavy work of building water conservation projects using whatever simple tools they had at hand—shovels, picks, and hoes. In some cases, as many as ten thousand peasants were transported to a single dam or canal-site from more than a dozen nearby villages. Since the commuting distances involved often exceeded twenty miles, and were too great to complete on foot in a single day, temporary barracks were erected for the laborers at the work sites, where they would remain for weeks, or even months at a time, returning home only infrequently.[134]

Despite a shortage of skilled workers, during the Anti-Rightist Campaign and the GLF, many educated people were marked by "black" class backgrounds (e.g., landlords, capitalists, bourgeois intellectuals) and faced discrimination or worse. Policies that placed those with "red" class backgrounds (i.e., workers, peasants, soldiers) in charge of those with "expert" know-how lowered the effective amount of human capital in the rural economy at a time when it was already scarce.[135] Skilled workers were dispirited or worse, and vast quantities of poor-quality physical capital and infrastructure were constructed, which in turn began depreciating at an accelerated rate. "The Communist political leadership," Wu and Sheeks observe, "courted failure through their indiscriminate and technically incompetent application of otherwise sound principles to improve and stabilize output." The CPC's "centralist organization and command structure" not only placed political slogans above science and technology but also discouraged all dissent from below.[136]

During the GLF, red-over-expert policies led to the widespread misallocation of investment and denuded both physical and human capital stocks at a time when both were already scarce. Baum cogently summarizes the sometimes-tragic consequences of rapid capital depreciation and the collapse of many GLF-era investments in the years that followed:

Although the initial crop harvest in the summer of 1958 was, in fact, larger than average, a number of serious problems had already begun to emerge. When the first heavy summer rains fell in 1958, many of the dams, canals, dikes and reservoirs hastily constructed in the previous winter began to fail, causing inundation of hundreds of thousands of acres of cropland. *Of the 500 largest reservoirs under construction in the winter of 1957–58, over 200 were abandoned within two years.* Nor did the Great Leap's water management failures end there. In 1975 a huge dam built in 1958 in Henan province collapsed, causing an estimated 200,000 deaths—the largest single dam disaster in human history. *The main causes of failure were inadequate engineering know-how and the routine use of substandard construction materials.* The Maoist emphasis on mass mobilization over careful planning, ideological "redness" over technical "expertise," had created not miracles, but vast misfortune.[137] (Italics added for emphasis)

The rapid depreciation of capital during the GLF exacerbated the preexisting scarcity of agricultural capital that had characterized rural China before collectivization. The immediate response to the famine was to reduce the extractive capability of the communes, which saw their size, mandate, and coercive controls shrink in the early 1960s as some political leaders (among them Deng Xiaoping) adopted policies to boost household consumption. After the crisis abated, however, China returned to similar macroeconomic conditions that had precipitated the communes' creation in the first place: low savings rates, rising population growth rates, falling arable land, and severe undercapitalization. Facing another looming crisis, beginning in the mid-1960s, China introduced the Dazhai model, which promised to increase household savings rates using the workpoint remuneration system. It was only after the reforms to agricultural research and extension system were completed in 1970, however, that the commune was able to successfully channel household savings into investments in *productive* physical and human capital.[138]

POLICY RESPONSES

Physical Capital Investment
WATER MANAGEMENT   In 1970s rural China, as elsewhere, irrigation increased yields, reduced labor hours, and opened old fields to new crops. Investments in water management and storage made farmers less dependent

on rainfall, thereby making grain output more predictable. Figure 3.14 illustrates how expanded investments in irrigation infrastructure made during the 1970s began to stagnate after 1977.

In the 1970s, large wells with electric pumps became critical to irrigation and thereafter had a major effect on agricultural productivity and drought reduction in northern China.[139] In 1965, China had about half a million mechanized irrigation and drainage systems, and by 1970, it had nearly 1.5 million systems. That number increased four times during the 1970s—to 4.3 million in 1976 and 5 million in 1978—before leveling off in the early 1980s. Moreover, the power of these systems also grew exponentially during this period—increasing from 9 million horsepower (hp) in 1965 to 18.2 million hp in 1970, 54.2 million hp in 1976, and 65.6 million hp in 1978—before leveling off in the early 1980s.[140]

Under the commune, the amount of land irrigated with mechanized water distribution systems rose as a percentage of total irrigated land. In 1965, China had 33 million ha of "well-irrigated lands" consisting of 31.9 percent of total cultivated land. Of those well-irrigated lands, 8 million ha (or 24.5 percent of China's total arable land) used mechanized irrigation systems. In 1970, 36 million ha of well-irrigated lands accounted for 35.6 percent of total cultivated land. Of this total, 15 million ha (41.6 percent) were irrigated using mechanized systems. By 1976, 45 million ha (45.3 percent of China's total cultivated land) were effectively irrigated, and 44.9 million ha (53.9 percent) were irrigated using mechanized systems. This peak in both nominal and percentage levels remained constant through the end of the decade and into the next.[141] When combined with new technologies, such as hybrid seeds and chemical fertilizers, investments in irrigation helped propel crop yields per land unit to unprecedented levels.[142]

AGRICULTURAL MACHINERY During the 1970s, China invested heavily in the production and distribution of agricultural capital equipment, including large and handheld tractors and all types of engines and vehicles. Local industrial enterprises under the commune and brigade provided machinery and tools to more Chinese farmers than ever before.[143]

Agricultural machinery and vehicles, transportation infrastructure, technology, and power generation became widely available for the first time in the 1970s. According to figure 3.15, in 1965, 15 percent (15.6 million ha) of all cultivated land was under machine cultivation, rising to 18 percent

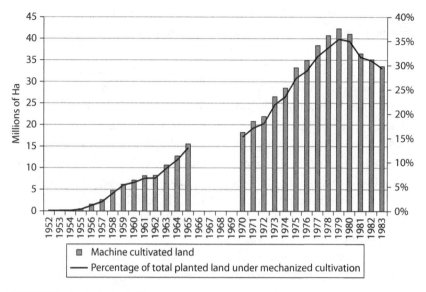

FIGURE 3.15. Mechanized cultivation.
Source: Agricultural Economic Statistics, 290.

(18.2 million ha) by 1970. By 1976, this figure had more than doubled to 35 percent (34.9 million ha). The percentage of agricultural land under mechanized production peaked in 1979 at 41.3 percent (42.2 million ha), but by 1983, it had fallen below 1976 levels.[144] Total agricultural horsepower, which in 1957 was only 1.65 million, increased to 15 million in 1965, 29.4 million in 1970, 117.3 million in 1976, and 159.8 million in 1978. The amount of tractor tailing furrow-makers (for digging furrows for planting) increased from 258,000 in 1965 to 346,000 in 1970. By 1976, production had nearly tripled to 985,000, and by 1978, there were 1.2 million furrow-makers.[145] This massive infusion of farm capital improved agricultural productivity (a conclusion demonstrated by the results of the statistical analysis presented in chapter 6) and freed up millions of farmers from backbreaking labor.

After the water pump, the tractor was probably the most important agricultural machine in 1970s China. According to commune-era statistics, tractors were divided into two categories: large and midsize tractors (*dazhong tuolaji*) and small handheld tractors (*shoufu tuolaji*). During the 1970s, tractors gradually replaced animal power in many areas, but the effect of tractor use was uneven. In the large fields of Heilongjiang and Henan, large and midsize tractors were invaluable, whereas in mountainous and swampy regions, the small handheld tractors proved more useful.

Figure 3.16 illustrates the precipitous rise in the number of tractors that began around 1970.[146] In 1952, China had only 1,307 large and midsize tractors. This number ballooned to 72,599 by 1965, more than doubled to 150,179 in 1971, and rose steeply to 397,000 in 1976 and to 557,385 by 1978. Meanwhile, the number of small handheld tractors rose even faster. National-level statistics report no small handheld tractors until 1962, when the country had only 919 of these tractors. By 1965, China had just 3,956 small handheld tractors, but by 1971, the number jumped to 133,550. Between 1971 and 1976, the number of small tractors rose to 825,000, and by 1978 China had 1.37 million of them.

Other farm machines that aided in planting, harvesting, and other field-work included planters, sprayers, harvesters, mills, and furrow-makers. Many machines were labor saving, like the electric grain grinder. After being introduced in Weihai, Shandong, in 1976, this grinder liberated women and children from countless hours of slow and tiresome work.[147]

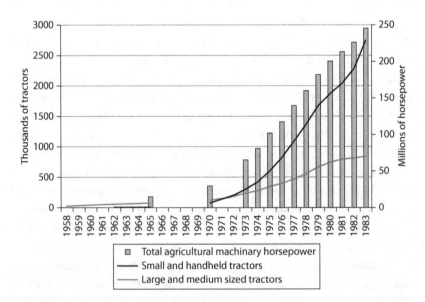

FIGURE 3.16. Tractors and agricultural horsepower.
Source: Agricultural Economic Statistics, 286–87.

Threshers separate grain from stalks and husks. As shown in figure 3.17, these machines were first introduced in 1962, and by 1965, the country had only 114,000. By 1970, however, the number of threshers reached 455,000; by 1976, there were 1.8 million; and, in 1978, there were 2.1 million. Reaper machines, which cut and gather crops, became available after threshers. In 1972, just 3,517 threshers were available nationwide; by 1976, however, 41,518 were available, and in 1978, there were 63,002 of them. The number of machines that combined threshing and reaping also proliferated, but these machines remained less common. In 1965, there were just 6,704 such machines; in 1970, there were 8,002; by 1976, there were 14,233; and by 1978. there were 18,987.[148] Farm equipment that helped expand animal husbandry increased quickly during the 1970s. National-level data for feed-mixing machines begin in 1973 and indicate that 676,000 were available nationwide; by 1976, 1.1 million were available; and in 1978, 1.3 million were available. Similarly, official records for sheep-shearing and cow-milking machines also began in 1973, when there were 980 and 399; by 1976, there were 1,178 and 868; and by 1979, there were 2,069 and 1,304, respectively.[149]

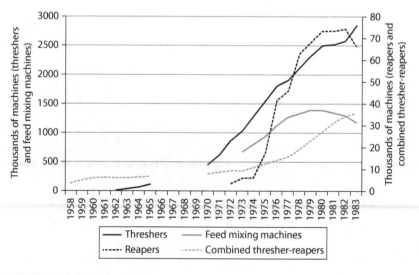

FIGURE 3.17. Agricultural machinery.
Source: Agricultural Economic Statistics, 287–88.

ELECTRICITY GENERATION   Although the number of kilowatt-hours (kWh) used in agriculture continued to rise steadily, it pales in comparison to urban electricity generation, both as a nominal figure and per unit of agricultural land. Although more than 80 percent of China's population was rural in 1965, only 3.71 billion kWh of electricity (5.62 percent overall) was produced in rural areas—an average of only 36 kW/ha per year. By 1971, 7.55 percent or 10.4 billion kW of China's electricity was produced in rural areas, an average of 103.5 kWh/ha per year.

Figures 3.18 and 3.19 reveal the extensive investments made in rural electricity generation throughout the 1970s. By 1976, the amount of kilowatt-hours used in rural areas had nearly doubled to 20.5 billion (or 10.09 percent of total Chinese electricity production), an average of 205.5 kWh/ha. In 1978, Chinese agriculture received 25.3 billion kWh, or an average of 255 kWh/ha, and by 1983, that number had risen to 43.5 billion kWh and 442.5 kWh/ha—more than 10 times the amount 18 years earlier. The distribution of electricity to power agricultural machines and to provide light for additional work at night helped boost rural productivity throughout the 1970s.[150]

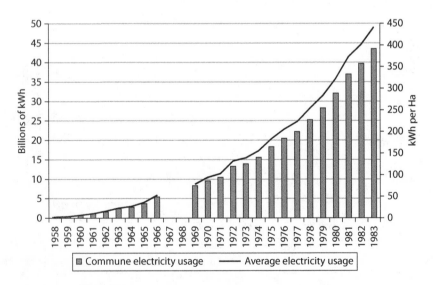

FIGURE 3.18. Commune electricity production and usage.
Source: Agricultural Economic Statistics, 294.

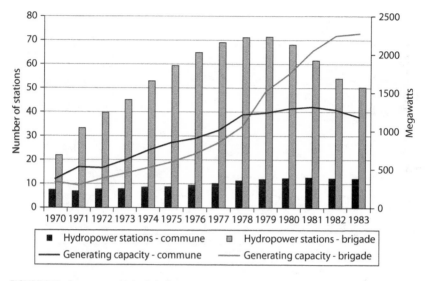

FIGURE 3.19. Commune and brigade hydropower.
Source: Agricultural Economic Statistics, 295.

Communes and subordinate brigades were encouraged to develop hydro-power resources within their jurisdiction, and the number of hydropower stations and dams, which often powered irrigation systems, increased substantially. As shown in figure 3.19, pre-1970 statistics on hydropower stations are not available, but that year, China's 7,297 commune-controlled power stations produced 374,000 kW, and its 21,905 brigade-administered stations produced 335,000 kW. In 1976, communes operated 9,348 hydropower stations, producing 706,000 kW, and brigades oversaw 64,777 stations, producing 904,000 kW. By 1978, communes directed 11,256 stations, producing more than 1 million kW. The number of commune stations rose slightly until 1981 and fell thereafter (although the number of kilowatts produced continued to rise steadily). By contrast, the number of hydropower stations under brigade control peaked in 1979 at 71,384 and subsequently dropped consistently. In 1979, as decollectivization began, brigade-controlled power stations produced more than 1.2 million kW.[151] Thereafter, however, reduced investment in rural electricity provision inhibited the expansion of agricultural mechanization, particularly electric water pumps critical to expanding irrigation networks. In the 1980s, power generation for urban centers became a policy priority.[152]

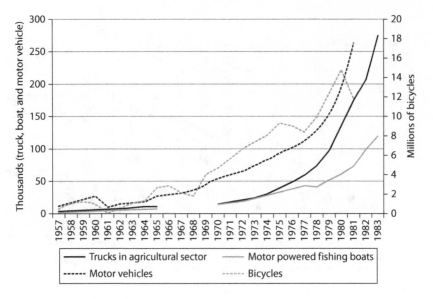

FIGURE 3.20. Rural transportation capital.
Source: Agricultural Economic Statistics, 295; Willy Kraus, *Economic Development and Social Change in the People's Republic of China* (New York: Springer-Verlag, 1982), 339–40.

TRANSPORTATION CAPITAL Rural transportation capital saw sizable increases during the 1970s and early 1980s. Figure 3.20 shows that the number of trucks, motor-powered fishing boats, motor vehicles, and bicycles grew rapidly over the course of the decade. In 1965, China had about 11,000 trucks in the agricultural sector; by 1970, it had about 15,000; and in 1979, it had more than 97,000—an average of about two trucks per commune. Exponential growth continued throughout the decade into the early 1980s, and by 1983, China had nearly 275,000 trucks in the agricultural sector. The number of boats likewise rose rapidly from about 7,800 in 1965 to 14,200 in 1970, to 52,000 in 1976, and to 120,000 in 1983. The increased carrying capacity of these boats also can be measured in horsepower, which expanded from 992,000 hp in 1970 to 3.129 million hp in 1979 and rose continuously throughout the decade.[153] These increases enhanced the mobility of productive factors and finished products in the countryside in ways that improved agricultural productivity throughout the 1970s and 1980s.

CONCLUSION

Using previously unexploited official Chinese data, this study identifies three primary economic challenges China faced in the 1970s: rising rates of population growth, falling arable land, and high capital depreciation rates. The chapter also describes and evaluates the policies adopted to alleviate these challenges. Beginning in 1970, China initiated a decade-long nation-wide investment campaign intended to modernize agriculture, improve basic education, and expand small-scale rural industrialization. This strategy kick-started a virtuous cycle of rural development that produced the sustained increases in grain, pig, and edible oil production documented in chapter 1 (chapter 1, figures 1.1–1.3). Agricultural investments undertaken via the 1970s agricultural research and extension system were essential drivers of productivity increases both under the commune and after its dissolution.

During the 1970s, China reformed the commune and adopted a set of agricultural policies that enhanced population control, reinvested profits locally, improved the quality of agricultural capital and inputs, and expanded application of these inputs. China's increased agricultural output came from the nationwide application of these improved agricultural inputs, which—when used together—substantially increased food production. Year after year throughout the 1970s, the commune increased agricultural production by extracting resources from households and investing them in agricultural capital and technology via the agricultural research and extension system. This effort was supported by thousands of commune- and brigade-owned enterprises that employed and trained the growing workforce, increased rural production, and diversified and capitalized the rural economy. According to Louis Putterman, these enterprises "lay the foundation for one of the most dynamic sectors of Chinese industry in the reform era, the township and village enterprises which would grow to account for nearly 20 percent of national industrial output in 1989."[154]

PART II

Sources of Commune Productivity

Chapter Four

ECONOMICS

Super-Optimal Investment

INTRODUCTION

This chapter uses neoclassical and classical economic growth models to explain patterns of productivity under the commune (1958–1983). It reveals how China revived agricultural production after the Great Leap Forward (GLF) famine and lackluster productivity in the 1960s and generated sizable increases in food output in the 1970s. High rates of income extraction from households (i.e., forced savings), productive investment, and technological progress drove increased food output under the commune. This process was akin to the "transformation in techniques" that E. L. Jones argued English agriculture experienced before that country's industrial revolution.[1] As detailed in chapter 3, between 1970 and 1979, higher savings rates underwrote investments in more and better agricultural capital and technologies (see chapter 3, figures 3.6–3.20) that increased agricultural production (see chapter 1, figures 1.1–1.3).

The key question for a developing country with an extremely large or fast-growing population is how to increase savings rates and make productive investments that take advantage of high returns to capital. The commune extracted an increasing percentage of household savings to finance productive capital and technology, thus kick-starting a continuous development process that produced rapid growth in food production. Through the extraction of household savings, Chinese communes funded investments that increased agricultural productivity. The workpoint remuneration system constituted a "kabuki theater" that used a multitude of meetings about job allocations, work evaluations, and workpoints to attract members' attention toward the size of their portion relative to others and away from the system's extraction of their savings. The agricultural research and extension system, which was covered in chapter 3, targeted investments into land and labor-saving capital improvements and technical innovations and rewarded locally appropriate, results-driven investments. Meanwhile, the formal recognition of household—the basic accounting unit before 1958 and again after decollectivization—private plots, cottage industries, and rural markets (i.e., the Three Small Freedoms) ensured at least a minimum consumption floor to prevent the return of famine.

I use a neoclassical economic growth model (i.e., the Solow–Swan model) to identify six distinct phases of savings and investment during China's collective agriculture era:

1. Pre-commune: undersaving
2. GLF Commune (1958–1961): oversaving with *unproductive* investment and high capital depreciation rates
3. The Rightist Commune (1962–1964): return to undersaving
4. The Leftist Commune (1965–1969): high savings rates but *without* increases in investment productivity
5. The Green Revolution Commune (1970–1979): high savings rates *with* increases in *productive* investment
6. Decollectivization (1980–1983): a return to undersaving

Phases 2–5 correspond with the four phases of commune development examined in chapters 2 and 3. This analysis reveals, among other things, how decollectivization delivered a consumption boost to impoverished rural households.

This chapter has two sections. The first section uses the Solow–Swan neoclassical economic growth model and the Lewis modified classical model to explain how a country like commune-era China—that is, a closed economy with an essentially unlimited and fast-growing labor supply, scarce land, quickly depreciating capital, and rising savings rates—could have generated sustained increases in agricultural output. These theories of economic growth clarify how changes in per capita rates of savings (s), consumption (c), population growth (n), capital (k), and relative capital productivity (α), as well as total factor productivity (A) and capital depreciation (δ), affect levels of per capita agricultural output (y).

The second section explains how the commune could increase savings rates without pushing households below minimum levels of consumption. It identifies variations in savings rates over the life of the commune and explains how household resources were extracted: the workpoint system, ad hoc equality-promoting policies, and rural credit cooperatives (RCCs). The chapter concludes with a discussion of the Three Small Freedoms and how they helped prevent a return to the overextraction that occurred under the GLF Commune.

THE TRANSITIONAL DYNAMICS OF PRODUCTIVITY GROWTH UNDER THE COMMUNE

This section applies insights from both the Solow–Swan neoclassical economic growth model and the Lewis modified classical model to explain how extracting household savings and investing them in productive capital and technology can generate long-run increases in agricultural output. These economic models identify explanatory variables—rates of savings, population growth, capital accumulation and depreciation, and technological progress—and their influence on agricultural output during the commune period. Note that when applying any theory to a complex empirical phenomenon, questions of "fit" inevitably arise. Being mindful that a perfect fit is not possible, it is important to recall that the limited aim of this exercise is to apply basic insights from the Solow–Swan model and the Lewis model to organize and explain patterns observed in the empirical data. These economic growth models provide internally consistent structures that may explain the long-run consequences of policies adopted during the commune period. They help identify causal variables that explain the trajectory of economic growth over time. With the help of my colleague at the University of Texas at Austin, economist Richard Lowery, I was able to represent these stylized displays using consistent numerical specifications.

These two models are particularly well suited for this case for two reasons. First, both assume a closed economy in which households cannot buy foreign goods or sell their goods abroad. Chinese communes were highly self-reliant and, with rare exceptions, were entirely insulated from foreign trade. In a closed economy, output equals income, and the amount invested equals the amount saved. Indeed, in 1970s China, the resources communes extracted from households (i.e., labor, grain, cash) were almost always spent or invested *within* the locality itself, such that savings and investment were practically identical.[2] Communes lacked access to outside equity or debt markets, sustained deficit spending was impossible, and local financial institutions (e.g., the RCCs) could not lend beyond their deposits.

Second, both models assume one-sector production (i.e., agriculture) in which output is a homogeneous good that can be consumed or invested to create new units of capital. Again, this condition fits with the commune's "grain first" mandate and its reliance on animal husbandry, especially swine. Thus, both the simple Solow–Swan neoclassical economic growth model and the Lewis modified classical model are well suited to explain why the commune was successful in increasing productivity.

The Solow-Swan Neoclassical Economic Growth Model

According to the neoclassical economic growth model, if an economy experiences increased rates of population growth and capital depreciation and responds with policies that increase the savings rate and channel resources into productive capital and technology, then returns to capital will remain relatively high and output will likely increase over a *sustained* period of time. To observe this, consider an aggregate production function including total factor productivity,[3] which is given by:

$$Y = Af(K, L) \tag{4.1}$$

Equation (4.1) represents total output, Y, as a function of the level of technological progress, A, capital input, K, and labor input, L. The level of technological progress is assumed in the Solow–Swan model to change at a steady rate that is exogenously given. I argue that there was an increase in the pace of technological advance attributable to institutional changes in the commune system introduced by the Communist Party in the 1970s.[4] K is an aggregate index of capital goods and should be interpreted broadly to include both human and physical capital.[5] L varies over time based on population growth. The Solow–Swan model assumes population growth is exogenous and occurs at a constant rate, $n = \Delta L/L \geq 0$. An increase in A, K, or L will lead to an increase in output. Multiplying both sides by $\frac{1}{L}$ yields an expression in per capita terms given by:

$$y = Af(k) \tag{4.2}$$

This differential $\partial k/\partial t$ refers to the derivative of the per worker capital stock with respect to time. In steady state, k is constant so that $\partial k/\partial t = 0$. In steady state, the levels of K, L, and C grow at the same rate as population growth, n, so that the per capita quantities k, y, and c do not grow. In figure 4.1, this point is determined by the intersection of the $s * A * f(k)$ curve and the $(n + \delta) * k$ line. The curve reflects the increase in capital per worker from saving that is invested, whereas the line reflects the decrease in capital per worker resulting from a growing population and capital depreciation. The capital stock is constant at the point at which the curve and line intersect. Any given positive level of s and A has a steady-state equilibrium.

According to neoclassical economic theory, the savings rate, s, is determined by households through a cost–benefit analysis of the utility of consuming today versus consuming at a future time. Thus, s is the fraction of output saved and $1-s$ is the fraction of output consumed. The determination of s is complex; Robert Barro and Xavier Sala-i-Martin claim it is "a complicated function for which there are typically no closed-form solutions."[6] Under the commune, cadres determined the level of extraction, not the households themselves. Thus, in the current application, I assume s is given exogenously, such that $0 < s < 1$.

At any point in time, a constant fraction of capital stock is exhausted and becomes unproductive so that capital depreciates at rate δ. If s were zero, k would decline because of a combination of capital depreciation at rate, δ, and growth in the labor force, L, at rate n. Because a constant proportion of output (i.e., the portion saved) is invested, we can represent the change in capital per worker as:

$$\Delta k = sy - (n + \delta)k \tag{4.3}$$

Substituting equation (4.2) into equation (4.3) yields:

$$\Delta k = sAf(k) - (n + \delta)k \tag{4.4}$$

Equation (4.4) constitutes the Solow–Swan model's fundamental nonlinear differential equation determining the change in capital per worker. At any time, the change in capital per worker is equal to gross investment minus the effective depreciation rate.

Figure 4.1 illustrates the workings of equation (4.4). The upper curve is the production function, $Af(k)$, which determines total output. The curve for gross investment, $sAf(k)$, reflects the share of total output that is saved, s, and invested as capital. This capital accumulation curve begins at the origin: if the capital stock is zero, then output is zero so that savings and investment are also zero. For any given level of k, gross output is given by $Af(k)$. Gross per capita investment is equal to the height of the $sAf(k)$ curve, and per capita consumption, represented by the dotted line, is equal to the vertical difference between the $Af(k)$ and $sAf(k)$ curves. Reflecting the model's assumption of diminishing marginal returns to capital, the $sAf(k)$ curve has a positive slope, but it flattens out as k increases. The right-hand term in equation (4.4) determines the effective rate of capital depreciation, $(n +\delta)k$, needed to maintain a constant capital stock per worker. It appears in figure 4.1 as a straight line from the origin with positive slope $n + \delta$. If the capital stock is zero, effective depreciation is zero. The constant slope reflects the constant rate of effective depreciation per unit of capital per worker.

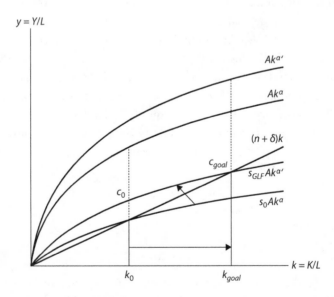

FIGURE 4.1. GLF Commune Goal, 1958–1961.

Figure 4.1 represents the stated objective of the GLF Commune (1958–1961): increase savings rates, capital formulation, and capital productivity to lift per capita consumption. The impact of these actions is indicated by an increase from α to α', which lifts the production curve, and by an increase in s_o to s_{GLF}, which rotates the savings function upward. Equilibrium k now increases from k_o to k_{goal}. GLF planners had hoped the capital built during the GLF would be of consistent quality with previous investments; hence, the depreciation line does not rotate. Planners had intended for the level of capital accumulation to increase from k_o to k_{goal} and for the level of consumption to rise from c_o to c_{goal}.

Figures 4.2–4.5 provide a stylized graphic representation of the five-stage transitional dynamics that I argue occurred throughout the commune era and decollectivization (1958–1983).

Tragically, the GLF Commune did not work as expected. Figure 4.2 captures the resulting famine. As planned, savings rates increased from s_o to s_{GLF}, while households saw their share of total collective income (i.e., consumption) fall 13 percent—from 63.7 percent in 1956 to 50.7 percent in 1959 (figure 4.8). However, the poor quality of capital constructed and the

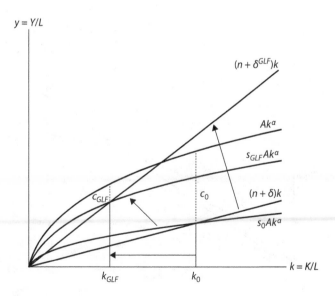

FIGURE 4.2. GLF Commune Reality, 1958–1961.

maltreatment of skilled workers during the GLF produced a sizeable counterclockwise rotation in the constant capital stock per worker line around the axis. This caused a collapse in the capital stock, represented by the decrease from k_o to k_{GLF}. The GLF famine, represented by a sizable reduction in per capita consumption from c_o to c_{GLF}, was caused by over extraction combined with poor quality investments that pushed consumption below minimum caloric levels. However, because a large portion of the 15–30 million people who perished during the GLF were either old or young—that is, not of childbearing age—population growth rate fell only briefly.[7]

During the Rightist Commune (1962–1964; captured in figure 4.3), China, led by Liu Shaoqi and Deng Xiaoping, pursued a strategy to increase consumption to alleviate the famine. To guarantee a consumption floor for households, the government introduced contract farming, household-administered private plots, and cottage industries and expanded free markets. By 1961, households had returned to consuming more than 60 percent of total collective income, and between 1962 and 1965, household consumption remained relatively high, averaging 57.3 percent (figure 4.8.) Lowering the GLF high savings rates shifted the saving function downward to its original position. The result of this strategy was an increase in per capita

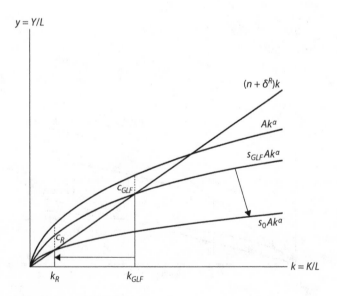

FIGURE 4.3. Rightist Commune, 1962–1964.

consumption (as indicated in figure 4.3) because c_R, the vertical distance between Ak^α and $s_0 Ak^\alpha$ evaluated at k_R, exceeds c_{GLF}, the vertical distance between Ak^α and $s_{GLF} Ak^\alpha$ evaluated at k_{GLF}. This increase in consumption was made possible by a reduction in capital formation, as indicated by the fall from k_{GLF} to k_R.

Although less capital was built during this period, what was built was of better quality and depreciated less rapidly than shoddy GLF capital. Meanwhile, after the famine subsided, population growth rates rebounded (chapter 3, figure 3.3). Considered together, these effects offset each other, such that the constant capital per worker line remained unchanged. As capital per worker and output per worker fell, a collateral effect was an increase in the marginal product of capital (given by the slope of the production function). That increase had important future consequences: it meant investment became more productive, in the sense that it had a higher yield.

During the Leftist Commune (1965–1969; depicted in figure 4.4), the Maoists regained control of rural policy and increased the savings rates (figure 4.8). This policy is represented as an increase in the rate of saving from s_0 to s_L, which shifted the investment curve upward. The results of this increased investment included an increased rate of capital accumulation,

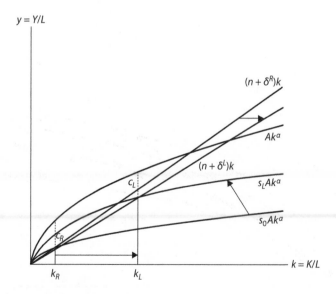

FIGURE 4.4. Leftist Commune, 1965–1969.

a slower rate of capital depreciation, and a rise in both steady-state capital per worker and output per worker. During this phase, the Cultural Revolution and the overhaul of the agricultural research and extension system (described in chapter 3) initially slowed new capital formulation; however, the farm implements and simple machines that were made during the Leftist Commune period were of better quality than those made during the Rightist Commune period. Meanwhile, the population growth rate remained high, thus offsetting much (but not all) of the effect of falling capital depreciation rates. As a result, throughout this period of rapid investment (indicated by the rise in capital stock from k_R to k_L), we observe a transitional period of continued low consumption, culminating in a slight reduction from c_R to c_L.

The Green Revolution Commune (1970–1979), which was initiated after policy reforms adopted at the 1970 Northern Agricultural Conference, is represented in figure 4.5. Household savings rates increased in the 1970s as represented by a return from s_L to s_G. By 1971, households' share of gross collective income had dipped to 55.9 percent and it continued to fall to a low of 50.7 percent in 1976—the same rate as in 1959, the height of the GLF (figure 4.8). The primary reason for the reduction in the members' share

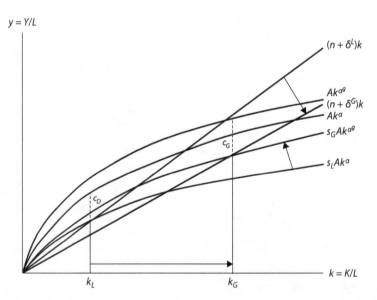

FIGURE 4.5. Green Revolution Commune, 1970–1979.

appears to be an increase in the percentage of collective income used for production costs (*shengchan feiyong*). Meanwhile, as shown in chapter 3, successful institutional changes in the workpoint remuneration system and the agricultural research and extension system contributed substantially to the expanded use of hybrid seed varieties, chemical fertilizers, mechanization, and irrigation. Figure 4.5 depicts how these institutional changes combined to increase the rate of technological innovation and improve capital productivity from a to a^g, which caused both the production function and aggregate saving function to rotate counterclockwise. With capital more productive, a given saving rate now generated more productive investments. The higher quality capital built during this period, together with the nationwide introduction of birth control, produced a clockwise rotation of the constant capital per worker line around the axis. Taken together, high savings rates, more productive capital, rapid technological progress, lower depreciation rates, and reduced population growth rates had the cumulative effect of increasing the steady-state equilibrium capital stock per worker from k_L to k_G, while consumption per worker rose only modestly, from c_L to c_G. Although the transition path during this period involves spells of reduced consumption, the result is a slightly higher consumption level because the capital stock was more productive and of superior quality. Under China's Green Revolution Commune, output per worker rose, enabling a simultaneous acceleration of capital formation along with a small increase in consumption per capita.

Decollectivization (figure 4.6), that is, the nationwide reintroduction of household-based agriculture, began in earnest with the power transition at the Fifth Plenum of the Eleventh Party Congress in February 1980 and ended in October 1983 with the "Circular on separating the local government from communes and establishing township governments" (see appendix C). During this period, savings rates fell back to approximately precommune levels, from s_G to s_o, thus causing the savings function, which drives capital accumulation, to shift downward. As communes were dissolved, although the depreciation and population growth rates remained constant, the pace of rural capital construction fell off considerably, which reduced the stock of per capita rural capital from k_G to k_D. This fall can also be observed in the amount of total investment in agriculture (chapter 3, figure 3.1), machine cultivated land (figure 3.15), irrigation systems (figure 3.14), technical and teacher training (figure 3.6), and pesticide production (figure 3.12).[8] If we compare figure 4.1 with figure 4.5, it appears that

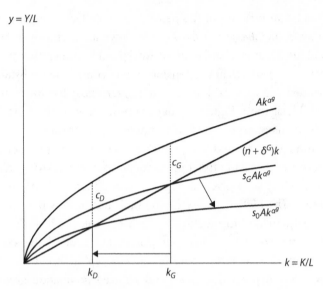

FIGURE 4.6. Decollectivization, 1980–1983.

between 1970 and 1979 Chinese policymakers achieved the goals promulgated during the GLF. They were able to induce higher savings rates and invest wisely in more and better agricultural capital and technologies that increased agricultural production.

Politically, the most important aspect of this period is the transition path of increased per capita consumption from c_G to c_D, which consolidated the reformist faction's political control by securing grassroots support for additional anti-Maoist reforms while also keeping as many farmers as possible in the countryside.[9] Between 1980 and 1983, as the workpoint system was gradually ended, household consumption increased as a percentage of collective income from 53.1 percent to 73.9 percent (see figure 4.8). This consumption increase was accompanied by a rise in the procurement price of grain purchased from now-independent household producers, and the widespread privatization of formerly collective lands and property, which often went to former commune and brigade cadres-turned-entrepreneurs. In economic terms, the early 1980s was a transitional period during which decollectivization allowed rural localities to consume the output of the existing capital stock without reinvesting.

To summarize, the transitional dynamics of growth during the commune were as follows: Initially, excessive extraction of rural household labor and savings was coupled with large-scale investments in poor quality capital and techniques, which caused the GLF catastrophe. Reforms taken in 1962 increased consumption rates, but at the expense of capital investment. After 1970, consumption was again constrained but, unlike during the GLF and the Leftist Commune period, the funds were put toward *productive* investments, while sideline private plots helped prevent the overextraction of household resources. Finally, during decollectivization, household consumption returned to pre-commune levels, a change illustrated in figure 4.6 by a return from s_G to s_o. That boosted per capita consumption from c_G to c_D while reducing capital investment from k_G to k_D.

In the next section, I examine how China—a poor county with a large and growing population—was able to increase savings rates to fund productive investments and innovations. But first, I will show how, under the same conditions, the modified classical economic growth model yields similar predictions to the neoclassical framework.

The Lewis Modified Classical Model[10]

The Lewis modified classical model assumes unlimited labor supplies and can explain the sustained output growth in commune-era China. "An unlimited supply of labour," writes Lewis, "exists in those countries where population is so large relative to capital and natural resources, that there are large sectors of the economy where the marginal productivity of labour is negligible, zero, or even negative." Lewis observes that the assumption of unlimited labor supplies best explains "the greater part of Asia [where] labour is unlimited in supply, and economic expansion certainly cannot be taken for granted." Under such conditions, "new industries can be created or old industries expanded without limit at the existing wage; or, to put it more exactly, shortage of labour is no limit to the creation of new sources of employment." This is because, despite surplus labor supplies in traditional rural economies like precommune China, "the family holding is so small that if some members of the family obtained other employment the remaining members could cultivate the holding just as well."[11]

According to the Lewis model, an unlimited pool of labor means that returns to capital would not diminish over time, as the Solow–Swan neoclassical model predicts would occur without technical innovation. Instead, in the classical model, returns to capital continue to grow unabated until surplus labor is used up. Lewis theorized how sustained high savings rates under conditions of unlimited labor supplies can kick-start a continuous cycle of capital accumulation:

> The key to this process is the use which is made of the capitalist surplus. In so far as this is reinvested in creating more capital, the capitalist sector expands, taking more people into capitalist employment out of the subsistence sector. The surplus is then larger still, capital formation is still greater, and so the process continues until the labour surplus disappears.[12]

This development process is illustrated in figure 4.7, which is reproduced from Lewis' original text. OS represents average subsistence earnings levels, and OW represents actual earnings levels after providing for additions to productive capital. The marginal productivity of labor is captured by the curves denoted NQ, with higher curves corresponding to production with a larger capital stock. The economic surplus available for investment is the area above the OW line and below the marginal productivity of labor schedule.

Because a fixed percentage of the economic surplus is reinvested, the quantity of capital increases at a constant rate, causing the marginal

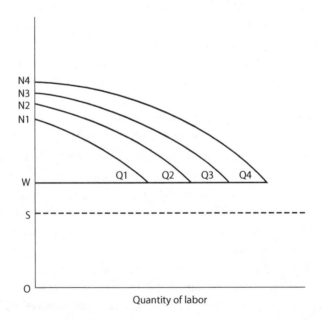

FIGURE 4.7. Lewis modified classical model.

productivity of labor schedule to shift right from N_1Q_1 to N_2Q_2. Both the surplus and the percentage of workers earning income at OW are now larger. Further investment pushes the marginal productivity of labor to N_3Q_3 and then to N_4Q_4 and beyond, until all surplus labor is exhausted. At this stage, known as the Lewis turning point, wages start to rise above OW because of the emergence of labor scarcity.[13] This simple diagrammatic framework reveals how, once started, China was able to maintain continuous and sizeable increases in agricultural output throughout the 1970s.

As with the Solow–Swan neoclassical model, the classical model considers that investments in both agriculture capital and technology are determined by savings. This savings requires refraining from consuming a portion of current output today and investing it in "capital goods which the introduction of new technology requires."[14] The big difference, however, is that the classical model assumes unlimited labor supplies at a constant real wage, which means capital per worker (k) can increase at a constant rate in perpetuity. This is because, for any quantity of K, a corresponding amount of L can be made available at the current subsistence wage rate. Income remains stable throughout the economic expansion and practically the whole profit generated by capital accumulation goes back to capital holders—or, in China's case, the commune. Labor welfare improves because more workers benefit from being employed at a wage above subsistence. Agricultural workers may also benefit from skills training they receive during the development process and from a higher caloric intake thanks to improved food quality. In this fashion, an economy with unlimited labor and a growing capital stock can experience unlimited capital widening, while aggregate output continues to grow. This contrasts with the Solow–Swan neoclassical growth model, in which growth raises the capital-to-labor ratio, thereby raising the marginal productivity of labor and compelling capital holders to pay a higher wage.

According to Lewis, capital holders consume a portion of their profits and use the rest to support further capital formulation to generate continued returns, which, in turn, increases their capacity to make future productive investments. This means that if an agricultural revolution led by capital expansion and technical innovations were to occur in times of sustained high savings and unlimited labor supplies—as occurred in 1970s China—practically the whole surplus would become available to capital holders (i.e., the commune) for subsequent rounds of productive investment.[15]

The classical framework takes capital accumulation and technical progress as part of a unified development process and does not distinguish between the distinctive effects of each. Lewis argues that capital and technological progress come together with new capital embodying the latest technology. Thus, Lewis directly incorporates technical innovation into his model and stresses its importance as a source of sustained returns to capital that is inseparable from capital itself: "If we assume technical progress in agriculture, no hoarding, and unlimited labour at a constant wage, the rate of profit on capital cannot fall. On the contrary it must increase, since all the benefit of technical progress in the capitalist sector accrues to the capitalists."[16]

Building on this, Nicholas Kaldor explains that technology is regularly applied in tandem with agricultural capital in ways that increase the productivity of both labor and land:

Since land is scarce, increases in production, using the same technology, are subject to diminishing returns to capital and labour, but with the passing of time, agricultural output per acre rises as a result of land-saving changes in technology (which does not exclude that many of the inventions or innovations are labour-saving as well as land-saving) and their adoption requires capital investment for their exploitation (a tractor, or a combine harvester, or even a new type of seed which promises higher yields but it more costly than previous types).[17]

The problem of increasing land scarcity worried David Ricardo, who observes that economic development inevitably increases the relative scarcity of land.[18] According to Kaldor, in a land-scarce country with unlimited labor, unless "offset by land-saving innovations," increasing capital investment in agriculture will cause marginal productivity of labor to decline.[19] Thus, assuming that most surplus labor is employed in agriculture, the objective of technological innovation is to increase output per unit land. Agricultural economist Bruce Stone operationalizes this concept for China, arguing that "yield growth of principal staple food crops" is among "the principal criteria for judging technical change at the initial stage of modern agricultural development in a large but land-scarce peasant economy."[20] Expanding on Lewis, innovations that increase output per unit land are the *only* type of technological progress necessary to explain "a constant rate of growth [when] labour exists in super-abundance," argues Kaldor.

The critical factor in continued economic growth is the persistence or continuance of *land-saving innovations*—man's ability to extract more things, and a greater variety of things, from nature. Thus, in the simple model just presented, land-saving technical progress in agriculture is the only kind of technical change assumed, and this is sufficient to keep the system growing at a constant rate of growth, at least as long as growth is not hampered by the scarcity of labour—so long as labour exists in super-abundance.[21]

In both the neoclassical and classical models discussed previously, increased savings rates are essential to support capital accumulation. The problem for countries that have scarce capital and land but an abundant and fast-growing labor supply living near subsistence levels is how to generate the savings rates necessary to take advantage of high returns to capital. If an economy has unlimited workers living at subsistence and very little capital—as China did when the communes were created—how can it extract the resources necessary to kick-start development? Thus, "the central problem in the theory of economic development," according to Lewis, is how an economy with an unlimited labor force living at or just above subsistence can cut consumption and save more. "People save more because they have more to save," he concludes. "We cannot explain any industrial revolution until we can explain why saving increased."[22]

INVESTMENT UNDER THE COMMUNE

Increased Savings Rates

The commune's coercive extraction of the savings of participating households funded the 1970s agricultural modernization scheme. It removed resources from total income ex ante—that is, before the remuneration of commune members. First costs—both managerial and production—were removed, next state taxes were removed, and then a portion was set aside for public services and good works. Only after the collective took its share was the remainder distributed to members based on the number of workpoints they earned that season. By taxing households before remuneration, this process disguised austerity; it reduced consumption and ensured the high savings rates necessary to finance agricultural modernization.

During team meetings, commune members were informed of relevant agricultural modernization plans—such as mechanization and infrastructural, educational, and technological improvements—and were obliged to "vote" for them. The only agricultural investments controlled by households were those on their small sideline private plots, which accounted for 5–7 percent of total agricultural lands. These household-administered private plots, which were first introduced after the GLF and reaffirmed in 1970, guaranteed a consumption floor for households by preventing the overextraction that had pushed them below subsistence levels during the GLF. Placed in terms of the neoclassical model, during the GLF (figure 4.2), overzealous policymakers extracted too much and pushed consumption below minimum caloric levels, thus causing millions to starve. By guaranteeing household control over small private plots, officials helped reassure households that overextraction would not happen again.

Over the course of three years in the mid- to late 1950s, farmers saw their share of total collective income (i.e., consumption) fall 13 percent— from 63.7 percent in 1956 to 50.7 percent in 1959.[23] By 1961, households had returned to consuming more than 60 percent of total income, and between 1962 and 1965, household consumption remained relatively high, averaging 57.3 percent. Data are unavailable for the 1966–1969 period, but by 1971, the members' share of gross income had dipped to 55.9 percent. This share continued to fall to a low of 50.7 percent in 1976, which was the same rate as in 1959 at the height of the GLF. Consumption remained low at 51.4 percent in 1977, but beginning that year (the year after Mao's death) the percentage of income allocated to commune members rose quickly, until it peaked at 73.9 percent in 1983, the commune's last year (figure 4.8).[24]

The primary reason for the reduction in the members' share between 1961 and 1977 was the increase in production costs (*shengchan feiyong*). For a decade, between 1956 and 1965, production costs remained constant at about 25–26 percent of total income. Statistics are unavailable for 1966–1969, but they were 27.9 percent in 1970, before jumping from 27.3 percent to 30.1 percent between 1971 and 1972. Production costs continued to rise, peaking in 1978 at 32.3 percent, before falling precipitously to a nadir of 22.9 percent in 1983.[25]

Decollectivization, begun in earnest in 1980, marked a return not only to traditional patterns of organization (i.e., village, township, county) but also to traditional rates of rural undersaving and high consumption.[26] Between

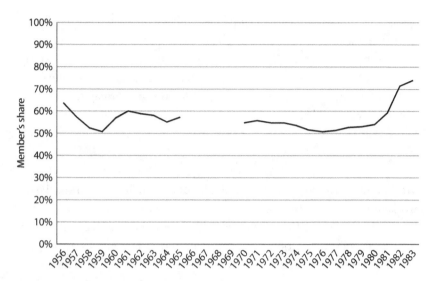

FIGURE 4.8. Commune collective income distribution.
Source: Agricultural Economic Statistics 1949-1983 [Nongye jingji ziliao, 1949-1983] (Beijing: Ministry of Agriculture Planning Bureau), 515.

1979 and 1983, the percentage of household consumption of total collective income rose 20.8 percent—from 53.1 percent to 73.9 percent (figure 4.8). As early as January 1978, in response to "low standards of living," farmers were again favoring "immediate consumption as against collective savings to be devoted to agricultural innovations," observes agricultural economist Lau Siukai.

One of the most important reasons for the resistance to innovations encountered in the rural areas in China is the preference of many peasants for immediate consumption as against collective savings to be devoted to agricultural innovations in the future and this phenomenon can be readily evidenced in the controversy over agricultural mechanization within the communes. Given the low standard of living of the peasants at the present moment, it is understandable that they would opt for a higher consumption/saving ratio.[27]

The excessive extraction of rural household labor and savings coupled with large-scale investments in poor-quality capital and techniques caused the GLF catastrophe. Consumption was again constrained in the

1970s, but unlike during the GLF, the funds were put toward *productive* investments, and sideline private plots helped prevent the overextraction of household resources. During decollectivization, household consumption increased as a percentage of total income. This change is illustrated in figure 4.6 by a return from s_G to s_o, which boosts per capita consumption from c_G to c_D.[28]

THE WORKPOINT SYSTEM

Workpoints ensured that the rural economy remained autarkic. People worked locally, received and redeemed points locally, and consumed locally. In the 1970s, the workpoint remuneration system served as both a cure for collective action problems common to communes everywhere and as a scheme for distracting households' attention away from the extraction of their savings. The former function, which is discussed in chapter 5, is among the incentive-generating mechanisms adopted to counter the impulse of members to shirk collective labor or slack off. The latter function, which is explained just below, was essential to extracting household savings to fund agricultural investment.

The value of the workpoint was a function of income *after* the commune extracted all costs, taxes, fees, and community funds. Regardless of how many workpoints were awarded to members or which method was used to disburse points, about half of gross collective income was extracted before members were allowed to squabble over the remainder (figure 4.8). Workpoints were important to members because what they could control of their household incomes depended on their point allotment relative to other members. Collective funds, however, remained unaffected by the number of workpoints or their relative allocation among members.

Introduced in 1965, the Dazhai remuneration system, which factored collective commitment and enthusiasm into workpoint calculations, was the Maoist ideal. After 1970, however, implementing the system was accepted as an evolutionary process and could vary considerably among communes and their subunits. Material incentives and performance-based compensation could determine the size of each member's slice of the collective pie, as Leslie Kuo observed in 1976: "Material incentive schemes that had been branded a 'capitalist trend' during the Cultural Revolution were officially vindicated and recommended as a means to boasting peasants' initiative and production in rural areas. Much was said about concern for people's livelihood."[29]

With the initial introduction of the Dazhai model in 1965, task rate remuneration, which awarded workpoints based on a specific assignment (e.g., plowing a field or moving a pile of earth), had been repudiated, but this remuneration was reintroduced in 1970 and 1971. Still, some teams were "reluctant to go out on a limb [for] fear of plunging into a danger-ous political blunder," Jonathan Unger explains. To push risk-adverse cadres to return to task rates, in 1973, the Guangdong provincial authori-ties announced the slogan "Repudiate Liu Shaoqi's task rates; permit Mao Zedong's task rates."[30]

Commune farmwork, unlike factory work, included dozens of differ-ent tasks during different seasons that varied substantially in complexity. The 1970s workpoint system encouraged communes to choose the desired mixture of task, time, and piece rates as well as overtime rates and count-less other impromptu compensatory arrangements that produced the most output under local conditions.[31] A piece rate awarded workpoints based on the amount completed, such as seed planted, corn husked, or baskets made; a time rate awarded workpoints for the amount of time spent on a specific job, like tending cattle or herding sheep; and a task rate awarded workpoints based on a particular job, such as plowing a field or transport-ing materials.[32]

Workpoints also could be awarded on an ad hoc basis, using an individ-ual labor contract (*lianchan daolao*) or through a specialized task agreement (*zhuanye chengbao*).[33] Any work or training that might increase agricul-tural productivity could be eligible for workpoint compensation (e.g., road or canal construction, attending tractor repair or driving lessons, testing seed varieties, or serving as a schoolteacher for a neighboring brigade or commune).[34] The most difficult jobs received the most points, making it possible for stronger or ambitious members to earn more income. Occa-sionally, competition among members for assignments that allotted more workpoints or were considered relatively easier became heated.[35] After the work was finished, recorders would review and award workpoints based on the applicable remuneration rate.[36]

Methods for awarding workpoints and the criteria used varied among different locations and could change over time.[37] Local cadres continued to tinker with their workpoint systems throughout the 1970s, and most adopted hybrid remuneration systems intended to maximize agricultural productivity. Gordon Bennett has observed that after 1970 many teams in Huadong Commune abandoned the original Dazhai remuneration system, and Unger has noted that by 1973 Chen Village in Guangdong had also returned to task rates.[38] Steven Butler reports that Dahe Commune in Hebei used the Dazhai system until 1979.[39] Li Huaiyin explains that "many production teams in Henan" adopted a variable time rate system called *lunsheng*.[40]

Peggy Printz and Paul Steinle's 1973 account describes how workpoint remuneration took place in Guang Li Commune's Sui Kang Brigade in Guangdong. First, agricultural workers were ranked in three grades: A for the best workers, B for slower workers, and C for older workers. Those in the same category made the same amount for an average day's work in the fields. During the busy season, workers assigned to the same level would earn varying amounts of workpoints depending on how much labor they performed and what they did. These grades and specific jobs were assigned four times a year at "self-education sessions." Members also gathered twice a year at lengthy mass meetings to assess each job's workpoint value. According to Printz and Steinle, who attended one such session: "It was a painstaking process. The leaders would read aloud the name and work grade evaluation of each worker, and a lengthy discussion would follow."[41] In Nan Huang Commune in Weihai, Shandong, members depicted themselves as drowning in "ocean meetings" (*huihai*) that were as numerous as they were tedious.[42]

To ensure active participation, workpoints were awarded on a daily basis, thus requiring an endless and "bewilderingly complex array of accounts," according to Bennett.[43] The team accountant posted each member's workpoints outside the team office for all to see. Li describes the close attention team members paid to this bulletin:

All team members checked the bulletin frequently. Some women checked it almost every day to make sure that their hard-earned points were credited. Barely literate, they were nevertheless able to identify their name on the form or at least remember the line where their names were located. They also had no problem reading Arabic numerals and therefore could check their workpoints for any date. Once a team member found that his or her work was not credited, the person would immediately complain to the accountant.[44]

Although tedious, detailed public accounts on workpoint allocations did provide a check on team leaders who may have wanted to favor their relatives and friends, while assigning tough or dirty jobs to those they disliked. After conducting extensive survey research in Henan, Li found that such preferentialism was rare because the aggrieved team members "would lose their interest in working hard and with care, and would even rebel."[45] He identified three checks that deterred team leaders from playing favorites: long-term reputational costs among other team members, the recurrent political campaigns against grassroots cadre corruption, and remuneration transparency under the workpoint system.[46]

The meetings and accounting of the 1970s workpoint remuneration system constituted a "kabuki theater" that distracted the attention of commune members from the extraction of their savings. Job allocations, subjective work evaluations, and the final exchange of points for cash or grain payments required countless hours of long, dull, numerous, and mandatory team meetings. These meetings diverted members' attention away from total team income relative to the members' collective share and directed it toward the size of their portion relative to other members—that is, the relative difficulty of their job and how many workpoints they received compared with other team members. Team accountants were agnostic about the total number of workpoints awarded or who received them. The important question was which rate system—time, task, or piece—best incentivized workers, a decision generally taken based on the type of work being performed. But no matter how many total points were awarded or which remuneration method was used, roughly half of total income (50–55 percent during the 1970s) had already been removed from the collective pot before their value in cash or kind was calculated (see figure 4.8).

REDISTRIBUTIVE POLICIES

Policies ostensibly established to promote more equal resource distribution gave commune cadres an additional smorgasbord of mechanisms to ensure that every possible *fen* of household savings was extracted for agricultural modernization. Although there were countless local schemes, two that appear to have been particularly common were the requisition of household or team resources by higher units and arbitrary income limits. Everyone had to work, but authorities could require wealthier households to contribute funds based on the principle of "mutual benefit and equivalent exchange" (*ziyuan huli, dengjia jiaohuan*), which required large-scale capital construction projects be completed based on "voluntary participation." In practice, however, each commune's functional autonomy and official mandate to build productive capital increased cadres' temptation to violate the "equal exchange" principle and extract more household resources in the name of "mutual benefit."[47]

Arbitrary income limits lowered disparities among households by capping the incomes of relatively better-off families and investing the excess resources in collectively owned capital. Peter Nolan and Gordon White explain how the requisitioning of wealthier household resources in the name of redistribution—a process known as "equalization and transfer" (*yiping erdiao*)—occurred in Laixi, Shandong: "Alarmed by a pattern of uneven per-capita income distribution ranging from 150 yuan in the rich brigades to 60 yuan in the poor. [Laixi cadres] therefore set an upper limit of 150 yuan and ordered that the residuum be channeled into public accumulation."[48]

Some commune leaders compelled wealthier brigades to provide interest-free loans to impoverished brigades and repaid these loans using profits from the commune tractor station.[49] Nolan and White explain how excess income was skimmed off and reinvested: "The residual income of the rich brigades was fed into their public accumulation funds. If these funds were well invested and managed, they would in fact lay the basis for even higher future incomes."[50] After decollectivization, by contrast, the commune and its subunits disappeared, and households kept all their income, thus increasing inequality and total consumption, but reducing the funds available for investment.

RURAL CREDIT COOPERATIVES

The RCC, according to Barry Naughton, was one of the commune's "surrounding institutions which both supported and taxed the rural economy."[51] It was a functionally independent subinstitution that accepted household deposits and lent them to the commune and its subunits for productive investments. After the growing season and any ad hoc income equalization schemes were applied, members exchanged their workpoints for cash or kind. To ensure the "safety" of their savings, households were strongly encouraged to deposit any excess funds with their local RCC, which aimed to absorb any resources that remained after the collective extracted its share and households consumed theirs.[52] RCCs also helped ensure that profits from sideline plots and cottage enterprises were reinvested rather than consumed or squirrelled away by risk-adverse households.

"By the late 1960s," Naughton observes, "the rural credit system had become fairly linked to rural savings." The RCCs were localized such that loans were increased apace with household deposits, which kept profits local and incentivized borrowers to repay their loans and encouraged households to increase deposits. RCC loans were essentially "good" if they could be paid back and "bad" if they could not be. This localization of lending is consistent with the implementation of the post-1970 agricultural modernization campaign, which decentralized agricultural investment decisions to better utilize local knowledge—in this case, credit worthiness.[53]

During the late 1960s and 1970s, RCCs "played a vigorous, continuous, and increasing role in the development of rural economy," according to Naughton, who estimated that they received about 3 percent of household income annual.[54] This estimate suggests that if households received about half of total collective income (50.7 percent in 1976, as seen in figure 4.8), then only about 1.5 percent of all collective income was deposited in RCCs that year; if a portion saved came from income earned on the household's private plot, then a lower percentage of collective income was deposited. The small size of RCC deposits, as compared with the overwhelming percentage of the total collective income captured by the workpoint system, underscores the effectiveness of the commune's ex ante extraction of household savings. It seems that the collective remuneration system simply did not leave much behind for households to deposit in their RCC accounts. As Harry Harding observes, the system stressed, "the mobilization of every possible available resource—be it human, monetary or material."[55]

The Three Small Freedoms

"The commune and later the production teams replaced the family as the basic unit of farming," Kate Xiao Zhou observes.[56] While this, strictly speaking, is true, it also overlooks the importance of household sideline farming, animal husbandry and cottage enterprises, and rural markets (i.e., the

Three Small Freedoms) under the commune system. Throughout the 1960s and 1970s, the household remained a legally recognized accounting unit charged with managing private sideline production. Household production and the rural markets it supplied were organized and regulated under commune auspices. They provided households with a baseline food security guarantee. By the mid-1970s, household production that took place on 5–7 percent of arable land accounted for about 10–25 percent of total household income.[57] Any attempt to remove household plots would have faced pushback from team leaders or risked widespread household noncompliance. Particularly in those provinces that suffered the most during the GLF famine, shared memories created a strong social and political inertia in favor of the Three Small Freedoms.[58]

Sideline plots were allotted by the team and were usually, but not always, adjacent to the family home. In 1961 and 1962, they were allocated on a per capita basis, but probably because of increasing land scarcity and a desire to avoid arguments, they generally remained unchanged despite births, marriages, or deaths. On the collective fields, the team's production plan determined which crops were grown and the methods used; on the private plots, the household decided. The primary collective crop was grain, and households planted mostly vegetables, although each family could grow anything, including grain, fruit, mulberry trees, and tobacco. Sometimes, to cut costs, several families planted or harvested their private plots together or pooled their resources to purchase inputs or rent farm equipment from the team or brigade to aid production or transport their produce to market.[59]

Given the commune's collectivist ethos, one might reasonably ask why authorities tolerated private household sideline plots, cottage businesses, and markets—even small ones under their supervision? Although some more radical Chinese leaders maintained the fig leaf of eventually eliminating all household private sideline plots and cottage industries, after the GLF, such policies were *never* officially sanctioned. One reason was to avoid waste, the cardinal sin amid conditions of land and capital scarcity and population growth. To ensure that all productive factors were used, cadres encouraged household to employ any remaining resources (e.g., older or disabled members, productive inputs, or sideline lands) that could not be collectivized or were left over from collective production. Households made better use of these small-scale or scrap resources than larger collective enterprises.

Unlike grain production, which was collectivized and modernized, small-scale vegetable cultivation and animal husbandry benefited from the daily hands-on oversight that households could provide.[60] The elderly often were excused from fieldwork, and they increased household income by making traditional handicrafts, tending household private plots and animals, watching their grandchildren, and selling their products, produce, or small livestock at regularly scheduled brigade or commune free markets (see figures 4.9–4.11). In this way, the household private sector could increase productivity without competing with the collective for scarce productive inputs. Because communes and brigade enterprises were primarily engaged in light industrial goods production, expanding cottage enterprises made basic consumer products cheaper and more widely available throughout the vast countryside. The household private sector also helped reduce local income inequality, because households with many dependents normally received less income from collective work.[61]

Team payments were often made in grain, making the households' sideline plots and cottage enterprises an important source of cash for home construction or health-care expenses. Sometimes the amount of cash a household earned from its private production would equal or exceed its total annual cash payments from the collective. Figures 4.9–4.11 depict scenes from a commune or brigade market in Guangdong taken by Printz and Steile in 1973. An indoor market in Hebei in 1971 was captured by Michelangelo Antonioni in his documentary *Cina*.[62] These images reveal that these were not black markets. They were public venues organized at regular intervals and supervised by commune and brigade cadres, who decided what could and could not be sold. During an interview, the former leader of Shangguan Xiantang Brigade, Yuhui County, Jiangxi, explained the rules regarding the sale of agricultural products in his commune:

Teams and households could sell excess household production at the free market for cash. But they could sell some things but not others. There were three types of agricultural products: grains, which could not be sold at all; poultry and fish, which could be sold if there was excess beyond the production quota; and fruits, vegetables and eggs, which could be sold freely.[63]

Throughout the 1970s, China permitted labor-intensive cottage industries, including tailoring, basket weaving, embroidering, knitting, shoe repair, fishing, hunting, bee raising, baby sitting, and firewood collecting. The most popular sideline enterprise was small-scale animal husbandry, which often included raising a pig or two, or a few chickens or ducks, for both meat and eggs. Often, the chickens of several households would live together in one coop, which if large enough could be operated by the team.[64] Throughout the commune era, eggs, in addition to being an essential source of protein, were among the most important exchange commodities for households.[65]

Raising a hog—the most common sideline animal—was a simple and economical source of household income and natural fertilizer. In 1969, through a combination of collective and private production, China produced 172.5 million swine, which by 1979 had reached 319.7 million (appendix A). In 1975, an official press article instructed cadres to support household pig raising, lest productive factors went untapped. This article pointed out that households had the labor, experience, scraps, and space necessary for pigs, making them well suited to the task.[66] Household-reared pigs lived in a small sty, often attached to the family home. Because of individual care, protection from the cold, and better food, they attained market weight more quickly than pigs raised by collective units.[67] Although their average weight was substantially below that of their U.S. counterparts, by 1979, up to 90 percent of red meat consumption per capita was pork.[68]

Families could purchase piglets, chicks, or ducklings using cash or on credit. Depending on the locality, these micro credit loans might come from the team or brigade. To support small-scale animal husbandry, brigades often supplied households with feed and breeding, veterinary, and immunization services.[69] After the animal was brought to market, the family would repay the team or brigade the purchase price plus any additional costs. In addition to its sale price, households gained income by selling pig manure or using it on their sideline plot.[70] In a 1975 article in *Science* magazine, George Sprague describes how household animal husbandry helped make use of scrap food materials:

In China, swine are raised primarily as a private household enterprise, although some are raised in large-production brigade units. In the private sector, swine are valued almost as much for their manure as for their meat. They are fed on waste materials not suitable for human food: vegetable refuse, ground and fermented rice hulls, corn husks, sweet potato and soybean vines, water hyacinths, and so forth.[71]

The economic role of the household and the proper size of the private sector remained contentious issues throughout the 1970s. Brigade and team leaders struggled to maintain the proper balance and relationship between the collective and household private sector. A mix of competition and cooperation was ever present between collective production and household private production. To limit the household private sector's ability to compete with the collective, teams restricted the scope of eligible products and prohibited them from hiring workers. In 1975, the Communist Party of China reiterated its longstanding policy protecting household private production and rural markets, which was first acknowledged in point five of the Urgent Directive Concerning Present Policy Problems in Rural People's Communes issued in November 1960, and later expanded on in detail in article forty of the *Sixty Articles* (see appendix C):

Under conditions which guarantee that the commune's collective economy progress and that it occupy a decisively superior position, *commune members may operate, in small amounts, private plots and household sidelines.* As for the household sidelines products, except for the first and second category goods, other *products may be taken to the free market and sold.* But Party policy also prescribes that as much as possible household sidelines be coordinated with the collective economy or the state economy; moreover, that *market management* be strengthened.[72] (Italics added for emphasis)

The average male commune member was officially supposed to work twenty-eight days per month on the collective fields and women were to work twenty-four days. Private sideline plots and enterprises were to be tended only on days off, in the morning before work, and in the evening after work or by those who did not participate in collective labor. By the mid-1970s, however, the expansion of agricultural modernization, rapid population growth, and falling arable land had left rural workers with less and less to do. Falling labor demand in the collective agricultural sector as a result of mechanization and overpopulation was partially alleviated by household cottage enterprises, which used any remaining productive factors to create various income-generating opportunities to supplement their collective income.

As rural sideline income rose, both the supply and the demand for consumer goods and services increased faster than communes could accommodate. In more lucrative sectors—brickmaking, for instance—tensions arose between the collective and private sectors. In the Shanghai suburbs, families built private kilns, and individual artisans hired out their brickmaking and carpentry skills.[73] In 1978, as household contracts were being introduced in some communes in Anhui and Sichuan, Butler observes that "burgeoning rural industries have overloaded rural transportation networks and peasants can earn ready cash by leaving the collective and hauling goods."[74] In some regions, new sayings emerged to capture the concept of increasing private household income relative to stagnant collective remuneration. They included the following: "If the horse doesn't eat night grass it won't get fat; if people don't obtain wealth from outside they won't prosper"; or "rely on the collective for grain; rely on yourself for spending money."[75]

FIGURE 4.9. A market-goer in Guang Li Commune makes a cash purchase, 1973.
Source: Photo provided by Peggy Printz.

FIGURE 4.10. A seller in Guang Li Commune market weighs out a sale, 1973. The bare feet and simple clothes of these rural residents suggest they had very little surplus income.
Source: Photo provided by Peggy Printz.

FIGURE 4.11. A shopper in Guang Li Commune market buys a goose, 1973.
Source: Photo provided by Peggy Printz.

CONCLUSION

This chapter explains how post-GLF China—an economy with an essentially unlimited, fast-growing population; scarce and rapidly depreciating capital stocks; and falling arable land—successfully funded a nationwide agricultural modernization program that substantially increased agricultural output. The key question for a developing country with unlimited or fast-growing labor supplies is how to increase savings rates to the level necessary to take advantage of high returns to capital. Thus, before launching a nationwide agricultural modernization scheme, China first needed a way to pay for it. Under the commune, rural wage rates were suppressed and coercive measures (e.g., restrictions on labor mobility) kept labor at essentially unlimited levels. Investments in agricultural modernization, made amid essentially unlimited labor supplies, produced commensurate increases in output without suffering diminishing marginal returns.

During the GLF, China undertook a disastrous overextraction of household savings and invested in poor-quality capital that depreciated quickly. After the famine, China's leaders prioritized increased household consumption, but by the end of the decade, the leftists had returned to power and reinstituted high savings rates. Throughout the 1970s, communes used the workpoint remuneration system to extract household savings and channel them into productive agricultural capital and innovations that increased output. Ad hoc measures ostensibly to increase income equality were also used to increase savings rates, and households were encouraged to deposit any unconsumed resources in their local RCC. The commune, in short, extracted an increasing percentage of household savings to finance agricultural capital and technology, thus kick-starting a continuous development process that produced rapid growth in food production.

The improved agricultural productivity experienced during the early 1980s was not primarily the result of "big-bang" market reforms; instead, it was largely the result of the previous decade of painful, forced household austerity that underwrote agricultural modernization. Productive investments also freed up workers to move, first into rural industry and later into coastal factories. Decollectivization not only increased household consumption but also destroyed the rural savings and investment systems nested within the commune that had improved agricultural productivity throughout the 1970s and that had laid the foundation for continued growth in the decades that followed.

Chapter Five

POLITICS

Maoism

INTRODUCTION

This chapter explains how Maoism, the commune's pervasive collectivist ideology, helped increase agricultural productivity. By incorporating elements of religious communes that increased the willingness of members to place collective over individual interests, the egalitarian politics of socialist communes, and a high-modernist doctrine that propagandized development, the Chinese commune created powerful bonds among team members that endured for more than two decades. This commune-based political architecture—which included Maoism's religiosity, the people's militia, self-reliance, social pressure, and collective remuneration—mitigated the collective action problems that threaten all communes. Until decollectivization destroyed these five aspects of the political architecture, they functioned together in ways that increased commune members' willingness to work hard and sacrifice for the greater good.

The next two sections introduce the different types of communes and the collective action problems they all face. After identifying the essential attributes of long-lived communes (i.e., ideology, collective isolation, and shared rituals), I explain how the Chinese commune included these and other elements (e.g., workpoints) that allowed it to extract more from its members than they otherwise would have tolerated.

COMMUNE TYPOLOGIES

Rural communes have existed in dozens of cultural and geographic contexts around the world and can be traced back to the Essenes community, in which Jesus supposedly lived. Lewis Mumford divides communes into two broad types: "utopias of escape" or "hippie communes," which offer refuge from the troubles of existing society (these institutions fall beyond the scope of this book); and "utopias of reconstruction," which are "purposeful, intentional communes oriented around a strong set of shared values and goals."[1] These latter institutions, which include the Chinese commune, seek to build a better world.[2] They are distinguished by the three overlapping collectivist ideologies they use to promote shared values: religion, socialism, and high modernism.

The religious view holds that life in modern society runs contrary to basic human values, preventing people from recognizing the value of life and being close to God. Working, sharing, and worshipping together in a religious commune promises members a more meaningful *spiritual* existence. The Shakers, for instance, attracted followers to their vision of "heaven on earth" and espoused an ideology that emphasized hard work under slogans like "Put your hands to work, and your heart to God," and "Work as if you had 1,000 years to live, and as if you were going to die tomorrow."[3] Members of religious communes are unified by collective work and by their group worship services (depicted in figure 5.1), which, like the Maoist rituals described later in this chapter, included ritualistic songs, dances, passwords, and gestures as well as the memorization and recitation of sacred texts.[4]

Socialist communes seek to create a *fairer* society. Their collectivist ideology is rooted in discontent over the distribution of power and resources in capitalist societies. According to the socialist view, because the "haves" dominate the "have-nots," most people are prevented from sharing fully in the output derived from their labor and from making important decisions that affect their lives. Ideological distinctions between religious and socialist communes are reflected in their organizational structures and remuneration systems: the former are generally more hierarchical, whereas the latter are more egalitarian.

Robert Owen's New Harmony commune, which began in Indiana in 1825, was based on the belief that an individual's character was shaped by

FIGURE 5.1. Shakers performs collective dances and songs as part of their worship.
Source: Shakers Near Lebanon State of N. York, Their Mode of Worship, 1830, the Library of Congress, California, https://www.loc.gov/item/00650589/.

his or her environment. By controlling members' environment, particularly their education, Owen believed his communes could create and replicate a new utopian social order. New Harmony introduced a remuneration system it called "Labor for Labor" that used time rates called "time money" to compensate workers with nontransferable "labor notes" at "time stores." The objective was to motivate workers while promoting a more egalitarian income distribution—the more one worked, the more commodities he or she received.[5] Unlike workpoint values in the Chinese commune, which were disclosed only at the end of the year, "labor notes" were exchangeable for set amounts of commodities (e.g., ten pounds of Indian corn).[6]

Under high-modernist communes, income extraction, prudent investments, economies of scale, and product specialization are intended to increase agricultural productivity. Because modern society is individualistic, it keeps people from forming meaningful social bonds and thus hinders workers from cooperating to achieve maximum productivity. A motivated workforce supported by a large, all-encompassing high-modernist commune, by contrast, inspires members through its commitment to improve their collective performance. To elevate members' performance, these institutions promulgated a state-sponsored collectivist ideology that propagandized development and offered material incentives for increased output.

One of the first visions of a high-modernist commune was elucidated in Plato's *Republic*. The commune was conceived as a disciplined, hierarchical, and authoritarian institution that recognized different levels of commitment and status.[7] Plato's *Republic* was administered by "guardians" who lived "in common barracks, with communal meals, a minimum of privacy, no private property, and a large number of regulations governing daily life."[8] The guardians, like cadres and militiamen in the Chinese commune, were society's best elements, who, like the institution itself, represented purity in an impure world.

[Members will] produce corn and wine and clothes and shoes and build houses for themselves. They will work in summer commonly stript and barefoot. They will feed on barley and wheat, baking the wheat and kneading the flour, making noble puddings and loaves. And they and their children will feast, drinking of the wine which they have made, wearing garlands on their heads, and having the praises of the gods on their lips, living in sweet society.[9]

More than two thousand years later, Plato's *Republic* and the Chinese commune still shared six essential elements: an emphasis on grain production, self-reliance, small-scale light industry and handicrafts, local capital construction, collectivist rituals, and collective poverty.

Traditionally, James C. Scott observes, the state's primary objective has been to produce "a concentrated population, within easy range, producing a steady supply of easily transportable, storable grain and tribute and providing a surplus of manpower for security, war, and public works."[10] This objective was achieved through the construction of irrigation and other public works, codifying religions, enforcing settlements, and empowering select local leaders. In the twentieth century, revolutionary leftist governments established high-modernist communes to achieve these age-old aims. Under these new regimes, however, communes became institutions for power consolidation, sovereignty building, economic development, and political indoctrination.[11]

Revolutionary states (among them Maoist China) tend to be ambitious, and thus they require extensive knowledge about local conditions to enact their plans. "Legibility," Scott observes, "is a condition of manipulation. The greater the manipulation envisaged, the greater the legibility required to effect it."[12] He continues, "[If the state] wants to extract as much grain and manpower as it can, short of provoking a famine or rebellion, if it wants to create a literate, skilled, and healthy population, if it wants everyone to speak the same language or worship the same god—then it will have to be far more knowledgeable and far more intrusive."[13]

In the 1920s and 1930s, social engineers and agricultural planners around the world believed that large-scale collective farming could cure hunger. Agricultural modernization and political enlightenment, many argued, could be achieved through vertical integration, economies of scale, and centralized authority. Writing in the *New Republic* in 1931, Michael Gold opined: "Collectivization is posed by history and economics. Politically, the small farmer or peasant is a drag on progress. Technically, he is as antiquated as the small machinists who once put automobiles together by hand in little wooden sheds."[14]

High-modernist communes expand government administration, monitoring, and taxation in rural areas, which enhance direct political control over localities.[15] They use coercive state power to prevent members from leaving; "rationalize" the layout of buildings; promote mechanization for major grain crops; and standardize farm machinery and tools, crop varieties, and chemical inputs.[16] This conception of rural communes as massive "food and fiber factories" led them to replicate the features of the modern factory. Unlike small agricultural producers, most high-modernist communes specialize in a particular crop, which makes it easier to assess productivity and expand state control.[17] Such communes, according to Scott, help the regime gain an "accurate or detailed map of society," without the help of the previous ruling class. The aim was "to create institutional forms and production units far better adapted to monitoring, managing, appropriating, and controlling from above."[18]

High-modernist communes upended the preexisting political hierarchy, thus rendering rural communities more amenable to party control.[19] According to Katherine Verdery, this was accomplished in Eastern Europe through "a protracted process of struggle, attempted imposition, and modification of rules."[20] These high-modernist communes were nationwide revolutionary political-economic-administrative systems designed to displace existing social structures. Masked in the rhetoric of development, collectivism, and improved social services, they affected a political and economic revolution and the coercive appropriation of household resources. As they did in China, high-modernist communes in Eastern Europe undid "old society," explains Verdery.

What emerged from this process everywhere was that the tie between peasant households and their land was broken; kinsmen and co-villagers had been used against one another, rupturing earlier solidarities; the influential members in each village had been humiliated and dispossessed; the former poor now held political advantage; and land was no longer the main store of wealth.[21]

COMMUNE COLLECTIVE ACTION PROBLEMS

Communes are created as alternatives to long-standing social norms and mores, and they are in open tension with "old" society. These alternative communities employ a pervasive collectivist ethos, an emphasis on group isolation, and a more egalitarian remuneration system to induce members to place the collective above their individual interests. "Communes are social orders designed to counteract the fragmentation of human life," Rosabeth Kanter explains. "They are vehicles for bringing fragments together into unity, for making connections between people and parts of life, for developing the 'whole person.'"[22]

All communes endeavor to cultivate a commonly held belief among members that through reciprocity they can build *togetherness*, or what Plato called wholeness or integration among members, and what social psychologists call "a sense of community." Communes promote a uniform set of goals and values to ensure that the fates of their members are closely bound. They add meaning to members' lives through the promulgation of shared beliefs and interactions that build a group identity.

Values typically associated with communes include *perfectibility*—the perfect community is possible here and now; *order*—meaning and purpose can be embodied in a plan for life; *camaraderie*—sharing and familiarity can create harmonious relationships; and the *fusion of mind and body*—integrating the physical and spiritual aspects of life can lead to self-fulfillment. Taken together, these elements connect people to each other and the institution, reinforce its centrality in their lives, and counteract the instinctive urge to place individual over collective interests.[23]

Commune primacy is instilled in all aspects of everyday life via regular group ceremonies, meetings, and work. According to Ran Abramitzky,

Communes [are] communities striving for internal equality while mitigating the inherent problems associated with a high degree of equality/redistribution, namely the tendency of more productive members to leave (brain drain), the tendency of less productive individuals to join (adverse selection), and the tendency to shirk or slack on collective duties (moral hazard).[24]

The problems of brain drain and adverse selection assume commune membership is voluntary and that resources are more equally shared among members. Moral hazard indicates insufficient worker oversight and a lack of member commitment. Throughout history, those communes that were able to successfully mitigate these three collective action problems were more productive and lasted longer.[25]

Communes face inherent tensions between voluntary participation and more equal sharing. More equal sharing threatens commune survival because people instinctively want to exert less energy and consume more. When members share more equally, less productive members tend to receive more collective assistance, that is, they "free ride" on the labor of others, making them the first to join and the last to leave (i.e., adverse selection).[26] Meanwhile, more productive members seek to conserve energy by working less hard (i.e., moral hazard), and they have an incentive to seek better compensation outside the commune (i.e., brain drain).[27] These problems are aggravated when an observable gap emerges between economic conditions inside the commune and those outside it. When membership is voluntary, inside-outside disparities are readily observable; thus, less productive members are incentivized to join the commune, whereas the most productive workers are lured away by higher wages. Stripped of its top contributors and inundated with weaker members, commune productivity and social cohesion are inevitably degraded, resulting in the institution's ultimate disintegration.

When participation is compulsory, however, as it was under the Chinese commune, the party-state can use residency requirements, local remuneration, and other policies to mitigate, although never entirely eliminate, brain drain and adverse selection. Yet the aforementioned moral hazard problem remains, and it is exacerbated if excessive income equalization causes members to perceive a weak link between their relative labor contribution and remuneration. The problem worsens if those who shirk their collective responsibilities or slack off on the job continue to disproportionately receive collective benefits.[28] If commune leaders fail to redress shirking and slacking, this behavior can spread rapidly among members and threaten the institution's economic and political viability.

ATTRIBUTES OF COMMUNE RESILIENCE

Ideology

Commune resilience is predicated on the ability to redress the three aforementioned collective action problems: brain drain, adverse selection, and moral hazard. "One characteristic of short-lived communes is that members did not share ideological training," Abramitsky observes.[29] The collectivist ethos promulgated in all communes—although utopian at first blush—is essential to mitigate the collective action problems that undermine their sustainability. Each commune's longevity is predicated on the effectiveness of its collectivist ideology, as Abramitsky explains:

A member with a high level of ideology is inherently less likely to leave or shirk than is a member with a low level of ideology, thus the presence of ideologically motivated members is important for the stability of communes. When ideology is high for all members, the commune can maintain a high degree of equality while avoiding brain drain and moral hazard.[30]

Collective ideology tends to be more powerful in religious communes because it is difficult to live by a strict religious code for an extended period of time.[31] Because religious beliefs are harder to fake, the group cohesion of spiritual communes is generally higher, and as a result of this cohesion, brain drain and moral hazard are more readily alleviated. To prove their loyalty, new candidates for the Ephrata Cloister, for instance, had to spend a year immersed in spiritual and physical training.[32] Group cohesion and commitment to the collective are catalyzed by constant references to an omnipresent God or gods and often sermonized by an all-powerful cleric.[33]

Like religious communes, the more long-lived socialist communes placed an emphasis on ensuring that all members shared the same ideology.

To ensure devotion, new members often underwent tests before acceptance. At New Harmony, Owen built an educational system to indoctrinate children and adults into his philosophies. Yet, as Katherine Hogan explains, without religion, New Harmony's socialist ideology proved insufficient to bond members to the institution and to each other:

But although Owen provided New Harmony with everything he could imagine that it would need to succeed, it was missing the essential component that made other communities, like the Shakers, cohesive. Because Owen did not believe in God, their [sic] was no central covenant that committed the residents of New Harmony to their enterprise. Although they were united by their communal labor, and to the idea of utopian life, the very rational concepts upon which Owen had based the community were antithetical to communal life. Because they lacked the strong central belief which served to unite other utopian groups, the members of the community were lacking the commitment to carry out the mission that Owen envisioned.[34]

The relative durability of religious communes also can be attributed to their ideology, which, unlike socialist ideology, is not based on equal sharing and thus creates less remuneration-related tensions among members. The more egalitarian the commune's remuneration system, the stronger the incentive to free ride, and hence, the more pervasive the collectivist ideology required to keep it together.

Many religious communes were hierarchical and had strict gender roles, which increased their longevity, as rising inequality does not challenge collectivist ideology, and in some cases, may actually enhance it. Because members are expected to progress gradually into greater spiritual awareness, equality is neither required nor expected. Newcomers to the Shakers, for instance, first joined a neophyte order called the "gathering family," in which they retained their property and family relationships. Next came the "junior order," when they dedicated the use of their property, which would be returned if the member withdrew. In the highest order, the "church family," time, service, talent, and property were irrevocably passed to the collective.[35]

Collective Isolation and Shared Rituals

Group rituals, when performed repeatedly while in collective isolation, bring a sense of normalcy and belonging to members, which in turn increases their sense of well-being and the attractiveness of the commune. When members routinely practice religion together, it becomes a "club good" that increases the membership's value.[36] Shared values and beliefs are conveyed using *proprietary* group activities, rituals, and holy texts that provide instructions for making life's most mundane activities an expression of collective devotion and togetherness. Leaders use group prayers before work, meals, and leisure time to cultivate unity among members and to give meaning to their daily lives. Edward Andrews explains how this occurred in Shaker communities: "Union of the various groups was achieved by common customs and practices, a common code of manuscript statutes, worship in common on the Sabbath day, and a strongly centralized system of government."[37]

First-generation members are often the most committed to the commune; for them, it is a chosen alternative to an unsatisfactory way of life that they have known firsthand. They are likely to steadily intensify their beliefs and eventually become the core group of motivated members. Founders of kibbutzim, for instance, often shared ideological training in the Zionist movement before moving to Israel. The initial cohesion of many American religious communes was similarly forged in their persecution in Europe.[38]

Later generations tend to remain committed only if they are sufficiently isolated from outside temptations to allow constant social pressure and ideological training. They did not choose commune life, had no hand in creating the institution, and have no memory of the ills of "old" society. Thus, compared with founding members, their cost-benefit calculations tend to be more individualistic and their use of ideology is more instrumental. Many communes (e.g., Amana, Zoar, Icaria, Oneida, and some kibbutzim) collapsed because older members failed to sufficiently transmit their devotion and values to their children. In Oneida, as in many kibbutzim, the younger generation abandoned the commune. In Amana, the children broke rules set by elders, including playing sports and wearing the color red.[39]

Over time, the indoctrination of later generations becomes increasingly difficult, so to maintain togetherness, despite declining noninstrumental adherence to collective ideology, long-lived communes have emphasized group isolation.[40] Collective isolation becomes increasingly important for commune survival, yet during the nineteenth and twentieth centuries, rapid technological change—particularly the invention of the automobile and telephone—made it increasingly difficult to maintain this isolation.[41]

To maintain collective isolation and indoctrinate younger members, the Shakers created a "children's order," which placed youth under a caretaker, usually a deacon or trustee, who closely monitored their progress in the faith and limited outside influences.[42] The Hutterites, whose ideology also "finds its roots in the biblical teachings of Christ," developed an educational system to transmit their values and vocational skills to their children and allowed only a select few to pursue higher education outside the commune. Hutterite communities gradually increased their isolation and today remain reluctant to accept outsiders unless candidates demonstrate strong commitment to the collective. To remain economically viable, they have adopted modern agricultural capital and techniques.[43]

POLITICAL SOURCES OF COMMUNE PRODUCTIVITY

The Chinese commune combined the religiosity of spiritual communes (i.e., the Shakers); the politics of socialist communes (i.e., Robert Owen's New Harmony); and the nationwide scale, obsession with development, and remuneration methodologies of high-modernist communes (i.e., the Soviet *kommuna*). Five aspects contributed to its unique collectivist ethos: Maoism's religiosity, the people's militia, self-reliance, social pressure, and collective remuneration. Together, these five aspects constituted the institution's essential political backbone, which allowed it to maintain higher household savings rates than members would normally have accepted without becoming disenchanted and resorting to slacking or shirking. Members' shared sense of community enabled the institution to overcome the collective action problems inherent in all rural communes: brain drain, adverse selection, and moral hazard.

Maoism's Religiosity

The Chinese commune, among other things, was the church of Mao.[44] China's top leaders—Liu Shaoqi, Zhou Enlai, Chen Boda, Kang Sheng, Lin Biao, Hua Guofeng, Chen Yonggui, Jiang Qing, and many more—all promoted Maoism as the political ideology to bind commune members to the institution, the nation, and, ultimately, the party. Maoism delegitimized the traditional social structure and replaced it with an ethic of self-sacrifice and collective devotion to create what David Zweig called a "moral incentive economy to generate higher levels of political consciousness and a willingness to work for moral rather than material rewards."[45] As in religious communes, group worship became a collective good that made people feel closer to Mao, to each other, and to the institution—which, according to Zweig, "mobilized peasant labor and imposed high rates of forced savings."[46] Compulsory political rituals that depicted Mao as a savior and commune members as "rust-proof screws in the revolution" prioritized the collective over the individual, which, in turn, increased members' tolerance for income extraction and made shirking and slacking a form of political, as well as economic, misconduct.[47]

Maoist rituals and symbols became the emblems of a single moral community that united all members as "part of a common holy enterprise."[48] According to Madsen, these rituals made members "susceptible to the urgings of the work team," which compelled them to "work harder and faster on collective undertakings and devote less time to private affairs."[49] Those in charge of Maoist propaganda met almost every day with the leaders in charge of agricultural production to ensure that selfless adherence to Maoism improved worker performance. Collective unity around Maoism produced a "renunciation of self in favor of the collective" that inspired hundreds of millions of Chinese to work hard to improve agricultural output.[50]

"The Maoist model," Marc Blecher observes, "emphasized, probably more than its Soviet progenitor, the importance of ideological work in the development and maintenance of Party discipline and control."[51] This emphasis was given by creating a "strict political atmosphere," such that all members' activities were judged publically by official standards of thought and behavior as well as by pervasive social pressure, which was mobilized to support and prevent members from deviating from those official norms.[52] The goal was to make the nonconformist feel that the entire group was against him or her and to use the norms of mutual criticism to push others to do their fair share. To that end, as discussed in chapter 6, the "structural properties" of the commune were adjusted over time to improve "the ease of supervision within the organization."[53]

As noted earlier, rituals counteract adverse selection by demanding hard-to-fake commitment signals to the group.[54] Cadres, teachers, and militia preached Maoism as China's state religion and promulgated shared rituals intended to build a new type of community. To enhance the speed and effectiveness of indoctrination and enshrine political rituals as central activities within the organization, Maoism blended traditional cultural norms, like ancestor worship, patriotism, and community solidarity, with socialist values and Mao's personality cult. Even menial group activities were made to relate to national goals.[55] "When they participated in solemn rituals to study Mao's teaching," explains Madsen, commune members "were really focusing their attention on the person of Mao himself and on a few of Mao's more noble-minded teachings. [This] led to a heightened sense of unity and common purpose, at least for a time."[56]

By changing the way members interacted with each other and as a group, commune rituals supplanted traditional hierarchical social practices with more egalitarian Maoist practices. When existing traditions could not be co-opted to serve the party, the commune became the institutional venue through which traditional religious practices and beliefs were destroyed and replaced with new Maoist rituals and norms. In this way, the party created a spiritual vacuum in rural society and then used the commune to fill it with Maoism. Gradually, members' coerced compliance induced their willing participation. Ceremonies may have begun as mimicry, but over time, they took on deeply personal significance for many participants. As Wang Tuo observes: "The constant repetition invested the new rituals with weight and importance. From this point of view, the rituals do not require participants' emotional dedication, only their physical participation."[57]

Collective Mao worship and the recitation of the chairman's teachings were central to the commune's collectivist ideology. Shared social interactions created a tight-knit community, within which peer acceptance determined each member's self-worth.[58] The goal was to create a largely self-disciplined form of social control that reduced shirking while also simplifying worker supervision. Physical participation, including songs and dances, recitation of Mao's writings while placing them to one's chest, and oral incantations venerating Mao, put each member's relationship with the chairman and his collectivist ideology on public display.[59] Members regularly watched, judged, and joined performances that praised those who sacrificed their individual interests for the collective. Madsen compares these Mao Zedong Thought Training Sessions to "religious revival meetings" in the United States: "They aimed not to teach a rationally coherent system of abstract doctrines but to proclaim a few fundamental ideas, to endow them with compelling moral and emotional power, and to call for personal and communal conversion to a life structured around them."[60]

The Loyalty Campaign (*zhongzihua yundong*) launched in 1969, taught members "to worship and glorify Mao and promote his thought through daily life."[61] Chen Ruoxi explains how the campaign's rituals glorified the Great Helmsman:

[The] objective was to worship and glorify Mao and promote his thought through daily life. At the beginning and end of each work day, everyone shouted "Long live Chairman Mao," recited his teachings, sang songs of praise, and danced before his picture. Every school and factory had a Loyalty Room in which were displayed many types of handicrafts, all with one subject—Mao; and in every household the walls were covered with objects related to him.[62]

Teams and brigades transmitted Maoism using numerous official sources, including Mao's writings, propaganda art, performances, films, radio broadcasts, and news bulletins. Collectively, these materials constituted a Maoist canon, more akin to a national religion and hence more powerful than the collectivism practiced in the Soviet *kommuna* or socialist communes like New Harmony. Mao's god-like status was enshrined in the first verse of China's unofficial national anthem, *The East Is Red*:

> *The east is red and the sun emerges;*
> *From China Mao Zedong arises*
> *He creates fortune for the people,*
> *He is the savior of the people!*[63]

The religiosity of Maoism developed apace with the commune's emergence as China's foremost rural institution. China's 1954 constitution, which was generally tolerant of religion, was replaced in 1966 with a call to destroy the Four Olds—old thinking, old culture, old customs, and old habits (figure 5.2). Throughout China, items and customs associated with the feudal system were destroyed, including temples, icons, scripts, art, and ritual objects. "Maoists believed, as did the Calvinists before them, that great leaps of faith and continuous warfare against Satanic forces could bring about the ideal society," explains Zweig.[64]

Radios carried Maoism into every commune via speaker systems, and broadcasts were followed by written "news" reports that instructed readers on the proper response to what had aired. The newspaper *Hongweibing*

FIGURE 5.2. "Destroy the Old World; Forge a New World," 1967.
Source: Destroy the Old World; Forge a New World [dasui jiu shijie, chuangli xin shijie], 1967, Beijing, Creature and Creator, http://creatureandcreator.ca/wp-content/uploads/2014/10/destroy-the-old.jpg.

(*The Red Guard*), for instance, reported that after hearing the 1966 broadcast "Demolish the Old, and Create the New," teams in Gaixian, Liaoning, brought all religious items to the brigade headquarters. According to another report, one member who listened to the broadcast tore down her traditional deity and put up Mao's picture and said, "From now on, I will only believe in Chairman Mao!"[65] Setting aside the campaign's grotesque cultural devastation, the elimination of previously venerated religious objects successfully demonstrated the destruction of the old social order.

Images and statues of Buddha were replaced with posters, paintings, and busts of Mao, which adorned every rural home. For tens of millions of barely literate older Chinese in the 1960s and 1970s, Mao's image was the most visible and valuable aspect of the commune's collectivist ideology. Between 1966 and 1976, not including unofficial reproductions, 4.18 billion copies of Mao's image were printed. Rusticated youth and cadres were encouraged to bring their Mao posters and busts and promulgate Maoist rites in their new teams.[66]

Ubiquitous at official meetings and events, Mao's picture often appeared next to other top communist leaders, including Marx, Engels, Lenin, Stalin, and Mao (figure 5.3). This lineage-based depiction of Mao established the legacy and international acceptance of the leader and his collectivist ideology, thus conveying legitimacy and authority upon both.[67] Mao was also frequently depicted as a glowing sun in the sky. His image became the center of the people's adoration, conveying warmth and strength in ways reminiscent of some portrayals of Christ (figure 5.4).[68] On a lapel pin (figure 5.5a), Mao is depicted as the sun, overseeing high-modernist agricultural development, in the form of electrification, water control, and terraced fields. In another lapel pin (figure 5.5b), Mao is depicted along with a machine gear, stem of grain, and what looks like a bowl of food, an allusion to the productivity of the worker-peasant alliance. In figure 5.5c, another pin, the Chairman is pictured above a handheld tractor—the most common agricultural machine in Maoist China. Mao's iconic profile combined with images of agricultural modernization and food production were unambiguous messages that all commune cadres should, as is embossed on the back of figure 5.5b, "Grasp the revolution, promote productivity!" (*zhua geming cu shengchan*).

Mandatory, repetitive political ceremonies were another element of Maoist indoctrination that enshrined and reified the commune's collectivist ethos. Among these rituals were the daily Mao reading (*tiantiandu*), painting

FIGURE 5.3. "Mao Zedong Thought is the peak of contemporary Marxism and Leninism," 1968.
Source: Wang Zhaoda, *Mao Zedong Thought Is the Peak of Contemporary Marxism and Leninism*, Zhejiang People's Fine Art Publishing House, Zhejiang.

FIGURE 5.4. "Achieve greater victories on the road to continuous revolution!" 1970.
Source: In Following the Revolutionary Road, Strive for an Even Greater Victory (Shanghai: Shanghai Publishing System Revolutionary Publishing Group, 1970).

A

B   C

FIGURE 5.5A. Lapel pin that depicts Mao overseeing agricultural modernization and hydropower genera-
tion. The back of the pin is embossed with the text "Long live Chairman Mao" (*Maozhuxi wansui*), undated.
Source: The author purchased this pin from an old farmer in a street-side market outside of Guangzhou on
December 7, 2016.
FIGURE 5.5B. Lapel pin that depicts Mao above a stalk of grain, a machine gear, and a bowl of food.
The back of the pin is embossed with the text "Grasp the revolution through productivity," 1968.
Source: The author purchased this pin at an antique store in Beijing on July 20, 2017.
FIGURE 5.5C. Lapel pin that depicts Mao above a handheld tractor. Beneath the tractor it reads: "The Fun-
damental Solution in Agriculture Lies is Mechanization," 1968.
Source: The author purchased this pin at an antique store in Beijing on July 20, 2017.

the sea red (*honghaiyang*), the transmission of Mao's orders (*zuigao zhishi buguoye*), and statue making (*lisuxiang*).[69] Sometimes "morning requests/ evening reports" (*zaoqingshi, wanhuibao*) were supplemented by a short recitation before each meal that wished the chairman a long life.[70] Other times, a Mao reading was given before or after fieldwork (figures 5.6 and 5.7).

The morning request/evening report was the most important Maoist ritual. Every morning, hundreds of millions of Chinese told Mao's image their work plan, and every evening, they gave a progress report. Jin Chunming, a professor at the Communist Party of China's Central Party School, called the practice "formal conduct for worshipping Mao Zedong" and provided this description:

Every morning, when everyone arrived at work, before they started to work or study, people were all to stand at attention in front of Mao Zedong's picture, looking up at the picture, with the quotation book [i.e. *The Little Red Book*] in front of their chests, shouting loudly at the leader, "Sincere wish for a long life to Chairman Mao! A long life! A long life!" While shouting people held their quotation book in front

FIGURE 5.6. At times the atmosphere of Maoist worship was akin to a religious revival.
Source: China's New Footprint: Impact of the 1970s [Xin zhongguo jiaoyin: Qishiniandai yingxiang], 1967, AFP/ Getty Images, http://chenmodemaque.blog.163.com/blog/static/16389212920129174522870/.

FIGURE 5.7. Farmers recite from Mao's *Little Red Book* before starting work, 1967.
Source: China's New Footprint: Impact of the 1970s [Xin zhongguo jiaoyin: Qishiniandai yingxiang], 1967, AFP/
Getty Images, http://chenmodemaque.blog.163.com/blog/static/16389212920129174522870/.

of them and waved it rhythmically. Then the leader would instruct the crowd to say
to Chairman Mao's picture, "Respected and beloved Chairman Mao, today we will
follow your teaching about such and such, we are determined to do such and such."
After this the crowd would be dismissed, and everyone would begin to work. This
was *zaoqingshi*. The *wanhuibao* was a similar routine to *zongqingshi*, with the exception that it took place after the day's work and before bedtime. People were to make a
report to Chairman Mao's image on their daily activity, such as quotations they had
studied, journals they had written, their experience and thoughts, and their plans for
the future, viewing themselves in light of Mao's "great teaching."[71]

Zhang Dong recalls how "morning requests" (*zaoqingshi*) were conducted
in the commune:

Every day before we go out to work a commune member will stand in front of the
Chairman Mao bust at the commune office, and request will all due seriousness:
"Beloved Chairman Mao, our mission today is to reap wheat, does your honor have
any instructions?" Then wait a bit. Seeing that Chairman Mao had no reply, he
would take his silence as acquiescence, and go on with his business.[72]

These rituals simulated direct communication between commune members and the Great Helmsman, akin to traditional ancestor worship. This building of Maoism on the ruins of tradition helped ease the population's transition from old to new. Rather than praying and confessing to their forefathers, people would pray and confess to Mao, whose watchful eye and wise teachings would help improve their work performance. Because everyone, from Politburo members to average team members, was accountable to Mao via their morning requests/evening reports, the ritual implied collective submission to the Great Helmsman.

As with the Shakers, choral songs and dances were important Maoist rituals. Collective singing, which often preceded Mao Thought Training Sessions, was a new ritual in rural China that created new modes of social interaction and instilled a sense of camaraderie. Singing together established a shared rhythm and enthusiasm among the group that helped open members to receive the new collectivist ideology.[73] Stories and slogans of self-sacrifice were put to song, to charge them with "emotional and moral value, making them fundamental symbols of the meaning of life," Madsen explains. "Then the stories, filled with a deeply felt sacred value, were used to criticize the normal 'selfish' patterns of life engaged in by most villagers and evoke resolutions of repentance."[74] The objective was to "imbue the parables containing Mao's moral teachings with an aura of holy goodness and make Mao himself a symbol of salvation."[75]

Many former commune members can still perform zealous tunes with Mao-glorifying lyrics, such as *Sailing the Seas Depends on the Helmsman* and *The East Is Red*. So strong is the nostalgia for these songs that amid his attempt to expand his political power in 2011, former Chongqing party boss Bo Xilai began a "Red Songs Campaign."[76] One Maoist song, *Chairman Mao Is the Red Sun in Our Heart*, encourages members to confess and sing to Mao's image:[77]

> *Respectful Chairman Mao, red sun in our hearts;*
> *Respectful Chairman Mao, red sun in our hearts;*
> *We have so many things to confess to you, We have so many songs to sing to you.*
> *Millions of red hearts are facing Beijing; Millions of smiling faces are directed toward the red sun.*
> *We sincerely wish you a long life, a long life, a long long life.[78]*

Maoist loyalty dances (*zongziwu*) sometimes accompanied these songs. *Zongziwu* were group performances that portrayed the relationship between the people, "us," and Mao, "our god." These dances were simple, had similar movements, demanded no special costumes, and required only minimum skill or training. For instance, every time participants sang Mao's name, they gestured their hands from in front of their chest toward their upper right or left side. Whenever the song mentioned "us," dancers gestured toward their chest with both hands (figure 5.8).[79]

The citation of Maoist quotations and texts was another essential component of the collectivist ideology of Chinese communes. The foremost Maoist scripture, *Quotations from Chairman Mao* (*Maozhuxi Yulu*), colloquially known as the "red treasure book" (*hong baoshu*) or known in English as the *Little Red Book*, was officially printed more than a billion times between 1966 and 1971—second only to the Bible.[80] China began publishing the book in May 1965, and by the second half of 1966, hundreds

FIGURE 5.8. Performers sing songs glorifying Mao.
Source: China's New Footprint: Impact of the 1970s [Xin zhongguo jiaoyin: Qishiniandai yingxiang], 1967, AFP/ Getty Images, http://chenmodemaque.blog.163.com/blog/static/16389212920129174522870/.

of new printing houses had been built specifically to print the *Quotations from Chairman Mao* and the Ministry of Culture had begun nationwide distribution.[81]

During the Cultural Revolution, Maoist quotes replaced daily greetings, making them essential to maintain interpersonal interactions and facilitating their popularization. Maoist quotes (like the Essenes' oath of entry) were passphrases that indicated group membership and emphasized ideological correctness.[82] As Wang explains, this ritual expanded the sense of community under the faith and helped define the parameters of group membership.

Reciting Mao functioned both as a question and as proof. The required routine proposed every individual one met as a potential suspect. In uttering a quote from Mao, one was asking a question—was he or she truly a revolutionary?—and at the same time positioning oneself as an ideological police officer. In answering the accusation with Mao's words, one rebutted the charge of not being revolutionary while issuing a counter-charge. Mao's words were the charge, the trial, the acquittal, and the counter-charge. Performing [this recitation] authorized people's everyday activities as being properly framed by the revolution as encapsulated in Mao's quotations.[83]

Mao's quotations were even used in rural markets, according to Sun Yixian, who recalls that "customers had to recite quotes before buying things. One would say 'To rebel is justified!' and the other would reply 'Long Live the Cultural Revolution!' then they could talk business. I didn't know how to exchange quotes, so I didn't dare buy anything." Another memoir recalls: "You had to know the quotations for the salespeople's exam, if you fail[ed] they would not sell you anything."[84]

Beginning with the Socialist Education Campaign in 1965 and continuing unabated until Mao's death in 1976, the Chinese commune sought to counteract noninstrumental adherence to ideology, which, as noted earlier, is common among children born into communes. To this end, one well-known ritual was to "recall sufferings in the old society and rejoice in the new" (*yikusitian*; see figure 5.9).[85] During *yikusitian* meetings, often held in dark meeting halls that evoked the darkness of "old" society, old farmers would recount tales of tyranny before "liberation" under conditions that vested these tales with deep emotional significance. Those who had suffered would tell their stories and occasionally sobbed with emotion.

FIGURE 5.9. An old farmer explains the hardships of old society during an *yikusitian* meeting.
Source: China's New Footprint: Impact of the 1970s [Xin zhongguo jiaoyin: Qishiniandai yingxiang], 1967, AFP/
Getty Images, http://chenmodemaque.blog.163.com/blog/static/16389212920129174522870/.

The audience would punctuate the speaker's tales of bitterness with such slogans as "Down with old society!" "Down with the landlords!" and, of course, "Long Live Chairman Mao!" Afterward, participants of varying ages would form small discussion groups to recount past injustices and express their gratitude to Chairman Mao. After the meeting, a special meal was prepared using the bitter wild herbs that peasants had eaten in the old days, and older people sometimes wept while they ate.[86]

Tang Ying recalls her experiences as a child between 1969 and 1973, in Cheng Guan Commune, Yong Chun County, Fujian, where her mother, a cadre with the grain bureau, had been sent to help improve agricultural productivity:

All the team members and their children would gather together, seated on benches or squatting, for the annual communal meal to reminiscence "the bitterness of the past," by eating such things as boiled rice husks, sweet potato leaves, and vegetable stalks. My mother, who was a sent-down cadre from the grain bureau in Fuzhou city, told me how to behave: "Don't complain, but also don't smile or laugh. Just sit quietly and eat the bitter foods." This was important because my behavior at the *yikusitian* would be interpreted as an indicator of my mother's ideological correctness. If I acted improperly, she might face criticism.[87]

Not surprisingly, however, despite extensive interventions, the system could never engender absolute adherence from all members, and over time, Maoism's coercive power was gradually reduced in some localities.[88] One member recalls: "The morning request/evening report was statutory for the workers. However, whenever there was only one person on duty, he always 'forgot' to do it."[89] Another form of grassroots pushback was using the term "morning request/evening report" in everyday parlance to mean a henpecked husband, which sarcastically portrayed members as nagged by cadres to report to Mao.[90] Given China's vast size and closed system, however, it is unclear how many commune members had become lapsed Maoists by the time decollectivization began.

People's Militia

The people's militia linked Maoism with the prestigious People's Liberation Army (PLA).[91] The militia was created as a semiautonomous local military institution nested within the commune and its subunit, the brigade. In August 1958, amid the GLF, the PLA bombarded Quemoy Island, precipitating the Second Taiwan Strait crisis. "It was in the midst of these military operations and while the great drive to establish the communes was in full course, that the related campaign to make 'Everyone a Soldier' was begun," explains Ralph Powell. Beijing claimed that "aroused by U.S. provocations," the commune-based militia system was created and rapidly expanded thanks to the masses' determination to defend the homeland.[92]

Despite its purported tactical value to the military, Mao's reasons for establishing the militia were primarily political: to create an informational conduit accountable to him alone, through which Maoism was transmitted into the commune and local reports were transmitted back up to Mao via the military—rather than the party—bureaucracy. Richard Thornton suggests that the commune and militia proposals were so important to

Mao that in 1958 he traded his chairmanship of the state to ensure their adoption:

The issue of party control of the militia was discussed in the December 10, 1958 party resolution, the same meeting at which it was decided that Mao would not stand for reelection to the chairmanship of the state. The connection of these events suggests the possibility that Mao agreed to step down from the state post in return for acceptance of his commune and militia proposals. The militia was to be an independent military organization, the armed instrument of the self-supporting commune, which was directly responsible to the party center, that is, to Mao.[93]

The *Sixty Articles* affirmed the militia's role as an integral component and proponent of Mao's collectivist ideology under the commune. Each team had a militia platoon of twenty-five or so members, but the brigade battalion ran most of the militia activities.[94] First in 1964 and again in 1966, state media linked the Dazhai agricultural model to the militia-led "learn from the PLA" movement.[95] Mao argued that "the establishment of the militia divisions on a large scale is not purely a question of mobilization of manpower, collective action and fulfillment of production tasks. It is a question of having the masses militarize and collectivize their life."[96]

The Four-Good Campaign, which embodied Chinese patriotism, reinforced the PLA's support for Maoism.[97] Initiated as part of the PLA emulation campaign in 1969 and led by army veterans, the campaign focused on four areas: political thought (i.e., Mao Zedong Thought as explicated by Lin Biao), work style (i.e., placing collective before individual interests), production, and military training. Leaders designated select communes as models for the army-led campaign to heighten revolutionary consciousness. In late 1969, the head of the armed forces department in Wugong Commune, Raoyang County, Hebei, instructed all commune and brigade militias to establish a Four-Good platoon. Once formed, Wugong's Four-Good platoons held Mao quote memorization contests, and the winners joined the Mao propaganda team and toured the commune, and some were offered party membership.[98]

Like Plato's guardians, the militiamen's ideological commitment placed them in the distinguished position of enforcing both the commune's collectivist ethos and its external security. A propaganda poster from 1967 (see figure 5.10) portrayed the militia as both the protector of Maoist ideology

毛主席教导我们：我们不但要有强大的正规军，我们还要大办民兵师。

FIGURE 5.10. "Chairman Mao Teaches Us: We Should Not Only Keep a Strong Formal Army, But Also Organize Contingents of People's Militia on a Big Scale," 1967.
Source: Militia in the Red Era [Hongse shidai de minbing] (Shanghai: Shanghai People's Fine Arts Publishing House, 1967).

and an essential part of China's national security. An article published in the *Peking Review* the same year explained that the "most important and fundamental" objective was to spread Maoism through "studying and applying Chairman Mao's works."

[The Four-Good Campaign] is a fundamental measure for strengthening the build-up of the [four-good] companies, a revolutionary, socialist emulation campaign of immense vitality among collectives. We must make the companies fine schools of Mao Zedong thought through the sustained development and improvement of this "four-good" campaign. We must attain these four things: good political and ideological work; a good "three-eight" working style; good military training; and a good arrangement of everyday life. *The most important and fundamental thing of all, however, is to strive for good political and ideological work, and especially doing a good job of studying and applying Chairman Mao's works creatively.* Only when this is accomplished, resulting in the revolutioniza-tion of people's minds, can other fields of work be really done well.[99] (Italics added for emphasis)

Militia units conducted political propaganda and study sessions using the *Little Red Book* and other approved texts.[100] The PLA published and distrib-uted manuals and propaganda to militia units to help explain the main les-sons of these works and suggested stories to illustrate them.[101] Commune and brigade militiamen began such meetings by standing at attention with Mao's *Little Red Book* clutched in their right hand. They conducted their morning requests and sometimes performed a skit. Then, waving the book, they would shout, "Long Live Chairman Mao!"[102] In the fields, militiamen would call for everyone to work hard in accordance with Mao's teachings. They would praise those who had worked hard and speak out against those who "preferred the light and shirked the heavy."[103]

Self-Reliance

Under the mantra of self-reliance, the commune enforced collective iso-lation through local production and political conformity within its geo-graphic jurisdiction. By unifying all economic, political, and administrative control under one institution, the party enhanced its leadership, reduced bureaucracy, and ensured each unit's isolation. Nothing was beyond the leaders' purview, and as a result, they could operate with broad local knowl-edge and minimal outside interference. Under self-reliance, collective iso-lation and social pressure were used in tandem to ensure indoctrination and make people accept low living standards.

The household registration (*hukou*) system restricted labor mobility and limited public goods to members. When isolation was hermetic—as it was for many households—better outside conditions could not tempt more productive members and brain drain was largely mitigated. Strict controls on labor mobility also alleviated adverse selection by ensuring that weaker workers could not move to more profitable teams or cities in search of a better life. By keeping workers in their teams, the *hukou* system ensured that communes remained self-reliant and maintained labor at essentially unlimited levels, which (for reasons explained in chapter 4) kept labor costs down and increased productivity. The system also improved legibility (as defined by Scott), which facilitated resource extraction and enabled economic planning on a massive scale.

Propaganda about conditions outside the commune was used to reduce members' temptation to leave. In Cheng Guan Commune, in Fujian just across the strait from Taiwan, members were constantly told about the "hardships" faced by their Taiwanese compatriots and reminded that they should cherish their comparative well-being and security. This theme, which appears to have been common throughout rural China in the 1960s and 1970s, was captured in the slogan about the need to liberate Taiwan people from "deep waters and infernos" (*shuishen, huore*). By repeatedly telling commune members how bad outside conditions were, cadres sought to counter attempts by the Taipei regime to penetrate the collective isolation of communes via radio broadcasts, propaganda leaflets, and boxes of treats with notes tied to balloons that were floated over the strait. Conversely, during decollectivization, the reformers pursued the opposite policy—they constantly reminded the Chinese of their country's backwardness relative to Japan and Western countries, which they blamed on underdevelopment and poor productivity during the 1970s.[104]

All but the most remote communes could not isolate *all* members, however. Households on the commune's geographic periphery, Sent-Down cadres and youth, members of the agricultural research and extension system, brigade-level teachers, and tractor and truck drivers were among the individuals who had varying amounts of knowledge about conditions beyond their teams. Commune and brigade sales and procurement officers who bought and sold goods with other communes and state suppliers were also exposed to outside conditions. Especially after 1970, the expansion of household sideline and handicraft production meant that rural markets became important, albeit limited, venues where members could interact with people beyond their team. In the 1970s, rural markets were not spontaneous or secretive gatherings. Instead, they were organized at regular intervals by the brigade or commune, which limited their size and the types of items available. A commune market held in an open amphitheater in rural Guangdong in 1973 is shown in figure 5.11.

Although limited, outside knowledge threatened commune stability because it revealed options that, if deemed to be better, undermined worker enthusiasm.[105] But clamping down could backfire. One former member recalls how, when leaders closed her brigade market, she feigned illness

FIGURE 5.11. Markets convened by communes and brigades, like this one in the Guang Li Commune amphitheater in 1973, were opportunities for interaction between members of different teams and brigades. *Source:* Photo provided by Peggy Printz.

and snuck out before dawn to sell her family's excess sideline production at a brigade market in a neighboring commune. While there, she learned that team members from that commune enjoyed a higher workpoint value than members in her own team, a fact she later relayed to her family to their great displeasure.[106]

Social Pressure

To ensure that teams were close-knit, social pressure was applied uniformly to all members. "One basic tenet of Mao's political theory," Blecher explains, "is that subjective attitudes can matter more than objective factors. Another is that the exercise of naked authority or coercion is not an effective way to achieve results."[107] Within the commune, team meetings, political study sessions, and numerous other mandatory gatherings all emphasized the collective above the individual. Constantly doing things together and excluding outsiders ensured that peer judgments and pressure were powerful, ever present, and inescapable. Nonconformists would eventually be identified and publicly shamed into submission. Because members could not leave their team, they would face unrelenting social pressure to acquiesce to social norms or at least to remain silent.[108]

To disseminate propaganda, some brigades positioned broadcast systems with speakers throughout the unit, and others used a bullhorn. After 1966, the speakers in Chen Village in Shunde, Guangdong, ran for two hours in the morning and two hours at night. Half of each broadcast was dedicated to identifying people or teams that had acted in an especially collectivist or individualistic manner. A worker who lagged behind (known as a *moyang-gong*) would soon hear their "laziness, selfishness, and lack of appreciation for Chairman Mao's Thought broadcast over the loudspeakers."[109] Writing in 1974, William Liu explained the all-encompassing power of peer pressure in the Chinese commune at the time: "Since peer group pressure is extensive and intensive, reactions to pressures tend to be circular, involving not one or two individuals as in the case of intergenerational pressures, but a larger number of friendship circles, all of which are proximate, and their collective force far exceeds singular pressure."[110]

Rather than punish wrongdoing outright, by the 1970s "struggle meetings" (*pidou hui*) were generally used to reinforce the primacy of the collective. For instance, in 1972, the Sui Kang Brigade in Guang Li Commune, Guangdong, held a struggle meeting against a former landlord accused of "serious crimes," to wit: "publicly carping that private property was better than collective ownership." His punishment was to continue working under poor peasants' supervision.[111] Similarly, a woman given to "petty theft and spiteful damaging of collective property" and nagging her husband for "not spending enough time on his private plot" was "reformed," rather than punished. According to one local cadre,

We expended a great deal of time helping his wife reform. If she did anything well, we immediately praised her during general meetings. When we went to her house, we told her good points, encouraging her to become good in other respects. It was the same process that a school uses to make small children Red. So after a fairly short period of time, she was very good. She didn't steal things and was more manageable. So the team was happy.[112]

Leaders extolled those who worked hard and took care of collective property. Praise might also be directed at "backward" workers who had made progress. This practice reminded the group that the person had been inadequate, thus opening him up for future criticism if he began to slack off again. In this way, praise was both encouragement for good work and "a subtle means of threatening shame for backsliding."[113] Doling out both public criticism and praise in Mao's name increased devotion to the collective in ways that counteracted moral hazard. According to Madsen,

People showed up for work more promptly and instead of quitting early even stayed past quitting time. While at work, they worked harder. In some production teams, fields that used to take five days to harvest could now be harvested in three. During the agricultural slack season, production teams found it easier to convince people to work on public works projects. There was less pilferage of collective night soil for use on private plots.[114]

At school, children were under constant pressure to conform. Parents faced similar pressure at mandatory town hall–style parent-teacher conferences, where teachers singled out some parents for praise and others for criticism based on their child's performance.[115] Classrooms featured large portraits of Chairman Mao in the front of the room, and his quotations appeared on the blackboard in the back.[116] According to Leo Orleans, this omnipresent emphasis on the collective over the individual ensured that "young people are well indoctrinated and prepared to accept the bidding of the state with maximum cooperation on any national policy."[117] After visiting a rural classroom in 1971, Arthur Galston agreed: "The propagandistic nature and rigidity of much of the curriculum disturbed us and made us question whether these young minds were being trained for inquiry or molded into a single line of thought."[118] Figure 5.12 is an example of the Maoist indoctrination of young children at this time.

A short story underscores the power of social pressure under the commune: While playing in the family garden, four-year-old Jingjing whimsically utters, "Chairman Mao is a Rotten Egg." Other children then report the "reactionary slogan" to a teacher, who after interrogating the boy, visits his mother and instructs her: "You have to start from the beginning and teach him to love Chairman Mao. You must guide him into loving our leader." To which the mother replies, "As if I haven't . . ." and she wept "at the injustice of the insinuation."[119]

FIGURE 5.12. A child shouts "Long Live Chairman Mao!" 1970.
Source: China's New Footprint: Impact of the 1970s [Xin zhongguo jiaoyin: Qishiniandai yingxiang], AFP/Getty Images, http://chenmodemaque.blog.163.com/blog/static/16389212920129174522870/.

Collective Remuneration

The Chinese commune's primary economic objective, like that of all high-modernist communes, was to introduce development to increase agricultural productivity. In 1958, sociologist Fei Xiaotong had observed that as long as rural households had sufficient food and clothing, they would not rebel.[120] The goal, therefore, as discussed in chapter 3 and 4, was to extract as much as possible from households for investment without inducing famine, revolution, or excessive foot-dragging. Extraction was achieved by disguising the amount of total collative income and focusing households' attention on their share relative to their neighbors. To this end, collective remuneration methods enhanced worker self-supervision.

The use of workpoints, regardless of how they were awarded, provided three advantages over direct cash payments that mitigated collective action problems. First, workpoints disincentivized labor mobility and kept workers in their teams, which augmented the *hukou* residency system and helped alleviate brain drain and adverse selection. Their local distribution and redemption simplified the provision of public goods and services. "People earned locally, spent locally, and consumed locally," Tang explains.[121]

Second, unlike physical currency, workpoints were recorded and untradeable, which increased members' propensity to cooperate. When people are exposed to money—even *fake* money or *reminders* of money— their behavior becomes more individualistic. Kathleen Vohs has found that people become less cooperative when exposed to simulated (i.e., Monopoly) money. Paul Piff has found that merely reminding people about money encourages them to behave more selfishly, and when exposed to cash, they tend toward unethical behavior. He concludes that "just the very thought of money gets people to put their own individual interests above the collective."[122]

Third, the flexibility of workpoints allowed each team to set and adjust its savings and consumption rates depending on the harvest, its households' long- and short-term needs, and the amount required to support capital investment. Each team could adjust its workpoint value on a harvest-by-harvest basis, and the composition of member remuneration could be given in cash, grain, or a combination. Using workpoints rather than direct cash payments ensured sufficient savings were set aside for investment, while also providing enough consumption to avoid famine. Flexibility in workpoint values also produced uncertainty among members about their actual income, which eased slacking. Because workpoint value was determined after the harvest, it was unclear during planting how many points a household would need to earn to avoid taking a loan from their team. Thus, members were incentivized to work *more* than they might otherwise have worked to ensure that they had sufficient income to avoid the financial and social costs of debt. After conducting interviews with former members in 1974, 1975, and 1978, Blecher explained:

The frequently heard argument that Chinese agricultural collectives did not provide labor incentives is dubious both in theory and in practice. An economic model of rational behavior under conditions of uncertainty can suggest, on the contrary, that the payment structure of Chinese collectives gave farmers incentives to work too hard. Since they did not know until the end of the year how much their work points would be worth, farmers worked harder and longer than made sense from the point of view of labor efficiency. This theory conforms to practice. During the 1970s, farmers and rural cadres did not complain primarily about indolence among their fellow villagers; on the contrary, their biggest complaint was that they worked very hard but did not seem to be reaping much in the way of rewards.[123]

The value of each worker's accumulated workpoints was calculated as a fraction of each production team's total annual income. No matter how many points a worker earned, if other team members slacked off, their value would suffer. In other words, the bigger the whole pie, the bigger the size of each slice.[124] This mitigated moral hazard because members were incentivized to monitor each other, and small team size (150–170 members) ensured that they had enough local knowledge to do so. The decision about how many points to allocate came at regular appraisal meetings, during which each worker was given a workpoint ranking to determine how many points he or she would be entitled to for a full day's work. In Chen Village, men received between 8.5 and 10 points; females received between 6 and 7.5 points.[125]

The task and piece rate remuneration methods used during the early 1960s rewarded people for quantity, not quality, and caused bickering over assignments and workpoint allotments.[126] Some experiments, however, were conducted with "group task work," whereby the team was awarded workpoints based on its combined production. After the harvest, as discussed in chapter 4, a meeting was held to appraise the labor contribution of members and allocate workpoints accordingly. After 1965, communes promulgated a revised remuneration system known as the Dazhai workpoint system that expanded the concept of group appraisals into a team-based wage distribution program intended to reinforce the commune's collectivist ethos. Under Maoism, collectivism was inherently better than individualism; thus, this strategy, which was reminiscent of socialist communes, was politically attractive. But the Maoists also believed that the Dazhai workpoint system would increase productivity and improve living standards.[127]

Named after the model Dazhai Brigade in Shaanxi discussed in chapter 2, the initial Dazhai system introduced in 1965 considered both a member's labor contribution and devotion to the collective when determining his or her workpoint allocation.[128] By employing social pressure, rather than material incentives via assorted rate systems, Dazhai remuneration reduced the difficulties associated with recording workpoints for differently skilled workers across a range of tasks.[129] Dazhai's "underlying idea," Jonathan

Unger observes, "was to structure remuneration in ways that induced people to concentrate their attention upon the gains that would accrue from a larger pie."[130] This system changed the basis upon which workpoints were awarded, but it did not change how household income was calculated, which remained as percentage of total team income.

Between 1965 and 1967, the Four Cleanups work teams simultaneously promulgated both Maoist indoctrination and the Dazhai workpoint system in a manner that was mutually reinforcing. "The key to making the Dazhai system work was maintaining the public spirit generated in the Mao study rituals," Madsen explains. As long as the spirit of Maoism remained strong, team members treated each other as comrades, worked hard, and remained willing to carry out impartial Dazhai workpoint evaluations.[131] Unger describes how local cadre leaders used Maoism to introduce Dazhai remuneration into teams.

Daily study sessions were inaugurated in which the work team cadres had a group of urban-educated youths who had settled in the village taught Mao's quotes and incessantly impressed upon the peasantry the sanctity and relevance of the quotes. A perfervid atmosphere somewhat like a religious revival was whipped up—and put to the service of the new wage system. The rhetoric of the Mao study sessions and of the new village broadcasting system repeatedly intoned: fight personal selfishness, devote yourself to the collective.[132]

The initial success of Dazhai workpoints in increasing productivity validated Maoism and reinforced public support for the collectivist ideology. According to one production team leader in Chen Village, "When production increased and things did not turn bad [people] began to believe in Mao Zedong Thought. Even the old generation had to believe because they had eyes to see that since the work team had come, production had increased. The increase in production proved that the campaign had been successful."[133]

Under the Dazhai workpoint system, a "social contract" was erected among members. "Under its ground rules, anyone overly careless could be loudly reprimanded. The threat of public embarrassment now helped keep potential offenders in line," Unger explains.[134] Combined with the social norm of active collectivism cultivated under Maoism, improved worker self-supervision did redress, at least for a time, the "culture of submissiveness" that had long been pervasive in old Chinese society.[135]

The difficulty with Dazhai remuneration as practiced from 1965 to 1967, however, was that judgments about a person's dedication to the collective are subjective in ways that judgments about labor productivity are not. Once farmers' enthusiasm for the collective became a determinant of workpoint allocations, remuneration became a measure of social status and gradually became intertwined with clan loyalties, kinship relationships, and personal rivalries, making group appraisals increasing unwieldy and unpleasant. For team leaders, it was often easiest to settle these disputes by increasing the complainer's workpoints.[136] Although this response alleviated the immediate problem, it also rewarded complaining, increased income equalization, and deflated the value of the workpoint, which left better workers discontented, thus exacerbating moral hazard. To reduce the propensity to slack among the best workers, single men and women in their late teens and twenties were often called upon during Mao study sessions to set the pace for collective work.[137]

To address the moral hazard problems that emerged under the Dazhai workpoints system, a more flexible remuneration policy was adopted at the Northern Districts Agricultural Conference in 1970, and Dazhai was rebranded it as investment-led growth. The new remuneration system allowed each commune to select the combination of workpoint methodologies (i.e., piece, time, and task rates) that best improved production. As discussed in chapter 4, the decentralization of workpoint remuneration methodologies to the commune produced extensive local variation. Throughout the 1970s, as the rural economy became increasingly diversified, communes continued to tinker with their workpoint systems to maintain and enhance their effectiveness.

Yet, although a return to performance-based workpoint remuneration systems during the 1970s rewarded worker productivity, it also produced similar drawbacks to the early 1960s system. These problems were exacerbated as the rural economy became increasingly diversified, which made measuring worker performance ever more difficult. Commune and brigade enterprises introduced numerous tasks, such as animal breeding, noodle making, beekeeping, fertilizer production, seed testing, machine repair, and tractor driving, which complicated workpoint allocations. After 1970, workpoint recorders needed to catalog dozens of chores that varied by location, season, and worker skill level, and then they had to review the work that was done, by whom, and at what rate.[138] The team accountant also had to keep pace with the dizzying array of time rates, overtime rates, piece rates, cash reward payments, and compensatory arrangements.[139] Sometimes the complexity and subjectivity of workpoint evaluations created disputes among members, which undermined the institution's collectivist spirit.[140]

In the 1970s, households were deeply concerned with their relative slice of the collective pie—that is, their workpoint allocation relative to others. The new culture of candor and local activism unleashed under the original Dazhai workpoint remuneration system inspired each household to vigorously monitor its workpoints and push others to contribute to increase collective income. If "a team member found that his or her work was not credited, the person would immediately complain to the accountant," explains Li Huaiyin.[141] The return to material incentives in remuneration after 1970 may have gradually turned members' healthy self-supervision into what psychologists call "egocentric bias," whereby group members systematically overemphasized their own contribution to the collective and thus were regularly dissatisfied with their compensation relative to other members.[142] It seems unlikely that households' discontent over collective remuneration alone could have induced decollectivization; after the process began, however, their dissatisfaction after more than two decades of hard work and austerity almost certainly catalyzed it.

CONCLUSION

Throughout history, long-lived communes have required a powerful collectivist ethos to promote hard work and cooperation.[143] Religious communes, which prioritize spiritual fulfillment over material wealth and are hierarchical institutions, have generally had the most effective collectivist ideologies. The commune was, among other things, the church of Mao. Beginning with the Socialist Education Campaign and the introduction of the Dazhai model in 1965, its leaders promoted Maoism as a national religion that for over a decade bound members to each other, the institution, the party, and the nation. Mao's image, group ceremonies and rituals, song and dance, and holy texts (e.g., the *Little Red Book*) were used to indoctrinate members. Maoism was so pervasive that four decades after the chairman's death millions of elderly rural residents throughout China still prominently display his image in their homes.

Self-reliance was the clarion call of the commune era; it strongly disincentivized workers from leaving their teams and thus eased adverse selection and brain drain. The linchpins of self-reliance were the *hukou* system and information control, which kept members producing and consuming locally and ensured that they remained largely ignorant of outside conditions. The commune's collective remuneration system countered brain drain and adverse selection by incentivizing workers to remain local, and mitigated moral hazard by encouraging worker self-supervision and rewarding those who put collective above individual interests. Meanwhile, commune members faced excessive and unceasing ideological indoctrination and social pressure from local leaders, militiamen, and fellow team members to conform to official norms that prioritized collective investments over individual consumption. The commune's collectivist ethos increased agricultural productivity because it bound members to the institution and to each other. Members' devotion made it possible to extract more from them to support agricultural investment than they otherwise would have tolerated without resorting to foot-dragging or outright rebellion.

Chapter Six

ORGANIZATION
Size and Structure

INTRODUCTION

This chapter measures the effects of the commune's organizational size and structure on its economic productivity. In addition to super-optimal investment and Maoism (see chapters 4 and 5, respectively), it identifies the structure of the commune and the relative size of its subunits as the third significant source of agricultural productivity. By examining the interaction effects among commune subunits and their influence on agricultural productivity, it applies and tests existing theories about the influence of organizational size and structure on institutional effectiveness. This analysis expands our understanding of the relationship between changes in organizational structure and agricultural productivity during the commune era, a period researchers have generally treated as a monolith, rather than a time of institutional change.

Between 1953 and 1962, as discussed in chapter 2, collective agriculture evolved from simple, traditional forms, into a complex, multitiered institution with control over all local economic, political, and administrative affairs: the commune. In the early 1950s, China implemented a nationwide land-to-the-tiller program. Next, Beijing encouraged Mutual Aid Teams (1953–1955)

This chapter reuses some text and tables from Joshua Eisenman and Feng Yang, "Organizational Structure, Policy Learning, and Economic Performance: Evidence from the Chinese Commune," *Socius: Sociological Research for a Dynamic World* 4, no. 1 (2018): 1–18.

based on traditional kin-based labor-sharing schemes; then it created Agricultural Producer Cooperatives (1956–1957), the countryside's first collective economic institution. When the Great Leap Forward (GLF) began in 1958, these cooperatives were merged to form large communes and their mandate was expanded to include Maoist politics and public administration.[1]

After the devastating GLF famine, the commune's structure was substantially altered to increase agricultural productivity. These reforms reduced its size and introduced two levels of administrative subunits: the production brigade and its subordinate production team. In the decade after its creation, the size of the commune and these subunits were continuously adjusted. This chapter examines how these organizational changes affected agricultural output under the commune. As the data reveal, before decollectivization (1958–1979), the size of the commune and its subunits was a significant determinant of the temporal and geographic variations observed in agricultural output.

This conclusion is based on an empirical model that uses heretofore unavailable data covering all 117 counties in Henan Province.[2] The model includes various agricultural inputs (i.e., land, labor, machine power, and fertilizer), which, not surprisingly, all remained positive and statistically significant at or above the 90 percent ($p<0.1$) confidence level. This empirical finding demonstrates the causal relationships assumed by the economic growth models presented in chapter 4. Unlike in chapter 4, however, the primary objective of this chapter is not to assess the contribution of agricultural inputs to productivity but rather to isolate the independent effects of structural variables. In so doing, this chapter explains how variations in the size of the commune and its subunits over time and space affected its economic performance.

Together, the relative size of the commune (i.e., the number of brigades per commune) and its subordinate production teams (i.e., the number of households per team) were significant determinants of the institution's ability to grow crops. Although I did not find strong evidence that commune relative size *per se* influenced agricultural output, I did find a sizable and significant interaction effect between commune size and team size. When average team relative size was small, smaller teams had higher agricultural output; however, as the average commune size increased (to the medium level), the effect was mitigated and even reversed. Small communes with large teams and big communes with small teams were the least productive types.

Over the course of the commune era, agricultural output exhibited considerable temporal and regional variations. The boxplots in figure 6.1 plot the distribution of total agricultural output of counties against years, and reveal that the median county-level output declined from 1958 to 1961 but increased thereafter. The whisker length of the boxplots indicates heterogeneity of agricultural output among Henan counties for each year, which changed as well. For instance, from 1961 to 1965, the within-year variation is larger than from 1970 to 1979, suggesting that variation in commune and subunit size diminished in the latter period.

To interpret the magnitudes of the marginal effect of changes in team size, imagine that two similar counties differ only with regard to the relative size of their communes: County A has a smaller average commune relative size and is in the 5th percentile of the sample, whereas County B's commune relative size is in the 95th percentile of the sample. In County A, enlarging team size by 10 percent will decrease per capita crop production by 0.9 percent. In County B, by contrast, the marginal effect of team size is positive, 0.06, and is not statistically significant. This effect implies that larger communes mitigate the negative effect of big teams.

In the next section, I present a brief history of the relationship between commune structure and economic performance. I lay out the general

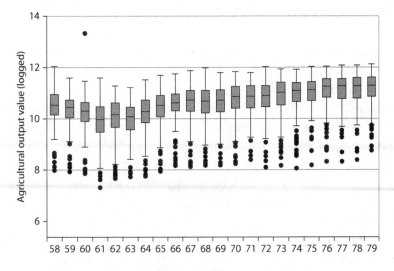

FIGURE 6.1. Distribution of agricultural total output across Henan counties, 1958–1979.

arguments in the existing literature about how and why organizational size and the size of subunits influences economic performance. Then, I discuss how those arguments have been applied to the Chinese commune and generate hypotheses about how the size of the commune and its subunits affect agricultural productivity. To test these hypotheses, I first develop a model that uses newly uncovered county-level data, then present and discuss my findings, and finally offer some plausible explanations for these results.

COMMUNE STRUCTURE AND ECONOMIC PERFORMANCE

Under all but the most ideal conditions, effective worker oversight and remuneration are necessary for any organization to be productive. The challenge, put succinctly, is how to get members to work hard. For communes, Rosabeth Kanter argues that the answer is smaller "face-to-face units" (or "teams" in the Chinese context) of about 150–200 members under the jurisdiction of a larger commune:

The group [should] be large enough to get its work done and implement common purposes, but small enough to maintain intimacy and face-to-face contact. Larger ones generally have somewhat smaller face-to-face units. The size of communal villages—groups that attempt to constitute comprehensive communities offering most life services—is between 150 and 200 members, a number that recurs often in the anthropological literature on communal societies.[3]

Subunits provide the local information necessary to identify and punish shirkers and slackers, address workers' problems or disputes, and reward hard work and devotion to the collective. They also take advantage of differences in scale that affect the productivity of various agricultural products. The less attention the crop requires (i.e., wheat), the more appropriate it is for large-scale collectivization, whereas the more attention a crop needs (i.e., raspberries), the better suited it is to smaller subunits or household production. Without subunits, communes are ill suited to improve output in vegetables, small livestock, and other labor-intensive forms of agricultural production.[4]

Nearly all large, long-lived communes have had subunits. The Hutterites peaked with more than 17,000 people living in 150 communities—that is, 113 members or about 15 families per subunit.[5] Shakers, which founded their first commune in 1787, created twenty-two villages in the American Northeast. Amana (1843–1933) had seven subunits, as did Synanon (1913–1997). New Harmony was subdivided into about ten subcommunities. In China, the lowest level commune's subunit, the production team, averaged between 150 and 170 members throughout the 1970s.[6] Plato's imagined *Republic* had about five thousand members, small compared with most Chinese communes, but without subunits, Kanter reasons, it probably would have been too big to effectively monitor and pay workers.[7]

To ensure sufficient oversight and facilitate accurate remuneration, the Shakers created three levels of administration. Five "bishoprics" (each with its own ministry) were responsible to the central leadership. Beneath them were eleven "societies," which were further subdivided into "families." Each "family" was a semi-independent economic unit consisting of thirty to one hundred members, and governed by four leaders who prioritized the "spiritual care of the group and oversight of all the family's affairs," Edward Andrews explains.[8] "Family leaders were appointed and supervised by an all powerful, self-perpetuating central ministry, and in the other societies by the branch ministries." To stress the centrality of the collective, families were named based on their location in relation to their local church (e.g., East family, South family), where meetings and ceremonies were held.[9]

Chinese policymakers recognized early on the need for commune subunits and the close relationship between subunit relative size and agricultural productivity.[10] In response to the GLF famine, policymakers moved quickly to reduce the communes' size and introduced subunits that expanded its single-level administration into a three-level organizational structure that included the commune, the production brigade, and the production team.[11] Figure 6.2 presents the structure of rural governance after the brigade and team were created and the structure in which it existed until decollectivization.

First promulgated in April 1961, the *Working Regulations of Rural People's Communes (Nongchun renmin gongshe gongzuo tiaoli)*, also known as the *Sixty Articles on Agriculture (Nongye liushi tiao)*, were adopted in September 1962 by the Community Party of China Central Committee and remained the commune's legal working guidelines until the institution was abandoned Article 5 mandated that the size of the commune and its subunits should maximize "production, management, and unity" (appendix C).

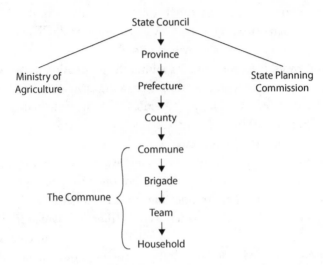

FIGURE 6.2. Rural governance structure in commune-era China.

The size of the various levels of a people's commune should be decided. . . . to benefit the various levels of a people's commune in production, management, and unity. . . . In deciding the size of a production team, it is necessary to consider the area of its land, the distance between plots, the density or scattering of residential quarters, its labor force, the balance between its draft animals and farm implements, conditions for developing diversified undertakings and so on.[12]

In keeping with these instructions, cadres in Henan adjusted their communes' size extensively throughout the early to mid-1960s. After the failure of the excessively large GLF communes in 1958 and 1959, between 1960 and 1963, the average number of communes per county in Henan rose dramatically, growing from ten in 1960, to thirty-two in 1961, to thirty-nine in 1962, and peaking at forty-three in 1963 (see figure 6.3). This change, which was accompanied by a reduction in average commune relative size from twenty-four brigades per commune in 1960 to nineteen in 1963 (figure 6.4), appears to have been an overcorrection that was redressed by a sharp increase between 1964 and 1965 followed by a gradual increase until plateauing around twenty-three brigades per commune in 1966 (figure 6.4). Team size, by contrast, was stabilized after 1962 and thereafter the gradual increase in team size (as measured by the number of households per

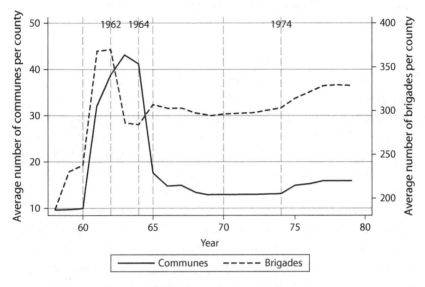

FIGURE 6.3. Average numbers of communes and brigades in Henan counties, 1958–1979.

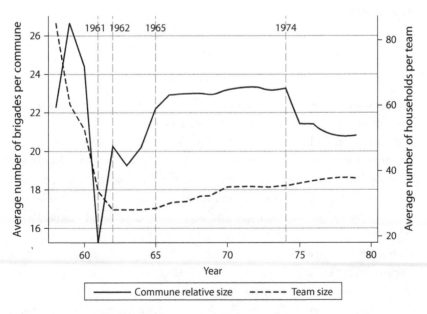

FIGURE 6.4. Average commune relative size and average team size in Henan counties, 1958–1979.

team) can be attributed primarily to population growth. Benedict Stavis explained how the size of the commune and its subunits influenced agricultural productivity:

Economically, the commune level coordinated agricultural production planning among its subunits, and mobilized labor for the construction of large-scale capital and infrastructure projects. The brigade's primary responsibility was to oversee its subordinate teams in agricultural production. It also handled small-scale capital construction and farm machine ownership and repairs, elementary education, veterinary services, basic healthcare and population control, etc. The team was the "principle accounting unit" responsible for the vast majority of agricultural production and household remuneration. They assigned jobs, monitored work performance, and compensated households based primarily on the number of members in each household and the number of workpoints they earned. *The efficient coordination of economic responsibilities among these three administrative levels were among the primary determinants of the institution's productivity.* The relative size of each commune's subunit influenced its capacity for resource extraction, the scope of capital investment, and its capacity for worker supervision and remuneration.[13] (Italics added for emphasis)

THEORY TESTING

In this section, I test the assumption that the size of an organization (i.e., the commune) and its subunits affects its economic performance.

Several non-China-related studies have found that an organization's size (measured in terms of the number of workers) is positively correlated with absolute levels of organizational performance, for example, total profits.[14] Economists and organizational theorists have identified a positive relationship between organizational size and economies of scale.[15] Because larger organizations are more likely than smaller ones to possess munificent discretionary resources they have the wherewithal to make investments that improve productivity.[16] Larger organizations' greater resources make it possible to acquire control over the "environmental entities that mediate critical resources," explain Richard Gooding and John Wagner III, and "thus, larger organizations might be more able to produce a degree of resource certainty that insures continued productive viability."[17]

Organizations with more discretionary resources can use them to make collective investments (e.g., irrigation networks) that mitigate their environmental resource constraints (e.g., water scarcity) and thus increase productivity. Yet, there appear to be limits on an organization's ability to increase its productivity through enlargement. Gooding and Wagner III argue that "diseconomies of scale associated with increasing workforce size might consume other scale economies . . . resulting in diminishing net returns on size-related economies of scale."[18] They find, in contrast to other economists and organizational theorists assumptions, that "any positive size-related economies of scale in organizational performance to be absorbed by counteracting diseconomies, [resulting] in the absence of net change in organizational efficiency."[19] This argument may explain why some studies have identified a curvilinear relationship, such that midsize organizations outperformed both larger and smaller ones.[20] Constraints on the positive relationship between organizational size and productivity may help explain the failure of China's large GLF communes.

Social psychologists who have studied the relationship between group size and group performance have generally found an insignificant or negative relationship between larger subunit size and economic performance.[21] After analyzing a sample of 234 regional metropolitan branches of a large financial services organization in the United States, Phoebe Carillo and Richard Kopelman found that "by keeping units to a small size, productivity may be enhanced."[22] Specifically, they found that smaller subunits increased overall productivity by 17 percent.[23] They explain this phenomenon, by arguing that workers in smaller subunits

(a) are more accountable because they cannot hide or pass the buck; (b) are more resourceful, given lower organizational slack; (c) have greater psychological ownership and commitment; (d) are more creative, risk accepting, and decisive (e) have greater information, because sharing information is easier; (f) have a feeling of control and empowerment; and (g) are more motivated and fast acting.[24]

Several theorists have attributed the loss of productivity associated with larger subunits to members' opportunistic behavior (i.e., slacking or loafing).[25] Others have identified a positive correlation between organization size and worker absenteeism (i.e., shirking).[26] Such free-riding is characterized as the rational single-minded pursuit of outcomes that are selectively allocated, that is, personally received and consumed. Simply put, free riders avoid contributing to the acquisition of shared "public goods," yet they continue to reap disproportionate collective remuneration.[27]

In larger subunits, the greater number of workers serves as a "behavioral mask" by making free-riding harder to detect and punish.[28] This problem is likely to grow worse as fellow workers observe their leaders' inability to sanction slackers and shirkers.[29] As an increasing number of workers become free riders, the subunit's total productivity is further reduced. A lack of oversight in larger subunit size thus increases the likelihood that workers will free ride, and, in turn, lowers collective productivity.

Researchers have tended to discount the possibility that some members might value the well-being of their group and thus might "irrationally" work hard even in a larger group.[30] Yet, Gooding and Wagner III observe that "'irrational' contributions to the acquisition of public goods can occur to a modest extent in large groups."[31] This finding corroborates reports from Chinese agricultural economists, former commune members, and Western experts that pervasive collectivist ideologies (e.g., Maoism) can induce workers to work hard despite a lack of material compensation.

In sum, the existing literature suggests that through economies of scale larger organizations are able to improve overall economic performance. Yet, at the subunit level, evidence indicates an inverse relationship between size and performance because smaller workgroups mitigate free-rider problems.[32]

To explain these conclusions, John Kimberly recognizes size as a multidimensional construct and identifies differences in the "operationalization of size" as the reason for different outcomes among studies.[33] What at first blush appears to be an inconsistency arises from "attempts to combine findings based on minimally correlated size measures."[34] As Gooding and Wagner III explain, "Defining size as the number of employees or the log of the number of employees might reflect the degree to which the availability of human resources facilitates or constrains performance."[35] To redress this problem, Dalton et al. have called for researchers to identify the "level of analysis" when conducting assessments of the productivity of organizations and their subunits.[36]

But do changes in the size of the commune and its subunits actually help explain the temporal and regional variations in agricultural productivity observed in figure 6.1? The behavior of previous communes, the *Sixty Articles*, Stavis, and the theoretical literature on the relationship between organization and subunit size and economic performance all suggest they should. Until now, however, because of a paucity of systematic data, it had not been possible to test the extent to which variations in organizational size affect agricultural productivity. To answer this question, I developed four hypotheses based on the existing literature, which are expressed—in accordance with Dalton et al.'s suggestion—in terms of the three relevant "levels of analysis": the commune, brigade, and team.

HYPOTHESES ABOUT THE RELATIONSHIP BETWEEN THE SIZE OF COMMUNE SUBUNITS AND AGRICULTURAL PRODUCTIVITY

Commune Size

HYPOTHESIS 1 (H1): AS COMMUNE SIZE INCREASES, CAPITAL INVESTMENT INCREASES, CAUSING AGRICULTURAL PRODUCTION TO RISE.

The commune system used coercive household income extraction to fund investments in agricultural physical and human capital. The commune-level coordinated the construction of infrastructure projects that were beyond the capacity and geographic jurisdiction of a single brigade or team. Larger communes had a greater capacity than small ones to invest in what Victor Lippit calls, "self-reliant industrialization projects," allowing them to better mitigate environmental and resource constraints.[37] Water-management systems and hydropower generation, for instance, reduced the stochastic influence of weather patterns on agriculture, thus improving yields.[38] A larger commune could take advantage of economies of scale in the purchase and maintenance of agricultural equipment via its numerous subinstitutions and enterprises, (e.g., its agricultural machine and tractor station and fertilizer production facilities). Similarly, the commune's capacity to harness workers to construct productivity-enhancing infrastructure was determined by the size of the labor force under its jurisdiction. Larger communes could deploy both skilled and unskilled labor across a larger geographic area and spread staffing costs across more teams, thus increasing the scope of benefits while reducing the burden on each subunit.

Brigade Size

HYPOTHESIS 2 (H2): AS BRIGADE SIZE FALLS, SUPERVISION OVER TEAMS IMPROVES, CAUSING AGRICULTURAL PRODUCTION TO RISE.

The brigade's most important responsibility was to monitor its teams' policy implementation and report economic performance–related data up to the commune. Every project or policy—whether initiated in Beijing or at the commune headquarters—required brigades to supervise team implementation. Brigade leaders were at the crossroads of a complex web of interdependent and competing team-level problems, objectives, and interests, Steven Butler observes.[39] I hypothesize that the more teams a brigade had, the harder it was to supervise them, and thus, all else being equal, smaller brigades had better oversight and were more productive.

To improve oversight and ensure that teams were meeting their production targets, the commune (with support from the county) could increase the number of brigades, thus reducing the number of teams under each one's jurisdiction. In Henan between 1960 and 1962, the average number of brigades per county increased sharply from 237 to 370 (see figure 6.3). After a sharp decline in 1963, the average number of brigades per county rose again from 284 in 1964 to 307 in 1965. One former team leader explained how subdividing brigades, thus reducing their size and increasing their total number, improved their supervisory capacity:

There were definite advantages in splitting up the previously large brigade. It was easier to inspect production. Previously it took four or five days to make an inspection, but after splitting the brigade it could be done in one day. It prevented the team from covering up the situation and strengthened the control over the team leadership. Splitting the brigade also had an effect on profiteering: the brigade controlled the team head. Previously even the team head could engage in profiteering. Before splitting the brigade, field management was not controlled as strictly.[40]

Team Size

*HYPOTHESIS 3 (H3): AS TEAM SIZE FALLS, SUPERVISION OVER WORKERS
IMPROVES, CAUSING AGRICULTURAL PRODUCTION TO RISE.*

After 1961, the production team was the principal accounting unit of the
commune system and was responsible for nearly all day-to-day field management, worker supervision, evaluation, and income distribution.[41] The
team administered the workpoint remuneration system, which required an
accurate recording of each worker's contribution to the collective. After
the harvest, the team accountant would tally each household's workpoints
and exchange them for a portion of the collective agricultural output that
remained after deducting all production, management, investment, and
welfare costs. Some researchers have argued that collective agriculture
under the commune undermined worker supervision, thus prompting
them to engage in excessive free-riding, which resulted in low labor productivity and falling agricultural output.[42]

During decollectivization, the commune was replaced by the Household
Responsibility System (HRS), which returned rural China to household-
based farming.[43] As discussed in chapter 1, numerous studies have made
cross-institution comparisons between collective agriculture under the
commune and HRS. Most attribute improved agricultural productivity
after decollectivization to economic "rational choice" theories that prioritize conceptions of the self-interested peasant. James Kai-sing Kung succinctly summarizes this view, which is supported by national-level data
that show agricultural output increased after decollectivization:

Collective agriculture was seen as suffering from problems of labor supervision within
the institutional context of a team, which prevented the adoption of payment systems that would sufficiently differentiate and reward farmers' actual contributions
to total output, such as the use of piece rates. In the Chinese case, the difficulties of
monitoring led to the adoption of a time-based payment system, with a very narrow spread of earnings. While that system was simple to administer, it provided
only a tenuous link between effort and reward. *This weakness of incentives led to
extensive free riding behavior, which was cured only by the eventual replacement of
the collectives by family farms.*[44] (Italics added for emphasis)

On the basis of the aforementioned general literature on subunit size and existing studies of agricultural reform in China, I hypothesize that opportunistic free-riding was a greater problem among larger teams than smaller ones. Hence, smaller team size is correlated with improved commune economic performance.

After 1962, the number of production teams remained stable in Henan; however, across counties, wide-ranging variation in team size remained for several reasons.[45] First, because teams were usually natural villages and team members were neighbors, subdivision would have disturbed social networks and the rhythms of daily life. Second, team subdivision was administratively troublesome, requiring the appointment of new inexperienced team leaders. Third, economically speaking, team subdivision meant the partition of land and labor, changes that would have abruptly altered workpoint values, and thus each household's collective income. Fourth, politically, the collectivist ethos of Maoism favored larger work units as more "socialist," thus making subdivision politically unattractive.[46] Given these difficulties, before redrawing team boundaries, brigade leaders needed approval from commune cadres who feared that subdividing teams could incite grassroots tensions or hurt worker cohesion or enthusiasm, which, in turn, would reduce productivity.

The relatively stable size of production teams after 1962 makes it hard to measure their effects on commune productivity per se. This does not necessarily mean, however, that the variable does not help explain the variance observed in agricultural production. As illustrated in the next section, team size interacts with commune and brigade size and thus plays a divergent role under different conditions.

Interaction Effects

HYPOTHESIS 4 (H4): THERE IS AN INTERACTION EFFECT BETWEEN OTHER ORGANIZATIONAL STRUCTURE VARIABLES (I.E., COMMUNE SIZE AND BRIGADE SIZE) AND TEAM SIZE SUCH THAT WHEN COMBINED WITH LARGE COMMUNES AND/OR SMALLER BRIGADES, LARGE TEAMS ARE LESS DETRIMENTAL TO AGRICULTURAL PRODUCTION.

The interaction effect among the size of the commune and its subunits can elucidate the role organizational structure played in determining its economic performance. When commune size is too small to mobilize enough resources to take advantage of the efficiencies generated by economies of scale, I hypothesize that team size has a strong negative effect on agricultural production. As commune size increases enough to benefit from economies of scale, however, the favorable macro-level production environment improves economic performance and thus reduces the need for extensive worker supervision at the team level. As worker supervision becomes a less powerful determinant of economic performance, there is, in turn, less pressure to maintain a small team, thus shrinking the productivity gap between communes with big teams and those with small teams. Therefore, I predict the following: smaller communes with smaller teams perform better than smaller communes with bigger teams, but the advantage of smaller teams diminishes as commune size increases.

This same logic can be applied to brigade size. When brigade size is too large to effectively supervise teams, I hypothesize that large team size had a stronger negative effect on agricultural production. Smaller brigades, by contrast, provide increased supervision and thus reduce the importance of team-level oversight; hence, larger brigades with smaller teams perform better than larger brigades with larger teams.

In sum, when commune size is small—which hinders capital investment (H1)—or brigade size is large—which hinders team supervision (H2)—the relatively poor production environment highlights smaller teams' ability to better supervise workers. Conversely, when and where commune size is large enough or brigade size is small enough, I predict the negative effects of large team size will be mitigated.

EMPIRICAL STRATEGY

Why Study Henan Counties?

Below I test my hypotheses and examine how differences in the average size of communes and their subunits among Henan counties affected their levels of agricultural productivity. To do this, I present heretofore-unavailable data on the often-overlooked county level, that is, the level just above the commune. Using the *Henan Agricultural Statistics, 1949–1979*, I constructed a balanced county-level panel data set (with missing observations), including county-level data on agricultural input and output for all 117 counties in the province's 10 prefectures covering the years from 1958 to 1979.[47]

FIGURE 6.5. A map of China indicating the location of Henan Province.

I chose Henan, first, because it is a large (approximately 63 million people), densely populated agricultural province located in the center of China (figure 6.5). These attributes minimized variations in climate, soil type, topography, and population density and placed the focus on the production of one product type: grain.

Second, in Henan, considerable variation existed on both the dependent and independent variables. During the GLF famine, several Henan counties experienced a drastic decline in agricultural output. According to the *Sixty Articles*, in the wake of the agricultural crisis, localities were instructed to adjust the size of their communes and their subunits to stimulate productivity. Moreover, as Dali Yang argues, in areas where the famine was particularly severe, local officials had greater autonomy to adopt measures to revive productivity.[48] Between 1958 and 1979, total agricultural output nearly doubled in Henan (see appendix A). Moreover, Henan counties also exhibited large variations in the size of communes and their subunits over both time and geographic space. These variations make it easier to observe whether the adjustment of commune and subunits size can explain patterns of productivity.

I conducted a county-level analysis for three reasons. First, to gain comparative leverage over my research question, I wanted to quantify how changes in the average size of communes, brigades, and teams affected agricultural output across Henan. County-level (as opposed to prefectural or provincial-level) data provide the granularity necessary to reveal the regional and temporal variations required to explain how these changes affected economic performance.

Second, according to official regulations, the size of communes was determined at the county level.[49] County leaders could increase the size of a commune by adding or subdividing brigades, or they could shrink the commune by combining brigades or removing them and adding them to an adjacent commune.

Third, examining the agricultural sector from the middle of the Mao era governance structure—rather than top-down or bottom-up—has distinct advantages. Communes in some counties performed much better than others, suggesting that differences in commune structure across time and space can help explain performance. Given the consistency of national policy under the *Sixty Articles* from 1962 to 1979, if I hold economic inputs—land, labor, and capital—constant, I should be able to observe how variations in the size of communes and their subunits helped account for changes in economic performance across counties and over time.

Variables

DEPENDENT VARIABLE: AGRICULTURAL PRODUCTION

Throughout the chapter, unless otherwise specifically stated, the dependent variable is the logged value of annual crop production of each county (rural per capita) for each year, expressed in thousands of yuan and in 1970 prices. To check the robustness of my operationalization, I also tested the model using the total value of agricultural production (rural per capita), including crop, livestock, forestry, fishery, and sideline production, as an alternative dependent variable. As reported in table B.2 in appendix B, the alternative measure yielded similar results.

INDEPENDENT VARIABLES

I measured the effect of commune, brigade, and team size as well as their interaction on agricultural production. Accordingly, the two salient independent variables are average relative size of communes and average team size per county per year. The former combines commune and brigade size into a single measure. It is calculated by dividing the number of brigades for each county in each year by the number of communes in that county, which is equal to a ratio of average commune size over average brigade size in a county (shown in equation 6.1). I then take a natural log to reduce the skewness. The latter is measured with logged average number of households per team for each county in each year.

$$\frac{\#bridages}{\#communes} = \frac{\frac{\#teams}{\#communes}}{\frac{\#teams}{\#brigades}} = \frac{average\ commune\ size}{average\ brigade\ size} \qquad (6.1)$$

I use the relative size of communes rather than the absolute size of commune and brigade, that is, the number of teams under their jurisdiction. If the absolute size of either commune or brigade is added into the regression, neither the variables per se nor their interactions with team size is statistically significant.[50] I suspect this null effect is caused by the strong correlation observed among these absolute variables.[51] I used the relative size of communes because it both mitigates this multicollinearity problem and allows us to study the interaction effects among the commune's three levels. After the transformation, the correlation between commune relative size and team size decreases to −0.03 (p-value = 0.19).

The commune relative size measure has a large value if there are many brigades and only a few communes in a county for a given year and has a small value otherwise. For reasons explained earlier, I anticipated a positive effect of commune size on production (because large communes take advantages of economies of scale) and a negative effect of brigade size on production (because small brigades have better supervision over their teams); thus, this measure can capture their joint effect. When the interaction between commune relative size and team size is included in the regression, I expect the interaction coefficient to be positive because large communes combined with small brigades mitigate the disadvantage of large production teams (H4).

Econometric Method

To test these four hypotheses, I used a two-way fixed effect model, which includes both county fixed effects and year fixed effects. This model can rule out the influence of time-invariant county-specific factors, such as culture and natural endowment, and year-specific factors, such as national or provincial policies, which affected all counties.

$$
\begin{aligned}
output_{i,t} = a_i &+ c_1 M\,C\,commune_{i,t} + c_2 M\,C\,team_{i,t} \\
&+ c_3 M\,C\,commune_{i,t} \times M\,C\,team_{i,t} + X'_{i,t-1}b + d_t + e_{i,t}
\end{aligned} \quad (6.2)
$$

In this model, i denotes counties, and t denotes years. The dependent variable *output* is the natural log of the value of crop production in each county for each year. To examine the coefficient of team size when commune relative size is fixed at its average level and that of commune relative size when team size is fixed at its average level, I rescaled both variables by subtracting their sample means.[52] Thus, the mean centered commune relative size variable (*MCcommune*) measures the deviation from mean logged average relative size of communes of the sample and mean centered team size (*MCteam*) is the deviation from mean logged average size of teams in the sample, both of which are measured in each county for each year. I also included an interaction term between the two variables of interest to test the interaction effect.

In the set of control variables (X), I included the conventional inputs, such as the area of planted land (logged), the total agricultural machine horsepower (logged), commune labor (logged), and metric tons of fertilizer per hectare of planted land (logged). For a more precise definition of these variables see the table B.1 in appendix B. I also controlled for the size of rural population (logged). To mitigate the problem of reverse causality, the conventional inputs and the rural population are lagged to the previous year (although regressions without lags generated almost the same results). I did not lag the commune relative size variable and team size variable because in the early 1960s they exhibited drastic changes from year to year, and a lag cannot capture such an immediate effect. Although this strategy may enhance endogeneity, I conducted several additional robustness checks to ensure that variations in prefectural-level policies did not affect the association among the size variables and agricultural production.

I included county fixed effects (a_i) in the specification to capture time-invariant county characteristics that may be related to both changes of size of commune and subordinate units and agricultural output. I also include year-fixed effect (d_t) to capture provincial or national wide policy changes that may simultaneously affect commune sizes and agricultural output; eit is the disturbance term and the disturbances can be correlated across years for the same county.

EMPIRICAL FINDINGS

Table 6.1 summarizes my findings. First, in the absence of the interaction variable, I did not find strong evidence supporting H1, H2, or H3. In table 6.1 columns 1 and 3, coefficients of both commune relative size and team size are negative and the estimates are not statistically significant at the conventional 95 percent confidence level. More than sixteen of the twenty year dummies are statistically significant individually, and a joint F-test for their significance resoundingly rejects the hypothesis that they are zero. The statistical significance of these year dummies implies that national or provincial policies that vary over time but affect all counties have a significant impact on agricultural production outcomes. These results suggest that interactions between team and commune size must be considered when evaluating the effects of commune size on agricultural production.

I did find evidence to support the interaction effect postulated in H4. In table 6.1, columns 2 and 4, when the interaction between commune relative size and team size is introduced, the marginal effect of team size diverges conditionally on different commune relative size. In both columns, the coefficients for commune relative size and team size are not statistically significant at the conventional confidence level. Because both commune relative size and team size are mean centered, the coefficients of commune relative size suggest that when team size is fixed at the average level, commune relative size does not have a strong effect on agricultural production. Similarly, the coefficients of team size indicate that when commune relative size is fixed at the sample average, team size does not have a statistically significant effect on agricultural production. The interaction variable's positive and statistically significant coefficients, however, suggest that if two counties both exhibit small average commune relative size, the one with smaller average teams will outperform the one with larger average teams. But if both counties' communes are relatively large, then the negative association between team size and agricultural production will be weaker, and if they are very large, then the positive association between team size and agricultural production will be weak.

Figure 6.6 plots the marginal effects of team size against commune's relative size based on table 6.1 column 4, with the x-axis ranging from the minimum to the maximum values of the commune's mean centered relative size in the sample. When commune relative size takes the value of −0.78 (the 5th percentile of the sample), the team size's marginal effect on agricultural output is −0.09 (−0.006+(−0.78) * 0.108= −0.09; p-value= 0.029): increasing average team size by 10 percent decreases crop production per capita by 0.9 percent. In my sample, among the 1,163 county-year observations whose commune relative size is smaller than the sample median, 36 percent (417) experienced a decrease in their average team size, which I argue may have been driven by the production benefits of small communes with small teams. As relative commune size increases, however, the detrimental effects of large teams on crop production are mitigated. When commune relative size is in the 95th percentile (0.61), the effect of team size is 0.06 (−0.006+0.61*0.108=0.06; p-value= 0.37), and the estimate is not statistically significant.

Figure 6.7 plots predicted agricultural output against team size with commune relative size as a moderator. When a county exhibits small average commune relative size—indicated by the dashed line with a negative slope—reducing average team size improves agricultural production. When a county's average commune relative size is medium or large, however, indicated by the dotted line or solid line with positive slope, reducing average team size does not enhance agricultural production.

Moreover, with conventional inputs fixed, the most productive communes were those that were relatively small and had small teams (see top left of figure 6.7). The institution was least productive, however, when small communes were combined with large teams, or when large communes had small production teams (see bottom right and bottom left of figure 6.7, respectively). Numeric examples provided in table B.3 in

TABLE 6.1
Commune Dynamics and Agricultural Output (Baseline Results)

VARIABLES	Value of crops		Value of crops per capita	
	(1)	(2)	(3)	(4)
Institutional structure				
MC commune relative size	−0.035	−0.036	−0.046*	−0.047*
	(0.024)	(0.025)	(0.027)	(0.027)
MC team size	−0.037	−0.012	−0.033	−0.006
	(0.045)	(0.047)	(0.042)	(0.048)
MC commune relative size × MC team size		0.100**		0.108**
		(0.039)		(0.043)
Conventional inputs				
Land	0.251**	0.247**	0.271**	0.267**
	(0.123)	(0.121)	(0.123)	(0.121)
Machine power	0.035*	0.035*	0.038*	0.038*
	(0.020)	(0.020)	(0.020)	(0.020)
Labor	0.185	0.179	0.166	0.160
	(0.138)	(0.137)	(0.137)	(0.136)
Fertilizer	0.020*	0.021*	0.022*	0.022*
	(0.011)	(0.011)	(0.011)	(0.011)
Rural population	0.072	0.090	−0.687***	−0.668***
	(0.266)	(0.270)	(0.229)	(0.232)
County fixed effect	Y	Y	Y	Y
Year fixed effect	Y	Y	Y	Y
Observations	2,030	2,030	2,030	2,030
R-squared (within, R^2)	0.653	0.654	0.429	0.432
No. of counties	117	117	117	117

Note: Dependent and all independent variables are logged; constant is included in the model but not reported here; robust standard errors in parentheses are clustered at county level; *** $p<0.01$, ** $p<0.05$, * $p<0.1$

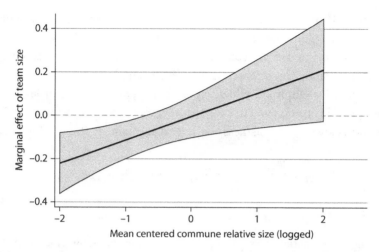

FIGURE 6.6. Marginal effects of team size conditional on mean centered commune relative size.
Note: Estimated based on table 6.1, column 4. The gray area indicates the 95 percent confidence interval of estimated marginal effect of team size.

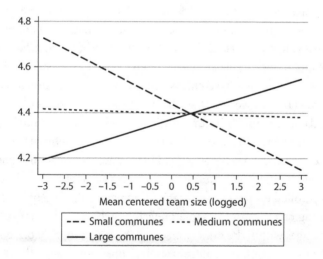

FIGURE 6.7. Predicted crops production against mean centered team size, conditional on commune relative size.
Note: Estimated based on table 6.1, column 4; small, mean, and large commune relative size take the value of the 5th percentile, sample mean, and 95th percentile, respectively.

appendix B quantify this finding. For instance, when small communes (–1.16) and small teams (–0.64) are combined, they produced 14 percent (p-value=0.01) higher agricultural output per capita than when commune relative size and team size were used at their sample means.

In sum, the empirical evidence does not support H1, H2, or H3, but it does provide strong evidence for the interaction effect postulated in H4. Following are some robustness checks that substantiate this finding.

ROBUSTNESS AND FALSIFICATION ANALYSIS

Controlling for High-Level Policy Changes

Among the potential confounding factors, I am particularly concerned with political policy "winds" and policy adjustments at the higher administration levels (i.e., national, provincial, or prefecture) that could influence either the size variables or agricultural production. As noted, to mitigate the endogeneity problem, I used a two-way fixed effect model to rule out the influence of county-specific time-invariant factors and year-specific county-invariant factors. Thus, county-specific factors, such as local culture or natural endowment, are less likely to bias the estimation. Moreover, because Henan is the only province in the sample, the effect of provincial- or national-level policies will be absorbed by year fixed effects and will not bias the estimation.

It is possible, however, that the prefectural government may have instructed counties under its jurisdiction to implement agricultural policies that could influence the size of communes and their subunits or agricultural output, and that such policies could vary across prefectures and years. Because systematic prefectural-level data on policy changes are unavailable, I controlled for the change of the mean per capita crop production for neighboring counties in the same prefecture, which served as a proxy for policy changes within the same prefecture. As shown in table 6.2, column 1, including these additional control variables does not change the results.

Lagged Effect of Size Variables

In the main analysis reported in table 6.1, I did not use lagged measures to capture the contemporaneous effect of the size variables. But do changes in commune relative size and team size have an immediate effect on crop production, or is there a lagged response to such changes? To address this question, in table 6.2, column 2, I included the mean centered size variables with one-year lags as additional control variables. These results lend more credence to the previous estimation: The lagged size variables are not statistically significant, while the main results remain unchanged. Moreover, in a test not shown here, when only including lagged size variables, neither the two size variables per se nor their interaction term is statistically significant. In sum, changes in commune relative size and team size are more likely to cause immediate changes in crop production and the contemporaneous size measures are more likely than the lagged measures to capture these effects.

Excluding the GLF Famine

Another concern is whether my empirical findings across the whole commune period might have been driven largely by the drastic fall in productivity associated with the GLF famine. To check whether this occurred, I drop the years before 1962 in table 6.2, column 3. The salient results remain unchanged, and the magnitude of the interaction coefficient gets even larger, suggesting that my findings are not driven by the first three years of the commune era.

Falsification Test

To evaluate the validity of my results, I employed a falsification test using the previous year's crop production as the dependent variable. Because commune relative size and team size and their interaction should not affect crop production in the previous year, I expect a null effect of the three variables on previous crop production. By contrast, if any statistical association is found between them, this result suggests an opposite causal direction—that is, agricultural performance effects commune relative size and team size, rather than vice versa.

In table 6.2, column 3, I conducted this falsification test using the size variable of one year and the previous year's crop production value as the dependent variable and found no statistically significant association between them. Although the falsification test per se should not be viewed as direct evidence for causation, the consistent result increases my confidence in these findings.

TABLE 6.2
Robustness and Falsification Analysis

| VARIABLES | DV: Crop per capita | | DV: Crop per capita in previous year |
	Additional control variables	Excluding GLF and famine	Falsification test
	(1)	(2)	(3)	(4)
Per capita crop production in neighboring counties	0.276*			
	(0.159)			
Institutional structure				
MC commune relative size	−0.050*	−0.042*	0.001	−0.043*
	(0.026)	(0.025)	(0.034)	(0.026)
MC team size	0.020	0.011	0.124	0.023
	(0.055)	(0.050)	(0.109)	(0.073)
MC commune relative size × MC team size	0.094**	0.104**	0.319**	0.073
	(0.045)	(0.040)	(0.153)	(0.055)
MC commune relative size (lag = 1)		−0.010		
		(0.022)		
MC team size (lag = 1)		−0.020		
		(0.035)		
MC commune relative size (lag = 1) × MC team size (lag = 1)		0.002		
		(0.033)		
Conventional inputs				
Land	0.220**	0.273**	0.288*	0.163
	(0.100)	(0.122)	(0.167)	(0.104)
Machine power	0.041*	0.039*	0.045	0.038*
	(0.021)	(0.021)	(0.027)	(0.020)
Labor	0.116	0.162	0.194	0.219*
	(0.136)	(0.137)	(0.153)	(0.128)
Fertilizer	0.012	0.023**	0.018	0.022**
	(0.008)	(0.011)	(0.012)	(0.011)
Rural population	−0.600***	−0.678***	−0.603**	−0.550***
	(0.208)	(0.238)	(0.268)	(0.207)
County fixed effect	yes	yes	yes	yes
Year fixed effect	yes	yes	yes	yes
Observations	2,030	2,004	1,731	2,006
R-squared (within, R^2)	0.451	0.432	0.360	0.423
No. of counties	117	117	117	117

Note: Neighboring counties are defined as other counties under the jurisdiction of the same prefecture; dependent and independent variables are logged; constant is included in the model but not reported; robust standard errors in parentheses are clustered at county level; *** $p<0.01$, ** $p<0.05$, * $p<0.1$.

DISCUSSION AND CONCLUSION

Using two decades of county-level data from Henan Province, I examined how changes in the size of the commune and its subunits affected the institution's agricultural productivity. Based on existing economic and social science theories, I developed hypotheses about the effects of commune size, brigade size, and team size on agricultural productivity and tested them using a detailed data set. This analysis reveals a potent interaction effect among communes, brigades, and teams of varying sizes on commune economic performance. This conclusion corroborates much of the existing theoretical literature on the relationship between organization and subunit size and productivity.

These results show that the marginal effect of team size varies with a commune's relative size: when commune size is small, smaller teams are more productive; when commune size is large, the negative effect of large teams is mitigated and even reversed. Reduced worker supervision in large teams seems to be mitigated by large communes that through economies of scale in public goods provision can improve agricultural productivity. Without sufficient capitalization, however, farmwork is more labor intensive, and the better worker supervision offered by small teams can produce more output. Hence, when teams are large, having larger communes can simplify agricultural planning and improve the allocation of productive factors.

Because different size subunits were assigned different tasks according to their relative size, local cadres were able to create interaction effects that strengthened or weakened certain features in ways that influenced agricultural productivity. In this way, the relative size of communes and their subunits constituted a third source of commune productivity—one that is not as readily observable as super-optimal investment and Maoism but nonetheless is a significant determinant.

But if there was an ideal commune-team ratio for each locality, why did some counties achieve a more productive balance than others? I observe a convergence toward an optimal commune-team ratio in some Henan counties, but not in all. For instance, of the 1,163 county-year observations whose average commune relative size is smaller than the sample median, 417 (36 percent) of them reduced their average team size. Accordingly, during the first half of the 1960s, commune relative size was frequently adjusted in many counties (figure 6.4), which may reflect county leaders' search for a "Goldilocks commune" that would maximize productivity. Since different size subunits had different tasks I argue that by varying their relative size local cadres were able to create interaction effects that strengthened or weakened certain features in ways that improved agricultural productivity. In my forthcoming article with Yang Feng in *Socius*, we provide strong evidence that such policy learning did indeed occur among the county-level officials who determined the size of the communes and its subunits.

Figure 6.8 suggests, that in accordance with the *Sixty Articles* discussed previously, local cadres' sought to create a commune organization structure that improved productivity. Each dot or circle's distance from zero represents the estimated advantage (if above the zero line) or disadvantage (if below the zero line) for agricultural production of a particular county-year observation compared with one with the combination of sample mean commune relative size and sample mean team size for that year. The solid dots represent those observations for which the commune organizational structure's estimated advantage or disadvantage is distinguishable from zero over the sample mean at a 95 percent confidence level. The circles indicate observations with insignificant estimated advantage or disadvantage, or those commune organizational structures that did not improve agricultural production by adjusting the size of the commune or team. The line,

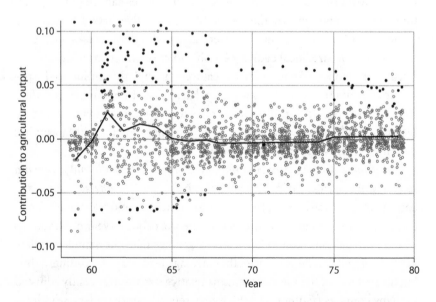

FIGURE 6.8. Predicted (dis)advantage of each observation in comparison to a pseudo case with sample mean commune relative size and mean team size.

which is computed based on table 6.1, column 4, averages all of the dots and circles, which represent the contribution of commune organizational structure to productivity for each year.[53]

The line indicates that the average contribution of commune organizational structure is the lowest in 1959, increased considerably until 1961, fluctuated during the first half of the 1960s, and remained stable for the duration of the commune era.[54] From 1959 to 1961, the annual average productivity contribution of commune organizational structure increased by 2.6 percentage points [0.023 − (−0.003) = 0.026]. Though by itself, this change is not statistically different from zero, but joint hypothesis testing reveals that I can reject (p-value = 0.023) the hypothesis that commune organizational structure contributes the same in each year of the first half of the 1960s (i.e., 1961–1965) as it did in 1959. Another joint test indicates that the productivity contribution of commune organizational structure in the first half of the 1960s is statistically distinguishable from an observation with sample mean commune relative size and team size (p-value = 0.024).

In counties that could not, for whatever reason, decrease team size, adjusting the relative size of communes was another way to increase productivity. When team size was large (i.e., the logged value exceeds 0.5), combining them with large communes was more productive than combining them with smaller communes (figure 6.7). In counties where commune size remained either too high or too low relative to team size, it seems likely that noneconomic considerations took precedence (see observations below the zero line in figure 6.8). One reason might have been topography of the land; another reason could be when political or military aspects of the commune's institutional mandate distorted the size of its subunits beyond their optimal economic ratio.

Unlike firms, whose optimal size is determined entirely by cost-benefit calculations, the commune's size was a product of its tripartite economic, political, and administrative mandate. The optimal commune size when all three components are considered may have been different than if only economic objectives had been considered. For instance, a smaller commune with smaller teams might have been best to improve economic performance, the dependent variable of this study, but in counties where military considerations were paramount, they may have had more influence on commune structure. In short, where and when political or military considerations, or just poor management, held sway, the commune's organizational structure was likely to be less productive.

Chapter Seven

BURYING THE COMMUNE

Implementing the household land contract scheme nationwide would not have been possible without Deng Xiaoping's support. The fact that it did not meet much resistance from central leaders had a lot to do with Deng's attitude. Though he did not comment much on the issue, he always showed support for views held by me, [Hu] Yaobang, and Wan Li.

—ZHAO ZIYANG[1]

INTRODUCTION

The notion that people at the lowest levels of society can unite to effect nationwide economic and political change is intoxicating. Chinese and foreigners alike are captivated by the story of the poor farmers who cast off the yoke of commune oppression: "disorganized, atomized individuals [who] behaved as if acting in concert."[2] People power, particularly for those raised in liberal democracies, just *feels* right. Unfortunately, however, especially in autocracies, the poor, weak, and vulnerable cannot effect peaceful, systematic change. The "truth," especially as it is presented to foreigners in official Chinese publications and meetings, is manipulated from above, such that, as Frederick Teiwes has observed, Western studies that adopt "the logic of official (or quasi-official) Chinese viewpoints" have serious "shortcomings."[3] The conventional view of commune abandonment detailed in chapter 1—that "the household responsibility system, enthusiastically embraced by peasants, spread throughout rural China [and] the central government acknowledged reality and officially endorsed the new system"—is among the more striking instances of foreigners echoing official Chinese interpretations.[4]

Decollectivization, like collectivization itself, was initiated by China's leaders and was cast as a popular movement to lend it legitimacy.

Households and low-level cadres could complain or drag their feet while implementing distasteful policies, but they could not coordinate dissent beyond their team, let alone bring down the entire nationwide commune system. The Chinese proverb that "on the top there is policy and on the bottom there is pushback" was as well known to Chinese farmers then as it is today. Indeed, among the dozens of former commune members interviewed for this study, *none* foresaw the institution's abandonment before it occurred in their locality, let alone believed that they or their local leaders had played any role in the decision to decollectivize. One former militia leader in Henan was unequivocal: "The order to decollectivize came from the provincial level."[5] In short, Chinese farmers chose neither to collectivize nor to decollectivize—just as they were forced into communes in 1958, they were forced out of them beginning in 1979.

An anti-commune faction led by veteran party leader Deng Xiaoping dismantled the commune for a distinctly *political* reason—that is, to gain control over China from a rival pro-commune faction led by Mao's chosen successor, Hua Guofeng. Among the three distinct political factions that existed on the eve of Mao's death, the commune was the primary policy disagreement. Ultimately, its fate was not decided by its economic performance or by grassroots demands, but rather by the political preferences of the winner of the factional struggle: Deng. To lend legitimacy to decollectivization, Deng's strategy to abandon the commune *intentionally* created, and then publicized, the perception that the farmers themselves initiated it. He encouraged allies at the provincial level to promote household farming, privatize commune enterprises, and expand rural markets and then broadcast farmers' improved living standards—first via provincial-level official press outlets and later using the national media. Recalling his decollectivization strategy in 1992, Deng said that many people had opposed a return to household-based agriculture, but rather than attack them, he waited until households began enjoying higher levels of consumption before expanding the practice nationwide.[6]

Setting the Stage

The previous chapters have set the stage for the dramatic conclusion of the commune, which this chapter tells in three acts. The chapter begins by identifying the three main rival political factions seeking to take over

China after Mao, along with their distinct visions for the commune—the radicals led by Jiang Qing, the loyalists led by Hua, and the reformers led by Deng. These three factions grew out of, but were not identical to, the three distinct economic policy lines of the late 1960s (i.e., the leftists, supporters of overall balance, and advocates of planned proportionate development, respectively) that were examined in chapter 3.

Act I documents the struggle to control the commune that took place in the two years preceding Mao's death. The big question throughout 1975 until Mao's death in September 1976 was who would lead the Dazhai movement. In a speech to the 3,700 participants at the September 1975 Dazhai Conference—the largest such gathering since 1962—Jiang publically challenged her rivals to revise the *Sixty Articles* (see appendix C), which had been the working regulations for the commune since 1962. In late 1975 and early 1976, as Deng worked to rehabilitate leaders ousted during the Cultural Revolution, he again came under criticism, and in April 1976, Jiang and Hua teamed up to remove him from office. At the end of Act I, in the summer of 1976, it seemed the radicals and their vision of an institution committed to "class struggle" had prevailed.

Act II opens with the death of Mao and the purge of the radicals, also known as the "Gang of Four." As Deng remained on the sidelines, Hua's loyalists took charge. They advocated their commune-based investment strategy and lobbed a continuous barrage of public attacks at both the radicals and reformers. At this point, Hua was working to fill Mao's big shoes, publicize his support from Mao, and identify the critical policy difference between him and Deng—that is, Hua's support for the commune, and Deng's longstanding opposition to it. Meanwhile, throughout 1977 and 1978, Deng's reform faction built support for decollectivization at the provincial level and gradually increased pressure on Hua's loyalists, who held sway in Beijing. The year 1978 was one of mixed messages, with loyalists calling for more agricultural investment under the commune, and Deng's faction advocating for more household consumption and team autonomy.

Act III concludes the story of the commune. The struggles of 1978 culminated in Deng's skillful manipulation of the Democracy Wall Movement to unseat his rivals at the Third Plenum of the National Party Congress' Eleventh Central Committee that December. After the crackdown on Democracy Wall, and under the guise of calling for greater team autonomy, improving the people's livelihoods, and ensuring continuity under the *Sixty Articles*, Deng's reform faction promoted the reintroduction of household production contracts as a means to increase consumption. Once reintroduced, household-based remuneration (known as *baochan daohu*) destroyed the commune's ability to extract resources for capital investment. These incremental steps toward decollectivization culminated at the Party Secretariat Work Conference in September 1980, with the release of Official Document No. 75, "Several Issues on Further Strengthening and Improving the Agricultural Production Responsibility System" (see appendix C). Promoted by Deng, Zhao Ziyang, Hu Yaobang, and Wan Li, among others, and over the objections of pro-commune provincial leaders, this document, more than any other single official directive, crippled the commune and spread decollectivization nationwide.

Meanwhile, Deng's reformers worked gradually and systematically to erode Maoism, the collectivist ideology that bound commune members to each other and the institution. At first, this was done by leveling indirect criticism at Maoist precepts (e.g., attacks on volunteerism and household austerity), then by placing Mao's wife and close associates on trial, and ultimately by aiming direct criticism at Mao's "erroneous left theses" in the "Resolution on Certain Questions in the History of Our Party" released on June 27, 1981. To replace Maoism, the reformers substituted improved household living standards as the determinant of political legitimacy under the slogans "practice is the sole criterion of truth" and "to get rich is glorious."

Finally, with its remuneration system destroyed, its "god" humanized, and its collectivist ethos and economic theories publically discredited, the commune collapsed. Collectively owned land, capital, and enterprises were distributed (primarily to local cadres-cum-entrepreneurs), prices for agricultural products were increased, the commune and its subunits were eliminated, and workpoints were abolished. The result was an increase in household consumption, a fall in rural investment, and annual fiscal deficits each year from 1979 to 1985.[7] Throughout decollectivization, this commune death dividend bought Deng and his political allies the time they needed to unseat their rivals and consolidate power. The last step was codified in October 1983, when the township was officially reestablished and the union of economic, political, and administrative authority that had existed for a quarter century under the commune was formally dissolved (see appendix C).

Factional Politics and Commune Abandonment

Factions (*zongpai*) in Chinese politics are informal networks of interdependent personal relationships that are neither fixed in membership nor immutable in ideology and policy preference.[8] Over time, factions change. However, between 1975 and 1979, the period when the commune's fate was decided, three principal political factions operated within the Communist Party of China (CPC) leadership: the "radicals," led by Jiang, the "loyalists" led by Hua, and the "reformers" led by Deng. Before Mao's death in September 1976, the radicals and the loyalists coexisted in an uneasy pro-commune coalition. After the radicals fell in October 1976, however, the struggle between the loyalists, who supported the commune, and the reformers, who did not, determined whether or not the institution survived.

Both the radicals and the loyalists supported the commune, but they had different visions for it. The radicals wanted to use the institution, first and foremost, to promote the idea of "class struggle" and to prevent a "capitalist resurrection" in the countryside. They believed that the 1970s commune was too capitalist, and they wanted to extinguish private plots, household cottage industries, and rural markets (i.e., the Three Small Freedoms), which, they argued, had produced dangerous "capitalist tendencies." On the other end of the political spectrum were the reformers, who wanted to forsake the commune entirely and return to household-based agriculture. In the middle were the loyalists, who supported the existing commune and the policies adopted at the 1970 Northern Districts Agricultural Conference (NDAC), which suppressed household consumption in favor of investments in capital and technologies that increased agricultural productivity. They fought to preserve and expand the existing commune system—first against attacks from Jiang's radicals on the political left, and then from Deng's reformers on the right. Simply put, the loyalists won the first struggle against the radicals in 1976, but they lost the second one against the reformers in 1978–1979. Ezra Vogel summarizes the loyalist position:

Until he fell from power, Hua Guofeng continued to support the Dazhai model and to advocate improving agricultural production by introducing new seeds, more chemical fertilizers, as well as water pumps, tractors, and other machinery. His goal was within five years to have a large tractor in every brigade and a small tractor in every production team.[9]

Before proceeding, it is important to identify the leading members of each faction and their respective positions on the eve of the September 1975 Dazhai Conference.

Jiang, China's first lady and a Politburo member, led the radicals. This faction also included Vice-Premier Zhang Chunqiao, a Politburo Standing Committee member and director of the General Department of the People's Liberation Army (PLA); Wang Hongwen, Vice-Chairman of the Central Committee and a Politburo Standing Committee member; Yao Wenyaun, editor of *Liberation Daily* (*Jiefang Ribao*), an official publication of the Shanghai Committee of the CPC, and editor of *Red Flag* (*Hongqi*), the party's leading journal; Mao Yuanxin, Mao's nephew and his Politburo liaison, who had been vice-chairman of Liaoning Revolutionary Committee; and Zhang Tiesheng, a member of the Standing Committee of the National People's Congress (NPC).

Led by Vice-Premier Hua, the loyalist faction (dubbed the "whateverists" because they were loyal to whatever Chairman Mao advocated) sought to preserve Mao's legacy and the commune system. This faction included a combination of senior party and military leaders who had either risen during or survived the Cultural Revolution. Among them were Beijing Mayor Wu De; Beijing Military Region Commander Chen Xilian; Mao's long-time personal bodyguard and Politburo member Wang Dongxing; Vice-Premier and Politburo member Ji Dengkui; and, most important for rural policy; Vice-Premier and Politburo member Chen Yonggui. Chen, it is worth recalling from chapter 2, served as party secretary for the famous Dazhai Brigade in the early to mid-1960s and was the person most closely associated with the 1970s commune's investment-driven growth strategy.[10]

First Vice-Premier Deng led a motley group of reformers—which Richard Baum has dubbed the "rehabilitated cadres faction" or the "practice faction"—whose "most vital common characteristic was their intense opposition to the Cultural Revolution, its leaders, and its legacy."[11] Prominent reformers included Guangdong Party Secretary Zhao Ziyang; Minister of Railways Wan Li; Vice-Chairman of the NPC Standing Committee Bo Yibo; Director of the State Council's Political Research Office Deng Liqun; Vice-Premier Wang Zhen; and former Vice-Premier Chen Yun, who remained a Central Committee member. Hu Yaobang, the former head of the Young Communist League, remained on the political sidelines in 1975, but he became a leading reformer after his rehabilitation. The reform faction was bound together by its members' shared experience of abuse during the Cultural Revolution and—after the fall of the radicals in late 1976—by their opposition to Hua's "loyalists" and the commune.[12]

Although they held diverse political and economic views, members of Deng's faction did agree on one overarching policy prescription: decollectivization. Achievement of this objective required the adoption of two sub-policies—one political and the other economic—each of which subverted the commune: an end to Maoist ideological indoctrination, and a return to the household as the basic accounting unit of rural China.

ACT I: LOYALISTS VERSUS THE RADICALS (1975-1976)

Scene 1: The 1975 Dazhai Conference

Between 1970 and 1975, the commune enjoyed broad political support and was not a major source of conflict in elite politics.[13] In June 1970, the Ministry of Agriculture and Forestry was established, and from August to October, the NDAC was held to promote Mao's commune-based development strategy. As the conference reconvened in Beijing, Mao's instructions to the delegates appeared in the *People's Daily*: "If Xiyang [county, the locale of Dazhai] can do it, why can't you do it? If one year isn't enough, isn't three years enough? Four or five years should surely be long enough."[14] From August to September 1971, Hua convened a national conference on farm mechanization, and in early 1972, he directed the Ministry of Agriculture and Forestry to prepare another major Dazhai Conference. In July 1974, the ministry held a preparatory meeting, and a year later, in mid-August 1975, Hua and Chen Yonggui led the small group that developed the conference agenda. The conference objectives, which did *not* include revising the *Sixty Articles*, were as follows:

- Exchanging experiences on learning from Dazhai and expanding the model to the county-level;
- Further developing the Dazhai campaign and rapidly transforming poor production teams; [and]
- Exchanging experiences of agricultural mechanization in order to reach Mao's goal of complete agricultural mechanization by 1980.[15]

Throughout 1975, as Mao's health worsened, a struggle emerged among the three factions about who should succeed him. Deng, who had been relegated to foreign affairs throughout 1974, was nominated by Mao and became first vice-premier in January 1975. Over the course of that year, as Premier Zhou Enlai's cancer worsened, his role became increasingly limited. Deng became de facto premier and accelerated his efforts to quietly rehabilitate comrades who had been branded as "rightists" during the Cultural Revolution and to cultivate a new generation of reform-minded provincial leaders.[16] As he gathered strength, Deng avoided confrontations and kept a low profile. Meanwhile, Jiang's radicals clashed with Hua's loyalists for control over the commune.

Between January and September 1975, in the run-up to the Dazhai Conference, the radicals and the loyalists struggled for control over the movement. That January, the Fourth NPC reaffirmed the protection of household sideline plots outlined in *Sixty Articles* as a necessary adjunct of the socialist economy. It also promulgated a new constitution, which at Mao's request included the Four Big Freedoms: the right to speak out freely, to air views fully, to hold debates, and to write big-character posters.[17] At this time, just as in the period from 1970 to 1971, "economic development superseded class struggle," observes Zweig.[18]

The radicals responded in February 1975 with a series of editorials in the *People's Daily* criticizing the Three Small Freedoms, which they claimed produced dangerous "capitalist tendencies," and advocating the eradication of rural markets.[19] In the spring of 1975, the loyalists responded with articles in *Red Flag* magazine and other outlets that supported rural markets, backed the team as the basic accounting unit, and opposed restrictions on private plots and household sidelines.[20] On July 2, 1975, Jiang sent a letter to the All-China Conference on Professional Work in Agriculture calling on delegates to promote class struggle and avoid revisionism. At the conference, these comments were trumpeted by Wang Hongwen, thus setting the stage for a confrontation between the radicals and the loyalists at the 1975 Dazhai Conference, which began on September 15.[21]

The 1975 Dazhai Conference, which included the party chief from every county in China, became the venue for a showdown over the commune. Like the NDAC five years earlier, it began with a visit and conference at Dazhai Brigade in Dazhai Commune, Xiyang County, Shaanxi, between September 15 and 22, and concluded with meetings among top central agricultural officials and provincial leaders in Beijing from September 23 to October 15. As the conference got under way, Mao told former British Prime Minister Edward Heath that he was anxious to increase economic development.[22]

Deng, Hua, and Jiang each sat at the dais and addressed the delegates. To avoid any surprises, all county-level leaders' reports were scripted in advance by writing groups.[23] Senior PLA representatives also attended the conference, and in the summer of 1975, the navy's political department established a Dazhai study group. "Whatever the precise mix of belief, calculation, or simply following orders, this reflected a broad elite predisposition to accept the legitimacy of the Dazhai model," Teiwes and Warren Sun explain.[24] Figures 7.1 and 7.2 depict images from the 1975 Dazhai Conference.

According to Wu Jicheng, a senior member of the leaders' guard under Wang Dongxing who was present at the conference, the radicals sought to co-opt "the red banner of Dazhai" to serve their own purposes. Rather than attack Dazhai, Jiang—recognizing Mao and Zhou's strong support for the conference—instead sought to capture the movement by "attacking Hua and Dazhai for selling out to revisionism."[25] To serve her political ambitions, Jiang aimed to change the commune's focus from economic development (i.e., capital construction and agricultural productivity) to revolutionary politics (i.e., class struggle and antirevisionism).[26] "I've come

FIGURE 7.1. The 1975 National Conference on Learning from Dazhai in Agriculture.
Source: Zuo Xiaoqin, *National Conference on Learning from Dazhai in Agriculture,* Voice of China, accessed December 6, 2016, http://bbs.voc.com.cn/archiver/tid-2754371.html.

FIGURE 7.2. Hua (right) and Chen Yonggui (left) inspect grain on the sidelines of the 1975 Dazhai Conference. *Source: The Great Life of Chairman Hua*, undated, 51.

to fight the revisionist line," she reportedly told participants, "Dazhai is lag-ging behind politically and following the revisionist line."[27]

Jiang's attacks began on September 12, three days before the start of the conference, when she gave an unscheduled two-hour lecture to county leaders. In using the novel *The Water Margin* to launch a metaphorical attack on Deng, Jiang was suggesting that he was quietly working to make Mao a "figurehead."[28] "He acted according to the principle of 'concealment.' That is, concealing his fierce appearance and waiting for the opportunity to come," Jiang reportedly said, adding: "The enemy is buried deep within the Party in disguise. Therefore, don't underestimate the discussion of this novel or take it as a matter belonging only to literary and art circles. The purpose of criticizing *Water Margin* is to warn the people about capitula-tors inside our Party."[29]

When the conference began, Jiang "severely disturbed" the proceedings with repeated calls to turn Dazhai into a revolutionary political struggle against the "capitalist class." On the first day of the conference, she gave another speech that emphasized the threat of a "capitalist restoration" in the countryside and that warned delegates that "peasants still cherish the ideology of a petty agricultural economy."[30] To "thoroughly get rid of the pernicious influence of Liu Shaoqi's revisionism," Jiang placed an empha-sis on "class struggle" and advocated for a "mass rectification campaign among the people." In Mao's name, she called for revising the *Sixty Articles* to strip the commune of its capitalist vestiges: "The capitalist restoration in agriculture is dangerous. It is reported that in some production teams there still exists the revisionist policy of the Three Small Freedoms and One Guarantee (*sanzi yibao*). Isn't it strange?"[31]

Jiang's attack on the One Guarantee (i.e., *yibao* or household contract farming) was significant because it relinked that policy, which Deng had advocated in the early 1960s, but Mao had condemned, with the Three Small Freedoms (*sanzi*), which both Mao and Hua had supported and had remained national policy under the *Sixty Articles* since 1962. In this way, Jiang sought to tie the loyalists to the reformers and to cast both as "revi-sionists" and "capitalist-roaders." When word of Jiang's comments reached Mao, he prohibited them from being distributed: "Don't publish the talk, don't play the recording or print the text," he reportedly instructed.[32]

Although Mao had ordered Deng to represent the government at the con-ference, this directive was probably his way of coercing Deng's compliance with the conference's commune-led, investment-based development agenda.[33] In his September 15 opening speech, Deng identified agriculture's importance as one of the Four Modernizations, and called the Dazhai Conference the most important meeting of leading cadres from various levels since the 1962 conference of seven thousand cadres that ended the Great Leap Forward (GLF).[34] As Deng began his remarks, Jiang interrupted him, saying, "Vice-Premier Deng was sent by Chairman Mao, who asked him to deliver some remarks."[35] Jiang's comment implied that Deng did not attend the Dazhai Conference by choice. In a similar ploy, although she knew the provincial party secretaries were not invited to the first part of the conference, Jiang criticized them for failing to attend and for paying insufficient attention to agriculture.[36] Jiang interrupted Deng several more times during his speech, including once to dispute his claim that in some prefectures and counties grain production had not reached pre-1949 levels.[37] Deng maintained his composure and did not respond publicly to Jiang's provocations.[38]

Whether or not Deng had wanted to do so, he could not openly oppose Mao's beloved Dazhai model in 1975. His desire to keep a low profile while he rehabilitated his allies required that he support the campaign as a "political fact of life, a requirement of political survival," Teiwes and Sun explain.[39] Deng, who together with Liu Shaoqi, had tried and failed to undermine Dazhai in 1964–1965, attended at least four sessions of the 1975 Dazhai Conference. On September 15, Deng delivered his "important remarks," on September 27 and again on October 4, he delivered his speech "Things Must Be Put in Order in All Fields," and on October 15, he was present when Hua gave his full conference report.[40] In his September 27 and October 4 speeches, Deng advocated increasing household consumption: "Commune members' income is very low, and some owe debts. Under these circumstances, can we be satisfied?"[41] He also called for party consolidation, urged delegates to link Maoism to "practice," and warned against an overemphasis on "class struggle" at the expense of "scientific development." Deng's speech cautioned:

[Mao Zedong] has talked about the four modernizations and has said that class struggle, the struggle for production, and scientific development are the three basic components of social practice. Today, the last component has been dropped and people are even afraid to discuss it, its very mention being regarded as a crime. How can this possibly be right? I'm afraid that the problem of how to study, propagate and implement Mao Zedong Thought systemically exists in quite a few fields. Mao Zedong Thought is closely bound up with practice in every sphere, with principles, policies and methods in every line of work.[42]

Later, during the small high-level meetings in Beijing, several reformist provincial-level leaders (including Zhao Ziyang and Zhejiang's Tan Qilong) disputed whether the Dazhai model should be expanded to the county level and whether brigade-level accounting should be introduced. Unable to stomach criticism of his cherished Dazhai model, Chen Yonggui lost his temper and a shouting match ensued. Under these circumstances, the issue of brigade accounting was shelved, but expansion of the Dazhai model to counties was not.[43]

On October 15, Hua gave the final conference report titled "Mobilize the Whole Party, Make Greater Efforts to Develop Agriculture and Strive to Build Dazhai-Type Counties" (see appendix C). This report, which was published in the *People's Daily* and circulated throughout the party as Document No. 21, stridently advocated the Dazhai model of investment-led growth and said that the existing three-level commune structure and the use of the team as the basic accounting unit were "in harmony with the growth of the productive forces in the countryside."[44] Document No. 21 remained the loyalists' foremost agricultural policy directive until February 1978, when Hua announced his ill-fated Ten-Year Plan.

Hua's twin objectives were to build a winning political coalition and "trigger a 'high tide' in rural capital construction."[45] He promoted "the superiority of the people's commune as an institution large in size and with a high degree of public ownership," which he compared favorably to "features of small production." "The people's communes have great vitality and are promoting the development of all kinds of undertakings in the countryside."[46] Under them, Hua explained, "better conditions have been created for the development of mechanized farming. In the course of farmland capital construction, the collective concept and sense of organization and discipline of the peasants are greatly enhanced and they think more of the collective and show greater zeal in building socialism."[47]

Hua's speech called for expanding the existing commune-led investment strategy to improve "grain, oil-bearing crops and pig production."[48] He praised the expansion of agricultural investment that had taken place under the Dazhai model "since 1970"; reiterated Mao's call for the complete mechanization of agriculture by 1980; and advocated expanding "capital construction," "animal husbandry," "side-occupations," and "training a mighty contingent of people for mechanized farming."[49] To "raise labor productivity in agriculture," Hua was unequivocal that the commune had been a great success and should remain China's foremost rural institution: "The expansion of commune and brigade-run enterprises strengthens the economy at the commune and brigade levels; it has effectively helped the poorer brigades and teams, accelerated farm production, supported national construction and speeded up the pace of mechanization in agriculture."[50]

Echoing the 1970 NDAC report (see appendix C) and evoking notions of the worker-peasant alliance, Hua said more commune and brigade enterprises and agricultural mechanization would

bring into play the role of the people's commune as an organization that combines industry, agriculture, commerce, education, and military affairs, in enabling the commune to display its superiority—big in size and with a high degree of public ownership—and in narrowing the difference between town and country, worker and peasant and between manual and mental labor.[51]

Politically, unlike Deng, Hua supported Mao's collectivist ideology, self-reliance, and household austerity as components of a collectivist ethos that bound members to "the country and the collective," noting that "Dazhai's fundamental experience lies in its adherence to the principle of putting proletarian politics in command and placing Mao Zedong Thought in the lead, to the spirit of self-reliance and hard struggle and to the communist style of loving the country and the collective."[52]

Immediately after Hua's speech, Jiang confronted him and Chen Yong-gui and accused them of revisionism. "To put it mildly, that's a revisionist report!" she reportedly said.[53] The radicals' resistance to Hua's vision of the commune intensified as they sought to wrest control of the Dazhai movement. They viewed Hua's emphasis on production, capital construction, and mechanization as support for the repugnant "theory of the productive forces."[54] Yao Wenyuan prevented Hua's speech from being printed in the *Red Flag* and claimed that it "does not study how to attend to revolution in rural work."[55] He instructed the *People's Daily* not to "play up Dazhai in everything you print."[56] In February 1976, Yao ordered the national media organs under his control to criticize Hua's agricultural and rural industrial development program, and Zhang Tiesheng traveled to Dazhai to give a speech challenging Hua's approach.[57]

Meanwhile, in Shanghai, Zhang Chunqiao prevented party work teams from implementing Document No. 21, reportedly arguing, "who knows whether the education in the basic line is correct or not!"[58] In April, Chen reiterated Hua's position at a conference in Wuxi, Jiangsu, but at agricultural conferences in May in Suzhou and June in Shanghai, local cadres criticized him for abandoning class struggle.[59] Despite radical opposition, in the spring of 1976, under the old slogan "Grasp revolution by promoting production," Hua and Chen worked to maintain control over the Dazhai Campaign and to implement its investment-based agenda nationwide.

Scene 2: Deng's Purge

In late 1975, Deng came under substantial political pressure from Mao's fraying coalition of radicals and loyalists. In late November, Deng declined Mao's request to draft a Politburo resolution supporting the Cultural Revolution, thus precipitating the beginning of the "Counterattack the Right-Deviationist Reversal-of-Verdicts Trend" Campaign and his removal from managing day-to-day government affairs.[60] On February 17, 1976, Deng was accused of rendering class struggle secondary instead of taking it as the "key link."[61] On March 2, he was attacked in the *People's Daily* as "the unrepentant man on the capitalist road; who is the origin of the rightist wind of reversal of verdicts, the man who opposed collectivization and communization."[62] A week later, Deng was decried as "the person who blew the rightist wind to reverse verdicts, who before the great Cultural Revolution followed the revisionist line of Liu Shaoqi."[63]

On April 5, 1976, the traditional Chinese day of mourning known as *Qingming*, thousands of Beijing residents descended on Tiananmen Square to honor Premier Zhou, who had died with little fanfare in January. The mourners were brutally suppressed by security forces aligned with the leftists and loyalists, who then collaborated to frame Deng for the protests and, with Mao's approval, had him removed from all official and party posts.[64]

On April 7, based "on the proposal of Chairman Mao," the Politburo announced two resolutions. The first promoted Hua from "temporary and acting" premier to permanent status, and appointed him to the Politburo Standing Committee as "first Vice-Chairman." The second "dismissed Deng Xiaoping from all posts both inside and outside the Party, while allowing him to keep his Party membership so as to see how he will behave in the future."[65] Richard Thornton highlights the split between the radicals and loyalists that quickly emerged after Deng's ouster:

Up to this point, Mao had managed to hold together his diverse leadership coalition, including its "radical" element. The Politburo decisions of April 7 in particular could not have been made had the so-called Gang of Four been in opposition to Mao. Yet even as Mao was elevating his chosen successor to a position of prominence, his coalition began to crumble.[66]

Emboldened by Deng's departure and empowered by Mao Yuanxin's position as the gatekeeper to Mao, the radicals gained the upper hand in their struggle to assert control over the Dazhai movement and produced what Zweig calls "the most radical policy wind in rural China since 1968–1969." Yao Wenyuan argued that the new "Criticize Deng Campaign" and the effort to root out revisionists and class enemies should guide all party work, including the Dazhai Campaign. Around the country, high school students were organized by the hundreds to participate in mass rallies to attack Deng and support his removal from all posts (figure 7.3). In a meeting

FIGURE 7.3. High school students rally in Fuzhou, Fujian, in the spring of 1976 under a banner that reads, "Firmly support Communist Party Central Committee's decision to remove Deng Xiaoping of all party and government positions."
Source: Image provided by Tang Ying.

of representatives of provincial propaganda departments in June 1976, officials were told to support radical policies or risk being branded as capitalist
roaders.[67] Rural areas in a half-dozen provinces reportedly closed markets,
restricted private plots and sidelines, and introduced experiments with
brigade-level accounting. The triumph of the radicals proved to be short
lived, however. By September, Mao was dead, and the following month, Hua,
with support from the military and the reformers (represented by Ye Jianying
and Li Xiannian, respectively) had the Gang of Four arrested for treason.[68]

ACT II: REFORMERS VERSUS LOYALISTS (1977-1978)

Scene 1: Hua on Top

As Deng waited on the sidelines, he penned a letter to Hua congratulating
him on his ouster of the radicals and pledging his support for Hua as Mao's
successor.[69] Doubtful of Deng's sincerity, Hua worked to distinguish himself from his rival by demonstrating Mao's support for him, indicating his
own support for the commune, and painting Deng as a revisionist. At Mao's
funeral on October 10, Hua, flanked by members of his loyalist faction,
publicly attacked Deng and linked him to both Liu Shaoqi and Lin Biao:

Chairman Mao himself initiated and led the Great Proletarian Cultural Revolution, which smashed the schemes of Liu Shaoqi, Lin Biao, and Deng Xiaoping for
restoration, criticized their counterrevolutionary revisionist line, and enabled us to
seize back that portion of leading power in the party and state they had usurped.[70]

Hua's funeral message warned that "anyone who tampers with Chairman
Mao's directives . . . and anyone who practices splittism or engages in con-
spiracies is bound to fail."[71] Then, during a massive anti-Gang rally on
October 24, Wu De announced: "We shall continue to criticize Deng."[72] Two
days later, on October 26, Hua ordered the party's propaganda apparatus
to criticize the Gang of Four and Deng simultaneously. Criticisms of Deng
continued for more than a month, culminating with his condemnation by
Wu De in a speech to the NPC Standing Committee on November 30, 1976.[73]
    Another way Hua sought to discredit Deng was by approving the pub-
lication of the fifth volume of Mao's *Selected Works*, which contained
a previously unpublished speech from 1956 entitled "On The Ten Major

Relationships." After its release in December 1976, which coincided with the Second Dazhai Conference, the official press extensively quoted the speech within which Mao laid out two alternative economic development strategies: "One is to develop agriculture and light industry less, and the other is to develop them more. The second approach will lead to a greater and faster development of heavy industry and, since it ensures the livelihood of the people, it will lay a more solid foundation."[74]

Hua closely aligned himself with Mao's development strategy and reminded everyone that Deng had supported the other position. He created this association by releasing an editorial note Mao penned in 1971 titled "The Fundamental Way Out for Agriculture Lies in Mechanization," which illustrated the differences between Mao and Liu Shaoqi (and implicitly Deng). The article revealed that Mao had taken the position that collectivization should precede mechanization, whereas Liu had taken the opposite view. "Chinese leaders reading the article knew perfectly well that Liu and Deng were the two leaders who had opposed Mao's strategy, even though Deng's name was not mentioned," Thornton explains.[75]

With Jiang and Deng absent from the scene, the loyalists triumphantly convened the Second Dazhai Conference, which ran from December 12–27, 1976. In his conference report, Chen Yonggui, now in charge of agricultural policy, condemned the Gang as ultra-*rightists*, and sought to attract residual radical support to the loyalist camp. Although the politics of Chen's message were tricky, his policies remained identical to those he and Hua had advocated the year before: "Further consolidate and expand the collective economy of the people's communes, and make a leap from small-scale farming with animal-drawn farm implements to large-scale mechanized farming," said Chen, continuing that "it is necessary to give full scope to the people's communes' advantages of being bigger in scale and having more developed socialist nature than the former agricultural co-ops and consolidate and develop the people's commune system."[76] Furthermore, Chen, citing Mao, called for expanding commune and brigade enterprises:

We must follow Chairman Mao's instructions and energetically expand commune and brigade-run enterprises and strengthen the economy at the commune and brigade levels. Considerable progress has been made in developing commune and brigade-run enterprises since the start of the Great Proletarian Cultural Revolution. By 1975, 90 percent of the communes and 60 percent of the brigades in the country had set up enterprises totaling over 800,000. We should give wholehearted support to such newborn things as commune and brigade-run enterprises in line with Chairman Hua's instructions in his letter on the expansion of commune and brigade-run enterprises.[77]

While he enjoyed the upper hand in late 1976 and 1977, Hua continued to advance his commune-based rural development agenda. In the summer of 1977, he chaired the Rural Capital Construction Conference in Xiyang, Shaanxi, where Chen gave another speech calling for field and water conservation projects to be built to increase collective productivity, not for "narrow personal gains and losses." To create a "high tide" of capital construction, Chen argued for expanding competition among local units, with a cadre's redness to be determined by his enthusiasm for collective production. By October 1977, more than 390,000 such projects were under way, and by mid-November more than 80 million laborers were involved.[78]

On December 11, 1977, the *People's Daily* heralded yet another major conference calling for the acceleration of agricultural investment to increase output, and announced that "our historical experience proves that each new leap forward in the national economy is invariably preceded by a new leap forward in agriculture."[79] Following the conference, on December 19, 1977, the Central Committee published its "Outline Report for the Politburo on the Working Forum for Popularizing Dazhai Counties," which called for a "high tide" in agricultural mechanization and rural capital construction, and a "mini-Great Leap" in agricultural output, particularly in grain production.[80] The report also "recognized that team accounting was appropriate for most of rural China," but it offered an important olive branch to residual radicals by calling on party committees at all levels to "create the necessary conditions" for an eventual transition to brigade-level accounting.[81]

Scene 2: Deng's Return

Throughout 1977 and 1978, behind a public façade of "unity and stability," a factional struggle raged between Hua and Deng that ultimately determined the fate of the commune and its more than 800 million members. Each side claimed that its policies represented the will of the people, yet neither faction sought to empower the masses or give them a voice in policymaking or leadership selection. Even as the loyalist and reformist factions held contentious policy debates in Beijing and provincial capitals, both agreed that grassroots change would be dangerous. According to Baum, both "wanted the benefits of modernity without the destabilizing effects of spontaneous, uncontrolled social mobilization."[82] They agreed on "Four Cardinal Principles," which constituted the ground rules for their power struggle: unwavering allegiance to socialism, the people's democratic dictatorship, Communist Party leadership, and Marxism-Leninism-Mao Zedong Thought.[83] In short, all agreed that the CPC alone would determine China's economic and political policies in accordance with socialist (not liberal democratic) precepts. They disagreed, however, on who should lead the CPC and which policies should be adopted.[84]

In January 1977, after an investigation led by Ye Jianying, Deng's offense was downgraded from an "antagonistic contradiction" to a "contradiction among the people." Deng could now be rehabilitated, although the Politburo was deadlocked on what posts he should be given. Hua then directed each of the two hundred–odd Central Committee members to provide a written opinion on Deng's case. This directive not only delayed Deng's reinstatement, but also gave Hua a list of Deng's political supporters. By early March, the reports were in, and between March 7 and 21, 1977, the Politburo contentiously debated Deng's case. Li Xiannian, Wang Zhen, Xu Shiyou, Wei Guoqing, and Chen Yun all supported Deng's restoration, whereas Hua and his loyalists dissented. To resolve the deadlock, Ye Jianying brokered a compromise whereby Hua agreed to make two concessions: he would agree that Deng's work in 1975 had included both "successes and shortcomings" and that the April 4 Qingming protests had started as a "reasonable" peaceful homage to Premier Zhou. For his part, Deng agreed to reiterate his support for Hua, acknowledge his own shortcomings in 1975, and not besmirch Mao's legacy. Hua then agreed to reinstate Deng to the four posts he had held in 1976: first vice-chairman of the CPC, vice-chairman of the Military Affairs Commission, first vice-premier, and PLA chief of staff.[85]

After his return, however, Deng began quietly pursuing a half-dozen strategies to promote the same "household responsibility system" he and Liu Shaoqi had advocated in the early 1960s. In the name of improving rural living conditions, he initiated incremental changes alongside restatements of the commune's essential governing document, the *Sixty Articles*, which Deng himself had helped draft in 1961. Deng also mobilized provincial-level supporters to pressure the center, called on teams to resist extraction from the commune and brigade, used Hua's attempts to gain residual radical support in late 1976 and early 1977 to paint the loyalists as radicals, used Hua's unswerving adherence to Mao to call his judgment into question, questioned the value of Mao's collectivist ideology, and humanized the once venerated Chairman by identifying his shortcomings.

The decision to reinstate Deng in spring 1977 triggered a struggle over the provincial party secretaryships. The leadership of at least fourteen provinces hung in the balance, and when the smoke cleared, Hua had inserted his supporters into only two positions, whereas Deng's coalition had gained control of eleven provinces and kept Zhao Ziyang in Sichuan.[86] Deng and his provincial-level allies then proceeded to "create a rightist wind that popularized the policy changes even before central leaders, still strongly influenced by proto-Maoists, formally accepted them," Zweig explains.[87] Another result of the Dengist faction's control over the provinces was the expanded criticism of Hua in some regional press outlets. In Sichuan, Guizhou, and Yunnan, Deng's political powerbase, provincial press outlets painted Hua as a radical leftist.[88] For his part, Hua controlled the central media organs, which continued to condemn the Gang of Four and implicitly criticize Deng.

To boost household consumption, the reformers advocated piece rates, the *Sixty Articles*, and team autonomy. In fact, these policies had continued unabated in nearly all communes throughout 1976 and 1977, but such proclamations suggested that they were under attack by Hua's "ultra-leftist" Dazhai model. Wan Li, who became party secretary of Anhui in June 1977, was the most brazen critic of the commune. After touring Anhui's poorest areas in the summer of 1977, Wan advanced the "Provincial Party Committee Six-Point Proposal," which recommended that (1) production teams, depending on the circumstances and as long as production responsibilities were met, allow certain tasks in the field to be assigned to small workgroups or individuals; (2) the autonomy of production teams be respected by higher levels; (3) quotas assigned to the production teams and individual members be reduced; (4) produce be distributed to members according to their work, not their needs; (5) grain allocation reflect the interests of the nation, the collective, and the individual; and (6) households be permitted to work on their own private plots and sell the produce at local markets.[89] Although points 4, 5, and 6 merely affirmed existing policy, points 1, 2, and

3 challenged the investment-driven growth strategy advocated by Hua and Chen Yonggui a year earlier at the Second Dazhai Conference.

In November 1977, Wan Li assembled Anhui's county party secretaries and instructed them to implement his six-point proposal. Against push-back and "lingering concerns," Vogel notes, Wan stood firm and declared that "any methods or policies that interfere with the advancement of production are wrong."[90] He won the day, and in early 1978, under the guise of the *Sixty Articles*, Anhui implemented the proposal, which reduced the size of agricultural work units and permitted contracted production to households. According to Vogel, Deng approved Wan Li's six-point proposal:

At the time of Wan Li's six-point proposal, national policy explicitly prohibited contracting down to the household and Wan Li could not oppose national policy. But when Deng saw the Anhui Party Committee's six-point proposal, produced under Wan Li's leadership, he, like a number of other officials, immediately affirmed the value of the experiment.[91]

Meanwhile, in November 1977, Jilin fixed its commune extraction rates at a maximum of 10 percent, and in Sichuan, Zhao Ziyang promulgated a provincial document affirming the *Sixty Articles*. Gansu followed suit the following March.[92] In December 1977, the *People's Daily* praised Zhao for introducing a provincial initiative advocating the distribution of more collective income to the household.[93] The goal, as Zhao explained on Sichuan provincial radio, was to "press the center (the commune and brigade) and guarantee the two ends (the household and the state)."[94] On February 1, 1978, Deng met Zhao in Sichuan, told him about Anhui's six-point proposal, and encouraged him to follow Wan's lead. Zhao, who had already begun similar experiments, quickly developed his own twelve-point program.[95] By reaffirming the *Sixty Articles*, Deng's provincial-level supporters appeared to be reinforcing existing policy. In hindsight, however, is it clear that these proclamations provided political cover for them to promote household-based farming.[96]

Writings and speeches like Wan's six points, which conveyed the team's interests in ways that placed them at odds with the commune and brigade, tore the institution's subunits apart. Teams were told that they would be better off without the commune and brigades extracting their income. The critique of Mao's advocacy of selflessness (i.e., voluntarism) reasoned that farmers should support team rather than brigade ownership. "The reformers gave team leaders a stake in the reforms," Zweig explains, thus intentionally creating the misperception that decollectivization was initiated at the local level.[97]

Collective remuneration was attacked under the ostensibly innocuous slogan "Carry out rural economic policy" (luoshi nongcun jingji zhenge). To increase household consumption at the collective's expense, Deng's provincial-level supporters encouraged households to emphasize their private plot and cottage enterprises. In early 1978, even as Hua remained supreme in Beijing, opposition to the loyalists and support for household contract farming was galvanized using official provincial press outlets, public speeches, and provincial party meetings. In January and February 1978, the People's Daily reemphasized the role of the private sector in the rural economy under the Sixty Articles.[98] In April 1978, the People's Daily commended the party committee in Qidong County, Jiangsu, for ordering its communes and brigades to return 19 million yuan they had extracted from their teams.[99]

In March 1978, Deng told the Political Research Office at the State Council that he supported "payment according to labor" and opposed Dazhai workpoints.[100] In Red Flag, Wan Li advocated the "responsibility system" (zirenzhi). To improve worker oversight, Wan proposed that subteam workgroups, akin to the Mutual Aid Teams of the mid-1950s, be assigned specific tasks and rewarded a fixed number of workpoints.[101] This policy turned compensation into a private, rather than a public, process—one that was a small step from direct cash payments to households for agricultural products. Household contract farming eliminated the need for team meetings to evaluate worker performance and disseminate Maoism. Without regular interaction with other team members and exposure to a common collectivist ideology, commune members' sense of togetherness withered. Although many commune and brigade leaders were placated by the privatization of collective property, household contracting faced stiff resistance from committed local cadres whose power to extract and invest team resources was eroded. Peter Nolan and Gordon White observe that the "provisions for team autonomy, propaganda paeans to enterprising households and individuals, and a diminution of the power of higher levels to interfere" increased household income at the expense of local enforcement capacity.[102]

At the national level, Chen Yonggui, still vice-premier in charge of agriculture, accused Wan Li of secretly promoting family farming, and in

March 1979, the *People's Daily* called for "maintaining the three-level ownership structure with the team as the basic accounting unit" (i.e., the commune) and criticized those who supported a return to household-based agriculture.[103] Wan, emboldened by support from Deng, replied to Chen: "You say you are speaking from the Dazhai experience; I say Dazhai is an ultra-leftist model . . . You go your way and I'll go mine . . . Don't impose your views on me and I won't impose mine on you. As for who is right and who is wrong, let's see which way works best."[104] At another meeting in Beijing, Wan responded bluntly to another critic by comparing his physical appearance to a fat pig and shot back: "You have plenty to eat. The peasants are thin because they do not have enough to eat. How can you tell the peasants they can't find a way to have enough to eat?"[105] In June 1979, Deng advised Wan to be less confrontational: "You don't need to engage in debates, just go ahead, that's all. Seek truth from facts."[106]

The loyalists' counteroffensive looked strong in February 1978 at the Second Plenary Session of the Eleventh Central Committee, when Hua announced the long-delayed Ten-Year Plan (1976–1985), which was issued at the Fifth National People's Congress later that month. On the basis of a document drafted by the State Council in 1975, this ambitious investment plan marked the last time the commune and the Dazhai model were prominently featured in an official government directive. The plan included Hua's familiar calls to expand agricultural investment to increase production and "consolidate and develop the people's communes."[107]

We must mobilize all party members, greatly expand agriculture, deeply develop the movement to Learn from Dazhai in Agriculture and to universalize Dazhai Counties, *consolidate and develop the people's communes'* collective economy, administer state farms well, and build agriculture based on large-scale adoption of modern technology and mechanization, so that agricultural production has a big development.[108] (Italics added for emphasis)

The Ten-Year Plan and its investment-based growth strategy caused what Baum has called a "flying leap" in agricultural investment in 1978 (see figure 3.1). In response, Deng's supporters, including Chen Yun, called for a sharp reduction in capital investment and an increase in household consumption. Economic theorist Wu Jiang argued that the most important goal of a socialist society was to "secure the maximum satisfaction of the constantly rising material and cultural requirements of the people."[109] Under pressure from reformers, Hua's Ten-Year Plan was aborted, and the CPC Central Committee approved plans to increase household consumption on June 23, 1978. These plans were adopted as the "Movement to Lighten the Peasants Burden" and were promulgated as a directive and announced by the *People's Daily* on July 5, 1978.[110] The campaign was also known as the Movement to Study Xiangxiang Experience, a reference to a county 15 miles from Mao's birthplace and under Xiangtan Prefecture, Hunan, where Hua had once been party secretary. Observers might have been forgiven for suspecting that Hua, not Deng, had promulgated the initiative.[111]

In the run-up to the Third Plenum, Hua supported the proinvestment policies adopted at the 1970 NDAC and affirmed at the 1975 and 1976 Dazhai Conferences. Deng, by contrast, was quietly "initiating major agricultural reforms in the provinces" intended to increase household consumption and reduce capital investment.[112] These diametrically opposed lines made 1978 "a year of uncertainty," Zweig explains.[113] Contradictory and inconsistent instructions from the center and province encouraged communes in some areas (e.g., Jilin, Shaanxi, and Jiangsu) to experiment with brigade-level accounting, while others (e.g., Sichuan, Anhui, and Gansu) were encouraged to experiment with household contracting. The climax of incoherence came at the State Council's July 1978 Rural Capital Construction Conference, which—under the banner of the *Sixty Articles*—advocated both increased investment and team independence. Stuck between pro-commune and anti-commune lines, delegates called for a high tide of capital construction, while also forbidding the expropriation of team labor, material, and capital. They emphasized the need to improve existing capital and condemned careless new projects. Under these circumstances, Zweig observes, risk-adverse local cadres generally concluded that "it was safest to avoid any changes."[114]

ACT III: POWER CONSOLIDATION AND DECOLLECTIVIZATION (1979-1983)

Scene 1: Democracy Wall Movement

The Democracy Wall Movement, led by many former Red Guards and returned Sent-Down youth now in their late twenties and early thirties, unwittingly played a vital role in securing the reformers' victory. In the last months of 1978, Deng manipulated their discontent over the abuses of the Cultural Revolution to paint the loyalists as radicals. Then, after securing his position, he turned on his erstwhile democratic allies in early 1979, condemned them as anarchists and criminals, and threw their leaders into labor camps.[115]

Deng stoked the discontent of the Democracy Wall Movement, which was ostensibly protected under the Four Big Freedoms, and used it to undermine the loyalists and their Maoist ideology. The protest movement, which was in full swing during the December 12–22, 1978, Third Plenum, "was allowed to go on for so long because it was used in the leadership power struggle and it was helpful to Deng," Merle Goldman explains. "Deng took advantage of this dissent from below—the demands of the Democracy Wall activists for political and economic reforms—to help oust the Maoists."[116] Goldman describes Deng's tactics:

When wall posters appeared on Xidan Wall in the fall of 1978 denouncing Mao and other officials associated with the Gang of Four and demanding political and economic reforms, Deng, in interviews with foreign journalists in late November 1978, expressed approval of the posters. As these journalists then relayed Deng's approval to the demonstrators at the wall, their numbers swelled into the thousands and wall posters spread to other walls in Beijing and to other cities.[117]

After Deng secured his political position at the Third Plenum, however, he "no longer needed the grassroots support of the Democracy Wall Movement."[118] On March 29, 1979, Deng had Wei Jingsheng, one of the movement's leaders, arrested. Wei had published an article entitled "Do We Want Democracy or a New Dictatorship?" in which he warned that without political reform, Deng would become a new dictator. The day after Wei's arrest, Deng publicly announced the Four Cardinal Principles and reminded all Chinese that "we practice democratic centralism not bourgeois individualist democracy."[119] Six months later, at a one-day show trial, Wei was convicted and sentenced to fifteen years in prison.

In early 1979, Deng called for the abolition of the Four Big Freedoms, which had been reiterated in the State Constitution at the Fifth NPC the year before, so that, as Ye Jianying had argued, "China would in the future be able to avoid fascist rule."[120] On February 29, 1980, the Fifth Plenum proposed their elimination. This decision was approved at the Third Plenum of the Fifth NPC in September 1980, and the Four Big Freedoms were omitted from the 1982 constitution.[121] In place of Maoist politics, Deng promised more consumption. As Maurice Meisner observes, "The Deng government set forth no new social and political ideals to strive for, but rather simply promised a better material life."[122] Deng's reformers promoted household consumption as the new yardstick of success, thus subverting the austerity-driven agricultural development strategy of the loyalists.

Scene 2: Document No. 75

The December 1978 Third Plenum began the loyalists' fall from power and marked the beginning of the end for the commune.[123] Years before household quotas were formally accepted in Beijing, Deng's provincial-level protégées (e.g., Wan Li and Zhao Ziyang) had encouraged this practice, and Deng used the pressure they created to push the center to accept household farming. For this reason, formal policy approval and guidelines for decollectivization lagged behind grassroots implementation, thus creating the erroneous impression that the center was responding to demands from below. As Zweig explains:

Informal policy mobilization kept the pace of decollectivization in parts of rural China well ahead of formal policy guidelines; while reformers in Beijing fought to authorize one form of the responsibility system, they concurrently experimented with more decentralized forms in localities under their control. As soon as the opposition acceded to one step on the path to decollectivization, new demands for another change arose from localities, keeping the pressure on the policy process in Beijing until collective agriculture was dismantled.[124]

The February 1980 Fifth Plenum of the Eleventh Party Congress officially changed the political leadership of China: loyalists Chen, Ji, Wu De, and Wang Dongxing, who had resisted decollectivization, were replaced with reformers.[125] In a public ceremony, Deng posthumously readmitted Liu Shaoqi into the CPC and denounced his purge as "the biggest frame-up our Party has ever known."[126] The Secretariat was reestablished and Hu Yaobang was placed in charge. Zhao Ziyang became premier, and Wan Li, who had initiated decollectivization, was named vice-premier, director of the State Agricultural Commission, and the member of the party Secretariat in charge of agriculture. To prevent Hua from influencing rural reforms, control over agricultural policy was removed from the Politburo (where Hua still retained some support) and placed under the authority of the reformist-controlled Secretariat.[127] "As head of the State Agricultural Commission, Wan Li, with Deng's permission, could extend the model of household production nationwide," Vogel explains.[128]

According to Vogel, in early 1980, Wan sought Hu's support for a central government resolution affirming the practice of household contracting: "[Wan] told Hu that it wouldn't work to have people at lower levels surreptitiously practicing contracting down to the household. Instead, they needed the full support of the top party leaders. Wan Li thus suggested to Hu Yaobang that they convene a meeting of provincial party secretaries to give clear public support for the policy."[129] On May 31, 1980, in a meeting before the conference of provincial secretaries, Deng for the first time publicly supported the household contract responsibility system. Yet, even in these baldly revisionist remarks, Deng insisted that the impetus for reform came from below and reassured readers that the collective would endure:

Now that more flexible policies have been introduced in the rural areas, the practice of fixing farm output quotas on a household basis has been adopted in some localities where it is suitable. It has proved quite effective and changed things for the better. Fixing output quotas on a household basis has been adopted in most of the production teams in Feixi County, Anhui Province, and there have been big increases in production . . . Some comrades are worried that this practice may have an adverse effect on the collective economy, I think their fears are unwarranted.[130]

In the summer of 1980, more than one hundred staff of the Central Committee and the State Agricultural Commission traveled across China to promote household farming. Then, between September 14 and 22, the first party secretaries of all provinces, cities, and autonomous regions convened in Beijing for the Party Secretariat Work Conference. On September 27, 1980, the delegates approved Central Document No. 75, "Several Issues on Further Strengthening and Improving the Agricultural Production Responsibility System" (see appendix C). Document No. 75, which Wan had drafted based on Deng's initiatives and statements between April 2 and May 31, approved household contracts and, according to Zweig, "signaled the demise of collective agriculture in China."[131] On Christmas Day 1980, Deng publicly endorsed the directive.[132]

At the September 1980 conference, Deng and his allies downplayed the momentous changes they were advancing. Wan called on Du Runsheng, deputy director of the State Agricultural Commission, to proclaim the success of household contracting in Anhui and to champion its nationwide implementation. In his speech on September 14, Du used the phrase "contracting production down to the household" (*baochan daohu*) because, Vogel explains, "this term reassured conservatives that there was still a local unit that was assigning responsibility." Although the objective was to quietly approve decollectivization, the adoption of Document No. 75 proved contentious.[133]

Some provincial secretaries—Guizhou, Inner Mongolia, Liaoning, Yunnan, Sichuan, Gansu, and Anhui—supported household contracting, yet a majority of provincial leaders refused to embrace it as a national policy. After Du finished his September 14 remarks, leaders from Guangdong, Fujian, Zhejiang, Jilin, Shanghai, Shaanxi, Jiangsu, and Heilongjiang remained silent.[134] But after Yunnan First Secretary An Pingsheng and Guizhou First Secretary Chi Biqing both declared they would implement household farming, an argument erupted among the delegates. During Chi's speech, Yang Yichen of Heilongjiang interrupted to protest that he would not permit household farming. During a break in the proceedings, however, Chi and Yang agreed that although Heilongjiang could take the "broad road" of collectivization, Guizhou would take the "single-plank bridge" of *baochan daohu*. The next day, Yang recognized "the need to start from realities and not prescribe a single way [or] one model."[135] Teiwes and Sun explain the profound consequences of this seemingly mundane acknowledgment: "In this, Yang accepted the reform principle of different measures for different conditions, the argument that underpinned the development of *baochan daohu*."[136]

Still, many provincial leaders remained unconvinced that household farming would facilitate agricultural modernization. These divisions are reflected in Document No. 75, which reaffirmed that "the collective economy is the unshakable foundation of our country's advance to agricultural modernization" and called for preserving the production team and strengthening its "core functions" in areas where household farming was adopted.[137] Under the principle of considering local conditions and in the interest of "the needs of the peasants," Document No. 75 approved household farming as a temporary measure in poor, backward, and mountainous areas.[138] Yet, as Teiwes and Sun explain, the document did *not* give households a choice:

Nowhere did Central Document No. 75 state that *baochan daohu* could simply be initiated where the masses wanted it, but it was replete with references to the desires of the peasants. The argument was that this new policy directive was not introducing a top-down process, but rather it was a process in which peasants' choice was to be respected. "Floodgates" notwithstanding, Central Document No. 75 provided considerable scope for officials seeking to extend household farming.[139]

Document No. 75's essential role was that it gave reform-minded provincial leaders license to decollectivize: "All in all, Central Document No. 75 was a skilled policy document that gave provincial leaders the flexibility they wanted, and created a new significantly enlarged opening for household farming when anything more direct would not have been approved by the conference."[140]

Although Wan Li had drafted Document No. 75, he had remained on the sidelines during the conference. Wan was initially dissatisfied with the final version, but Hu Yaobang reassured him that significant progress had been made. On the sidelines of the conference, Hu had held heart-to-heart talks with the Shanxi Provincial Party Committee in which he condemned the leftist mistakes of the Dazhai movement. Two months after the conference, the Shanxi Provincial Party Committee submitted a self-examination that was circulated as Central Document No. 83, along with instructions to eliminate all remaining Maoist ideological barriers to reform.[141]

After the conference, Hu Yaobang asked Du Runsheng to develop a plan to persuade residual loyalists to accept decollectivization. Support from provincial-level leaders was essential. In Guangdong, for instance, household contract farming was introduced within three months after Ren Zhongyi replaced Loyalist Party Secretary Xi Zhongxun in November 1980.[142] Throughout 1981, Hu traveled to the Northwest, Wan went to the Northeast, and Du visited several provinces to remove remaining opposition to decollectivization.[143] "Some provinces still sent people out to prevent the implementation of household land contracts, and at that point we issued administrative orders to stop them," Zhao Ziyang explains in his memoir.[144]

More than any particular policy directive, Deng's efforts to rehabilitate older cadres and cultivate reform-minded younger provincial and national leaders, led by the "reform trinity" of Zhao Ziyang, Hu Yaobang, and Wan Li, were essential to accomplish decollectivization. As Zhao later recalled: "Implementing the household land contract scheme nationwide would not have been possible without Deng Xiaoping's support. The fact that it did not meet much resistance from central leaders had a lot to do with Deng's attitude. Although he did not comment much on the issue, he always showed support for views held by me, [Hu] Yaobang, and Wan Li."[145] In his autobiography, former Vice Premier Li Lanqing, also underscored Deng's leadership over the reform process: "Deng was the irreplaceable nucleus of the nation's central leadership. To put it another way, the reform and opening would have been out of the question without Deng's third and final comeback to power."[146]

Scene 3: Burying Mao

During the Deng era, "ultra-leftism" became a political heresy. In late 1976 and early 1977, Hua and other loyalists had paid lip service to radical policies (e.g., brigade-level accounting) to bolster their coalition in the wake of the Gang of Four's fall. Hua had hastened to distinguish himself from Deng by vowing "to support *whatever* policy decisions were made by Chairman Mao" and "unswervingly follow *whatever* instructions were given by Chairman Mao."[147] He commissioned a new official hagiography to advance his claim as the guardian of Mao's collectivist ideology. Posters hailing Mao's selection of Hua as his legitimate successor appeared around the country, including the statement, which Mao had written on a note to Hua in April 1976, "With you in charge, I am at ease."[148] Songs and dances were commissioned to glorify Hua's past exploits and to act as paeans to his popularity and compassion for the people. Slogans glorifying the "Wise Leader Chairman Hua" were painted on buildings across the countryside (see figure 7.4).[149]

These decisions proved rash, however, as they associated the loyalists with radical policies and blind leader worship. They also locked Hua into a Maoist defense for all future policy decisions and precipitated the pejorative moniker "whateverists," which Deng skillfully juxtaposed with the reformers' slogan "Practice is the sole criterion of truth."[150] Deng used Hua's unconditional adherence to Maoism to paint him as a radical, question his judgment, and call Mao's collectivist ideology into question.

FIGURE 7.4. A home in rural Weihai, Shandong, with a worn slogan that reads, "Firmly Support the Wise Leader Chairman Hua."
Source: Picture by the author taken on June 29, 2016.

In his memoir, Li Lanqing (a reformer) recalled that, in 1977, Deng "on more than one occasion, spoke openly in opposition to the 'two whatevers.'" Hua, by contrast, "believed that the Gang's downfall was 'yet another great victory of the Proletarian Cultural Revolution' and that China 'should carry through to the end the continued revolution under the proletarian dictatorship.'"[151]

In July 1977, just after his third revival, Deng addressed the Third Plenary Session of the Tenth Central Committee. During this speech, Deng proposed an alternative yardstick to Maoism that could be used to gauge the correctness of policies: "seek truth from facts" (*shishi qiushi*). Although unobjectionable in itself, the phrase, which Mao had coined in his Yan'an writings, became the essential rhetorical weapon used to attack the loyalists and undermine Mao's legacy.[152]

In August 1977, at the Eleventh Party Congress, Deng again identified the need to "restore and carry forward the practice of seeking truth from facts."[153] The slogan's formal acceptance by the party at the Third Plenum meant that no truths were unassailable and that Maoist ideology and the leader's decisions, including his selection of Hua, could be questioned. Zweig explains the significance: "Reforms could not be judged on their political orientation; if they improved the peasants' situation they should be followed. Economic outcomes replaced political slogans as the criteria of policy evaluation."[154]

In this way, the reformers' coalition first declared that improved household consumption was the goal, then met that goal through the commune death dividend—that is, the distribution of collective property and reduced extraction rates, which were made possible by commune abandonment. Increased procurement prices, approved at the Third Plenum, also helped increase household consumption. The price of grain sold to the state was increased by 20 percent, whereas surplus crop prices increased by 50 percent.[155] Using an index of state procurement prices for grain taking 1950 as the base year, grain prices grew from 222 to 222.8 between 1971 and 1977, and then jumped from 224.4 to 271.8 between 1978 and 1979 and to 283.5 in 1981.[156]

Improved living standards validated the effectiveness of the reformers' polices, provided the window of prosperity they needed to unseat their rivals, and solidified their hold on political power. An unwelcome consequence of increased procurement prices and lower taxes on rural households, however, was a large national budget deficit. After a surplus of 10.1 million RMB in 1978, China's budget deficit was 170.6 million RMB in 1979, and fiscal deficits persisted until 1985.[157]

The Third Plenum jettisoned many of Mao's ideas and polices and called for a "reversal of verdicts" against those who had been persecuted under his rule. It did so, however, without any formal judgment on the leader himself. Rather, a torrent of implicit criticism of the chairman appeared in official publications and was reinforced by the explicit accusations of democracy activists, returned Sent-Down youth, and others that had suffered during the Cultural Revolution. Throughout 1979–1981, in the lead-up to Mao's formal assessment, his reputation and collectivist ideology were under continuous attack. In a speech on October 1, 1979, Ye Jianying commemorated the thirtieth anniversary of the People's Republic of China by condemning the Cultural Revolution as a decade-long calamity (1966–1976) perpetrated by "ultra-leftists." Mao was not mentioned by name, but instead "the personality cult" (sometimes called "modern superstition") was denounced and Mao Zedong Thought, rather than the chairman alone, was redefined as the creation of the entire party.[158]

The Third Plenum also established the Central Discipline Inspection Commission (CDIC) chaired by Chen Yun, with Hu Yaobang as vice-chairman. "The hundred-member CDIC was tasked with exposing and rectifying remnant ultra-Leftists, 'factionalists,' 'anarchists,' and 'smash-and-grabbers' within party organizations," Baum explains. Much credit for Deng's triumph belonged to Chen Yun's efforts to mobilize veteran party cadres and to Hu's network of supporters inside the Communist Youth League and the Central Party School. Baum explains the essential role cadres in these party organs played in vanquishing pro-commune loyalists:

It was they who had spearheaded Deng's "criterion of truth" campaign; they who led the drive to desanctify Mao and demystify "whateverism"; they who drafted the Third Plenum pathbreaking communiqué; and they who, along with such veteran party theorists as Liao Gailong, most ardently championed systemic structural reform.[159]

By 1980, the entire commune era was open to public scrutiny. Document No. 75 called for eliminating the "ultra-leftist line," and beginning on November 20, 1980, the radicals—including Jiang and Mao's onetime secretary, Chen Boda—were subjected to a show trial orchestrated by the Politburo. The trial in Beijing became the model for a series of less-publicized provincial trials against "followers of the Gang of Four." In Henan Province alone, after the loyalists fell, more than 1 million Maoists were detained and some four thousand were given prison sentences following closed-door trials.[160] For Deng and his allies, the trials were revenge for decades of mistreatment. But, as Meisner explains, "the most important political purpose of the highly ritualized spectacle was to raise the question of the role of Mao Zedong in the events for which his widow and onetime comrades stood condemned as criminals."[161] Jiang affirmed Mao's complicity by continually evoking him in her defense, and the chief prosecutor drove home the point in his closing statement, arguing that the Chinese people "are very clear that Chairman Mao was responsible . . . for their plight during the Cultural Revolution."[162]

On June 27, 1981, a day after accepting Hua's resignation as party chairman, the Sixth Plenum of the CPC Eleventh Central Committee issued its assessment of Mao, formally known as the "Resolution on Certain Questions in the History of Our Party Since the Founding of the PRC." The document, which was drafted in accordance with Deng's suggestions, sought to preserve Mao as a symbol of revolutionary and nationalist legitimacy while also condemning his "personality cult" and "erroneous left theses." It decried the Cultural Revolution as a decade-long debacle "responsible for the most severe setback and the heaviest losses suffered by the Party the state and the people since the founding of the People's Republic." Most important for the hundreds of millions of Chinese still living in communes, the document denounced Maoist collectivism as "utopian," "unscientific," and "divorced from reality," resulting in economic theories that "overestimated the role of man's subjective will." In a final blow to the commune's collectivist ideology, Deng humanized the infallible chairman by estimating that his Cultural Revolution had been 70 percent correct and 30 percent wrong.[163]

After the 1981 Resolution, the once sacred artifacts of Maoism (e.g., posters, statues, busts, paintings, and writings) became trinkets of a bygone faith. According to Meisner, the de-deification of Mao "provided a necessary ideological sanction for the abandonment of Maoist socioeconomic policies in favor of market-oriented economic reforms that Deng Xiaoping and others were preparing."[164] In rural areas, discrediting Mao and his ideology destroyed the collectivist ethos that bound commune members to the leader, to each other, and to the institution. With Mao and his collectivist ideology and development strategy discredited, unity of purpose among commune members was destroyed and the rural social structure that had existed for more than two decades collapsed.

By October 1981, more than half of all production teams were contracting work to households. Central Document No. 1, issued in January 1982, declared household contracting as "socialist," and by year's end, 98 percent of rural households worked on contracts.[165] The final blow came in the October 1983 "Circular on Separating Government Administration and Commune Management and Setting Up Township Government" (see appendix C), which once and for all ended the unity of political, economic, and administrative affairs that had existed under the commune and reestablished the township government. It declared:

At the present time, the priority is to separate government administration and commune management and set up township government. At the same time that township party committees are set up, suitable economic structures should be established. We must speedily change the situation in which the party does not handle party affairs, governments do not handle government affairs, and government administration is fused with and inseparable from enterprise and commune management.[166]

The battle was over, and the commune had lost. Between 1980 and 1983, depending on the province, the Chinese commune—under which a fifth of the world's population had lived for a quarter century—was silently abolished. Newly established township governments took over administrative responsibilities, and the communes, brigades, and teams were dissolved. Rural households no longer had a venue for political participation or collective coordination for agricultural investment. They could keep what they earned, and consume as they liked, but they were also atomized and subject to the vicissitudes of the weather, illness, and the market.

Individual enrichment became the primary measure of success. In the summer of 1984, a leading Shanghai newspaper published an article "Prosperous Girls Attract Husbands," which praised a group of women from a poor farming village who became the object of intense matrimonial desire when they became prosperous after shifting from collective to private household farming. "The moral was clear," Baum explains, "to snag a mate, one must be commercially successful."[167]

At the elite level, with the commune gone, the bonds among members of Deng's reformist faction began to erode. Conservative patriarch Chen Yun and Deng's liberal protégée Zhao Ziyang, who had worked together to "maintain central administrative control over the reform process, began to diverge appreciably by 1983–84."[168] Soon Deng's anti-commune coalition would rupture, and by decade's end, the hardliners had triumphed. Thousands of party liberals who had collaborated with them to eliminate the commune just a few years earlier (including top party leaders Hu Yaobang and Zhao Ziyang) were purged from their posts, or worse.

CONCLUSION

This chapter challenges the contention that China's leaders acquiesced to local demands to abandon the commune. Even if most Chinese farmers and team leaders had wanted to abandon the commune, which is unknowable, they still would have faced insurmountable barriers to collective action. Spread across the huge expanses of rural China, and facing a wide diversity of local conditions and dialects, local farmers and cadres lacked the knowledge and ability to coordinate their interests and intentions. Unable to act in concert and without assurances from higher levels, farmers and teams that did not conceal "illicit" behavior would have faced criticism from commune and brigade leaders, as they had throughout the 1970s. The difference, Zhao Ziyang explained, was that after the victory of the reformers at the Third Plenum, when household land contracts faced local resistance, "we issued administrative orders to stop them."[169]

Unified by their disdain for the Cultural Revolution and a desire to solidify their grip on power, Deng's reform faction set out to bury Mao's collectivist ideology, his economic theories, and his commune. To achieve decollectivization, Deng nurtured a new generation of provincial leaders and encouraged them to introduce household contracts and to criticize commune- and brigade-level extraction. After decollectivization was under way in some provinces, Deng brought his allies to Beijing to pressure the center to approve decollectivization under the pretext of acquiescing to grassroots demands. This effort was aided by a temporary alliance with Democracy Wall Movement activists, who Deng crushed after they had outlived their political usefulness. In 1980, the acceptance of household contracts in Document No. 75 gave Deng's supporters the go-ahead they needed to promulgate the practice nationwide.

An increase in state procurement prices for agricultural products and the "decollectivization dividend" (i.e., the disbursement of commune capital and the withering of commune extractive powers) increased the living standards of long-deprived rural households. Meanwhile, privatizing collective capital helped secure the support of local cadres who benefited most. Households' desire to consume more and local leaders' willingness to privatize commune and brigade property were essential to the commune's demise. Yet, the desire to consume more—perhaps the most fundamental human desire—is ever-present. The difference is that this desire was suppressed and punished under the commune, but then called forth and validated during decollectivization.

Ultimately, the faction that captured political power decided the commune's fate, and when offered the chance to consume more, long-deprived households and most low-level leaders were happy to comply. This strategy bought Deng's reformers the time they needed to consolidate political power and discredit their rival's investment-based economic growth model. Had Hua's loyalists prevailed over Deng's reformers, however, they almost certainly would not have abandoned the commune. On the contrary, under the "banner of Dazhai," they would have used the institution to implement the ambitious nationwide rural investment program detailed in Hua's 1978 Ten-Year Plan.

Chapter Eight

CONCLUSION

The aim of every revolutionary struggle is the seizure and consolidation of political power.

—MAO ZEDONG[1]

INTRODUCTION

This study began by presenting and evaluating two rival assessments of commune economic performance: the conventional wisdom, which holds that the commune's poor productivity led farmers to abandon it; and an alternate view, which argues that the commune successfully modernized agriculture and increased productivity, thus laying the foundation for rapid growth in the 1970s and beyond. These contradictory appraisals were evaluated in chapter 1 using newly acquired data on the national and provincial levels (see appendix A) and compared with data from other large agricultural countries (i.e., United States, Soviet Union, and India). The results of this examination indicate that the latter interpretation is more accurate.

China did *not* experience a V-shaped growth line with economic collapse narrowly avoided by life-saving rural reforms launched in 1979. To the contrary, improvements in Chinese agricultural productivity in the 1970s and early 1980s were built on painful, forced household austerity under the commune that underwrote agricultural modernization and basic education. These investments were made not just in better-off coastal provinces but also across a broad swathe of the country. Agricultural modernization created the surpluses that supported continuous rounds of productive investment in the 1970s and freed rural workers to move, first into the local rural light industrial sector, and later from the countryside to the cities. Commune members were poor and unfree, but for the first time in history, hundreds of millions of rural Chinese acquired the basic reading and bookkeeping skills, agricultural capital, and technology necessary to reach the first rung of the development ladder. Increased food production under the commune was an essential first step in China's industrial revolution.

The commune's institutional structure was altered over time to reduce the strain of collective action problems, which were brought about (as in all communes) by the need to maintain sufficient worker oversight and polices that increased income equality. The 1970s Chinese commune is distinguished from its predecessors and other commune experiments by its remarkable ability to increase household savings to support productive investments in agricultural modernization on a nationwide scale without inducing widespread slacking and shirking. Equality was a consequence of increased extraction from more well-to-do households, which had surplus resources that could be removed without pushing them into famine.

Like previous commune experiments, the Chinese commune used a unifying collectivist ethos, group isolation, and institutional subunits to entice members to work hard for the collective. Most important, however, it also developed several original innovations, including the workpoint remuneration system, the agricultural research and extension system, and the Three Small Freedoms (i.e., private household sideline plots, cottage enterprises including small-scale animal husbandry, and rural markets). After the Great Leap Forward (GLF), the Three Small Freedoms remained in place throughout the life of the commune and ensured that extraction for productive investments in capital and technology would never again push the populace below minimum consumption levels. Under the commune, growth through collective impoverishment kept rural households living in austere—often subsistence-level—conditions. But it also bankrolled the investments and innovations that generated the agricultural surpluses needed to kick-start the long-run cycle of productive investment and sustained output growth explained in chapter 4.

INSTITUTIONAL CHANGE

This book has analyzed the institutional origins and evolution of the commune from its inception to its demise over the course of a quarter century.

It identifies three nationwide challenges faced by the institution (i.e., rising population growth rates, rapid capital depreciation, and a fall in arable land) and discusses how the commune was reformed over time to address them. After its creation in 1958, the commune went through four distinct phases of institutional development, each one distinguished by its organizational structure, remuneration methodology, and investment policies. Evolutionary changes in these areas over the course of the commune's institutional life reflected political changes in the top leadership that influenced nearly every rural locality.

Over time, the commune's mandate was substantially altered. Yet many decisions regarding size, structure, priorities, and remuneration taken during the first three phases of the institution's life span proved sticky in its final, and most productive, phase. Political battles between leftists and rightists fashioned a compromise institution—the 1970s Green Revolution Commune—that combined elements of both collective and household production, economic planning and free markets, and collective and private remuneration.

The GLF Commune was created in 1958 and lasted until 1961. The institution was quite large (approximately twenty-three thousand members per commune[2]), had no subunits, and had an expansive social welfare mandate that included communal cafeterias and childcare. It instituted free-supply remuneration, collectivized all private plots, closed free markets, prioritized red politics over technical knowhow, and pulled millions of farmers off their fields to build large, often ill-conceived, infrastructure projects. The GLF Commune suffered from an overemphasis on political correctness, a shortage of skilled workers, overextraction of household resources, and excessive free-riding—factors that collectively produced a famine that killed millions. Still, the GLF did instill all Chinese with the notion that large-scale, high-modernist development was the yardstick of national virility and that everyone was expected to pitch in.

The institution's second phase, the Rightest Commune, rose from the ashes of the GLF disaster and lasted until 1965. The GLF famine drove policymakers to reform the commune in ways that increased household consumption. Its size was reduced by roughly a factor of three, and two more administrative levels (the brigade and the team) were added in an effort to reduce the free-rider problems that had plagued the massive GLF communes. Private household plots, free markets, and cottage enterprises, collectively known as the Three Small Freedoms, were introduced and remained throughout the life of the institution. These and other reforms were introduced in the November 1960 "Urgent Directive on Rural Work" (i.e., *The Twelve Articles*), and expanded upon in the "Regulations on the Rural People's Communes" (i.e., *The Sixty Articles*) drafted in March 1961 and adopted in September 1962 at the Tenth Plenum of the Eighth Central Committee (see appendix C). The *Sixty Articles* remained the commune's primary official functional guidelines until decollectivization two decades later.

Between 1965 and 1969, another round of institutional reforms produced the Leftist Commune. In 1965, Mao gained control over the Socialist Education Movement (i.e., the Four Cleanups) and changed it from an anticorruption campaign into a broader strategy to fund agricultural modernization via a more extractive workpoint system known as the Dazhai model. Under the Dazhai model, agricultural modernization was funded locally, decentralized to commune control, and expanded nationwide. The commune, Mao argued, should introduce agricultural modernization funded by high extraction rates and a remuneration scheme that rewarded workers for prioritizing collective over individual interests. Maoism, the commune's collectivist ideology, was propagandized with the help of the People's Liberation Army's veterans and people's militia units. Maoist indoctrination and Dazhai workpoints increased income extraction, but it was only after reforms to the agricultural research and extension system were completed in 1970 that the commune took on its final and most productive form.

This final phase—the Green Revolution Commune—was initiated at the Northern Districts Agricultural Conference (NDAC) from August to October 1970 under Premier Zhou Enlai's leadership. The Dazhai model was reformed to create a hybrid institution that included elements of collective and private production, ample local control over workpoint remuneration, and vertical integration of an agricultural research and extension system designed to target investment at productive capital and technological innovations. The reformed institution retained the Three Small Freedoms introduced in the early 1960s, along with the three-tiered organizational structure, collective ownership of capital, and the collectivist ideology of Maoism. Unlike the early 1960s, however, when the size of the commune and its subunits fluctuated considerably, in this final phase, the size and structure of the commune remained stable.

SOURCES OF COMMUNE PRODUCTIVITY

The 1970s Green Revolution Commune was productive for three reasons: its ability to generate super-optimal investment, its pervasive collectivist ideology, and its three-tiered organizational structure. This overlapping economic-political-organizational support structure was created and adjusted over the course of two decades as part of a national strategy to increase agricultural productivity. During decollectivization, these "three legs" of commune productivity were removed and replaced with a consumption-led growth strategy known as Reform and Opening Up.

Economics: Super-Optimal Investment

"The central problem in the theory of economic development," W. Arthur Lewis observes, is determining how an economy with an unlimited labor force living just above subsistence level could cut consumption and save more. "People save more because they have more to save," he concludes. "We cannot explain any industrial revolution until we can explain why saving increased."[3]

So how did 1970s commune-era China—a country with scarce capital and land and essentially unlimited labor at or near subsistence levels—raise savings rates and ensure investment in productive capital and technical innovation without pushing households below subsistence consumption levels? Simply put, reforms to the commune's remuneration and agricultural research and extension systems accelerated capital accumulation and technical change. Both systems were nested within the institution's subunits and worked in tandem, first forcing households to "save" and then investing locally in productive agricultural inputs and techniques.

From 1962 until decollectivization, the team administered the workpoint system, through which nearly all collective income was distributed. The fortunes of households rose and fell together, along with the value of the workpoint. The small size of teams—twenty to thirty households (or about 150–170 people)—ensured that workers could monitor each other's performance and single out slackers (reported in brigade-level statistics as *mouyanggong*) at mandatory team meetings where they would be subjected to intense, regular, and inescapable social pressure. Workpoints could be removed from habitual offenders or added for top producers, known as *kuofen* or *jiafen*, respectively.

After the harvest, each household exchanged its workpoints primarily for grain produced by the team. The value of the workpoint fluctuated with each crop, so households did not know their actual income until after the harvest. This scheme incentivized workers to work as hard as possible to both maximize the number of workpoints they earned and to increase their value. The flexibility and lack of transparency of workpoints disguised gradual increases in income extraction by local leaders to support agricultural modernization, which, in turn, produced surpluses that were reinvested in local capital and technology. This cyclical process of development and growth is detailed in chapter 3 and explained using both neoclassical and classical economic growth models in chapter 4.

Equality-promoting policies gave commune cadres additional mechanisms to ensure that the maximum amount was extracted from better-off households to support agricultural modernization. Policies ostensibly designed to promote more equal resource distribution, such as arbitrary income limits, lowered disparities among households by capping the incomes of relatively better-off families and investing excess resources in collectively owned capital. After the growing season and these ad hoc income equalization schemes were applied, members redeemed their workpoints. To ensure the "safety" of their savings, households were strongly encouraged to deposit any excess funds with their local rural credit cooperative, which aimed to absorb any resources that remained after the collective took its share and households consumed theirs.

The Three Small Freedoms were approved in the *Sixty Articles* in 1962, reiterated in the 1970 NDAC Conference report, and reaffirmed again in the 1975 National Dazhai Conference report and in other relevant documents (see appendix C). Small-scale household production and commune- or brigade-administered local free markets became essential parts of the rural economy and remained so throughout the 1970s.[4] These markets contributed to agricultural production, provided a consumption floor for households, and utilized leftover materials that otherwise might have been wasted. Households produced whatever foodstuffs (e.g., fruits, vegetables, eggs, or a pig or two) or handicrafts (e.g., shoe insoles, straw hats, or knitted garments) that met their needs, were permitted by local cadres, and would fetch the best price at market. Rather than compete, households worked with the collective, which rented them equipment, provided veterinary services for their sideline animals, and supplied agricultural chemicals and seed varieties for their private plots.

China's post-1970 agricultural research and extension system ensured that household resources were invested in productive capital and technology, and disseminated basic education and vocational skills on an unprecedented scale. The system rewarded applied, results-driven science over theoretical work. To familiarize themselves with local problems and conditions, researchers spent one year in the lab, a second year in a commune, and a third year traveling throughout rural areas to teach and learn various planting techniques. Agrotechnical experiment stations at the county, commune, brigade and team level constituted a vertically integrated agricultural research network that was intended to improve communication and empower local decision-making. Each level was semiautonomous, not merely an extension unit that blindly implemented instructions from above. Communes commonly supported a dozen or more staff and experts to test and improve agricultural capital and technology. They controlled test plots and planting schedules throughout the collective to determine which seed varieties and agricultural chemicals were best suited for local conditions. Brigade- and team-level agrotechnical small groups employed a three-in-one system that included older farmers, educated youth, and local cadres with the experience and incentive to evaluate each input at the grassroots level.

Politics: Maoism

Maoism was the second essential source of commune productivity. The Chinese commune was a hybrid institution that combined the dogma and structure of religious communes, the politics of socialist communes, and the development priorities of high-modernist communes. Five aspects of commune-era politics—its religiosity, the people's militia, self-reliance, social pressure, and collective remuneration—allowed the institution to overcome the collective action problems inherent to all rural communes: brain drain, adverse selection, and moral hazard. Together, they constituted the commune's collectivist ethos, which served as the institution's political backbone.

Throughout history, to promote hard work and cooperation, long-lived communes have required an all-encompassing collectivist ideology, often preached by an all-powerful leader.[5] The commune was, among other things, the church of Mao. Beginning in the mid-1960s, Maoism became a national religion that bound members to each other, the party, and the nation. Mao's image, group ceremonies and rituals, song and dance, and holy texts (most notably, the *Quotations from Chairman Mao*) were used to secure members' loyalty to the collective. Maoist group rituals and symbols became the emblems of a single moral community that united all members as "part of a common holy enterprise," which compelled them to "work harder and faster on collective undertakings and devote less time to private affairs."[6] Even today, four decades after his death, millions of elderly rural residents throughout China still prominently display Chairman Mao's image in their homes.

During the 1960s and 1970s, the military provided essential political support for Mao and the commune. Mao used militia units nested within every commune and brigade to expand political indoctrination. During the 1960s, all Chinese were told to "learn from the PLA [People's Liberation Army]," which, in turn, expounded the infallibility of Mao Zedong Thought. Militia members competed against each other to memorize and recite Mao's works. After their indoctrination was complete, soldiers and veterans led commune-based militias, which were at the forefront of Maoist political indoctrination. Militias led political study, put on patriotic plays, and printed and distributed propaganda to build grassroots support for Maoism. Militiamen, who were generally among the most capable in the brigade or commune, were also called on to lead the construction of large-scale infrastructure, assist in urgent or difficult fieldwork, and respond to natural disasters.

The commune enforced collective isolation, which kept members producing and consuming locally and ensured they remained largely ignorant of outside conditions. Self-reliance, the clarion call of the commune era, alleviated adverse selection and brain drain. The linchpins of self-reliance were the household residency registration system (*hukou*), relentless social pressure to influence members to place collective interests above individual ones, and strict information control. The commune's collective remuneration system kept labor local, incentivized worker self-supervision, and counteracted the propensity of members to place individual above group interests. The goal was to cultivate a shared sense of community among all commune members, which would allow the system to extract as much as possible without pushing households toward famine or revolt.

Organization: Size and Structure

After the GLF famine, the *Sixty Articles* instructed county-level officials to adjust the commune's organizational structure to increase agricultural productivity. The resulting reforms reduced the commune's size and introduced two administrative subunits: the production brigade and the production team. Because different size subunits had different tasks, by varying their relative size, county leaders could create interaction effects that strengthened or weakened certain features in ways that improved agricultural productivity. During the 1960s, the size of the commune and its subordinate units was adjusted to identify a "Goldilocks commune" that would maximize productivity. After 1970, however, the structure and size of the commune and its subunits remained stable and productivity expanded considerably.

Exploiting detailed county-level data from Henan Province for the years 1958–1979, I find that a commune's size and the size of its subunits were powerful and significant determinants of its agricultural productivity. In chapter 6, I present an empirical model examining both cross-sectional and over-time variation that reveals a consistent nonlinear relationship between the size of communes and their subunits and agricultural productivity. The model includes various inputs that affect agricultural productivity (i.e., land, labor, machine power, and fertilizer), which, not surprisingly, all remained positive and statistically significant above the 90 percent ($p < 0.1$) confidence level. This model also isolates the independent effects of structural variables to identify the effects of variations in the size of the commune and its subunits over time and space on commune productivity. Examining both cross-sectional and temporal variation reveals that smaller communes with smaller teams were most productive. As commune size increases, however, the effect of larger team size is mitigated and eventually reversed, such that large communes with large subunits were more productive than large communes with small subunits. Small communes with small teams, and small communes with large teams, were the most and least productive types, respectively.

Taken together, the relative size of the commune (i.e., the number of brigades per commune) and its subordinate production teams (i.e., the number of households per team) were significant determinants of the temporal and geographic variations observed in agricultural output. In a forthcoming study with Yang Feng, we uncovered additional evidence that to create a more productive commune, county-level officials learned from their most productive neighbors and adjusted the size of their communes under their juristiction accordingly. These results suggest that future studies on the relationship between organizational size and economic performance should include interaction effects among different size subunits in their statistical models, and explore whether policy learning took place among local leaders in close proximity. Sinologists studying the political economy of contemporary China also should pay more attention to changes in the size and structure of rural institutions. These effects are more difficult to observe than economic development or political campaigns as they require an extensive county-level data set, yet they ought not be overlooked.

DECOLLECTIVIZATION

From an intellectual perspective, it is understandable why many researchers are drawn to collective action arguments to explain the Chinese commune's demise. Communes around the world have generally failed because they were unable to sufficiently mitigate "the tendency of more productive members to leave (brain drain), the tendency of less productive individuals to join (adverse selection), and the tendency to shirk or slack on collective duties (moral hazard)."[7] For more than two decades, however, the Chinese commune adequately alleviated these pressures, and I found no indications in official or scholarly writings before 1979 that China's commune was an institution in crisis or on the verge of disappearing. By contrast, in February 1978, the Communist Party of China's Ten-Year Plan praised the commune system's performance and called for expanding its investment-driven growth model to the county level.[8] As late as March 1979, the front cover of the *People's Daily* proclaimed that the three-tiered commune was the economic and political foundation of rural China and criticized those who supported a return to household-based agriculture.[9]

The commune's elimination was the direct result of actions taken by its political opponents who *intentionally* exacerbated collective action problems by stripping it of its collectivist ethos and its best workers. Through the deliberate and ingenious methods detailed in chapter 7, Deng Xiaoping and his allies at the provincial level quietly created a crisis of confidence in the commune's collectivist ideology. They eliminated Maoism, expanded rural markets, encouraged private over collective enterprises, pitted the commune's subunits again each other, and permitted some urban migration (including the return of Sent-Down youth and cadres). These policies, taken together, constituted decollectivization.

Decollectivization was portrayed as a response to the deprived masses' calls to increase household consumption. But it was actually a deliberate decision taken by Deng's "reform" faction to consolidate its political power and defeat a rival, pro-commune "loyalist" faction lead by party chairman Hua Guofeng.

When Maoism was repudiated, the unifying ideology that bound commune members to each other and to the institution was destroyed. Mao's name and image were removed from public areas and ceremonies, and political indoctrination was ended, along with the chairman's cult of personality. Mao's *Little Red Book* was withdrawn from circulation in February 1979, and Maoism was officially removed from China's constitution in 1981.[10] These events were among the credible policy signals from the new leadership that undermined the commune's legitimacy and deliberately catalyzed the spread of the collective action problems that ultimately tore the institution apart.[11] Shirking on collective labor became increasingly prevalent after 1978 as households focused on their private sidelines and skilled workers abandoned rural areas for better opportunities in cities.

Decollectivization marked a shift from super-optimal investment under the commune to consumption-led growth under Reform and Opening Up. To generate support for its broader reform agenda, Deng's political coalition reduced extraction and increased procurement prices for agricultural products, thereby increasing incomes for impoverished rural households for the first time in nearly a decade. The commune's productive capital was either distributed to households (as was the case with tractors and other agricultural machines) or endured as in-field infrastructure (e.g., irrigation, wells, dams) that remained productive throughout the 1980s and beyond. Commune and brigade factories were privatized, renamed town and village enterprises, and their land and physical capital (e.g., farm machines) were placed under the control of former cadres-cum-managers.

These and other ad hoc capital and income transfers from the disintegrating collectives to private control were part of the reaping that occurred when the commune was dismantled. By increasing households' income, Deng's coalition won political support for decollectivization and maintained social stability throughout the transition from collective to household-based agriculture. But when the commune and its subunits were eliminated, so too were the workpoint remuneration system and the agricultural research and extension system that were nested within them. This crippled the ability of various localities to extract resources from households to support agricultural modernization. Rural investment fell from 3.2 billion yuan in 1979 to 1.8 billion yuan in 1982. Government revenues fell dramatically as well, producing a extraordinary reversal from a 10.1 million yuan surplus in 1978 to a 170.6 million yuan deficit in 1979. Fiscal defects continued nearly every year thereafter until 1985.[12]

CONCLUSIONS

This study offers three primary conclusions about the Chinese commune. First, during the 1970s, Chinese communes fed and employed the fast-growing Chinese population, which added nearly 158 million people during that decade. After the institutional reforms adopted at the 1970 NDAC, the commune produced substantial and sustained increases in agricultural output. Improved productivity was accomplished primarily through investments in human and physical capital (e.g., vocational education and farm machinery) and enhanced agricultural technology (e.g., pesticides and seed varieties). Maoism was the collectivist ideology that bound members to the institution and helped it alleviate collective action problems. Modifications to the commune's organizational structure and the size of its subunits also increased its productivity via economies of scale and helped mitigate free-rider problems.

Second, increases in rural productivity during the early 1980s were not "big bang"—that is, achieved "in less than three years."[13] The contention that decollectivization explains the lion's share of subsequent rural productivity growth ignores the extensive investments made under the commune. This study concludes that the post-1979 "harvest" would not have been possible without the increased rural savings rates and productive investments in agricultural machines and technologies made under the commune. Without the commune, it is hard to imagine how China could have kick-started the long-run development cycle that freed tens of millions of skilled rural Chinese workers to staff coastal factories during the 1980s and 1990s. In China, as elsewhere, increased savings rates and agricultural modernization heralded an industrial revolution.

Third, the highest levels of China's political leadership, not poor, powerless farmers, initiated the campaign to abandon the commune. Deng and his allies purposely eliminated the commune—an institution they had long opposed—for their political gain. To consolidate their coalition's control over China and vanquish their opponents, they disavowed Maoism, increased government procurement prices to boost household consumption, encouraged private over collective production, ended collective remuneration, and allowed local cadres to privatize collective property. These policies created the crisis of confidence in the commune's collectivist ethos that tore it apart, while galvanizing widespread political support for Deng's reform coalition.

NATIONAL AND PROVINCIAL AGRICULTURAL PRODUCTION DATA, 1949–1979

TABLE A.1
National and Provincial Grain Production, 1949-1979 (millions of metric tons)

	National	Anhui	Beijing	Fujian	Gansu	Guang dong	Guangxi	Guizhou	Hebei	Heilong jiang
1949	113.20	6.39	0.42	2.83	2.06	7.29	4.05	2.97	4.70	5.78
1950	132.15	6.75	0.54	3.11	2.20	7.35	4.33	3.00	6.06	6.86
1951	143.70	8.78	0.63	3.38	2.52	7.89	4.78	3.19	5.80	7.05
1952	163.90	8.92	0.74	3.72	2.68	8.60	5.30	3.45	7.72	8.04
1953	166.85	9.08	0.80	3.88	2.62	9.36	5.64	3.80	6.86	7.14
1954	169.50	7.77	0.58	3.77	3.17	9.92	6.01	4.07	6.78	7.04
1955	183.95	11.53	0.74	3.90	3.31	9.87	5.97	4.26	7.71	8.21
1956	192.75	9.09	0.57	4.44	3.80	10.74	5.90	4.87	6.82	7.93
1957	195.05	10.27	0.79	4.44	3.16	10.94	5.85	5.36	8.19	6.65
1958	200.00	8.85	0.85	4.46	3.40	10.27	5.86	5.25	8.38	7.88
1959	170.00	7.01	0.58	4.00	2.90	8.96	5.45	4.24	7.40	8.51
1960	143.50	6.75	0.55	3.29	2.01	8.95	4.97	3.16	6.23	5.34
1961	147.50	6.29	0.61	3.24	1.96	8.97	5.00	3.25	5.93	4.75
1962	160.00	6.71	0.79	3.59	2.10	9.98	5.23	3.66	6.63	5.83
1963	170.00	6.98	0.86	3.94	2.90	10.99	4.75	3.72	5.52	6.98
1964	187.50	8.12	0.98	4.34	3.04	11.47	6.10	4.56	7.48	7.05
1965	194.55	9.67	1.19	4.56	3.72	13.25	6.67	4.90	9.65	8.83
1966	214.00	9.58	1.10	4.50	3.06	13.31	6.79	4.74	10.95	10.39
1967	217.80	10.08	1.14	4.34	3.93	13.75	7.19	5.16	10.63	12.23
1968	209.05	10.69	1.28	4.21	3.43	13.09	7.01	4.86	9.78	10.87
1969	210.95	9.33	1.16	4.64	3.66	13.96	7.52	4.65	11.06	7.92
1970	239.95	12.64	1.41	5.67	4.12	13.90	8.20	5.17	12.73	11.97
1971	250.15	13.61	1.43	5.86	4.29	15.57	8.98	5.58	12.81	12.01
1972	240.50	13.68	1.18	6.22	4.45	15.36	9.49	4.29	11.55	9.00
1973	264.95	15.54	1.53	6.05	3.99	14.85	10.04	5.99	13.88	10.97
1974	275.25	15.55	1.71	6.32	5.00	16.72	10.35	5.44	15.69	12.94
1975	284.50	15.36	1.84	6.41	5.50	16.26	11.27	5.39	15.44	14.09
1976	286.30	16.84	1.71	6.01	4.81	15.92	10.75	5.70	14.80	11.23
1977	282.75	15.01	1.51	6.53	4.77	17.52	11.15	6.66	13.12	11.37
1978	304.75	14.83	1.86	7.26	4.91	16.32	10.83	6.44	16.88	14.78
1979	332.10	16.10	1.73	7.63	4.62	17.38	11.73	6.23	17.80	14.63

Average annual growth rate (%)

	National	Anhui	Beijing	Fujian	Gansu	Guang dong	Guangxi	Guizhou	Hebei	Heilong jiang
GLF (1958–1961)	−6.32	−11.29	−4.61	−7.28	−10.07	−4.69	−3.76	−10.98	−7.50	−5.45
Rightist (1962–1964)	8.34	9.01	17.44	10.23	16.69	8.58	7.95	12.28	10.19	14.49
Leftist (1965–1969)	2.48	3.34	4.08	1.48	5.41	4.22	4.36	0.58	8.93	4.47
Green Revolution (1970–1979)	4.77	6.22	5.19	5.35	2.91	2.44	4.66	4.16	5.61	8.51

TABLE A.1

National and Provincial Grain Production, 1949–1979 (millions of metric tons) (*Continued*)

Henan	Hubei	Hunan	Inner Mongolia	Jiangsu	Jiangxi	Jilin	Liaoning	Ningxia	Qinghai	Shanxi
7.14	5.78	6.41	2.13	7.49	3.88	4.59	4.06	0.32	0.30	2.60
8.42	6.36	7.48	2.22	8.49	4.49	5.54	5.14	0.34	0.32	3.01
10.53	7.15	8.34	1.77	9.31	4.29	4.69	4.64	0.42	0.34	3.19
10.07	7.48	10.32	3.49	9.98	5.75	6.13	5.44	0.48	0.37	3.84
10.91	8.18	10.34	3.60	10.64	5.76	5.62	5.60	0.43	0.33	4.32
11.43	6.68	9.29	4.00	10.49	5.75	5.31	6.08	0.61	0.53	4.12
12.50	8.96	11.27	3.33	11.79	6.27	5.57	6.17	0.62	0.59	3.73
12.11	9.83	10.36	4.66	10.82	6.62	4.94	7.43	0.76	0.61	4.34
11.80	9.86	11.33	3.03	10.64	6.72	4.30	5.87	0.56	0.59	3.57
12.65	9.87	12.28	4.78	11.29	6.63	5.29	7.00	0.70	0.59	4.63
9.75	7.65	11.09	4.34	9.93	6.27	5.27	5.90	0.64	0.52	4.08
8.87	7.98	8.03	3.59	9.60	6.07	3.95	3.60	0.47	0.42	3.37
6.85	7.34	8.04	3.44	9.04	6.10	3.99	4.04	0.49	0.39	3.54
9.03	9.60	10.25	3.26	9.66	6.04	4.37	4.60	0.49	0.42	3.75
7.88	10.63	9.10	3.38	11.15	6.38	5.02	5.68	0.71	0.61	4.18
9.51	10.43	10.87	4.30	13.50	7.01	4.92	5.63	0.75	0.63	4.89
11.66	12.41	11.02	3.82	14.14	8.03	5.25	6.71	0.84	0.67	4.63
12.28	12.02	12.64	4.27	15.74	8.06	5.98	6.56	0.81	0.60	4.72
13.82	11.22	12.75	4.40	15.20	7.69	6.48	6.95	0.90	0.67	4.76
13.31	11.24	13.18	3.87	15.33	8.30	6.22	6.99	0.73	0.51	4.34
13.22	10.25	13.10	3.52	15.55	8.67	4.99	6.50	0.78	0.56	4.86
15.56	12.69	14.82	4.70	16.83	9.86	7.39	8.71	0.72	0.65	5.19
16.47	13.35	15.89	4.54	19.07	9.95	7.13	7.94	0.91	0.64	5.99
16.27	13.57	15.39	3.22	19.01	9.95	5.57	6.71	0.87	0.80	4.25
18.72	14.74	16.84	4.97	20.59	9.42	7.83	8.75	0.76	0.84	5.75
18.62	15.76	17.02	5.03	15.67	9.87	8.58	10.33	1.18	0.86	5.90
19.42	15.62	18.09	5.20	20.35	10.57	9.07	11.20	1.10	0.93	7.00
21.22	16.98	18.19	5.12	22.24	10.25	7.56	10.87	0.76	0.89	7.05
19.48	16.17	18.20	4.76	19.05	10.92	7.29	10.38	0.99	0.86	7.14
20.98	17.26	19.00	4.96	22.90	10.50	9.15	11.17	1.17	0.91	6.74
21.35	18.50	22.19	5.10	25.14	12.97	9.03	11.94	1.06	0.82	8.01

Average annual growth rate (%)

Henan	Hubei	Hunan	Inner Mongolia	Jiangsu	Jiangxi	Jilin	Liaoning	Ningxia	Qinghai	Shanxi
−11.88	−6.52	−7.19	6.77	−3.77	−2.37	−0.35	−5.81	−1.47	−9.56	1.36
13.26	13.21	11.91	8.56	14.45	4.84	7.47	12.15	16.84	18.74	11.46
7.22	0.11	3.94	−3.49	2.98	4.54	1.04	3.29	1.50	−1.30	0.13
5.17	6.32	5.58	5.84	6.04	4.44	8.25	7.36	5.83	4.33	6.49

(*continued*)

TABLE A.1
National and Provincial Grain Production, 1949-1979 (millions of metric tons) (*Continued*)

	Shandong	Shanghai	Shaanxi	Sichuan	Tianjin	Tibet	Xinjiang	Yunnan	Zhejiang
1949	8.70	0.70	3.31	14.95	0.24	0.00	0.85	3.93	4.30
1950	10.34	0.90	3.70	14.49	0.37	0.00	0.98	4.03	5.17
1951	10.24	0.86	4.24	15.36	0.46	0.00	1.08	4.18	6.26
1952	11.99	0.97	3.98	16.43	0.56	0.16	1.34	4.51	7.01
1953	10.50	1.12	4.82	17.91	0.52	0.16	1.42	4.79	6.94
1954	12.47	1.04	5.05	19.03	0.43	0.16	1.46	5.11	7.09
1955	12.76	1.13	4.52	19.61	0.63	0.16	1.48	5.42	7.61
1956	13.73	1.22	5.44	21.56	0.57	0.17	1.59	6.02	7.51
1957	11.26	1.02	4.44	21.31	0.72	0.17	1.47	5.83	7.65
1958	12.26	1.17	5.14	22.46	0.47	0.18	1.98	5.44	7.89
1959	10.49	1.10	4.74	15.82	0.52	0.19	2.01	5.07	7.79
1960	8.30	1.16	4.10	13.40	0.47	0.20	2.01	4.90	6.65
1961	8.41	1.15	3.76	11.55	0.47	0.22	1.79	5.00	6.54
1962	9.10	1.27	4.00	14.35	0.45	0.23	1.70	5.35	7.13
1963	9.93	1.41	4.41	17.01	0.65	0.24	2.24	5.37	8.17
1964	11.33	1.73	4.48	18.00	0.67	0.26	2.59	6.07	8.71
1965	12.50	1.76	6.08	20.56	1.17	0.29	2.65	5.87	9.21
1966	14.70	1.87	5.90	22.10	0.82	0.32	3.36	6.29	10.12
1967	14.66	1.84	5.59	21.53	1.02	0.34	2.74	6.34	9.37
1968	12.83	1.86	4.86	20.09	1.06	0.34	2.22	5.87	9.75
1969	14.50	2.08	5.73	20.21	0.85	0.29	2.59	6.51	10.48
1970	14.65	2.12	6.01	23.21	1.18	0.30	3.07	6.99	11.24
1971	16.08	2.19	6.60	25.08	1.19	0.32	3.17	6.71	11.02
1972	16.65	2.29	6.28	23.83	0.78	0.29	2.82	7.35	12.90
1973	17.75	2.45	6.75	25.71	0.99	0.38	3.10	7.99	12.50
1974	17.25	2.49	7.50	25.62	1.39	0.44	2.62	6.81	12.33
1975	26.00	2.30	8.11	25.81	1.30	0.45	3.14	7.99	11.22
1976	22.50	2.52	7.77	25.42	1.20	0.48	3.44	7.62	11.96
1977	20.99	2.10	7.77	29.23	0.88	0.50	3.27	7.30	12.24
1978	22.88	2.61	8.00	31.97	1.17	0.52	3.75	8.64	14.67
1979	24.72	2.59	9.10	33.62	1.39	0.43	3.94	7.93	16.11

Average annual growth rate (%)

	Shandong	Shanghai	Shaanxi	Sichuan	Tianjin	Tibet	Xinjiang	Yunnan	Zhejiang
GLF (1958–1961)	−6.28	3.33	−3.45	−13.32	−8.42	6.68	6.32	−3.70	−3.60
Rightist (1962–1964)	10.47	14.72	6.07	16.20	14.42	5.74	14.12	6.80	10.07
Leftist (1965–1969)	5.64	3.86	6.47	2.61	10.64	2.69	1.67	1.63	3.95
Green Revolution (1970–1979)	6.57	2.72	4.91	5.42	8.35	4.74	4.94	2.55	4.75

Source: Agricultural Economic Statistics, 1949–1983 [Nongye jingji ziliao, 1949–1983] (Beijing: Ministry of Agriculture Planning Bureau, 1983); *Thirty Years Since the Founding of the People's Republic of China: Agricultural Statistics of Henan Province, 1949–1979* [Jianguo sanshinian: henansheng nongye tongji ziliao, 1949–1979] (Zhengzhou: Statistical Bureau of Henan Province, 1981); *Agricultural Statistics of Jiangxi Province, 1949–1979* [Jiangxisheng nongye tongji ziliao, 1949–1979] (Nanchang: Agricultural Department of Jiangxi Province, 1996); *Achievements of the Thirty-Five-Year Socialist Construction in Jilin Province* [Jilinsheng sanshiwunian shehui zhuyi jianshe guanghui chengjiu] (Changchun: Statistical Bureau of Jilin Province, 1984); Statistical Bureau of Ningxia Hui Autonomous Region, ed., *Collection of Statistical Materials on Ningxia's Rural Areas* [Ningxia nongcun tongji ziliao huibian] (Beijing: China Statistics Press, 1998); Statistical Bureau of Zhejiang Province, ed., *Collection of Statistical Materials on Fifty Years of Zhejiang* [Zhejiang wushinian tongji ziliao huibian] (Beijing: China Statistics Press, 2000).

TABLE A.2
National and Provincial Pig Inventory, 1949-1979 (millions)

	National	Anhui	Guangdong	Guangxi	Hebei	Heilong jiang	Henan	Hubei	Hunan
1949	57.75	2.44	3.77		3.47		1.56	3.18	3.50
1950	64.01	2.78	4.33	3.70	3.88		1.79	3.48	4.17
1951	74.40	3.22	5.21	3.95	4.23		2.01	3.83	5.27
1952	89.77	3.18	5.42	4.20	5.03	2.75	3.23	4.11	6.84
1953	96.13	4.05	6.16	4.39	4.22		3.96	5.03	7.30
1954	101.72	3.75	6.57	4.93	3.98		3.88	4.37	6.75
1955	87.92	2.65	6.14	4.45	3.08		2.98	3.74	4.73
1956	84.03	3.33	6.11	4.14	4.44		3.72	4.94	6.09
1957	145.90	5.60	8.26	6.08	7.04	2.67	7.16	7.62	10.91
1958	138.29	4.27	7.46	6.61	6.88		6.40	6.67	12.78
1959	120.42	3.11	5.72	5.91	6.58		5.94	4.13	7.96
1960	82.27	1.99	4.90	3.02	4.15		4.32	3.45	4.39
1961	75.52	2.26	4.65	2.51	3.65		4.68	4.53	3.41
1962	99.97	4.03	6.33	4.02	5.24		6.48	6.29	5.33
1963	131.80	5.03	8.97	5.91	5.89		7.55	7.93	8.48
1964	152.47	4.99	12.25	6.59	6.78		7.33	7.16	9.40
1965	166.93	6.04	12.91	7.35	7.73	3.91	7.07	7.62	9.17
1966	193.36	8.07	13.20	6.98	9.30		9.58	10.19	10.16
1967	190.06	7.88	13.85	6.45	9.73		9.87	9.88	10.55
1968	178.63	7.08	13.45	6.82	8.03		9.79	8.95	10.87
1969	172.51	6.55	13.88	6.99	6.53		9.37	8.47	10.40
1970	206.10	7.95	15.89	8.72	9.24		11.48	10.64	12.50
1971	250.35	9.26	17.75	10.70	13.10		13.43	12.95	15.00
1972	263.68	11.03	17.62	10.41	12.79		14.73	14.24	16.45
1973	257.94	11.04	16.93	10.67	10.93		14.36	14.63	16.72
1974	260.78	10.67	17.27	11.40	13.20		14.61	14.29	16.80
1975	281.17	11.78	19.72	12.10	16.23		15.05	14.77	17.50
1976	287.25	13.54	19.70	12.25	16.12		16.53	15.92	18.00
1977	291.78	12.29	19.03	12.58	13.61		18.20	16.61	19.23
1978	301.29	11.66	19.81	12.46	12.46	8.35	17.25	17.06	19.45
1979	319.71	11.32	20.10	11.03	13.52		15.92	17.49	21.21

Average annual growth rate (%)

	National	Anhui	Guangdong	Guangxi	Hebei	Heilong jiang	Henan	Hubei	Hunan
GLF (1958–1961)	−14.50	−18.33	−13.10	−16.88	−13.95		−9.21	−8.97	−21.93
Rightist (1962–1964)	26.63	34.07	38.12	39.49	23.72		17.38	18.45	42.07
Leftist (1965–1969)	2.83	6.92	2.58	1.42	0.57		6.00	4.45	2.18
Green Revolution (1970–1979)	6.61	6.17	3.97	5.16	9.40		5.84	7.85	7.59

(*continued*)

TABLE A.2
National and Provincial Pig Inventory, 1949-1979 (millions) (*Continued*)

	Jiangsu	Jiangxi	Jilin	Liaoning	Ningxia	Shanxi	Shandong	Shaanxi	Sichuan	Zhejiang
1949	3.89	2.19	1.99	2.10	0.09	0.36	2.71	0.74	10.19	2.46
1950	4.25	2.19	2.15		0.10	0.52	2.95	0.95	11.36	1.97
1951	4.57	2.84	2.28			0.75	3.58	1.57	11.67	2.42
1952	5.57	2.84	2.40	4.09	0.12	0.66	5.27	1.79	13.78	2.78
1953	5.34	3.18	2.12	3.28		0.75	4.48	1.75	17.13	3.31
1954	5.14	3.12	2.26			0.85	3.30	1.85	21.44	3.72
1955	4.93	2.98	1.94			0.69	3.59	1.76	19.07	2.63
1956	6.25	3.11	1.74			0.82	4.97	1.98	20.00	3.74
1957	8.30	5.27	2.07	4.07	0.22	1.91	7.00	2.74	25.00	5.97
1958	7.06	5.33	1.89	3.25		2.18	6.12	2.61	26.00	3.50
1959	6.53	4.65	2.02	3.65		2.50	5.87	2.74	20.00	3.50
1960	5.17	4.29	1.88	2.28	0.13	1.54	4.14	2.46	12.00	3.30
1961	5.53	4.12	1.30	1.51		1.15	4.49	2.13	11.00	3.43
1962	6.72	4.32	14.25	2.52		1.25	7.05	2.32	12.50	4.75
1963	7.66	4.95	1.86	3.62		1.87	8.19	2.94	18.49	7.04
1964	8.79	5.47	2.52			2.60	6.95	3.18	24.90	9.05
1965	12.23	6.08	2.41	4.92	0.44	3.39	8.50	3.37	25.00	8.92
1966	15.09	6.48	2.57	4.82		3.12	13.84	4.84	30.59	9.92
1967	13.16	6.49	3.01			3.25	12.95	4.43	29.96	9.28
1968	12.96	6.17	2.84			3.34	10.45	3.41	27.63	8.04
1969	14.09	6.87	2.38			3.07	9.05	2.75	25.94	8.91
1970	15.66	8.79	3.02	5.33	0.36	3.57	11.49	4.48	29.66	11.12
1971	17.45	9.50	3.81	7.55		4.76	15.95	6.40	37.39	13.08
1972	18.57	9.31	4.88			4.88	15.17	8.19	39.13	12.85
1973	17.92	8.72	4.86			4.35	13.85	7.11	38.87	12.96
1974	18.30	8.40	4.90			4.74	15.32	6.11	37.78	12.99
1975	19.96	8.47	5.61	10.32	0.59	5.64	20.02	7.21	38.68	11.98
1976	20.53	8.74	5.67	12.08		6.81	22.64	8.30	36.70	10.85
1977	19.25	9.04	5.94	11.88		6.83	20.41	8.19	37.04	10.92
1978	21.61	9.44	5.82	11.85	0.73	5.79	19.92	7.89	42.63	13.35
1979	23.56	10.45	5.86	11.89	0.65	5.59	21.18	8.22	50.92	15.50
GLF (1958–1961)	−9.09	−5.81	−9.82	−19.82		−8.75	−9.44	−5.81	−16.85	−10.81
Rightist (1962–1964)	16.74	9.94	313.79	3.58		32.48	19.39	14.56	32.07	38.44
Leftist (1965–1969)	11.39	4.85	−0.51			4.24	9.21	−0.25	1.36	0.15
Green Revolution (1970–1979)	5.46	4.67	10.05			7.15	10.06	13.86	7.43	6.36

TABLE A.3
National and Provincial Oil Crop Production, 1949-1979 (thousands of metric tons)

	National	Anhui	Guangdong	Guangxi	Hebei	Heilong jiang	Henan	Hubei	Hunan
1949	2,564		74		264		243	134	72
1950	2,972		136	575	301		208	158	97
1951	3,620	208	143	714	312		314	186	83
1952	4,193	323	145	910	309	59	335	223	127
1953	3,856	236	147	896	266		349	263	131
1954	4,305	194	186	1,348	367		264	129	73
1955	4,827	272	168	1,930	402		321	239	90
1956	5,086	255	190	2,129	398		304	255	96
1957	4,196	264	190	1,802	296	31	317	253	100
1958	4,770	278	203	1,608	323		344	233	159
1959	4,104	188	143	1,756	292		287	129	104
1960	1,941	55	103	1,254	114		89	85	91
1961	1,814	35	116	794	115		92	135	46
1962	2,003	75	171	704	85		97	183	63
1963	2,458	88	182	865	116		73	186	85
1964	3,368	145	223	1,114	181		145	180	85
1965	3,625	164	285	1,099	179	28	127	223	130
1966		138	302	1,012	256		174	157	111
1967		157	365		233		163	184	133
1968		162	281		235		104	152	118
1969		151	389	1,146	195		130	143	129
1970	3,772	152	345	1,123	242		149	149	130
1971	4,113	204	299	1,061	246		146	195	170
1972	4,118	238	367	1,132	187		138	193	133
1973	4,186	249	277	1,291	207		202	204	109
1974	4,414	277	385	1,337	231		178	166	136
1975	4,521	301	364	1,328	241		154	214	149
1976	4,008	268	371	1,282	192		166	208	141
1977	4,017	237	356	1,172	156		139	195	154
1978	5,218	327	387	1,278	245	88	242	237	253
1979	6,435	446	441	1,567	323		369	321	

Average annual growth rate (%)

	National	Anhui	Guangdong	Guangxi	Hebei	Heilong jiang	Henan	Hubei	Hunan
GLF (1958–1961)	−14.89	−33.26	−9.48	−16.71	−15.18		−18.54	−6.74	−9.26
Rightist (1962–1964)	23.40	64.58	25.32	13.46	22.37		26.35	11.29	23.75
Leftist (1965–1969)		1.56	14.02		3.36		1.39	−2.43	11.26
Green Revolution (1970–1979)	6.75	12.78	2.77	3.57	7.81		14.62	9.80	−0.64

(*continued*)

TABLE A.3

National and Provincial Oil Crop Production, 1949-1979 (thousands of metric tons) (*Continued*)

	Jiangsu	Jiangxi	Jilin	Liaoning	Ningxia	Shanxi	Shandong	Shaanxi	Sichuan	Zhejiang
1949	159	88	11	26	21	35	554	56	236	117
1950	171	92	22	88		43	661	66	234	79
1951	190	129	42	177		48	736	68	229	101
1952	217	175	39	107	26	67	846	69	287	104
1953	201	165	22	133		59	798	63	278	
1954	262	100	35	203		61	1,050	55	359	
1955	319	147	26	195	42	43	1,059	59	421	
1956	279	141	28	225		50	1,299	72	407	
1957	253	139	24	160	35	48	701	63	407	93
1958	223	135	69	242		51	783	75	371	
1959	174	116	58	241		53	448	62	404	
1960	128	87	22	41	13	24	220	37	234	
1961	84	66	10	57		24	396	26	169	
1962	102	78	10	49		23	423	19	163	64
1963	113	105	16	92		39	510	34	251	55
1964	209	125	20	87		48	643	40	372	107
1965	197	141	18	100	31	46	670	55	393	107
1966	219	109	17	134		49	971	53	363	88
1967	212	127	18	146		44	821	48	413	80
1968	218	125	17	128		33	691	35	331	95
1969	205	144	15	85		48	472	45	309	101
1970	195	120	13	104	29	49	786	48	372	115
1971	231	139	23	118		42	927	50	461	134
1972	276	144	35	102		31	748	53	453	140
1973	285	105	62	86		46	874	59	454	103
1974	253	127	78	85		44	832	62	461	162
1975	267	146	87	105	25	57	840	75	440	116
1976	198	123	98	60		53	587	71	356	124
1977	170	136	109	63		70	677	68	434	118
1978	334	135	123	105	25	42	960	57	585	221
1979	379	199	142	172	22	76	1,090	96	652	270
GLF (1958-1961)	−23.74	−16.47	13.53	1.35		−11.00	−0.40	−16.88	−17.45	
Rightist (1962-1964)	39.03	24.04	25.28	23.02		29.24	17.79	22.08	32.88	
Leftist (1965-1969)	−0.14	4.06	−4.92	2.45		2.54	−2.77	4.92	−2.94	−0.45
Green Revolution (1970-1979)	10.06	5.30	28.26	12.08		10.11	11.87	9.92	8.88	14.95

Source (edible oil and pigs): Agricultural Economic Statistics, 1949–1983 (Beijing: Ministry of Agriculture Planning Bureau, 1983); *Thirty Years Since the Founding of the PRC: Agricultural Statistics of Henan Province, 1949–1979* (Zhengzhou: Statistical Bureau of Henan Province, 1981); *Agricultural Statistics of Jiangxi Province, 1949–1979* (Nanchang: Agricultural Department of Jiangxi Province, 1996); *Achievements of the Thirty-Five-Year Socialist Construction in Jilin Province* (Changchun: Statistical Bureau of Jilin Province, 1984); Statistical Bureau of Ningxia Hui Autonomous Region, ed., *Collection of Statistical Materials on Ningxia's Rural Areas* (Beijing: China Statistics Press, 1998); Statistical Bureau of Zhejiang Province, ed., *Collection of Statistical Materials on Fifty Years of Zhejiang* (Beijing: China Statistics Press, 2000).

SUPPLEMENTAL MATERIALS FOR CHAPTER 6

TABLE B.1
Summary Statistics

Variables	Definition	Obs.	Mean	Std. Dev.
Crop production	Natural logged value of crops production, expressed in thousand RMB and in 1970 prices	2,307	10.27	0.91
Crop production per rural capita	Natural logged value of crops production per rural capita, expressed in RMB and in 1970 prices	2,307	4.39	0.58
Total agricultural outputs	Natural logged value of agricultural outputs, expressed in thousand RMB and in 1970 prices	2,533	10.57	0.85
Total agricultural outputs per rural capita	Natural logged value of agricultural outputs per rural capita, expressed in RMB and in 1970 prices	2,533	4.71	0.51
Commune relative size	Natural logged average number of brigades per commune	2,473	2.99	0.46
Team size	Natural logged average number of households per production team	2,528	3.55	0.34
Land	Natural logged area of planted land (for grains and oil) in hectares	2,560	11.07	0.87
Machine power	Natural logged machine horse power	2,410	9.37	1.67
Labor	Natural logged average share of labor in rural population	2,529	−0.95	0.14
Fertilizer	Natural logged tons of fertilizers per hectare of planted land	2,574	−2.2	1.78
Rural population	Natural logged rural population in thousands	2,562	5.86	0.74

TABLE B.2
Estimation Using Alternative Dependent Variables

VARIABLES	Total output (1)	Total output per rural capita (2)
Institutional structure		
MC commune relative size	−0.030	−0.040
	(0.025)	(0.027)
MC team size	−0.032	−0.024
	(0.036)	(0.036)
MC commune relative size × MC team size	0.096***	0.103**
	(0.035)	(0.041)
Conventional inputs		
Land	0.175**	0.190**
	(0.082)	(0.082)
Machine power	0.029	0.033*
	(0.018)	(0.018)
Labor	0.433**	0.414**
	(0.174)	(0.171)
Fertilizer	0.019**	0.020***
	(0.007)	(0.007)
Rural population	0.179	−0.578***
	(0.212)	(0.189)
Year fixed effect	Y	Y
County fixed effect	Y	Y
Observations	2,184	2,184
R-squared (R^2)	0.795	0.615
Number of counties	117	117

Note: Dependent and independent variables are logged; constant is included in the model but not reported here; robust standard errors in parentheses are clustered at county level; *** $p<0.01$, ** $p<0.05$, * $p<0.1$.

TABLE B.3
Estimated Contribution to Agricultural Production of Various Organizational Structures

	Commune relative size	Team size	Contribution to agriculture output	p-value	2.50%	97.50%
Organizational structures	(1)	(2)	(3)	(4)	(5)	(6)
Small commune with small teams	−1.16	−0.64	0.14	0.01	0.04	0.24
Medium commune with small teams	0.06	−0.64	0.00	0.92	−0.07	0.06
Large commune with small teams	0.94	−0.64	−0.11	0.08	−0.22	0.01
Small commune with medium teams	−1.16	0.02	0.05	0.10	−0.01	0.11
Medium commune with medium teams	0.06	0.02	0.00	0.17	−0.01	0.00
Large commune with medium teams	0.94	0.02	−0.04	0.11	−0.09	0.01
Small commune with large teams	1.16	0.83	−0.05	0.15	−0.13	0.02
Medium commune with large teams	0.06	0.83	0.00	0.95	−0.08	0.08
Large commune with large teams	0.94	0.83	0.04	0.61	−0.10	0.17

Note: The contribution of commune organization structure to agricultural production is calculated based on the mean centered commune relative size (column 1) and mean centered team size (column 2), their interaction, and regression coefficients of the three variables reported in table C.1, column 4; small, medium, and large communes refer to the commune relative size variable taking values of −1.16 (1st percentile), 0.06 (median), and 0.94 (99th percentile), respectively; small, medium, and large teams refer to the team size variable taking value of −0.64 (1st percentile), 0.02 (median), and 0.83 (99th percentile), respectively; p-value (column 4) refers to the p-value of the estimated contribution in column 3; and columns 5 and 6 report the 95% confidence interval of the contribution estimate.

ESSENTIAL OFFICIAL AGRICULTURAL POLICY STATEMENTS ON THE COMMUNE, 1958-1983

I. COMMUNE CREATION

(a) Resolution on the Establishment of People's Communes in the Rural Areas[1]

Central Committee of the Chinese Communist Party
August 29, 1958

1. The people's communes are the logical result of the march of events. Large, comprehensive people's communes have made their appearance, and in several places, they are already widespread. They have developed very rapidly in some areas. It is highly probable that there will soon be an upsurge in setting up people's communes throughout the country and the development is irresistible. The basis for the development of the people's communes is mainly the all-round, continuous leap forward in China's agricultural production and the ever-rising political consciousness of the 500 million peasants. An unprecedented advance has been made in agricultural capital construction since the advocates of the capitalist road were fundamentally defeated economically, politically, and ideologically. This has created a new basis for practically eliminating flood and drought and for ensuring the comparatively stable advance of agricultural production.

Agriculture has leaped forward since right conservatism has been overcome and the old technical norms in agriculture have been broken down. The output of agricultural products has doubled or increased several-fold; in some cases, more than ten times or scores of times. This has further stimulated emancipation of thought among the people. Large-scale agricultural capital construction and the application of more advanced agricultural technique are making their demands on labor power. The growth of rural industry also demands the transfer of some manpower from agriculture. The demand for mechanization and electrification has become increasingly urgent in China's rural areas. Capital construction in agriculture and the struggle for bumper harvests involve large-scale cooperation, which cuts across the boundaries between cooperatives, townships, and counties. The people have taken to organizing themselves along military lines, to work with militancy, and to lead a collective life, and this has raised the political consciousness of the 500 million peasants still further. Community dining rooms, kindergartens, nurseries, tailoring groups, barber shops, public baths, "happy homes" for the aged, agricultural middle schools, and "red and expert" schools are leading the peasants toward a happier collective life and further fostering ideas of collectivism among the peasant masses. What all these things illustrate is that the agricultural cooperative with scores of families or several hundred families can no longer meet the needs of the changing situation. In the present circumstances, the establishment of people's communes with all-round management of agriculture, forestry, animal husbandry, side occupations, and fishery, where industry (the worker), agriculture (the peasant), exchange (the trader), culture and education (the student), and military affairs (the militiaman) merge into one, is the fundamental policy to guide the peasants to accelerate socialist construction, complete the building of socialism ahead of time, and carry out the gradual transition to communism.

    2. Concerning the organization and size of the communes, generally speaking, it is at present better to establish one commune to a township with the commune comprising about two thousand peasant households. Where a township embraces a vast area and is sparsely populated, more than one commune may be established, each with less than two thousand households. In some places, several townships may merge and form a single commune comprising about six or seven thousand households, according to topographical conditions and the needs for the development of production. As to the establishment of communes of more than ten thousand or even more than twenty thousand households, we need not oppose them, but for the present we should not take the initiative to encourage them.

As the people's communes grow, there may be a tendency to form federations with the county as a unit. Plans should be drawn up right now on a county basis to ensure the rational distribution of people's communes.

The size of the communes and the all-round development of agriculture, forestry, animal husbandry, subsidiary production, and fishery as well as of industry (the worker), agriculture (the peasant), exchange (the trader), culture and education (the student), and military affairs (the militiaman) demand an appropriate division of labor within the administrative organs of the communes; a number of departments, each responsible for a particular kind of work, should be set up, following the principle of compactness and efficiency in organization and of cadres taking direct part in production. The township governments and the communes should become one, with the township committee of the Party becoming the Party committee of the commune and the township People's Council becoming the administrative committee of the commune.

3. Concerning the methods and steps to be adopted to merge small cooperatives into bigger ones and transform them into people's communes. The merger of small cooperatives into bigger ones and their transformation into people's communes is now a common mass demand. The poor and the lower-middle peasants firmly support it; most upper-middle peasants also favor it. We must rely on the poor and the lower-middle peasants and fully encourage the masses to air their views and argue it out, unite the majority of the upper-middle peasants who favor it, overcome vacillation among the remainder, and expose and foil rumor-mongering and sabotage by landlord and rich peasant elements, so that the mass of the peasants merge the smaller cooperatives into bigger ones and transform them into communes through ideological emancipation and on a voluntary basis, without any compulsion. As to the steps to be taken, it is of course better to complete the merger into bigger cooperatives and transformation into communes at once; but where this is not feasible, it can be done in two stages, with no compulsory or rash steps. In all counties, experiments should first be made in some selected areas and the experience gained should then be popularized gradually.

The merger of smaller cooperatives into bigger ones and their transformation into communes must be carried out in close coordination with current production to ensure not only that it has no adverse effect on current production, but also becomes a tremendous force stimulating an even greater leap forward in production. Therefore, in the early period of the merger, the method of "changing the upper structure while keeping the lower structure unchanged" may be adopted. The original, smaller cooperatives may at first jointly elect an administrative committee for the merged co-op to unify planning and the arrangement of work; and transform themselves into farming zones or production brigades. The original organization of production and system of administration may, for the time being, remain unchanged and continue as before; and then later, step by step, merge, readjust, and settle whatever needs merging or readjusting and whatever specific questions demand solution during the merger, so as to make sure there is no adverse effect on production.

The size of communes, the speed of carrying out the merger of small cooperatives into bigger ones and their transformation into communes, and the methods and steps to be taken in this connection will be decided in accordance with the local conditions by the various provinces, autonomous regions and municipalities directly under the central authorities. But no matter when the merger takes place, whether before or after autumn, in the coming winter or next spring, the small cooperatives which are prepared to merge should be brought together from now on to discuss and jointly work out unified plans for post-autumn capital construction in agriculture and to make unified arrangements of all kinds for preparatory work for an even bigger harvest next year.

4. Concerning some questions of the economic policy involved in the merger of cooperatives. In the course of the merger, education should be strengthened to prevent the growth of departmentalism among a few cooperatives, which might otherwise share out too much or all of their income and leave little or no common funds before the merger. On the other hand, it must be understood that with various agricultural cooperatives established on different foundations, the amount of their public property, their indebtedness inside and outside the cooperatives, and so on will not be completely equal when they merge into bigger cooperatives. In the course of the merger, the cadres and the masses should be educated in the spirit of communism so as to recognize these differences and not resort to minute squaring of accounts, insisting on equal shares and bothering with trifles.

When a people's commune is established, it is not necessary to deal with the questions of reserved private plots of land, scattered fruit trees, share funds and so on in a great hurry; nor is it necessary to adopt clear-cut stipulations on these questions. Generally speaking, reserved private plots of land may perhaps be turned over to collective management in the course of the merger of cooperatives; scattered fruit trees, for the time being, may remain privately owned and be dealt with some time later. Shared funds etc. can be handled after a year or two, since the funds will automatically become publicly owned with the development of production, the increase of income, and the advance in the people's consciousness.

5. Concerning the name, ownership, and system of distribution of the communes. All the big merged cooperatives will be called people's communes. There is no need to change them into state-owned farms. It is not proper for farms to embrace industry, agriculture, exchange, culture and education, and military affairs at the same time.

After the establishment of people's communes, there is no need immediately to transform collective ownership into ownership by the people as a whole. It is better at present to maintain collective ownership to avoid unnecessary complications in the course of the transformation of ownership. In fact, collective ownership in people's communes already contains some elements of ownership by the people as a whole. These elements will grow constantly in the course of the continuous development of people's communes and will gradually replace collective ownership. The transition from collective ownership to ownership by the people as a whole is a process, the completion of which may take less time—three or four years—in some places, and longer—five or six years or even longer—elsewhere. Even with the completion of this transition, people's communes, like state-owned industry, are still socialist in character, where the principle of "from each according to his ability and to each according to his labor" prevails. After a number of years, as the social product increases greatly, the communist consciousness and morality of the entire people are raised to a much higher degree, and universal education is instituted and developed, the differences between workers and peasants, town and country, and mental and manual labor—legacies of the old society that have inevitably been carried over into the socialist period, and the remnants of unequal bourgeois rights which are the reflection of these differences—will gradually vanish, and the function of the state will be limited to protecting the country from external aggression but will play no role internally. At that time Chinese society will enter the era of communism where the principle of "from each according to his ability and to each according to his needs" will be practiced.

After the establishment of people's communes, it is not necessary to hurry the change from the original system of distribution, in order to avoid any unfavorable effect on production. The system of distribution should be determined according to specific conditions. Where conditions permit, the shift to a wage system may be made. But where conditions are not yet ripe, the original system of payment according to workdays may be temporarily retained (such as the system of fixed targets for output, workdays and costs, with a part of the extra output as reward; or the system of calculating workdays on the basis of output). This can be changed when conditions permit.

Although ownership in the people's communes is still collective ownership and the system of distribution, either the wage system or payment according to workdays, is "to each according to his work" and not "to each according to his needs," the people's communes are the best form of organization for the attainment of socialism and gradual transition to communism. They will develop into the basic social units in communist society.

6. At the present stage, our task is to build socialism. The primary purpose of establishing people's communes is to accelerate the speed of socialist construction and the purpose of building socialism is to prepare actively for the transition to communism. It seems that the attainment of communism in China is no longer a remote future event. We should actively use the form of the people's communes to explore the practical road of transition to communism.

(b) Urgent Directive Concerning Present Policy Problems in Rural People's Communes[2]

Central Committee of the Chinese Communist Party
November 3, 1960

Central Committee Letter to the Party Committee of Each Province and District:

1. At the present stage, make certain that ownership by the production brigade is basic in the three-level system of ownership.
2. Firmly oppose the "communist wind" of one equalization and two transfers [absolute egalitarianism and excessive transfer of personnel] and thoroughly rectify it.

3. Strengthen the system of basic ownership by the production brigade.

4. Stabilize the system of partial ownership by the production team. Carry out the "four fixed allocations" policy [fixed targets for output, workdays, and costs, with bonuses for over-fulfillment] and ensure peasant rights to subsidiary agricultural products.

5. Permit commune members to cultivate private plots and engage in family sideline activities.

6. Lessen deductions, enlarge distribution, and ensure income increases for 90 percent of the commune members.

7. Enforce the principle "from each according to one's ability, to each according to one's work," and divide income in the ratio of three parts free supply and seven parts wages.

8. Economize labor and strengthen the first line of agricultural production.

9. Handle the distribution of grain well and manage the communal dining halls well.

10. Restore rural free markets under proper leadership and stimulate the village economy.

11. Genuinely integrate labor and rest and put into effect the holiday system.

12. Boldly mobilize the masses and carry out readjustment of the communes.

We will not change the above measures for at least seven years. The entire nation must study, but cadres especially must study every year during the winter season. Continue this for at least three years.

(c) Working Regulations of Rural People's Communes (a.k.a., The Sixty Articles on Agriculture)[3]

Approved by the Tenth Plenary Session of the Eighth CCP Central Committee in September 1962

CHAPTER I THE CHARACTER, ORGANIZATION, AND SIZE OF A RURAL PEOPLE'S COMMUNE IN THE CURRENT PHASE

1. A rural people's commune is an organization merging government administration with commune management. It is a grassroots unit of our socialist society as well as a grassroots unit of our socialist government in rural areas.

A rural people's commune is constituted on the basis of the union advanced agricultural producers' cooperatives to accelerate production. For a fairly long period, a people's commune will serve as a collective economic organization of mutual aid and benefit, implementing the principles of "from each according to his ability," "to each according to work," "more pay for more work," and "one who does not work, neither should he eat."

Both the economy of collective ownership by the people's communes and the economy of ownership by the whole people are two forms of the socialist economy. They should support each other and jointly flourish with our national economy. The state should support the collective economy of the people's communes as much as possible in varying aspects, develop agricultural production, make gradual innovations in farming techniques, and fulfill farm mechanization and rural electrification based on agricultural collectivization within a period of several five-year plans.

2. The basic accounting unit of a people's commune is a production team. Depending on different local conditions, a people's commune may be composed of two levels—a commune and production teams; or three levels—a commune, production brigades, and production teams.

3. The organizations at various levels of a people's commune must enforce the state's policies and decrees. Under the direction of the state, they should manage and organize production rationally in a manner appropriate to local conditions.

The Party organizations at various levels in a people's commune must maintain close ties with the masses, consult the masses whenever problems arise, pay heed to their suggestions, and play a leading, central role among the organizations at various levels of a people's commune.

4. The organizations at various levels of a people's commune should act in line with the principles of democratic centralism.

The organs of state power of a people's commune are its people's congress, the people's congresses of its production brigades, and the general meetings of its production teams.

The administrative organs of a people's commune are management committees at various levels.

The supervisory organs of a people's commune are control commissions at various levels. Relatively small production teams may only appoint a controller instead of setting up a control commission.

All deputies to the people's congresses of a commune and members of management committees and control commissions should be elected by secret ballot after full deliberation by commune members.

5. The size of the various levels of a people's commune should be decided by commune members in a democratic way. The size decided should benefit the various levels of a people's commune in production, management, and unity, under the supervision of the masses.

The size of a people's commune is based on a town, either large or small. The size of each commune will remain unchanged for a long period once it is decided.

In deciding the size of a production team, it is necessary to consider the area of its land, the distance between plots, the density or scattering of residential quarters, its labor force, the balance between its draft animals and farm implements, conditions for developing diversified undertakings, and so on. The size of a production team will also remain unchanged for a long period once it is decided.

6. Regions that minority nationalities inhabit, pasturage areas, fishing areas, and forestry areas may formulate additional measures in accordance with the basic provisions of this regulation to cope with local situations.

CHAPTER II THE COMMUNES

7. The people's congresses of the communes are the people's congresses of towns. The deputies to the people's congresses of the communes are deputies to the people's congresses of towns.

Important matters concerning the whole communes should be decided by the people's congresses rather than by management committees. The commune people's congresses should hold at least two sessions each year.

8. Deputies to the commune people's congresses are elected for a term of two years. The deputies should extensively and properly include representatives of commune members engaged in different undertakings: old experienced peasants, rural professional workers, youth, women, minorities, nationalities, dependents of martyrs, army men transferred to civil work, dependents of overseas Chinese, and returned overseas Chinese.

Commune directors and members of the management committees and control commissions should be elected by the commune people's congresses for a term of two years and may be re-elected for a second term. When electing members to management committees and control commissions, the communes, production brigades, and production terms should ensure that old poor peasants and lower-middle peasants have a preponderance of members.

Communes or brigades that are composed of several different nationalities should make efforts to incorporate members of minority nationalities into the management work.

Incompetent commune directors or members of management committees and control commissions may be dismissed by the commune people's congresses at any time.

9. The management committees of the communes are the townspeople committees administration (also known as the townspeople governments). They are under the leadership of organs authorized by the county people's committees and exercise the functions of managing production, construction, finance, grain, trade, civil affairs, culture, education, public health, militia, and mediation in civil disputes.

The commune directors are the town heads.

10. The main tasks of commune management committees are to gear themselves to the needs of the production teams and to fully arouse the aggressiveness of the masses of commune members for boosting farm production, animal husbandry, forestry, side occupations, and fishing. In doing this, they should make investigations and studies, follow the mass line, handle problems correctly, and perform their duties conscientiously rather than monopolize or control everything:

a. They should implement the policies and decrees on the rural people's communes set forth by the central government; the communes must not violate or change the policies or decrees laid down by the central government; on the other hand, they must urge production brigades and production teams to execute these policies conscientiously and meanwhile check their performance.

b. They should advance their proposals for drafting production plans to the production teams, which should be based on the state's plans and the factual situation of various production teams but should pay equal attention to the state and collectives' interests; meanwhile, they may readjust the plans drafted by the production teams reasonably. The readjustment should be made through consultation rather than by force.

c. They should supervise and check the output of various production teams, help the teams solve production problems as soon as possible through discussion with commune members and cadres, improve administration and their work on financial accounting, help the production teams arrange income distribution, and provide support to the production teams that encounter more difficulties than other teams. Moreover, they are forbidden to convene telephone conferences except for urgent matters, to ask for statistics and reports of the production teams without proper reason, or to give blind directions for production.

d. They should popularize measures for increasing production that have been proven efficient through repeated experiments and advanced experience. In doing so, they should take local conditions into account and employ typical examples to show the way and then should advance proposals rather than compel the production teams to follow them.

e. They may coordinate production among the production teams, when necessary. In doing so, they should act in line with the principles of voluntariness and mutual benefit as well as of exchange at equal value. They are prohibited from commandeering labor force, capital goods, or materials without compensation.

f. They should assist and urge the production teams to arrange their capital goods properly: (1) They should select and reserve superior seeds and readjust the varieties of seed, when necessary, according to the principle of exchange at equal value; (2) they should formulate plans for the supply of farm implements, fertilizers, and insecticides, which should be based on the demands of the production teams and the sources of goods, after consulting the supply and marketing cooperatives; meanwhile, they should supervise the supply and marketing cooperatives performing supply work; in addition, they must ensure good quality and complete sets of farm implements and stress efficiency in supplying these capital goods, which should be purchased freely by the production teams themselves rather than be apportioned among the production teams; the production teams have the right to reject goods that are apportioned; (3) they may popularize improved farm implements and transportation means that have been proved efficient through repeated experience, and at the same time, best fit local conditions; and (4) they should take charge of and make the best of all large- and middle-scale farm implements and transportation means owned by the communes.

11. On the premise that it will not hinder the increase of production and the commune members' income of that year, each management committee

may build irrigation facilities and capital construction, such as afforestation, water and soil conservancy, and soil improvement for the whole commune or several production brigades or production teams, according to the demands of production and the possible manpower, material resources, and financial abilities. It may also build irrigation facilities and other capital construction to be used together by several communes. All of these construction projects should be decided after discussion by the people's congresses of the communes and brigades concerned and by general meetings of the members of the production teams concerned. The decisions are subject to approval at higher levels.

In carrying out construction, the commune management committees should sign contracts with the units concerned, specifying the rights and duties of each unit. They should apportion labor and capital among these units according to the benefits to be derived from the construction. Units that do not benefit from the construction but contribute labor, land, and appendages to the land should be paid or compensated rationally.

The commune management committees should also be responsible for managing and maintaining the irrigation facilities and other farmland capital construction collectively owned by the communes. The irrigation facilities and other farmland capital construction built by several production teams should be managed and maintained by a management organ to be elected jointly by the production brigades or teams concerned under the leadership and direction of the commune to which they are affiliated; a covenant should also be formulated to this end by the production brigades or teams concerned.

The commune management committees and the organizations at various levels of the communes must protect reservoirs, dams, irrigation canals, and ponds and also should make multipurpose use of construction to raise fish and ducks and to grow aquatic plants.

12. To protect, nourish, and utilize the resources of mountains and forests rationally, mountains and forests owned by communes should be transferred to production teams. Mountains or forests unsuited for transfer should still be owned by the communes or production brigades, but are generally to be managed by production teams under contractual arrangements. Mountains or forests unsuitable for management by production teams should be managed by specialized teams organized by the communes or production brigades. The ownership of the mountains or forests

and the authority to manage them should remain unchanged for a long term once they are decided.

No matter whether in mountainous areas, in semimountainous areas, in plains, in costal areas, or in other areas, the organizations at various levels of the people's communes must afforest, protect forests, and conserve soil energetically. Further, they must strictly forbid the wanton felling of trees and the opening up of wasteland at the expense of forests. It is also forbidden to destroy young forests through grazing. The communes, brigades, and production teams should stipulate the amount, items, timing, and places for felling trees each year, according to the resources of the mountains and forests, growth laws of trees, the state's plans for felling, and the demands of commune members' livelihood. The responsible units have the right to put a check on felling trees if such felling is inconsistent with state plans or stipulations. A strict system for approving the felling of trees should be established; any unit or individual violating this system should be penalized.

The organizations at various levels of the people's communes should formulate a covenant for protecting forests, which should be approved by commune members after discussion. Specific personnel for managing forests must be employed. The covenant should stipulate that any units or individuals must plant three trees for every tree they fell and must ensure the growth of the trees.

13. Generally, the commune management committees will not sponsor any enterprises within the next several years. Enterprises that have been initiated but have not measured up to the requirements for normal production and are unwelcome by the masses should be closed. Enterprises that are valuable if maintained should be transferred to handcraft co-operatives or production teams for management, or transformed into individual handicraft industries or domestic side-occupations. Arrangements of this kind should depend on different situations and should be decided by the commune people's congresses. The individual enterprises may be run continually by the communes or transferred to production brigades with the approval of the commune people's congresses and ratification by the county people's committees.

The enterprises operated by the communes should directly serve the development of agriculture and the life of the peasants. They should not hinder agricultural production or increase the burdens of the peasants, nor should they affect the state's requisitions of agriculture products. These enterprises must strive to carry out economic accounting and democratic management, and make public their accounts on schedule. They have to report the appointment of personnel, the status of production, the utilization of materials, and their revenue and expenditures to the commune people's congresses on schedule and seek suggestions from members. Embezzlement is prohibited among these enterprises. The cadres of communes or any other individuals are forbidden to capitalize on these enterprises, to eat or take more than their due, to hand out jobs to their associates, or to be extravagant and wasteful.

The profits of the enterprises operated by communes should be used to expand the output and to develop productive undertakings of the communes. Apart from these, part of the profits should be allocated to aid the production teams that encounter difficulties in production.

14. Commune management committees should energetically promote the development of the handicraft industry.

The rural handicraft producers' cooperatives and cooperative groups are independent units in operation and are under the joint leadership of the county federations of handicraft cooperatives and the communes. The communes should do their best to help the handicraft organizations solve their production difficulties and urge them to conform to the state's policies and decrees.

The commune management committees should solve the issues for food grain rations for craftsmen in the production teams and handle problems affecting their share in collective distribution in a reasonable way. For craftsmen engaged both in handicrafts and farmwork, the committees should assign farmwork that best fits their situation. Payment for labor contributed by skilled craftsmen should be calculated on a basis different from that of fieldwork and should be according to the particular situation prevailing.

The organizations at various levels of the people's communes should allow individual craftsmen who have been working around the countryside to continue to do so.

15. Based on the state's stipulations, the commune management committees should apportion in a rational way the tasks of requisitioning grain and other agricultural and sideline products for the state among the production teams and urge them to accomplish their tasks.

The communes or production brigades must not assign the production teams additional tasks such as requisitioning grain for occasional use or providing grain by themselves other than the tasks stipulated by the state. They are forbidden to assign additional tasks under any sort of classification.

16. Generally speaking, communes and production brigades will not draw public reserve funds and public welfare fund of the production teams within the next several years.

17. According to the basic principles of operating communes industriously and thriftily in a democratic way, commune management committees should check at all times the work of the production teams on finance and on managing materials and help them do a good job. Moreover, they must help the production teams set up a system for managing finance or improving the system that has already been established, urge them to act in line wit the system strictly, utilize capital rationally and prevent corruption and extravagance.

The departments concerned at the county level should frequently check the accounting and financial work of the various levels of the communes and offer assistance, and open training classes to train accountants.

CHAPTER III THE PRODUCTION BRIGADES

18. In the three-level people's communes [i.e., commune, production brigade, and production team] important matters affecting a production brigade should be decided by its people's congress. The brigade people's congresses should meet at least twice a year. The deputies to the brigade people's congresses should be elected every year. Just like the deputies to the commune people's congresses, the deputies to brigade people's congresses should also thoroughly represent the people of varying backgrounds.

The directors of the production brigades and members of the brigade management committees and control commissions shall be elected by the brigade people's congresses.

The directors of the production brigades and members of the brigade management committees and control commissions shall be elected for a term of one year and may be re-elected for a second term. Incompetent directors or members may be dismissed at any time.

19. The management committee of a production brigade shall manage the production and administrative work of its production teams under the

leadership of the commune management committee of the commune to which it belongs:

a. It should help the production teams prepare their production plans.

b. It should correctly direct, examine, and supervise the production, financial management, and distribution of the production teams, and help them to improve administrative work.

c. It should take the lead in building and managing irrigation facilities and other farmland construction utilized by the whole brigade or several production teams and organize the necessary coordination among the production teams to meet the demands of production, according to the principles of voluntariness, mutual benefit, and exchange at equal value.

d. It should take charge of all large- and middle-scale farm machinery, implements, and means of transportation owned by the brigade and make the best of them.

e. It should strive to administer mountains, forests, and enterprises owned by the brigade; conscientiously direct the enterprises jointly run by the production teams; and urge and assist the production teams to administer mountains, forests, and enterprises.

f. It should urge its production teams to fulfill the tasks of requisitioning rain and other agricultural and sideline products for the state, and help them arrange the livelihood of their members.

g. It should take charge of the civil affairs, militia, public order, culture, education, and public health of the whole brigade.

h. It should carry out ideological and political work and implement the policies and decrees set forth by the Party Central Committee.

In performing this work, the brigade management committees should abide by the regulations laid down in Chapter II; and while dealing with the enterprises operated by the brigades, they should adhere to the regulations concerning enterprises run by the communes laid down in article 13 of Chapter II.

Some production brigades still serve as basic accounting units. Efforts should be made to administer these brigades to a satisfactory extent so long as the masses agree. In handling their work, the production brigades should refer to the regulations laid down in Chapter IV on basic accounting units.

CHAPTER IV PRODUCTION TEAMS

20. A production team is the basic accounting unit of a people's commune. It carries out independent accounting and is responsible for its own gains and losses. It also organizes production and the distribution of its income directly. This system will remain unchanged for at least thirty years once it is determined.

21. The land within the scope of a production team should belong to the team. No land belonging to a production team, including private plots of its members and land used for residence and public centers, is allowed to be sold.

No unit or individual may commandeer the land owned by production teams unless this is approved by people's committees above the county level after investigation. Land already cultivated should be utilized carefully. Capital construction projects should limit to a minimum the commandeering of land already cultivated.

The labor force of production teams should be under the control of the teams themselves. The communes or production brigades must consult the masses of team members before the requisition labor forms the production teams. The requisitioning of labor will not be permitted without the consent of team members.

No communes or production brigades are allowed to requisition cattle, horses, and farm implements owned by the production teams. Farm implements, small-scale farm machinery, or cattle and horses that originally belonged to the communes or brigades but are better suited for ownership or use by a production team should be transferred to them. Farm implements, machinery, and cattle or horses not suitable for ownership or use by a production team should be retained by the communes or brigades, or may be collectively owned and managed by several production teams.

Mountains, forests, water surfaces, and prairies owned by the collectives but more suitable for ownership by production teams should be transferred to them. Production teams may assign team members the responsibility of managing scattered groves and forests and sign contracts with them, stipulating the distribution of earning from those resources or they may share the scattered groves and forests among team members.

The ownership of land, livestock, farm implements, water surfaces, and prairies stated above and the authority to manage them will remain unchanged for a long period once approved by general meetings of commune members or the people's congresses. Apart from these, other ownership or authority are also unchangeable for a long period once this is decided at general meetings of commune members or by people's congresses.

22. Production teams are vested with autonomous rights in production and income distribution.

On the premise that they accept that state's planning and direction and do not destroy natural resources, production teams have the right to plant and decide how to increase production in a manner and timing suitable to local conditions.

Assuming that they will not erode agricultural land, woodland, and prairies, production teams have the right to open up wasteland, to reclaim barren mountains, and to make full use of all possible resources.

On the premise that it has fulfilled the task of submitting and selling agricultural and sideline products to the state, a production team may distribute among its team members its products and earnings. The manner of doing so should be decided at general meetings of team members after discussion.

23. Based on local conditions, local methods of production, the rotation system, the requirements of the state's plans, and the demands of production and the livelihood of its members, a production team should prepare its plans for production with overall consideration for the ratio between grain crops and industrial crops as well as of the varieties of grain crops.

While preparing the plans for production, a production team should mobilize the masses to discuss, supplement, or revise the plans to the fullest extent; above all, it must seek the suggestions of the experienced peasants. The production plans should be approved by general meetings of team members.

After its plans for production are approved, a production team should organize the masses to review these plans on schedule so as to ensure their extension.

24. Usually, the production teams should place its main emphasis on developing the production of grain and meanwhile develop energetically the production of cotton, oil-bearing crops, and other industrial crops according to local conditions. Further, they must make full use of natural resources and sideline products of farm crops to develop animal husbandry, fishing, and other side occupations.

Production teams in centralized production areas for industrial crops should give first priority to the planting of such crops.

Production teams in fishing areas should concentrate solely or mainly on fishing.

Production teams in the pasturage areas should concentrate solely or mainly on animal husbandry.

Production teams in the mountainous areas or semimountainous areas should nourish and protect forests effectively and strictly prohibit the excessive felling of trees and the opening up of wasteland at the expense of forests. Furthermore, they must energetically afforest and develop, in a manner appropriate to local conditions, the production of timber, bamboo, economic forests, and firewood, as well as products of mountains and the sideline products of forests. The production teams in the centralized production areas for bamboo should grow bamboo primarily, combining the production of bamboo with the production of grain.

25. The production teams should energetically develop diversified undertakings.

In accordance with local demands and conditions, production teams should energetically develop workshops for processing agricultural and sideline products such as mills, flour mills, bean curd workshops, and oil workshops that have been in operation in the countryside; in addition, they should also develop handicrafts (the manufacture of farm implements, pottery, and knitwear) and cultivation (pigs, breeding cattle, ducks, geese, and bees), transportation, picking, fishing, hunting, and so on.

The diversified undertakings of production teams may adopt varying modes to meet their requirements: some may organize a labor force during slack farm seasons for short-distance transportation, fishing, hunting, or picking; some may organize team members possessing skills to run a variety of processing workshops; some may organize team members to engage in processing with raw materials supplied by production teams.

Production projects that were originally run by the communes or brigades should be taken over by production teams provided that the projects are better suited for operation by the teams and that they would not obstruct agricultural production. Projects too big to be run by a single production team may be jointly operated by several production teams or still by communes or production brigades.

In accordance with the principles of voluntariness and mutual benefit, the diversified undertakings of the production teams must carry out strict economic accounting and democratic management. Their accounts must be publicized on schedule. The products and income of these diversified undertakings should be distributed among team members according to proposals of the general meetings of team members. No one is allowed to eat or take more than his due.

26. The production teams should protect and breed draft animals, cattle, and horses conscientiously. They must employ cattle and horses rationally. Special attention should be paid to the rearing of female livestock, breeding cattle, and young livestock and improving the livestock breed.

Depending on various local conditions, there are various ways to feed the draft animals owned by the collectives. It is permissible to let individual contractors be responsible for feeding and using draft animals or to feed them in the same mangers. The ways of feeding should be decided by team members after discussion. The production teams should guarantee the supply of hay and other fodder for these draft animals.

The production teams should select animal keepers strictly through democratic nomination. Animal keepers who are rich in experience and who show genuine consideration for livestock should remain in their positions and should not be transferred lightly. The units or individuals who perform satisfactorily in using draft animals and in preventing and curing the diseases to which such animals are liable should be given rewards. The masses should investigate the death of draft animals caused by improper management, feeding or use and determine who should be held responsible; personnel involved in such cases should be properly punished.

The production teams should encourage team members to breed livestock. Personnel who are so engaged should be given grain or cash as rewards; or they may have a share of the livestock bred.

The livestock of the production teams may be marketed at trade fairs for sale or exchange. Earning from the sale of livestock may be included as part of the income distribution of that year.

Efforts should be made to train veterinarians especially country veterinarians and to nip various diseases of livestock in the bud.

27. The production teams should strive to take care of their farm implements and try their utmost to buy new farm implements.

Production teams should select team members with a strong sense of responsibility to take charge of farm implements and should strive to have those who use the implements maintain them in good order.

Production teams should train artisans in a planned way to repair farm implements. These artisans should be concurrently farmworkers.

Team members should prepare small-scale farm implements for their own use. Some middle-scale farm implements may also be purchased by team members themselves. Production teams should seek the consent of team members before they borrow farm implements from them and should pay a reasonable fee; in case the farm implements borrowed are damaged, the production teams should pay compensation.

28. The production teams should strive to increase their collection of manure. They should map out annual plans for storing manure and organize team members to store manure at all times. To acquire more backyard manure, production teams should encourage team members to rear domestic animals and poultry. In addition, they must encourage team members to gather manure of varied origin and quality. Some production teams also must enlarge the areas as much as possible for growing plants that can produce manure, if they are able to do so.

Production teams should prescribe reasonably the tasks for team members for submitting or selling manure to them, and pay them on basis of its quality. Payment for manure may be by workpoints or by cash. Team members who submit manure of good quality exceeding quotas prescribed should be given additional cash or goods as rewards.

29. The production teams should organize all able-bodied persons to participate in labor. They must assign, through democratic evaluation, all fully and partially able-bodied males and females the basic attendance dates they are required to contribute, according to the demand of production and individual cases. In stipulating the basic attendance dates for female team members, the teams should take into account their physical condition and household responsibilities. Production teams should also organize all those who are able to undertake auxiliary productive activities to participate in work befitting their physical state and pay them for the work they perform.

30. The production teams must strive to improve the farming techniques of team members. They should enable the old experienced and skillful peasants to play their part to the fullest, invite them as advisers, and listen to and study their suggestions conscientiously. Furthermore, they must

organize young people to learn techniques in a planned way and have old hands train greenhorns. In reviewing the course of production, the production teams must examine and evaluate the techniques applied. Team members who make contributions to the techniques and disseminate their technical knowledge enthusiastically should be given rewards.

31. To facilitate the organization of production, production teams should set up specific or temporary operation groups on a short-term, seasonal, or yearly basis by signing contracts with them and assigning them work. In doing this, a strict system of responsibility should be established. A similar system should also be carried out in animal husbandry, forestry, fishing, and other side occupations, as well as in managing livestock, farm implements, irrigation facilities, and other public property. Responsibility may be assumed by groups or individuals.

Groups or individuals who participate in labor energetically, are responsible in management, produce outstanding achievements, or fulfill tasks exceeding their quotas should be given proper rewards; groups or individuals who are unenthusiastic about their labor, irresponsible in management, or fail to fulfill their tasks should be punished by lowering their pay or by other proper penalties.

32. The production teams should pay team members for their labor based on the quality and the amount of work done. In doing so, they must avoid equalitarianism in calculating the labor payment for team members.

Production teams should stipulate various output quotas for labor and place control over the quotas. They should calculate workpoints on the basis of the output quotas. As to work in which a prescribed output is impossible, production teams should, depending on the actual situation, calculate workpoints by evaluating work done.

When stipulating output quotas, the production teams should set up rational standards for calculating workpoints on the basis of techniques needed in the course of work, hardship in working, and the importance of the work for production. Payment for farm at busy farm seasons should be higher than that in normal times; payment or work in farming and animal husbandry that requires high technical skills should be higher than that for ordinary work. Payment for professional activities in the handicraft industry, forestry, fishing, the salt industry, and transportation should be based on standards different from those for farmwork.

In stipulating output quotas or readjusting the standards for payment, production teams should consider not only the amount of fieldwork but also the quality of the work. Output quotas and standards should be approved by general meetings of team members after discussion.

In areas unsuitable for the imposition of output quotas, production teams should calculate conscientiously the workpoints by evaluating the work done.

Regardless of sex or age, cadres, or members, there should be equal pay for equal work. The workpoints earned by each member should be listed in his workpoint handbook on schedule. The workpoints earned by team members should be made public on schedule.

33. Production teams are obliged to fulfill their tasks requisitioning grain, cotton, and oil-bearing crops, as well as agricultural and sideline products for the state. In prescribing these tasks, the state should place equal emphasis on its own interests and on those of collectives and individuals so as to enable the teams that produce more to reserve more.

In accordance with the principle of exchange at equal value, the state should stipulate a rational proportion between the prices of industrial and agricultural products, providing as many industrial products as possible to the production teams in exchange for agricultural products. Areas in which more agricultural products are submitted or sold to the state should be given more industrial products. Areas in which more grain, cotton, and oil-bearing crops are submitted or sold to the state should receive greater attention from the state.

To encourage the development of agricultural production to meet industrial development, while maintaining the desired population proportion between the urban and rural areas, state taxation in agriculture and the total amount of grain requisitioned should be kept stable at an appropriate level within a certain period.

It is necessary to avoid equalitarianism in instituting a standard for grain to be reserved by team members. Production teams that submit more commodity grain on a per capita basis should enjoy higher food grain rations. Production teams that engage mainly in the production of industrial crops, vegetables, forestry animal husbandry, and fishing and thus lack grain should be ensured a food grain ration not lower than that for adjacent grain-producing areas.

34. Production teams must implement conscientiously the principles of "to each according to his work" and "more pay for more work," and avoid equalitarianism in distribution.

Production teams should make every effort to increase output, save labor force and expenses used for production, put expenditure for nonproductive use under strict control, and uphold more share in distribution rather than deduction. Further, they must try their best to raise the value of workpoints team members earn, thus increasing the income of the members.

Production teams may adopt various measures to distribute grain to team members, and at the same time must conform to their own situation and consider suggestions made by the majority of team members. It is permissible to use the practice of integrating basic rations with distribution based on workpoints, or to use the practice of distribution according to workpoints plus consideration for special cases, or adopt other proper measures. Whatever the case, the grain should be distributed as to stimulate the labor aggressiveness of team members and ensure normal food grain rations for the dependents of martyrs, of servicemen, of staff and workers, and of peasant households with too many members but little manpower.

Food grain rations for team members should be delivered to their living quarters and controlled by team members themselves.

According to the results of harvests, production teams may set aside some grain for reserves as decided at a general meeting of team members. Grain reserves are to be stored against war and natural disasters, or be used to aid other production teams when they are short of grain. The grain reserves borrowed must be returned in full. Also, they may be used to subsidize needy households and "five guarantees" households. Usually, the amount of grain reserves of a production team is less than 1 percent of the total amount of its distributable grains that are left over after it submits the stipulated amount of grain to the state. The amount of grain reserves should not exceed 2 percent at most. The grain reserves in good harvest may be more than in those normal harvest years. The grain reserves of production teams should be kept by the teams themselves. Communes or brigades are forbidden from requisitioning the reserves. The use of grain reserves should be decided at general meetings of team members after discussion. A system for managing grain reserves, which meanwhile facilitates supervision by the masses, should be established to prevent the cadres from eating or taking more than their due.

35. The amount of the public reserve funds of a production team should be decided at general meetings of team members after serious discussion on the basis of annual demands and possibilities. Usually, public reserve funds will be limited to less than 3–5 percent of its distributable revenue.

A few high-income production teams located in production areas for industrial crops, forestry, or suburbs may set aside relatively more income for public reserve funds. Production teams that suffer severe natural disasters may set aside less income for reserve funds or cancel them.

The use of public reserve funds should be decided at general meetings of team members after discussion rather than by a few cadres.

Expenditure in capital construction by a production team and its investment in expanding production should be drawn from its public reserve funds. Labor days for capital construction and for production should be calculated separately. With the approval of general meetings of team members, each able-bodied team member should contribute a certain number of labor days each year to capital construction projects for the use of production; this contribution should be regarded as the labor accumulation of the collective economy. Labor days of this kind should usually be limited to under 3 percent of basic attendance dates required as a contribution by commune members each year. Contributed labor days exceeding this stipulation deserve a payment that should be issued from public reserve funds.

The labor of production teams for repairing small-scale irrigation facilities, such as drains, ponds, and dams, and for improving the soil should be paid by workpoints in the same way as that for production and should have a share in the distribution of that year.

36. Production teams may set aside a certain amount of the distributable revenue for public welfare funds to be used for social security and collective welfare undertakings. The amount of public welfare funds should be decided at general meetings of team members after serious discussion in accordance with annual demands and possibilities; public welfare funds should be limited to less than 2 or 3 percent of the total distributable revenue.

The use of public welfare funds should be decided at general meetings of team members after discussion rather than arbitrarily by a few cadres.

Subject to approval of general meetings, production teams should support or subsidize team members who have lost their independence because they have aged; have become weak, orphaned, widowed, or disabled; or have met unfortunate difficulties in earning a livelihood. Proper preferential treatment should also be given to the dependents of martyrs and of servicemen and disabled servicemen who find it difficult to earn a livelihood. Households with too many members but inadequate manpower should be assigned appropriate work according to their capacity for work so that they are able to increase their income; in addition, production teams may issue them necessary subsidies with the approval of a general meeting of team members after discussion. All of these supports and subsidies should be drawn from public welfare funds. The subsidies for team members injured on official assignments or the pension for dependents of team members who died while discharging official assignments should also be drawn from public welfare funds.

37. Production teams should be run industriously and economically. They should be very careful in reckoning affairs, stress efficiency, and resolutely object to extravagance and wastefulness.

The production teams should set up a sound system for managing finances. All expenditures should be approved before they are used. Accountants have the right to reject any expenditure inconsistent with regulations. Production teams should make public the revenue and expenditure each month. Grain and other agricultural and sideline products belonging to production teams should be so scrupulously kept that embezzlement, misappropriation, and other losses are prevented. Specific personnel should be employed to take charge of grain, materials, finance, and accounting. Team directors should examine and supervise the work on finance and the storing of materials, but must not be in personal charge of cash and materials.

38. Production teams should be run in a democratic way and should arouse the enthusiasm of members for becoming masters.

Important matters of the production teams concerning output and distribution should be decided by general meetings of team members after discussion rather than by cadres. Before meetings, the production teams should outline their various programs to team members, clearly explain concrete measures for implementing the programs and seek their suggestions. After full discussion, the general meeting of team members should make decisions in a democratic way.

Team members should convene general meetings on schedule, at least once every month. Meetings may also be specially convened to meet the demands of production and distribution and the requests of team members.

The directors, accountants, and members of management committees and control commissions of the production teams should be elected at general meetings of team members for a one-year term and may be re-elected for a second term.

The direction of teams should be assumed by peasants who come from a good class, perform satisfactory work, have much experience in agricultural production, know how to consult the masses, and also are fair and just in conducting business.

Incompetent team directors, accountants, members of management committees and control commissions, or controllers may be dismissed at any time by general meetings of team members.

The team management committees should submit at least one work report to general meetings of team members each month. The work reports should include important matters in which team members are interested, such as the revenue and expenditure of the production teams, the amount of materials stored, the number of workpoints team members earned, the amount of manure offered or sold, and the amount of grain or cash distributed. All of these matters should be explained one by one to team members who have the right to raise questions, offer criticism, and make suggestions.

Team management committees should pay careful attention to various suggestions of team members at all times and act in accordance with suggestions by the majority, meanwhile safeguarding the democratic rights and economic interests of the minority.

CHAPTER V DOMESTIC SIDE OCCUPATIONS OF COMMUNE MEMBERS

39. The domestic side occupations of the members of the people's communes are necessary supplements to the socialist economy. They pertain to the economy of collective ownership as well as to the economy of ownership by the whole people, serving as their auxiliaries. On the condition that they would strive to develop the collective economy, not hinder the development of the collective economy, and guarantee the absolute preponderance of the collective economy, the people's commune should allow and encourage their members to avail themselves of their leisure time and the holidays to develop domestic side occupations, increase the output of society, augment the members' income, and enliven the rural markets.

40. The members of the people's communes may engage in the following domestic side occupations:

a. Cultivating private plots distributed by the collectives. The area of private plots normally accounts for 5–7 percent of the cultivated land of production teams. These private plots are for use by the households of commune members and will remain unchanged for a long time. In areas where there are wooded hills and barren slopes, the production teams may, based on the needs of the masses and old customs, allot to team members an appropriate number of private hills to be managed by them. The private hills, once allotted, will also remain unchanged.

b. Raising livestock and poultry, such as pigs, sheep, rabbits, chickens, ducks, and geese, or raising sows, cattle, and horses. To develop pig breeding so as to provide more manure for the collective economy, the production teams may, wherever needed and suitable, allot to their members an appropriate number of fodder plots in accordance with their local land conditions and after the discussion of team members. Fallow land or small lots of wasteland should be used as much as possible to this end.

c. After discussion by the general meetings of production teams and approval of communes or production brigades, fractional wasteland may be opened up under a unified programming. The acreage of land thus opened up may normally be the same as that of private plots. It may be a little less where there is a smaller population, and a little more where the population is larger.

In opening up wasteland, it is absolutely forbidden to destroy soil, mountains, forests, prairies, or irrigation facilities or to disrupt communications.

The combined area of private plots, fodder plots, and reclaimed wasteland owned by production team members varies with different local conditions. Under normal conditions, the acreage may account for 5–10 percent of the cultivated land of a production team, or 15 percent at most.

d. Engaging in domestic handicraft production, such as knitwear, sewing, embroidery, and the like.

e. Engaging in such side occupations as picking, fishing, hunting, sericulture, apiculture, and so on.

f. Managing private fruit trees and bamboos distributed by the collectives. Team members may plant fruit trees, mulberry trees, and bamboos around their houses or at other places specified by the production teams. These plants will belong to team members forever.

When engaging in domestic side occupations, team members should pay the collectives proper fees whenever they use the means of production owned by the collectives, such as livestock or implements.

41. The products and earnings that team members gain from domestic side occupations belong to, and are at the disposal of, the team members. After fulfilling the contracts of purchase they signed with the state, team members may sell the products at the fairs except those specifically restricted by the state.

The agricultural products grown by team members on their private plots and reclaimed wastelands are not included in the reckoning of the output and the food grain rations to be distributed by the collectives. The state will not impose farm tax on products of this kind, nor will they be subject to requisition.

42. The management committees at various levels of the people's communes should offer commune members who undertake domestic side occupations necessary instruction and assistance and should not interfere without proper reason. At the same time, they must instruct commune members to pay equal regard to the interests of the state and the collectives to actively participate in and show concern for collective production, to avoid infringing public interests, not to quit farming to go into business, and not to engage in speculation.

For team members who encounter difficulties in earning their living, the production teams should help them solve difficulties and increase their income by enabling them to undertake some side occupations, such as pig breeding, knitwear, and the like.

43. In accordance with the principles of voluntariness and mutual benefit, the organizations at various levels of the people's communes, the supply and marketing cooperatives, the handicraft cooperatives, and the state-run enterprises specified by the state may adopt a variety of ways, including processing, placing orders for their products, purchasing raw materials for them, marketing their products on their behalf, purchasing their products, or having team members rear public-owned livestock, to help team members develop domestic side occupations, combining domestic side occupations with the collective economy or the state-run economy.

CHAPTER VI COMMUNE MEMBERS

44. The members of the people's communes enjoy all the rights to which they are entitled within the communes in respect of politics, economics, culture, and welfare. The organizations at various levels of the people's communes should respect and safeguard all the rights vested in team members.

In the communes composed of several nationalities, commune members from different nationalities should have common respect for different customs and should befriend and cooperate with one another.

All means of subsistence including houses, furniture, clothes, bicycles, and sewing machines owned by individual commune members and their deposits in banks or credit cooperatives belong to commune members forever and should be safeguarded; no encroachment upon this ownership is allowed.

All the means of production including farm implements and tools owned by individual commune members and their livestock should belong to commune members forever and should be safeguarded; none is allowed to encroach upon this ownership.

A system for vacations should be carried out by arranging labor time in accordance with the usual farming practices and with the busy or slack farm seasons so as to achieve a proper ration between labor and leisure.

Concern must be shown for the physical health of commune members, and the security of commune members in labor must be safeguarded. Proper subsidy should be furnished to commune members injured while on official assignments. Dependents of commune members who died while carrying out official assignments should be given proper pension. Special care should also be taken of the physiological peculiarities of female commune members and the growing youths participating in labor. Female commune members on maternity leave who have difficulties in learning a living should be properly subsidized.

Commune members have the right to make suggestions, to take part in discussion and vote, to offer criticism, and to exercise supervision in the production, distribution, welfare, and expenditure of the communes or brigades. This right is under the protection of the people's government and is not to be violated by anyone.

Commune members have the right to indict to higher authorities any cadres of communes or brigades of violation of the law and discipline. This right is under the protection of the people's government; none is allowed to obstruct the exercise of such right or to resort to retaliation.

45. The houses of commune members belong to the members forever.Commune members have the right to buy, sell, or rent their houses. In doing so, a contract may be signed between the buyer and the seller or between the homeowner and the tenant, through a go-between assessing a fair and reasonable rental or price.

No units or individuals may compel commune members to move. Without commune members' personal consent or paying reasonable rental or price, no organs, groups, or units can occupy the houses of commune members. In case the houses of commune members must be commandeered for construction or other purposes, the regulations on commandeering private houses promulgated by the State Council must be strictly observed. Compensation must be paid and the moved households properly resettled.

The organizations at various levels of the state and the people's communes should offer commune members all possible aid in manpower and material for constructing their houses. The sites for commune members to construct houses should be mapped out by the production teams. Occupying cultivated land for residential purpose should be avoided wherever possible.

46. All members of the people's communes should heighten their socialist consciousness and fulfill their obligations to the communes. Each member is required to abide by the state policies and decrees and carry out the decisions made by the commune people's congresses and general meetings of commune members.

Each commune member must care for the collectives, voluntarily observe labor discipline, and struggle against the phenomena of impairing the collective economy and subverting labor discipline.

Each commune member must do his or her basic daily stint and complete the stipulated tasks of submitting or selling manure.

Each commune member should take good care of the public property of the state, communes, and brigades, protecting them from damage.

Commune members should heighten their revolutionary vigilance and guard against the restoration of feudal forces and the sabotage activities of counterrevolutionaries.

CHAPTER VII CADRES

47. The organizations at various levels of the people's communes must practice rigorous retrenchment, reducing, whenever possible, the number of those cadres who completely or partially turn away from productive activities and cutting to a minimum the number of the subsidized workpoints given to cadres. The number of the subsidized workpoints given to cadres of the communes or production brigades should be discussed and approved by the people's congresses or general meetings of commune members and ratified by the superior level, rather than arbitrarily decided by cadres.

The number of cadres at the commune level should be rigorously limited to that stipulated by the state in accordance with the size of the communes and the principle of retrenchment. It is forbidden to exceed this limit.

The number of cadres of a production brigade should be deliberated and decided by its people's congress in accordance with its size and the principle of retrenchment. After it is approved by the management committee of the people's commune to which it is affiliated, the number decided on should be submitted to the county people's committee (the county people's government) to be kept on record. The cadres of the production brigades must not completely turn away from productive activities; they can only partially turn away from their work in production.

The number of cadres of a production team should be decided by general meetings of team members in accordance with its size and the principle of retrenchment, and should also be too many. All the cadres of production teams are required to engage in production.

48. The cadres at various levels of the people's communes should establish the concept of serving the people, working as sincere servants of the people. They must show concern about the livelihood of the masses, always keep the masses in mind, share their joys and hardships and oppose individualization. They are prohibited from practicing graft, sharing bribes, or eating and taking more than their due.

The cadres at various levels of the people's communes should have a correct understanding of the identity of interests of the state and the masses, correctly combining their responsibility to the state with that to the masses. When encountering difficulties in executing the superiors' directives, they may report to the superior level and submit their own suggestions.

The cadres at various levels of the people's communes must implement conscientiously the three main rules of discipline and the eight points for attention laid down for all Party and state cadres. The three rules of discipline are: (1) conscientiously execute the policies set forth by the Party Central Committee and the laws and decrees of the state, and actively participate in socialist construction; (2) implement democratic centralism; and (3) reflect the true situation. The eight points for attention are: (1) show concern for the livelihood of the masses; (2) take part in collective labor; (3) deal with people on an equal footing; (4) consult the masses about work and be fair and square in conducting affairs (5) identify themselves with the masses and not hold themselves aloof from the masses; (6) have no say in matters without investigations; (7) act in accordance with factual situation; and (8) heighten the proletarian class-consciousness and meanwhile raise the political level.

49. The cadres at all levels of the people's communes must uphold the democratic work style and oppose decrees by force. They must establish correct leadership on the basis of democracy and oppose laissez-faire. They are forbidden to suppress democracy or seek revenge. They should discuss problems with the masses on an equal footing and let people with different opinions speak their minds freely. They should deal with commune members having different opinions by consultation rather than by force and refrain from making false accusations. They are strictly forbidden to beat or scold the people and impose corporal punishment in any shape or form. They are also strictly prohibited from punishing commune members by means of "withholding food rations," excessively deducting workpoints, or excluding them from fieldwork.

50. Cadres at all levels of the people's communes must learn administration, management, and production, raising their professional standard. At the same time, they must participate in labor along with commune members.

Depending on different working conditions, the cadres at the commune level should engage in collective labor in the production teams for certain days, sixty days at least in a whole year. Furthermore, they would ensure that their work reaches a certain standard in quality and quantity.

The cadres of the production brigades and teams should take an active part in labor in the capacity of ordinary commune members and their work should be evaluated and workpoints given in the same way as ordinary commune members. Each cadre of the production brigade had better always participate in labor in one particular production team. The cadres of the production brigades are required to work at least 120 days in a whole year.

To compensate the cadres of production teams for reduced income due to loss of work time for official reasons, fixed subsidies or subsidiaries for the loss of work time should be awarded according to the workload of each cadre after discussion and decision by team members. The subsidized workpoints for the cadres of production teams generally should be limited to no more than 1 percent of the total workpoints.

Cadres of the production brigades who partially turn away from productive activities can be subsidized either by the state or by the production teams with a certain number of workpoints. In the areas where the latter way is adopted, the total subsidized workpoints issued to the cadres of a production brigade and its production teams may be a little more than 1 percent of the total workpoints of the production teams, but should not exceed 2 percent.

In case counties or units above counties summon the cadres of the production brigades and production teams to conferences, they should not only bear these cadres' travel and food expenses, but also issue them proper subsidies. The production teams will give them no more workpoints.

51. The appointment and dismissal of the personnel at all levels of the people's communes and any reward and penalty should conform to the stipulated procedures. It is forbidden to appoint cronies or indulge in favoritism and corruption. Any appointment, dismissal, reward, or penalties inconsistent with procedures are invalid.

CHAPTER VIII SUPERVISORY ORGANIZATIONS AT VARIOUS LEVELS OF THE PEOPLE'S COMMUNES

52. The control commissions or controllers of the production teams and the control commissions of the production brigades are under the leadership of the control commissions of the communes, which are under the jurisdiction of the county people's committees. The central supervisory organs may directly oversee the work of the supervisory organizations at various levels of the people's communes.

53. The functions of the various levels of supervisory organizations of the people's communes are as follows:

a. Investigating whether or not the cadres of the management committees violate the state policies or decrees, the provisions of these Regulations, and the decisions made by the people's congresses and by the general meetings of commune members.

b. Investigating whether or not the cadres violate the civil and other rights of commune members, and whether there are other violations of the law and discipline.

c. Inspecting the accounts of cash and inventories of the management committees of the same and lower levels, enterprises, and collective welfare undertakings; checking whether or not their income and expenditure are proper or at variance with the fiscal system.

d. Investigating wrongdoings including favoritism, corruption, extravagance, wastefulness, eating or taking more than one's due, embezzlement, misappropriation, and destroying public property.

e. Accepting the accusations of commune members, their prosecutions, and complaints.

f. Attending the meetings of the management committees of the same or lower levels.

g. Interrogating the management committees and other organizations or personnel of the same or lower levels. The organizations or people interrogated should be responsible for giving prompt answers.

h. Organizing, whenever necessary, special personnel to conduct inspection and investigation. All units and personnel concerned are under obligation to supply information.

For serious problems, the supervisory organizations at various levels of the people's communes should submit their accusations or prosecutions to the superior supervisory organs and judiciaries, even up to the supervisory commission of the Party Central Committee, the Supreme People's Procuratorate, and the Supreme People's Court.

When encountering obstruction and resistance in their work, the supervisory organizations of the people's communes have the right to report to their superior levels, including the central supervisory organ for resolution.

54. Cadres serving on the management committees at various levels of the people's communes, accountants, cashiers and custodians of the communes, and the managers of enterprises and undertakings run by the communes or production brigades are ineligible for membership of the control commissions or for being a controller.

CHAPTER IX PARTY ORGANIZATIONS IN THE PEOPLE'S COMMUNES

55. According to its size and number of Party members, each people's commune may set up a Party committee, or a general Party branch committee, or a Party branch committee. According to its size and number of Party members, each production brigade may set up a general Party branch committee or a Party branch committee. The Party committees, general Party branch committees, and Party branch committees are the grassroots rural organizations of the Chinese Communist Party, serving as the nucleus of leadership in rural work.

56. The Party organizations in the people's communes must strengthen the leadership in the work of all levels and units of the people's communes in conformity with Party guidelines and policies, but must not take it upon themselves the duties of the management committees at various levels. The work and duties of the communes and brigades should be handled by the management committees. The Party organizations in the people's communes must give priority to the work on education and training of the cadres, especially those of the production teams.

The Party organizations of the people's communes should discuss and study periodically the work performed by the people's congresses, general meetings of commune members, management committees, and control commissions of various levels.

As for important issues concerning production, the life of the masses, the execution of the policies, decrees and plans of the state, etc., the Party organizations should first fully deliberate them within the Party, and then study together with commune members and non-Party cadres, and then bring the Party's proposals before the general meetings of commune members, the people's congresses, the management committees, or control commissions for discussion. Implementation should be ensured after they are announced.

57. The Party organizations in the people's communes should do a good job in ideological and political work.

They must propagate among Party members, League members, and the masses Marxism-Leninism, Mao Zedong Thought, as well as the Party's General Line for Socialist Construction, the Great Leap Forward, and the People's Communes. Further, they must educate them in socialism, patriotism, collectivism, and worker-peasant alliance, as well as current affairs and policies, so as to consolidate the people's communes ideologically and politically.

They must carry out regularly the class education of the proletariat and the education in the Constitution of the Party and that of the League among Party members and League members.

They must teach Party members, League members, and cadres to care for the opinions of the masses at all times.

They must teach Party members, League members, and cadres to correctly implement the Party's class line in the rural areas, rely on the old poor peasants and middle-lower peasants and firmly unite with other middle peasants. They must strengthen the solidarity among the laborers from different nationalities.

58. The Party organizations in the people's communes must assume the leadership in the work of the Communist Youth League and the Conference of Women's Delegates, enabling them to play well their part as links between the Party and the masses.

The Party organizations in the people's communes must strengthen their leadership in militia work, to ensure that the military equipment of the militia is in the hands of the activist elements of old, poor, lower-middle peasants who are politically reliable.

59. The Party organizations in the people's communes should improve their organized living, strengthen the Party's organization and discipline, and put an end to such phenomena as the shirking of responsibilities and laxity in organized living, with the Party branches playing the role of a fortress and Party members the role of a paragon.

They should periodically convene meetings of Party groups and rallies of Party branches, intensify Party members' study in the Party policies and the Party Constitution, examine Party members' work among the masses, and carry out criticism and self-criticism.

The Party committees of the communes and their affiliated general Party branch committees or Party branch committees should hold elections at intervals as stipulated in the Party Constitution. In doing so, they must give full play to democracy within the Party and listen attentively to the suggestions of the masses.

Recruiting or punishing Party members must be strictly in conformity with the procedures set forth in the Party Constitution.

The Party committees of the communes must do a good job in scrutinizing Party members, tighten up and purify the Party organizations, and guard against bad elements and elements of other parties worming their way into the Party.

60. The Party organizations in the people's communes must strictly observe democratic centralism and act upon the principle of combining collective leadership with division of labor and the sharing of responsibilities. All important issues should be discussed in meetings rather than being left to the personal decision of secretaries. During the discussion, individuals attending the meeting should be enabled to voice adequately their opinions. Decisions should be made collectively, abiding by the principle that the minority is subordinate to the majority. After the decisions are made collectively by the Party committees, Party organizations and personnel concerned must act upon them in an earnest and responsible manner.

II. COMMUNE REFORM AND GOVERNANCE

(d) Report of the State Council on the Northern Districts Agricultural Conference

Zhongfa [1970] No. 70

Chairman Mao's Instructions: Approved for Distribution

The Revolutionary Committees of all provinces, municipalities, and autonomous regions; all military regions, provincial military districts, and group armies; all headquarters, the military, and arms; the CPC Central Committee and all ministries and commissions:

The Report of the State Council on the **Northern Districts Agricultural Conference** (draft) brought back by provincial representatives attending the meeting for discussion and implementation has proved that it can advance the role of "grasping revolution and promoting production" and solve some urgent problems.

The central government now officially approves this report, expecting all provinces to enforce it based on local context. At the same time, agricultural development plans of all provinces, municipalities, and autonomous regions should be formulated in mid-December this year, in accordance with this report and the conception of the fourth Five-Year Plan for Agricultural Development.

CPC Central Committee

December 11, 1970

(Please circulate this piece to all counties)

To: Chairman Mao, Vice-Chairman Lin, and the CPC Central Committee

We held the Northern Regional Agriculture Conference from August 25 to October 5. The attendees included provincial-, city-, and county-level delegates from fourteen provinces, municipalities, and autonomous regions located in Northern China; lower and lower-middle peasants from progressive communes and brigades; and delegates from other provinces, municipalities, autonomous regions, and PLA Production and Construction Corps, totaling 1,259 people.

Delegates first went on a study tour to Dazhai Brigade and Xiyang County, and then to the conference in Beijing. They studied the important instructions from Chairman Mao and Vice- Chairman Lin, carried out large-scale revolutionary criticism, summarized and exchanged the experience of learning from Dazhai, studied the relevant policy issues in the current rural work, and discussed the design and measures of the fourth Five-Year Agricultural Plan.

During the conference, delegates enthusiastically studied the communiqué of the Second Plenary Session of the Ninth Central Committee of the CPC, the remarks made by Vice Chairman Lin at the celebration ceremony of twenty-first anniversary of the National Day, and the National Day's editorials published on central newspapers and magazine. The conference unanimously agreed to resolutely respond to the call of the Plenary Session, adhere to the continued revolution under the dictatorship of the proletariat, adhere to Chairman Mao's proletarian revolutionary line and policy, and continue to complete the fighting missions identified by the Ninth National Congress.

1. The New Upsurge in Agricultural Production Is on the Rise

At the present time, the situation is excellent both domestically and internationally. Under the unified and successful guidance of the Ninth National Congress, a new upsurge in the socialist agricultural production is on the rise.

First, the tasks of struggle, criticism, and correction are carried out step by step among the vast majority of communes and brigades. Large-scale revolutionary criticism, "One-Strike-Three-Anti Campaign,"[4] and the party-building movement continue to be deepened. The combat prepared-ness work has been greatly strengthened. The mass lower and lower-middle peasants have been improving their consciousness of class struggle and line struggle. An active revolution prevails in the countryside.

Second, the mass movement of Learning Agriculture from Dazhai has a new progress. There is an emergence of not only thousands of Dazhai-type communes and brigades, but also Dazhai-type counties.

Third, the agricultural production has experienced a bumper harvest for eight consecutive years and is anticipated to continue the trend this year. In 1969, the municipal grain yield per mu in Beijing, Shanghai, and Zhejiang exceeded the requirement of the "Program."[5] Among the fourteen provinces, municipalities, and autonomous regions in northern regions, there were 84 counties, 1,251, communes and 26,613 brigades that had more grain production than the requirement of the "Program." This year there will be more counties, communes, and brigades. Hebei, Shandong, and Henan Provinces, where food shortage pervaded for a long time, have ini-tially achieved food self-sufficiency through the Great Proletarian Cultural Revolution. This is a great thing with strategic significance.

Fourth, the farmland construction is developing rapidly. From last win-ter to this spring, the country's high-yielding farmland has increased more than 30 million mu, reaching 450 million mu, of which the fourteen north-ern provinces, municipalities, and autonomous regions added 13 million mu, totaling 150 million mu.

Fifth, the industries for agriculture, especially the "five small" industries, are developing rapidly. It is estimated that the national steel production of small iron and steel plants will reach 1.8 million metric tons and pig iron production will reach 3.3 million metric tons. About 90 percent of the counties around the country will be equipped with agricultural machinery repair factories.

Now, the collective economy of our people's communes is more consoli-dated. Food and most of the cash crops have been able to meet the basic needs of national construction and people's livelihood. This is the great victory of Chairman Mao's revolutionary line and the great victory of the Great Proletarian Cultural Revolution.

The conference pointed out that in the past, the development of agri-cultural production was largely affected by the disruption and destruction of the antirevolutionary revisionist line led by Liu Shaoqi, the renegade, traitor, and scab. Currently, China's grain yield per unit area is still relatively low. The capability of disaster resistance and management is not strong. The grain reserve is not adequate. The level of agricultural mechanization is not high. Especially in the fourteen northern provinces, municipalities, and autonomous regions with nearly half of the national population, the reliance on food delivery from southern China has not yet been completely reversed. This situation is incompatible with the requirements of "preparing against natural disasters for the people," the development of national economy, and the expectation that "China should make a greater contribution to the mankind." We must work harder and double our efforts to promote agricultural production and grab back the time delayed by a handful of counterrevolutionary revisionists like Liu Shaoqi.

2. Learning Agriculture from Dazhai

Delegates visited Dazhai, listened to the experience of Xiyang County, studied the editorial titled "Learning Agriculture from Dazhai" in *People's Daily*, and experienced a huge shock to their mind-sets. They have also enhanced their confidence, improved the morale, and solved two major problems:

First of all, it is clarified that which should be learned from Dazhai. That is to learn Dazhai brigade's consistent adherence to the principle of proletarian politics in command and Mao Zedong Thought in leadership, to learn its self-reliance and hard-working spirit, and to learn its communism-type patriotism and collectivism in the three revolutionary movements of class struggle, production struggle, and scientific experiments. In a word, that is to educate the peasants with the great Mao Zedong Thought like the Dazhai Party branch. This is the primary and fundamental experience of Dazhai. The material and spirit can be interchangeable. Once the masses master the Mao Zedong Thought, then there comes a direction, a driver, and a way through which we can change the people, the land, and the production and overturn the earth. As for some specific methods of operation, management, and production techniques, those should be the secondary lessons to be learned from Dazhai and cannot be replicated regardless of local conditions.

Secondly, it is clarified that in order to disseminate the Dazhai experience, we must firmly stick to the guideline of class struggle, starting from resolving the leadership problems underlying communes and brigades at all levels and the revolutionization issues within the leadership, particularly at the county level. Why are people from some communes and brigades unable to carry out the mass movement of Learning from Dazhai? Where does the resistance come from? According to the comrades of Xiyang County, this is mainly because some leadership teams are infiltrated by the rogues; some cadres cannot distinguish from the enemies whom they collude with; some are keen on the capitalism road; some are the so-called yes-men who show little enthusiasm about socialism and thus unleash the proliferation of capitalism. There are other Party members whose mind-set still stays in the stage of democratic revolution and cannot reach the gateway to the socialist revolution. Lower and lower-middle peasants from Xiyang made a good point about it. Their sayings include "Learn from Dazhai, chase after Dazhai, one cannot learn well without power in hand," "learn well or not, leadership is the pivot." Xiyang County firmly seized this key; scrutinized over four hundred county branches one by one; carried out large-scale revolutionary criticism, Party rectification, and "One-Strike-Three-Anti" campaigns in three years; and mobilized the masses to unveil the class struggle of the society and within the Party. Following Chairman Mao's guidance of "attacking less and educating more" and the policy of "getting rid of the old and bringing in the new," they have strictly differentiated two types of contradictions, united and educated the majority of cadres, removed a handful of rogues inside the Party leadership, saved a group of cadres from wrongdoings, and elected a large number of new leaders. As a result of these efforts, the spirit of leadership at all levels was renewed, the mass movement of Learning from Dazhai was spread across the county, the total grain production doubled in three years, the yield per mu surpassed the requirement of the "Program," and Xiyang turned into a Dazhai-type county. The conference believed that the experience from Xiyang was representative and other counties should study and promulgate it based on their own situations. Now, many counties have their own "Dazhai." While studying Xiyang's experience, they should ask themselves the following questions: If Xiyang can do it, why cannot we? If we cannot do it in one year or two, can we achieve it in three years? Or four or five years?

Dazhai is a red flag advocated by the great leader Chairman Mao. "Learning Agriculture from Dazhai" is the great call of Chairman Mao. All delegates agreed that determining whether to learn from Dazhai or not was of great importance in choosing the line of agriculture. All delegates expressed their resolution to say, "under the same dome, on the same ground, with the same sun and the leadership of Chairman Mao, what Dazhai is capable of, we can achieve as well."

3. Deepen Class Struggle and Two-Line Struggle

Chairman Mao taught us: "socialism is the only way for China's agriculture." Since the founding of the PRC, the intense conflict between the two lines in the rural areas has always revolved around the fundamental question of which line should be taken. Liu Shaoqi and his agents have long opposed Chairman Mao's proletarian revolutionary line, vigorously advocated a set of revisionist schemes, such as "three freedoms and one contract,"[6] "four big freedoms,"[7] and "material stimulus," attempting to disintegrate the socialist collective economy and restore capitalism. Renegade Liao Luyan has long dominated the Ministry of Agriculture, established an independent and dictatorial regime, sabotaged the Party's unified leadership, and strangled the passion of the local and the masses. He furiously opposed proletarian politics in command, objected to the mass movements transforming socialist agriculture, and deluded the public that the socialist collective economy was dying. He turned the previous Ministry of Agriculture into a "technical department" and a department of "retrogression." Through the Great Proletarian Cultural Revolution, a handful of traitors, spies, and unrepentant capitalists were apprehended, yet the counterrevolutionary revisionist line they pursue still exists. Hence, the current mission must be to put through a large-scale revolutionary criticism emphasizing the following issues.

 a. Eradicate the vestige of "three freedoms and one contract" and "four big freedoms," criticize the capitalism tendency, and adhere to the socialism principle.

Comrades attending the conference listed numerous facts and pointed out the intenseness of the current class struggle and line struggle in the rural areas. A small group of class enemies usurp a few communes and brigades. Landlords, rich peasants, revisionists, and rogues provoke a storm of trouble and initiate counterrevolutionary activities. In some communes and brigades where the capitalist tendency pervades, corruption, embezzlement, opportunism, farmland abandonment, and advocacy for businesses have severely undermined the consolidation and development of the collective economy. It has been proved that agriculture production decreases as capitalism rises and increases as socialist righteousness permeates. Wuji-aping, a brigade contiguous to Dazhai, used to be an advanced unit. After 1957, the unit was separated due to an uproar. Wujiaping became capitalist and its grain yield decreased from over 300 catties to 200 catties. Dazhai remained socialist and its yield increased from over 300 catties to 900 catties. Later, Wujiaping halted its capitalist trend and learned from Dazhai earnestly. It took three years to meet the requirement of the "Program," four years to cross "Yellow River," and five years to cross "Yangtze River."[8] In Qufu County, Chenjiazhuang, Shandong, grain yield per mu was 500 catties when the good was in charge, but after the revisionists took power, grain yield dropped from 500 catties to 300 catties. When the masses stood up to replace the bad with the good, grain yield grew from 300 catties to 600 catties and reached 1,000 catties last year through the Great Proletarian Cultural Revolution. Comrades pointed out that the "three freedoms and one contract" and "four big freedoms" were slogans representing the interests of the landlords and rich peasants and were the counterrevolutionary guideline to restore capitalism in rural areas. It is a basic task and a long-term mission of rural political and ideological work to eradicate the vestige of and constantly criticize the capitalist tendency.

  b. *Criticize the idea of "relying on the heaven and the state," and adhere to the principle of "self-reliance" and "hard work."*

In order to develop agriculture, should we depend on the lower and lower-middle peasants and be self-reliant, or should we count on the heaven and the state? This is a critical issue in the two-line struggle of the agricultural front.

Jiuyuangou of Suide County, Shaanxi Province, used to be a typical "state-funding and peasant-farming" commune. From 1953 to 1963, the state invested 960,000 yuan, but only built 2,600 mu of terraced fields and five dams. Since last winter, they mobilized the masses, criticized the thought of reliance on others, and consequently repaired 1,450 mu of horizontal terraced fields and constructed over twenty dams without a penny from the state.

Shenyang is a large industrial city with a total population of more than 4.2 million, of which nearly 60 percent is urban population. In the past, capitalists said, "Shenyang is built on industries and should not engage too much in agriculture." As a result, its food, vegetables, and meat have long been imported from other provinces. After the establishment of the provincial and municipal Revolutionary Committee, Shenyang achieved a "turnaround in agriculture," which can basically realize self-sufficiency in food and vegetables this year.

Two principles contribute to two consequences. Just as the lower and lower-middle peasants said, "the more one relies on the country, the lazier one becomes, the less grain can be produced; to learn from Dazhai, the more self-reliant one is, the wider the road one can walk through." This is exactly the conclusion.

> c. Criticize Rightist conservative thinking and the worldview of tardiness and cowardliness, improve the morale, and aim high.

Chairman Mao once pointed out in the upsurge of rural socialism in 1955: "The current problem is that people consider it impossible to do what they could have completed with hard work. Therefore, it is absolutely necessary to constantly criticize the Rightist conservative ideas that do exist." Yan'an County serves as a vivid example. Agricultural production there used to be at a low level for two decades, while only 18,000 mu of farmlands were irrigated. This year they re-learned Chairman Mao's responding message to the Yan'an people in 1949, criticized the Rightist conservative ideas in the leadership, and carried forward the spirit of Yan'an; 10,000 mu of farmlands and 30,000 mu of Dazhai farmlands were irrigated in approximately six months. What used to take two decades can be achieved in one year, can't it?

At present, in the face of a new upsurge in production, there are still some leaders and cadres who fall behind the situation, follow the old, are satisfied with the status quo, and lack the sensitivity to new things. They always find it impossible to do everything, stick to the old mode, and refuse to innovate. Some people put "fear" upon anything and are willing to do nothing at all. They disseminate the philistine philosophy that "upstream is adventurous, downstream is dangerous, midstream is safe and stable." Their so-called safe and stable philosophy is to ensure the safety of "private" interests and their political careers. This erroneous thought can put the Party and the people at risk if it is not rebuked.

> d. Eliminate the vestiges of ideas that are "Left" in form but Right in essence such as "proneness of bloating and exaggeration" and "arbitrary orders," and integrate the passion and ambition with the spirit of seeking truth from facts.

The delegates also enumerated a large number of facts, harshly reprimanding a handful of counterrevolutionary revisionists, including Liu Shaoqi, for using the approach that is left in form but right in essence to sabotage Chairman Mao's proletarian revolutionary line. They rebuked several capitalists for their arbitrary orders, "egalitarianism and indiscriminate transfer of resources" (*yiping erdiao*), and the "proneness of bloating and exaggeration" (*fukua feng*) during the Great Leap Forward, which seriously damaged the agricultural productivity. What they did, in essence, is the Kuomintang's approach to the masses, which deprives peasants, undermines the collective economy of people's commune, and destroys the worker-peasant alliance. "Historical experience is worth attention." The delegates talked about the fact that in the past, there were a few places that changed the basic accounting unit and retrieved reserved lands regardless of the conditions and the will of the majority of the people. The scale was not large, but the influence was not trivial, signaling the presence of the ideas that is left in form but right in essence among some leaders and cadres. It is necessary to remind the leaders at all levels to pay full attention.

The delegates evaluated the situation of class struggle in the rural areas according to the Directive of the Second Plenary Session of the Ninth Central Committee. It is agreed that we must follow Chairman Mao's guidance of "earnestly engage in struggle, criticism, and correction," deepen the "One-Strike-Three-Anti" campaign, and complete the party-building tasks. During this winter or next spring, according to individual condition, all need to organize the Mao Zedong Thought Propaganda teams consisting of the People's Liberation Army, revolutionary cadres, and lower and lower-middle peasant representatives. The teams must go inside the communes and brigades that have not completed "struggle, criticism, and correction"; rectify the Party branches one by one; resolve the leadership problems underlying the communes and brigades; "organize a revolutionary leadership closely tied with the people"; and consolidate the dictatorship of the proletariat to the grassroots level.

4. Implement the Party's Policies Correctly

In accordance with Chairman Mao's guidance that "policy and strategy is the life of the Party, leaders at all levels must pay full attention and never be negligent," the conference discussed how to correctly implement the Party's policies targeting the rural areas.

Chairman Mao personally presided over the formulation of the *Sixty Articles* of the people's commune, which played a significant role in consolidating the collective economy and improving agricultural production. After Great Proletarian Cultural Revolution, the situation has undergone a new development, but the basic policy of the *Sixty Articles* regarding the people's commune at the present stage is still applicable and must continue to be implemented. In December 1967, the Central Committee had made it clear that "the existing three-level and team-based system and the private land system of rural people's communes should generally be unchanged." In February 1969, *People's Daily* editorial reiterated, "policy issues newly emerged in the movement, particularly those involving ownership, should be treated cautiously and request for directives." We must strengthen the Party's policy concept and tackle the undisciplined and unorganized trends in some places. The Party policy is a concrete manifestation of Chairman Mao's proletarian revolutionary line. Only by earnest implementation of the policy would the Rightist and Leftist disruption be excluded.

All delegates agreed that we must follow the instructions of Chairman Mao, noticing one major tendency while also noticing another tendency that may be concealed. The cadres must be told clearly what they are permitted to do and what they are not under the Party's policies. We must resolutely eliminate the vestiges of the "three freedoms and one contract" and "four big freedoms." However, under the circumstances when the collective economy is guaranteed to develop and maintain the absolute advantage, commune members can operate a small amount of private plots and household sidelines. We must resolutely eliminate the vestiges of "material stimulus" and "workpoint in command," but also adhere to the principle of "distribution according to work" and oppose egalitarianism. We must criticize the erroneous tendency of "splitting up and using up," but also avoid accumulating so much that the commune members' income will be affected this year. Under the premise of following the unified national plan, we must allow the production teams to adapt to local conditions flexibly. We must promote socialist cooperation, and gradually develop the economy of the communes and brigades, yet we must not repeat the mistake of "egalitarianism and indiscriminate transfers of resources." The state-run enterprises or enterprises managed by production brigades and lower-middle peasants are allowed neither to dispatch labor, supply inventories, and other facilities of the production team without payment nor to increase the burden of the commune members. We must not draw excessive labor from the production teams in the name of mobilizing farmers to support the national construction, which impacts the production and management of the production teams. At present, some communes and brigades arbitrarily increase the nonproduction personnel and nonproduction expenses and reduce the income of commune members, which affects the enthusiasm of members. All governments must take effective measures to stop it.

5. Accelerate the Realization of Agricultural Development According to the "Program"

In line with Chairman Mao's strategic guidelines on "preparing the war against natural disasters for the people," the conference discussed the conception of the fourth Five-Year Agricultural Development Plan.

First, the goal is to "reverse the situation that Northern China must rely on the grains delivered from the South" and to meet the requirement of "National Program for Agricultural Development." In areas where the goal has been achieved, we should push the agricultural production toward a new pinnacle. We should also speed up the development of agricultural production in the third front and the northern areas with food insecurity.

Second, we must follow the guideline of "all-round development based on grain production." We must earnestly promote the production of grain, cotton, oil, hemp, silk, tea, sugar, vegetables, tobacco, fruit, medicine, and etc. Five industries including agriculture, forestry, animal husbandry, sideline, and fishery must be arranged comprehensively and mapped out with plans. We must emphasize the grain production while developing a diversified economy and preventing overconcentration. We must emphasize forestry and animal husbandry. "It takes ten years to grow a tree." It also takes several years for big livestock to grow up, so the work must start early.

Third, we must put great efforts into the farmland construction. As long as the basic conditions of agricultural production are unchanged, the grain yield cannot be stabilized and the passive situation underlying agriculture cannot be reversed fundamentally. The fourth Five-Year Plan is aiming to assure each person one mu of high-yielding field regardless of the weather and climate through the improvement of soil and water conservancy. Terraced fields must be introduced on the hills and mountains. Flat farmland and soil improvement should be introduced in plain areas. Water conservancy construction should be adhered to the small-scale, support-ive, and commune-based approaches. Flood control should be combined with soil improvement and alkaline modification. Drilling and studies on how to make use of the underground water should be encouraged.

Fourth, we should increase the use of fertilizer with a main purpose of boosting pig raising. We should earnestly promote pig raising via a col-lective approach and continue to encourage the commune members to participate. We should find reasonable solutions to pig feed and continue to implement the policy where the state subsidizes swine sales with an appropriate amount of pig feed. The commune members who feed the pigs should receive reasonable payment. We should increase feed mills, popu-larize saccharified pig feed, and prevent swine fever. Through the fourth Five-Year Plan, we should achieve one pig for each two people, striving for one pig per capita. "If we can achieve one pig per capita, one pig per mu, we can find the main source of fertilizer." We should grow more green fertilizer according to local conditions, and actively promote the use of fertilizers.

Fifth, we should fully implement the agricultural "Eight-Word Constitu-tion" on soil, fertilizer, water, cultivation, coverage, storage, management, and labor. We should actively promote high-quality seeds and appropriate close-spaced planting based on local conditions. We should take advan-tage of intercropping, actively develop pesticides, and prevent pests and diseases. We should frequently exchange and promote new technologies.

Sixth, "the fundamental solution for agricultural development lies in mechanization." With no agricultural mechanization and manual labor alone, it is impossible to increase agricultural productivity more quickly, it is impossible to change the situation of 600 million peasants struggling for food, and it is impossible to free up labor to speed up industrial construc-tion. It has been fifteen years since Chairman Mao proposed to "basically achieve agricultural mechanization within twenty-five years." We should pay close attention to the work of the next decade. During the fourth Five-Year Plan, the level of farming mechanization should reach about 50 per-cent of the arable land and the level of irrigation mechanization should reach about 60 percent.

Agricultural mechanization should adopt the principle of "walking with two legs." We should encourage all provinces, municipalities, and autono-mous regions to be more self-reliant based on local conditions and meet the requirements of intensive farming. We should utilize both domestic and foreign techniques and develop mechanization and semimechanization simultaneously. We should endeavor to advance "five small" industries from the raw materials and adhere to the direction of serving agriculture.

All provinces, municipalities, and autonomous regions should proceed immediately to formulate the agricultural development plan for 1971 and the fourth Five-Year Plan. "When devising the plan, we must mobilize the masses and pay attention to the flexibility of the plan."

The Five-Year Plan is grounded on the conditions of the first three years, the Three-Year Plan is grounded on the conditions of the first year, and the annual plan is grounded on the conditions of the previous winter. All governments should earnestly supervise the harvest and cultivation work this fall and the farmland construction between this winter and next spring.

6. Strengthen the Leadership of the Party

Chairman Mao taught us, "China has over 500 million agricultural population. The living condition of farmers is instrumental in developing national economy and consolidating the regime." To develop agriculture, we must strengthen the Party's unified leadership. The heads of the Party organizations and the Revolutionary Committee at all levels should be held accountable, take personal responsibility, and strengthen the leadership of the mass movement of Learning Agriculture from Dazhai. Particularly at the city and county levels, we should focus on guiding the rural work. For tertiary and food-insecure areas, we must boost agricultural production as soon as possible. We cannot take any initiative before the agricultural sector meets the requirement.

The development of agriculture is crucial for the Party and the people of the whole country. It is not only the issue of the agricultural sector. Other departments, including industry and transportation, finance, and trade, should see supporting agriculture as their glorious task and actively contribute to the development of agricultural production.

In the face of the current new upsurge of agricultural construction, we must prepare ourselves to be progressive. We should earnestly study Chairman Mao's philosophy, adjust the worldview, and improve the work style and working methods. We should promote dialectical materialism and historical materialism and oppose the idealism and metaphysics. We should have not only the vigor for revolution, but also the scientific attitude of seeking truth from facts. We should focus on pragmatism rather than the glorious fame. "There must be a driver, there must not be lies." We should improve the production and livelihood at the same time and balance between work and rest to prevent an overemphasis on one side. "We should be modest and prudent and to guard against arrogance and rashness." We should seek the masses for help and should not be capricious.

Right now, some leaders and cadres use the metaphysical view to tackle the relationship between revolution and production, politics and economics. They either see it as a parallel or a contradiction. They do not understand that politics is the commander and the soul and they do not have the proletarian politics in command rooted in their mind. Others use the revolution as a substitute instead of a driver of production. We must fully implement the principle of "grasping revolution and promoting production." To guide the agricultural work, we must rely on the lower-middle peasants and take the mass line. Cadres' participation in collective production work is an important measure to prevent and oppose revisionism, thus must be resolutely implemented. "We must emphasize the archetypes." "The surface of the work should be grasped a third first." We must carry out large-scale investigations and studies, summarize the experience in a timely manner, and extend it to broader scope. To streamline the conferences, we must oppose the "five excesses,"[9] and resolutely correct the superficial management style featured by "only appearing at the meeting, writing on the paper, and talking without practices." The agricultural and forestry departments of the central government must stick to the proletarian politics in command; deepen the reform into the grassroots; concentrate on studying the Party's principles, policies, and planning; and exchange the best practices. As for important issues, we must discuss with the local authorities, provide them with necessary assistance, and defeat the "dictatorship" with a resolution.

All delegates insisted that we must uphold the red flag of the great Mao Zedong Thought, follow the leadership of Central Committee of the CPC under Chairman Mao and Vice Chairman Lin, leverage the outcomes of the Second Plenary Session of the Ninth National Congress, and "unite for a greater victory!"

State Council

October 5, 1970

(Reprinted from original of Central Committee)

(e) CPC Central Committee Directive Concerning the Question of Distribution in the Rural People's Communes[10]

December 26, 1971

Zhongfa (1971) No. 82

Chairman Mao's Instructions: Published as Recommended

Under the guidance of the line of unity and triumph adopted in out Party's "Ninth Congress," and in compliance with our great leader Chairman Mao's directive concerning carrying out ideological and political education in the whole Party, the rural areas in the whole nation have unfolded a rectification movement to criticize revisionism. This education has in particular succeeded in smashing the counterrevolutionary conspiracy of careerist, conspirator, renegade, and traitor Lin Biao and his diehard followers; smashing the counterrevolutionary revisionist line of Lin Biao and Chen Boda; enhancing the consciousness of the broad masses of poor and lower-middle peasants, commune members, and revolutionary cadres in their class struggle and the struggle between the two lines; raising to a higher level the aggressiveness of socialist revolution and production; and enlarging to a wider scope the mass movement of "Learning Agriculture from Dazhai," thus promoting the overall development in agriculture, forestry, animal husbandry, sideline production, and fishery. After overcoming the serious natural disasters caused by drought, flood, typhoons, and pests, agricultural production this year scored a bumper harvest for the tenth consecutive year. At present, the situation of revolution and production in the countryside is excellent.

In this excellent situation, "we must take care of the national, collective, and personal interests" and at the same time, seriously make the Party's related policies take full effect, and do well the distribution work in the rural people's communes. This is of paramount importance in carrying out Chairman Mao's great strategic plan for "preparing against war, preparing against natural disasters, and doing everything for the people"; consolidating the socialist position in the countryside; intensifying the proletarian dictatorship; promoting the socialist aggressiveness of the broad masses of commune members; and supporting the nation's socialist construction.

On the whole, distribution word in the rural people's communes of the whole nation is excellent. In recent years [our comrades in] various areas have, in general, been able to correctly handle relations between the country, the group, and individuals, actively completed and surpassed national levying and purchasing tasks, thus strengthening the collective economy and increasing the commune members' income. However, we should also be able to see that on the question of distribution, the struggles between the two classes, two roads and two lines are still rampant. Some communes "partition all and eat all"; others increased production collectively, but commune members' income did not increase; and some others have many households that overdraw, making normal distribution impossible. Still others, having criticized "workpoints take command" and have exercised egalitarianism in paying for the labor. All these impaired the thorough implementation of Chairman Mao's revolutionary line.

In order to further improve distribution work in rural people's communes, we must summarize experience, enhance achievement, correct deficiency, and effectively solve the following problems:

1. Correctly handle relations between collective accumulation and distribution among commune members. The people's communes should gradually build up their accumulation on the basis of productive development. To do this, however, we should not accumulate too much at one time. "We should make every possible effort to enable the peasants to receive better personal incomes in normal situations from the increased production year after year." Those communes, production brigades, or teams that develop production faster and have a higher income level may, with the commune members' agreement reached through discussions, retain a more proportionate public accumulation.

In general, the commune or the production brigade should not draw the public accumulation from the production team. However, it also may, with the agreement of the team's assembly through discussions, draw a proper share of the public accumulation for establishing enterprises or purchasing agricultural machinery, provided that the drawing does not affect the team's plan for enlarging reproduction.

The public reserved fund should be used for enlarging reproduction; it should not be used for building offices, auditoriums, or hostels or for entertainment or gifts and other nonproductive expenditures.

2. Handle distribution of grains extremely well. The Central Committee's notice concerning the Five-Year Plan for continuously carrying out the levy and purchase of grains shall be seriously and thoroughly implemented with full effect. In carrying out this task, we should ensure timely accomplishment of the nation's levy and purchase missions, and at the same time, take

good care of the life of commune members. "Over purchase of grains is positively prohibited."

The production team must reserve sufficient grains for seeds and fodder. "There must be reserve grains. A little reserve a year will build up a great amount in the end." The reserve grains of collective organizations are to be used primarily for preparing against war and natural disasters, and cannot be used without sufficient reason. When the reserve grains must be used, the use should be decided through assembly discussions of the commune members.

For distribution of rations, we can use the general practice to integrate basic rations with distribution according to workpoints, or other proper systems supported by the majority of commune members. Whatever the case, the grains should be so distributed that it can facilitate mobilizing labor aggressiveness of the greatest majority of commune members and at the same effectively ensure that dependents of the martyrs, soldiers, staff, and workers and difficult households receive normal rations. Rations for commune members should be sent to the houses of individuals and controlled by commune members themselves. We shall educate the commune members to be industrious and frugal and to spend their rations according to their own plans.

The levy and purchase of grains or the unified marketing index for the areas where economic crops are concentrated should be properly arranged. We should resolutely pledge that commune members in these areas receive rations not less than that in the adjacent grain-producing areas. The rations for commune members in forestry, animal husbandry, and fishing areas should also be properly arranged.

3. Persist in the socialist principle of the "from each according to his ability and to each according to his work." A good system of payment for labor is the basis of "to each according to his work." In paying commune members for labor, we must persist in the proletarian politics taking command, steadily raise the consciousness of commune members to plant rice for revolution, and steadily struggle against capitalist inclination. In the current stage, attention must be paid to overcoming egalitarianism. We should pay commune members reasonably according to the quality and quantity of their labor. To learn from Dazhai's labor administration methods, we must start from the actual situation and discuss the matter with the masses, but not adopt the methods wholly without consideration. We must mobilize the masses to seriously summarize the typical experience, which proves good in their area, correct those complicated unreasonable things that restrict

aggressiveness of the masses, persist in those simple feasible measures that are welcomed by most of the masses, and steadily improve them.

The principle of equal pay for equal work of men and women must be practiced, and the feudal thinking of prejudice against women must be criticized and repudiated. In some areas, the "four category elements"[11] who have more men workers at home incite men and women to do the same amount of work with unequal pay and exploit the poor and lower-middle peasants by taking advantage of the old thinking of the cadres and the masses. Particular attention should be paid to this deviation, which must be exposed in time and resolutely struggled against.

4. Seriously carry out the policy of administering the communes through diligence and frugality, fostering the spirit of self-reliance and hard struggle. "[We] must very frugally use our manpower and material resources and strictly refrain from waste." The collective welfare enterprises conducted by the commune, brigade, or team should conform the economic development level. It will not be allowed to increase those individuals who are disengaged from production without good reason. The propaganda teams, broadcast announcers, and athletic teams should persist in various activities in their spare time. The barefoot doctors[12] should persist in participating in collective production labor. When necessary, they may, with the approval of commune members through discussions, be absent from work with workpoints granted.

The system of persisting in having cadres participate in collective production labor "is a great matter of basic nature under the socialist system." Some cadres in production brigades and teams participate in little labor. This situation must be resolutely corrected, and the cadres should be made "three nondisengaged."[13] The allowance for their additional workpoints should not exceed the amount stipulated in the *Sixty Articles.* [14]

The types of conferences should be simplified. Meetings should be made fewer in number and shorter in time. When governments of the county and above call cadres and commune members from the production brigade and team for conferences or study class training, those participants and trainees should be provided with allowances, food costs, and necessary travel expenses. The commune and brigade should try as much as possible not to use production time for meetings.

If the commune wants to utilize the labor from the production team, the commune must consult members of the team. If the national departments want to utilize labor from the production team, the use must have prior approval of Party committees at various levels and should be given reasonable reward. It will not be allowed to again commit the mistake of "production grading and sending up"[15] by using the capital and materials of the production team with no pay and launching a donation campaign or levying money among the masses.

If the national government conducts cultural, educational, medical, or other enterprises and activities, or delegates the administration of these enterprises and activities to poor and lower-middle peasants in the production team, the expenditure for these enterprises and activities should be provided by the national departments concerned, but not by other organizations of commune members. The national subsidies approved for schools sponsored by civilians and subsidized by the government and that for civilian-sponsored school teachers in various areas cannot be transferred to other uses without prior permission.

5. Thoroughly solve the problem of overdrawing households. At present, some communes, brigades, and teams have quite a few overdrawing households, rendering normal distribution impossible. They have even used up the accumulation of the group, partitioned the national loans, thus seriously battering the aggressiveness of the commune members' collective production, affecting the consolidation and development of the collective economy. This must be seriously regarded and treated. The reasons for the emergence of overdrawing households are several. The primary factor is agitation by the class enemy and the erosion of certain cadres by capitalist ideology. Therefore, we must tightly grasp the class struggle, strike the sabotage activities of the class enemy, and criticize and repudiate capitalist inclination; we must intensify the revolutionary construction of the leading group of communes, brigades, and teams, educate cadres to heighten their consciousness, change their working style and make them take the lead in repaying money they owe; we must establish the financial system in the organizations and units responsible for financial administration at various levels and in communes, brigades, and teams, and improve it with the objective that financial affairs have no secret, the accounts are published, and democracy is practiced in economy.

6. Thoroughly carry out the policy of "taking the grains as the key link to promote overall development." To develop production and increase income is the basis of distribution. When the people's commune grasps

the production of grains, it must properly arrange the plans for agriculture, forestry, animal husbandry, sideline production, and fishery, and properly treat the relations of grains, cotton, oil, linen, silk, tea, sugar, vegetable, tobacco, fruit, drugs, and other products, so that the success of the key link will prompt the development in other aspects, which will in turn promote one another and lead to overall development. They should make a fine line between multiple business and "money takes command" and should not mistake multiple businesses, which is allowed by the Party's policy, for the capitalist inclination, which must be criticized and repudiated.

The commercial departments should actively organize multiple businesses in communes, brigades, and teams and the justified household sidelines. They should also intensify the purchase of products and correctly carry out the Party's price policy and not reduce grade and price, so as to promote the development of multiple businesses in rural areas.In addition to this, the reasonable policy of reward for selling must be carried out continuously and cannot be changed at will.

The Central Committee hopes that the Party committees at various levels will grasp the distribution work in rural people's communes as a great task. They shall take the rectification movement for criticizing revisionism as the key link to persist in the mass line, engage in deep investigation and research, seriously grasp the models and the proper time to summarize experience so as to successfully grasp the final account and distribution work of this year.

(This directive will be distributed to various organizations down to county and regimental levels.)

(f) Mobilize the Whole Party, Make Greater Efforts to Develop Agriculture and Strive to Build Dazhai-Type Counties Throughout the Country[16]

Excerpts of the report by Hua Guofeng at the National Conference on Learning from Dazhai in Agriculture

October 15, 1975

Comrades:

Our conference has continued for a month and we have fully discussed the question of learning from Dazhai in agriculture. At the same time, we have studied the question of agricultural mechanization. Today I shall dwell on the following questions.

I. MILITANT TASK OF THE WHOLE PARTY

China's socialist revolution and socialist construction at present are in an important historical period of development, and the nationwide mass movement "In agriculture, learn from Dazhai" has also reached a new important stage. A great militant task before us is to get the whole Party mobilized, make ever greater efforts to develop agriculture and strive to build Dazhaitype counties throughout the country. This is an urgent task in implementing Chairman Mao's important directive on studying theory and combating and preventing revisionism and in consolidating the dictatorship of the proletariat; it is also an urgent task in pushing the national economy forward so that China will be advancing in the front ranks of the world before the end of this century, as well as an urgent task in racing against the enemy for time and speed and doing a good job of getting prepared against war. The whole Party must get mobilized vigorously, attain unity in thinking and pace, unite and lead the people of the whole country to accomplish this great political task.

To build Dazhai-type counties throughout the country means building every county in China into a fighting bastion which adheres to Chairman Mao's proletarian revolutionary line and the socialist road. In this way, the leading bodies at all levels in the country will be further revolutionized. The cadres and members of our Party and the masses of the people will greatly raise their understanding of Marxism-Leninism-Mao Zedong Thought. Our dictatorship of the proletariat and socialist-system will be further consolidated and developed. And we shall have greater might with which to smash attacks in any form by any enemy.

To build Dazhai-type counties all over the country means enabling every county in China to achieve stability and unity on the basis of Chairman Mao's revolutionary line and go all out to build socialism with millions united as one. It means that every county will implement the general principle of "taking agriculture as the foundation and industry as the leading factor" in developing the national economy, undertake large-scale farmland capital construction, basically realize the mechanization of agriculture, "take grain as the key link and ensure an all-round development" so that production of grain, cotton, oil-bearing crops, pigs, all industrial crops and forestry, animal husbandry, side occupations and fishery will surpass the targets set in the National Program for Agricultural Development and outstrip the state plans. We should see to it that the modernization of agriculture would more effectively push forward and guarantee the modernization of industry, national defense and science and technology so as to greatly strengthen the material base of our great socialist motherland for preparedness against war and natural disasters.

Take for instance Shanxi Province where Xiyang County is located. If every county in Shanxi is built into a Dazhai-type county attaining this year's level in Xiyang where every person on the average has produced 750 kilograms of grain and supplied 250 kilograms of marketable grain, then the total grain output in the whole province would increase 2.5-fold and marketable grain nearly fourfold compared with 1974. Generally speaking, natural conditions in Shanxi as a whole are not worse than in Xiyang and it is quite possible for the entire province to attain Xiyang's present level. From the example of Shanxi alone, we can see the prospects of how grain production will rise after Dazhai-type counties have been built all over the country.

The necessary conditions for building Dazhai-type counties throughout the country have been provided on a nationwide scale. As a result of the tremendous victories won in the Great Proletarian Cultural Revolution and in the movement to criticize Lin Biao and Confucius and the destroying of the two bourgeois headquarters of Liu Shaoqi and Lin Biao, Chairman Mao's revolutionary line has achieved brilliant successes on all fronts and the consciousness of the cadres and people in class struggle and the two-line struggle has risen to unprecedented heights. Since 1970, the Xiyang experience in building itself into a Dazhai-type county in three years has been popularized and the movement to learn from Dazhai in agriculture has gathered ever greater momentum. Dazhai-type communes and production brigades have emerged in great numbers, more than 300 counties in various parts of the country have excelled as advanced units in learning from Dazhai, and a revolutionary torrent involving vast numbers of people in learning from Dazhai has taken shape in many areas and a number of provinces. In the movement to learn from Dazhai, the cadres and people have mounted powerful attacks on the class enemies and capitalist forces and this has led to a tremendous rise in the socialist forces and a drastic fall in the capitalist forces. Farmland capital construction has been carried out on a large scale, and during the past four years some 100 million people have taken part in each winter-spring period, bringing an average of 1.6 million more hectares of land each year under irrigation. The rate of mechanization of agriculture has been gradually stepped up. The amount of irrigation and drainage equipment, chemical fertilizer and tractors supplied in the past four years exceeded the total supplied in the previous 15 years, and a number of production brigades, communes and counties have attained a relatively high degree of mechanization. Mass scientific experiment in farming has spread far and wide. Five provinces and municipalities, 44 prefectures and 725 counties have topped their targets for per-hectare yield of grain set in the National Program for Agricultural Development. Another 11 provinces and one municipality are nearing their respective targets. Thirty counties in the north have reached the target set for areas south of the Yangtze River, six of them topping the 7.5-ton-per-hectare mark, and four counties in the south have doubled the yield set by the program.[17]

At the same time, however, we must take note of the fact that the development of the movement is as yet not well balanced. So long as we strengthen the leadership, adhere to the correct line and take effective steps, the movement will get under way rapidly.

Learning from Dazhai in agriculture and building Dazhai-type counties throughout the country is a great revolutionary mass movement to continue the revolution under the dictatorship of the proletariat and build socialist agriculture with greater, faster, better and more economical results. Like the land reform, agricultural co-operation and people's commune movements, it is another great revolutionary movement in the rural areas. The whole Party, from the Central Committee to Party committees at provincial, prefectural and county levels, should firmly take it into their own hands, exercise centralized leadership, and organize all fronts and departments to make concerted efforts and strive for the victory of the movement.

II. KEY LIES IN COUNTY PARTY COMMITTEES

Dazhai is a standard-bearer established by Chairman Mao himself; it is a typical example in adhering to the Party's basic line, continuing the revolution under the dictatorship of the proletariat and achieving greater, faster, better and more economical results building socialist agriculture. Dazhai's fundamental experience lies in its adherence to the principle of putting proletarian politics in command and placing Mao Zedong Thought in the lead, to the spirit of self-reliance and hard struggle and to the communist style of loving the country and the collective. Dazhai has consistently used Marxism-Leninism-Mao Zedong Thought to educate the peasants and deepen the socialist revolution in the political, economic and ideological and cultural spheres. It has consistently practiced criticism and self-criticism and strengthened the revolutionization of the leading body. It has continually given full scope to the enthusiasm, wisdom and creativeness of the masses, thus ensuring the growth of agricultural production and progress in agricultural technique year after year. To build a Dazhai-type county means spreading Dazhai's fundamental experience throughout the county.

Through discussions and study at the conference the present standards for a Dazhai-type county are as follows: (1) The county Party committee should be a leading core which firmly adheres to the Party's line and policies and is united in struggle. (2) It should establish the dominance of the poor and lower-middle peasants as a class so as to be able to wage resolute struggles against capitalist activities and exercise effective supervision over the class enemies and remold them. (3) Cadres at the county, commune and brigade levels should, like those in Xiyang, regularly participate in collective productive labor. (4) Rapid progress and substantial results should be achieved in farmland capital construction, mechanization of agriculture and scientific farming. (5) The collective economy should be steadily expanded and production and income of the poor communes and brigades should reach or surpass the present level of the average communes and brigades in the locality. (6) All-round development should be made in agriculture, forestry, animal husbandry, side-occupations and fishery with considerable increases in output, big contributions to the state and steady improvement in the living standards of the commune members.

The key to building Dazhai-type counties lies in the county Party committees, which are at once leading and executive organs. Only when there are staunch county Party committees is it possible to set the pace for the communes and brigades.

That the key in building Dazhai-type counties lies in the county Party committees does not mean that the provincial and prefectural Party committees are relieved of the important or even primary responsibility they should assume. Whether a province or prefecture has a clear idea about taking agriculture as the foundation, whether it follows a correct orientation in building Dazhai-type counties, whether the measures taken are practical and effective and whether the pace of progress is fast enough, the leadership o! the provincial or prefectural Party committee plays a decisive role.

III. DEEPEN EDUCATION IN PARTY'S BASIC LINE

In the historical period of socialism, the principal contradiction always remains the struggle between the proletariat and the bourgeoisie and between the socialist road and the capitalist road. Deepening education in the Party's basic line in the countryside is the fundamental guarantee for building Dazhai-type counties. All provincial, prefectural and county Party committees must conscientiously do a good job in grasping this work, mobilize the masses fully, constantly raise the socialist consciousness of the broad masses of peasants and make consistent efforts to ensure the victory of socialism over capitalism.

The serious problem is the education of the peasantry. The peasants are willing to take the socialist road under the leadership of the Communist Party. We must unswervingly rely on the poor and lower-middle peasants, unite with the middle peasants and wage struggles against capitalism. With the growth of the socialist agricultural economy, the consolidation of the people's commune system and the improvement of the peasants' life, the overwhelming majority of the peasants have come to see more clearly than ever that only socialism can save China, and their enthusiasm for socialism has become still higher. We must be aware at the same time that in socialist society there are still classes and class struggle, and that the differences between town and country, between worker and peasant and between manual and mental labor still remain. Our country at present practices a commodity system, the wage system is unequal, too, as in the eight-grade wage scale and so forth. Under the dictatorship of the proletariat such things can only be restricted. Therefore, new bourgeois elements will invariably be engendered continuously. This is true of the countryside as well as the cities. The traditional influence of small production still remains among the peasants, and there still are fairly serious spontaneous tendencies towards capitalism among the well-to-do middle peasants. It is a long-term task constantly to imbue the peasant masses with the socialist ideology and to criticize the tendency towards capitalism, and at no time should we relax our efforts in this respect.

Many cases of the tendency towards capitalism in the countryside are problems among the people. They must be solved by means of persuasion and education, and criticism and self-criticism. It is also necessary to solve those problems concerning the consolidation and development of the collective economy appropriately in line with the Party's policies, and make constant efforts to consolidate and extend the positions of socialism.

IV. SPEEDING UP THE BUILDING OF LARGE-SCALE SOCIALIST AGRICULTURE

We must guide the cadres' and masses' socialist enthusiasm engendered in the course of vigorously criticizing capitalism on to the great drive to develop socialist agriculture.

In building Dazhai-type counties, it is necessary to undertake farmland capital construction as a great socialist task. We must carry forward the spirit of self-reliance and hard struggle, transform China in the spirit of the Foolish Old Man who removed the mountains, change the face of mountains and harness the rivers. This is a fundamental measure to increase our capabilities to resist natural calamities and achieve high and stable yields, and we must persistently and unremittingly carry out this work with the utmost efforts. The experience of the Dazhai-type counties in different parts of the country shows that where big progress has been achieved in farmland capital construction, the superiority of the people's commune as an institution large in size and with a high degree of public ownership has demonstrated fully, the old features of small production have undergone tremendous changes, and better conditions have been created for the development of mechanized farming than elsewhere. In the course of farmland capital construction, the collective concept and sense of organization and discipline of the peasants are greatly enhanced and they think more of the collective and show greater zeal in building socialism. "The more we do it, the better we like it and the greater our courage and ability to do it well." All this helps to further consolidate and develop the victory in vigorously criticizing capitalism and developing socialism.

In order to build themselves into Dazhai-type counties, all counties must map out overall plans for their farmland capital construction.

To equip agriculture with machinery is a decisive factor for achieving a great expansion of farming, forestry and animal husbandry simultaneously. In the course of building Dazhai-type counties throughout the country, the provinces, municipalities and autonomous regions must energetically develop their own form machinery industry in the light of local conditions so as to supply the communes and production brigades with equipment and other products needed for the mechanization of agriculture.

The prefectures and counties, for their part, must in the light of their own resources and other conditions set up small industrial enterprises producing iron and steel, coal, chemical fertilizer, cement and machinery in order to provide the rural areas with more farm machinery, chemical fertilizer and insecticide suited to local needs. We must publicize among the masses Chairman Mao's teaching that the fundamental way out for agriculture lies in mechanization, bring the enthusiasm and initiative of the hundreds of millions of people into full play, work energetically for the technical transformation of agriculture and raise the level of mechanized farming step by step and in a planned way. We must train a mighty contingent of people for mechanized farming, people who are both workers and peasants and well versed in modern techniques. The development of farm mechanization will greatly raise labor productivity in agriculture and enable the peasants to set aside plenty of time to develop a diversified economy and build a new, prosperous and rich socialist countryside. It will also have a great significance in bringing into play the role of the people's commune as an organization that combines industry, agriculture, commerce, education and military affairs, in enabling the commune to display its superiority— big in size and with a high degree of public ownership—and in narrowing the differences between town and country, between worker and peasant and between manual and mental labor. Therefore, the various departments concerned under the State Council and the leading organs or the provinces, prefectures and counties must make very great efforts to speed up the progress of this work so as to ensure that the great task of mechanizing agriculture will be accomplished in the main by 1980.

In order to build Dazhai-type counties and achieve high and stable yields, it is necessary to implement the Eight-Point Charter for agriculture[18] in an all-round way and go in for scientific farming. It is necessary to make big efforts to breed, propagate spread, purify and regenerate fine seed strains; to change the old cropping system, improve cultivation techniques and raise the multiple-cropping index; and to tap various sources of fertilizer, apply fertilizer rationally and do plant protection work well. We must work hard to promote scientific research in agriculture so as to change the present situation in which research lags far behind the needs of speeding up the expansion of large-scale socialist agriculture.

Each county must set up agricultural scientific experimental organizations at the county, commune, production brigade and production team levels and weld them into a complete network, encourage the masses to carry out widespread scientific experiments, and bring into full play the function of professional scientific and technical personnel. At the central, provincial, prefectural and county levels, the agricultural scientific research organizations must be reinforced and agricultural production and technical work given more guidance.

The expansion of commune- and brigade-run enterprises strengthens the economy at the commune and brigade levels; it has effectively helped the poorer brigades and teams, accelerated farm production, supported national construction and speeded up the pace of mechanization of agriculture. It constitutes an important material guarantee for the further development of the people's commune system. Party committees in all parts of the country must adopt a positive attitude and take effective measures to help the commune- and brigade-run enterprises develop still faster and better. In promoting the expansion of commune and brigade-run enterprises, it is necessary to keep to the socialist orientation and see to it that they devote their main attention to serving agriculture and the people's livelihood. Where conditions permit, these enterprises should also work for the big industries and for export. It is necessary to make the fullest possible use of local resources to develop the cultivation of crops and breeding as well as processing and mining industries.

The people's communes have great vitality and are promoting the development of all kinds of undertakings in the countryside. For most parts or China, the rural people's communes' present system of "three-level ownership, with the production team as the basic accounting unit" is in the main still in harmony with the growth of the productive forces in the countryside. However, we must also note that, with the spread and deepening of the movement to build Dazhai-type counties, with the expansion of large-scale socialist agriculture, and especially with the growth of the economy at the commune and brigade levels, this system of ownership will make a step-by-step transition to the system of ownership that takes the production brigade or even the commune as the basic accounting unit when conditions are ripe. In the still more distant future, the people's commune will undergo the transition from the system of collective ownership to the system of ownership by the whole people and then from the socialist system of ownership by the whole people to the communist system of ownership by the whole people. Therefore, although the economy at the commune and brigade levels today is only incipient and small, herein lie our great, bright hopes.

V. ALL-ROUND PLANNING AND THE STRENGTHENING OF LEADERSHIP

To build Dazhai-type counties throughout the country is a great march in which our Party leads millions upon millions of peasants to deepen the socialist revolution and speed up socialist construction. The Central Committee and the local Party committees at various levels should all map out all-round plans and effective measures and go all out to win victories, just as they did in leading the land reform and the movement for agricultural co-operation and in directing military operations.

After five years of hard struggle, that is, by 1980, more than one-third of the counties in the country are expected to become Dazhai-type counties, and more Dazhai-type brigades and communes should have been built up in the other counties. There are now more than 300 advanced counties in the country which have distinguished themselves in learning from Dazhai. While these counties must continue to consolidate their achievements and make further progress, an average of at least 100 new Dazhai-type counties should be built annually in the next five years. The provincial, municipal and autonomous regional Party committees and the prefectural Party committees under them should all work out their own concrete plans. All county Party committees in the country should regard the work of building Dazhai-type counties as their own goal of struggle and, on the basis of local conditions, draw up their own schedules and steps for accomplishing the task and strive to fulfill it ahead of time.

The various departments under the Party Central Committee and the government should make great concerted efforts and do a good job in building Dazhai-type counties. Agricultural departments must devote all their efforts to the movement to build Dazhai-type counties throughout the country, do a good job in investigation and study, and give timely reports to the Central Committee and the State Council on the movement's progress and problems. All other departments including those or planning, industry and communications, finance and commerce, culture and education, science, public health and family planning should make their contributions to building Dazhai-type counties throughout the country.

Building Dazhai-type counties is a great and arduous fighting task. We shall inevitably come up against many difficulties on our way of advance. But we shall certainly be able to overcome all kinds or difficulties and reach our goal so long as we earnestly carry out the political line, policies, principles and methods of work formulated by Chairman Mao and have faith in and rely on the masses. We Communists, revolutionary workers and staff members, poor and lower-middle peasants and educated youth who have settled in the countryside have high aspirations and ability "to change our world by our own hands through hard struggle and build our as yet very backward countryside into a thriving and prospering paradise."

III. DECOLLECTIVIZATION

(g) On Questions of Rural Policy 19

Deng Xiaoping
May 31, 1980

Now that more flexible policies have been introduced in the rural areas, the practice of fixing farm output quotas on a household basis has been adopted in some localities where it is suitable. It has proved quite effective and changed things rapidly for the better. Fixing output quotas on a household basis has been adopted in most of the production teams in Feixi County, Anhui Province, and there have been big increases in production. Nearly all the production teams in the same province's Fengyang County, which incidentally is the locale of the "Fengyang Flower-Drum" Opera, have been practicing an all-round contract system, which inside of a year has resulted in an upswing in production that has transformed the county's prospects. Some comrades are worried that this practice may have an adverse effect on the collective economy. I think their fears are unwarranted. Development of the collective economy continues to be our general objective. Where farm output quotas are fixed by household, the production teams still constitute the main economic units. What does the future hold for these places? It is certain that as long as production expands, division of labor increases and the commodity economy develops, lower forms of collectivization in the countryside will develop into higher forms and the collective economy will acquire a firmer basis. The key task is to expand the productive forces and thereby create conditions for the further development of collectivization. To be specific, the following four conditions should be realized: First, a higher level of mechanization, one that is relatively well suited to local natural and economic conditions and welcomed by the people (here I mean mechanization in a broad sense, not merely mechanized plowing, sowing, and harvesting). Second, a higher level of management, combining accumulated experience and a contingent of cadres with fairly strong management abilities. Third, a developed diversified economy that leads to the establishment of a variety of specialized groups or teams, which in turn leads to the large-scale expansion of the commodity economy in the rural areas. Fourth, an increase in the income of the collective, both in absolute terms and in relation to the total income of the economic unit involved. If these four conditions are realized, the localities that now fix output quotas on a household basis will develop new forms of collectivization. This sort of development won't come from above as the result of administrative decree, but will be an inevitable response to the demands of growing production.

Some comrades say that the pace of socialist transformation had been too rapid. I think there is some ground for this view. For example, in the cooperative transformation of agriculture, there was an upsurge every year or two, with one kind of organizational form being quickly replaced by another before the first one had time to be consolidated. The rapid, large-scale transition from elementary cooperatives to advanced cooperatives was a case in point. If the transformation had advanced step by step, with a period of consolidation followed by further development, the results might have been better. Again, during the Great Leap Forward in 1958, before cooperatives of the advanced type had been consolidated, people's communes were set up on a large scale. As a result, we had to take a step back in the early sixties and again make production teams the basic accounting units of the collective economy. During the rural socialist education movement, production teams of an appropriate size were arbitrarily divided into very small ones in some localities, while in others they were amalgamated into teams that were too large. Practice has shown this to be bad.

Generally speaking, the main problem in rural work is still that people's thinking is not sufficiently emancipated. This problem manifests itself not only in the matter of determining the organizational forms of collectivization. It also is apparent when it comes to developing production suited to local conditions. The latter means developing what is appropriate for a specific locality and not arbitrarily attempting what is unsuitable. For instance, many areas in northwest China should concentrate on growing forage grass in order to expand animal husbandry. Some cadres currently give little thought to planning new undertakings that would be suitable to local conditions and would produce economic gains and benefit the masses. Far from emancipating their thinking, these cadres still act according to fixed patterns. Thus there is still much work to do, even now that flexible policies have been adopted.

It is extremely important for us to proceed from concrete local conditions and take into account the wishes of the people. We must not propagate one method and require all localities to adopt it. In publicizing typical examples, we must explain how and under what conditions people in these localities achieved success. We should not describe them as perfect or as having solved all problems; and we should certainly not require people in other places to copy them mechanically in disregard for their own specific conditions.

(Excerpt from a talk with some senior officials under the Central Committee of the Communist Party of China.)

(h) CPC Central Committee Directive Concerning Several Issues in Further Strengthening and Perfecting the Production Responsibility System in Agriculture

Zhongfa (1980) No. 75

In a recent colloquium of the first secretaries of the provincial, municipal, and autonomous regional committees of the CPC, the issues regarding further strengthening and perfecting the production responsibility system in agriculture were discussed, with the following meeting minutes. The Central Committee agreed with the opinions in the meeting minutes, and now forwards them to you for prompt transmissions, discussions, clarification, and unification of thoughts, and implementation with regard to local conditions, in order to motivate the broad rural cadres and the masses to do their job well and enhance agricultural productions.

CPC Central Committee
September 27, 1980

Several Issues in Further Strengthening and Perfecting the Production Responsibility System in Agriculture

Meeting Minutes of the first secretaries of the provincial, municipal, and autonomous regional committees of the CPC, September 14 to September 22, 1980

First, since the Third Plenary Session of the Party's Eleventh Central Committee, localities throughout the country have liquidated the influences of the ultra-Left line, implemented two of the Central Committee's documents on agriculture, adjusted the agricultural policy regarding prices, taxation, credit, and purchase of sideline agricultural products, and relaxed restrictions on private plots, household sideline production and country fair trade. More prominent is the promotion of autonomy for production teams, thereby enabling them to develop a diversified economy suitable to local conditions, to establish various forms of production responsibility system, to improve measures of calculating payments for labor performed, and or rectify subjectivism in directing production and equalitarianism in distribution. These measures have effectively mobilized the power of initiative of the peasants, brought about a comparatively speedy recovery and development of agricultural production and an increase of income for the majority of peasants, and made the situation in the countryside better and better.

Our future tasks still are to continue to march ahead along the line, the guiding principle, and the policy decided upon by the Party's Central Committee at its Third Plenary Session, to study new circumstances, to solve new problems, to strive for an overall upsurge of agricultural production and a gradual improvement of livelihood for the peasant, and to realize overall agricultural modernization.

Second, the collective economy is the unshakable foundation on which to modernize our country's agriculture. It has the superiority that cannot be matched by individual economy, a fact that has been attested to by the history of agricultural development in the recent twenty years. Since the liberation of the whole country, our Party has led the broad masses of peasantry to affect two social reforms of far-reaching significance. First, it was the elimination of the feudalist system to carry out the land reform. Secondly, it was the implementation of socialist reform of the small peasant economy to lead several hundred million peasants onto the socialist road. This has in turn laid down the new basis for the worker-peasant alliance, released rural productivity, and initiated the peasants into the new era of agricultural socialist construction.

Although our country's agricultural collectivization has confronted some complications and developed some faults, generally speaking, it was primarily a success. The complications and faults we are talking about have been in the main caused by failures to do things in strict accordance with the principles of voluntary participation by, and mutual benefit of, the masses in the process of directing agricultural collectivization, which caused not a few localities to adopt more political coercion and administrative actions than measures of demonstration and attraction; and by failures to consistently follow the correct guiding principles of suiting measures to local conditions, giving different directions for different things, and following in order and advancing step by step, while practicing the erroneous way of cutting things with one stroke of the knife and cooking different things in the same pot. These problems had already emerged during the period of the establishment of advanced agricultural cooperatives and then developed to a larger degree and on a larger scale during the movement for people's communes, resulting in a nationwide "tendency to effect the transition to communism prematurely," the "proneness of bloating and exaggeration," and the "arbitrary orders" that caused even more serous losses. Aiming at these situations, the Party Central and Comrade Mao Zedong had conducted several adjustments of the system and policy concerning the people's commune to enable the collective economy to stabilize step by step. Now, after more than twenty years of efforts, the rural collective economy has been consolidated in the majority of localities and the orientation of agricultural collectivization is recognized and supported by the broad messes of peasantry. On the basis of agricultural collectivization, a bigger increase of agricultural productivity has been achieved and at the same time conditions for agricultural production have also been initially improved. At present, there are in the whole country 700 million mu of irrigated land, more than 600,000 large and medium tractors, and various kinds of agricultural machinery with a total motive power of 180 million horsepower, and more than 80 billion yuan of public properties held by communes and teams, while the total value of production by communal and team enterprises constitutes one-third of the total agricultural output value. By relying mainly on the collective economy, agricultural production has been continuously enhanced, with the total agricultural output value more than doubled as compared with that during the initial stage of the cooperative movement. Meanwhile, peasant livelihood has also been improved, and socialist industrialization and the development of other enterprises have been assured. Under the conditions that existed in our country—small-peasant economy divided into single households—it would have been inconceivable and impossible to build up a modernized agriculture, to achieve higher labor productivity, to increase production of commodities, and to free the countryside fundamentally from poverty and to attain general prosperity. Therefore, the orientation toward agricultural collectivization is doubtlessly correct and must be persisted in.

Of course, we must also realize that, owing to the shortcomings in the movement of collectivization, the ultra-Left interruptions, and the fact that for a long period of time the Party has not shifted its emphasis, bases for the collective economy are still comparatively weak. Meanwhile, there are also matters in need of improvement and perfection concerning the systems and structure of the people's communes, the weakest link being the management and administration work. For a long time, there have been no significant improvements and breakthroughs in implementing the principle of distribution according to work and in perfecting the system of job responsibility for production. This has caused suppression of the peasants' socialist initiative as well as insufficient exertion of the superiority of collectivization. Because the collective economy has not been doing satisfactorily, people in a few backward and poverty-stricken localities have been less faithful in agricultural collectivization. We must face these problems squarely and solve them aggressively and step by step. At present, it is necessary to regard improvement of management and administration, implementation of distribution according to work, and improvement and perfection of the system of job responsibility for production as the central links for further consolidation of the collective economy and for development of agricultural production. It is necessary to put in a lot of strenuous efforts to grasp it tight and grasp it well.

Third, under the moral encouragement of the Third Plenary Session, Party cadres and the masses of commune members have in the recent two years proceeded from actual conditions, liberated their thought and boldly explored, and established many forms of job responsibility system for production which can be generally divided into two categories: one is contracted work of small segments with payments according to fixed quotas, and the other is contracted work and production quotas with payments in accordance with actual production. Results of implementation indicate that most areas have increased production by acquiring some new experiences. Especially noteworthy is the emergence of the system of job responsibility that gives contracts to specialized persons and gives payment in accordance with actual production, which is widely welcomed by commune members. This is a very good start. Leadership at various levels should sum up the positive and negative experiences, together with the broad masses, and help the communes and brigades perfect and improve the system of job responsibility to energetically push further forward the management work of the collective economy.

Fourth, our country is geographically vast, economically backward, while developments are very unbalanced from place to place. Moreover, the agricultural production is different from industrial production in that is it is chiefly done by hand, with the labor force being scattered while the production cycle being considerably longer, and in many aspects being restricted by natural conditions. This requires that relations of production must be made suitable to the productivity levels of different localities and that the management of agricultural production must have larger adaptability and more flexibility. In different localities and communes or teams, even in the very same production team, things must be done on the basis of actual demands and actual conditions in order to permit co-existence of diversified management forms, diversified labor structures, and diversified measures for calculating payments. Along with the elevation of productivity levels, these measures and forms will have corresponding changes in different periods of developmental time. Therefore, all forms of the system of job responsibility that are favorable to encouraging the producer to give utmost attention to collective production, to increasing production, and to increasing incomes, are good and feasible ones, and should be supported. It is improper to rigidly stick to any form only and practice "cutting things with one stroke of the knife."

Fifth, the system of job responsibility of giving contracts to specific persons and giving payments in accordance with actual production is a system based on division of labor and cooperative work. Under the system, the labor forces who are good in agriculture receive contracts for arable lands according to their ability, while those who are good in forestry, stock raising, sideline production, fishery, industry, commerce, etc., receive contracts of various trades concerned according to their ability. Contracts for production of fixed quotas in various trades are assigned to teams, to labor forces, or to households, according to the principle of facilitating production and benefiting management. All operations in the process of production are to be centralized whenever centralization is suitable, and decentralized, whenever decentralization is good, by the production team. Centralized distribution of payment is made for the portions under fixed quotas, while rewards or penalties are given for production in excess of quotas or unfulfilled production. These are stipulated in the form of contracts for the current year or for the next several years.

This kind of system of production responsibility has many more merits than other forms of contracted production: It can satisfy the commune members' demand for calculating payments in accordance with production, stabilize the production team's position as the main economic entity, concretely consolidate both the mobilization of production initiative of individual commune members and the exertion of the superiority of centralized management as well as division of labor and cooperative work; it is favorable to the development of diversified business, popularization of scientific farming, and promotion of production of commercial items; it is good for men to exert their talents, things to exert their usefulness, and land to exert its potential; it is favorable for the commune members to take care of their sideline business; and it is convenient to make arrangements for production to ensure the livelihood of the four categories of bereaved households and the weak-labor households. This form is, on the one hand, applicable to areas currently undergoing difficulties while, on the other hand, can be developed into a system of job responsibility that further divides specialties by an ever-higher degree and with more socialist characteristics.

In addition, there are some agricultural production teams that have, on the original basis of in-the-field management and responsibility of the individual, developed into a system that calculates rewards and penalties in accordance with production quantities. This also has certain advantages of a system that gives contracts to specific people and gives payments in accordance with actual production. Moreover, the cadres and masses are more familiar with this system and are willing to accept it.

In the communes and teams located in Jiangsu, Zhejiang, and Northeastern provinces, and suburban areas of large cities, diversified management of business is comparatively advanced, with a higher level of mechanization. Some of them have expanded beyond the scope of production teams and are using the production brigade as the unit for implementing the system of production responsibility that gives contracts to specific people and gives payments in accordance with actual production. This is exactly a kind of new development.

Localities should lead the masses according to their voluntary will to gradually popularize the above-mentioned forms as local conditions permit. At the same time, they should help the concerned in perfecting various systems and solving various problems that might emerge during the process of development.

Sixth, at present, the question of whether the system of contracted production of fixed output quotas based on the individual households is applicable or not has caused widespread discussion among the cadres and masses. To facilitate work and to benefit production, it is necessary to work out corresponding measures in policy.

The collective economy in most localities in our country is solid or comparatively solid, but there are localities where collective economy is not doing satisfactorily and where the level of productivity is still very low and the livelihood of the masses is very hard, owing to such influences as Leftist policy or other leadership factors. In view of these conditions, different guiding principles should be adopted for different communes and production teams in different localities for the contracted production of fixed output quotas on the basis of individual households.

In remote mountainous areas and poverty-stricken and backward localities, masses in the production teams that have been for a long time "eating grains resold by the state, producing by relying on loans from the state, and living on relief" have lost their confidence in collectivization and thus have demanded implementation of a system of contracted production of fixed output quotas on the basis of individual household. It is necessary to support the demand of the masses to practice either the system of contracted production of fixed output quotas based on the individual households or the system of contracted work to the individual, and to keep the system thus adopted a stable one for a longer period of time. In view of actual situations in these areas, implementation of the system of contracted production of fixed output quotas based on the individual households is a necessary measure to line up the masses, to develop production, and to solve the problem of producing enough to wear and eat. In the whole country, implementation of the system of contracted production of fixed output quotas based on the individual households practiced under the leadership of the production team and under the conditions where socialist industry, socialist commerce, and collective agriculture are in an absolutely predominant position means dependence on the socialist economy that will not deviate from the track of socialism. Thus, it poses no threats of restoration of capitalism. Therefore, it is nothing to be afraid of.

In ordinary localities where collective economy is comparatively stable, production has increased, and the current system of production responsibility has satisfied the masses or will satisfy them after improvement, the system of contracted production of fixed output quotas based on the individual households need not be practiced. Vital energies of the leadership of these localities should be placed on how to further consolidate and develop the collective economy. Places that have implemented the system of contracted production of fixed output quotas based on the individual households will be allowed to continue, if the masses do not demand a change. Then these places should, based on the development of situation and the demand of the masses, adroitly guide action according to circumstances and utilize all transitional forms for further organization. Classification of the above-mentioned localities is to be determined by various provinces, municipalities, and autonomous regions, in accordance with the actual conditions of the local communes and production teams, after a careful investigation and study.

The communes and production teams that have practiced the system of contracted production of fixed output quotas based on the individual households should, through actual work and public discussion, achieve the following: (1) protect collective properties, not tear them down and divide them equally; promptly ascertain the property rights of woods and forbid wanton cuttings; (2) reiterate the prohibitions on selling lands, hiring labors, and practicing usury; (3) take proper care of dependents of military men and martyrs, of households enjoying the five guarantees,[20] and other households suffering hardship; (4) retain as much as possible the collective-operated production items that are welcomed by the masses and have yielded good economic results; (5) ensure that production teams and commune members strictly fulfill obligatory duties assigned to them, while credits and liabilities must be checked up and arranged in good order; and

(6) retain the organization of production teams and restrengthen the role of basic-level Party organizations as the center of actions.

Seventh, do a good job as much as possible at the production teams and communes that are in a medium status on the economic level and the management level. These teams and communes amount to a large number, about 50 percent of the total. There are many factors attributed to their internal instability and easily susceptible to outside influences. Only improvement of work in such teams and communes can help stabilize the whole situation.

There are many factors attributable to the protracted hardships in certain localities as well as to satisfactory operations of certain teams and communes. Do not use the system of contracted production of fixed output quotas to the individual households as the only way to solve their problems. Some of them need policy readjustments from many aspects in order to reduce their burden and to liven up the diversified economy; some of them need gradual improvement of conditions for production, transportation, and storage; some need readjustment of the scope of the teams and communes to simplify the organizational structure and straighten out the leadership squads; and some need adequate expansion of the auxiliary economy conducted by individual team or commune members, such as the private plots. All in all, it is necessary to solve the problems by "suiting the medicine to the illness."

Eighth, it is necessary to bring into full play the specialties of all kinds of handicraftsmen, small merchants, small retailers, and other tradesmen, by organizing them into enterprises of the teams and communes as well as other kinds of collective sideline production enterprises. The few who request individual operations can, upon approval by agencies concerned, sign contracts with the production teams and then take the permits to go outside to labor or to run business. It is necessary to encourage the commune members to develop household sideline production in order to liven up and develop the rural economy.

Ninth, in practicing a certain policy or taking up a certain work in the rural areas, the Party must make allowance for the peasants' economic interests and respect the peasants' democratic rights. In the process of establishing a sound production responsibility system, it is wrong to run counter to the wishes of the local masses and to arbitrarily push forward any single form while forbidding other forms. It is necessary to unite together the persistence in the Party's leadership and the respect to the autonomy of the teams and communes, in a way that will be good for both the exercise of democracy and effective leadership. It is necessary to associate together the expansion of autonomy of the teams and communes and the improvement of democratic supervision by team/commune members, to bring into full play the duties and functions of the commune members representative assembly and the management committees at various levels. All important matters that involve the interests of the team/commune members, including the establishment of the system of production responsibility, must be determined collectively through democratic discussions.

Tenth, it is necessary to strengthen the Party's leadership and improve the work style of the leadership. All comrades of our Party must understand that reformation of the small producers' ideology and habits is a long-term and arduous work which requires the time of a whole generation or even several generations and which can only be accomplished through a great deal of deep-going, meticulous ideological and political work as well as economic work. Any resort to coercion will be ineffective and harmful. It is necessary to be adept at applying methods such as persuasive education, demonstration by exemplary models, and economic incentives to continuously elevate the peasants' socialist consciousness and to establish close associations with the peasants.

Eleventh, it is necessary to conscientiously train cadres and cultivate a great number of talented persons who understand the Party's policy and the government's regulations and at the same time are familiar with operation and management of the socialist collective economy. Cadres engaged in agricultural work at various levels, especially those working in counties and communes, should penetrate into their professions and practice them continuously so that they can make, as soon as possible, themselves professionals managing the socialist collective economy.

Twelfth, in the instant winter and the coming spring, all provinces, municipalities and autonomous regions must take the establishment of sound production responsibility systems and further improvement of the calculation of labor payments as an important task which should be arranged in conjunction with the winter production drive as well as the production effort and relief measures in the disaster areas. Various provinces can carry out the above-mentioned principles and guidelines in accordance with the actual conditions in their localities. The key requirement is that they must achieve stability of the overall situation, develop an excellent situation, and raise a bumper harvest in 1981.

(i) Circular on Separating the Local Government from Communes and Setting Up Township Governments[21]

Party Central Committee and State Council
October 12, 1983

As economic structural reform continues in the countryside, the unsuitability of the present structure in which government administration is combined with commune management becomes more and more apparent. The constitution stipulates that township governments should be established in the rural areas, and that government administration and commune management should be separated. To carry out this reform in a controlled and planned way, you are herewith advised of the following:

First, at the present time, the priority is to separate government administration and commune management and set up township government. At the same time that township Party committees are set up, suitable economic structures should be established in accordance with the needs of production and the wishes of the peasants. We must speedily change the situation in which the Party does not handle Party affairs, governments do no handle government affairs, and government administration is fused with and inseparable from enterprise and commune management.

The work of separating the government from the commune and setting up township government should proceed along with the election of Township People's Representatives, and should be largely completed by the end of 1984.[22]

Second, the scope of a township should generally be based on the area formerly under commune jurisdiction. It could also be smaller if the commune was too large.

In setting up townships, particular attention must be paid to market towns. Where conditions are ripe, governments should be set up in market towns to promote economic and cultural development of surrounding rural areas.

The establishment of township governments should be streamlined and the number on their staffs should not exceed that of the present commune level. Concrete arrangements should be made by the provinces. Municipalities, or autonomous regions concerned after all-round considerations.

Township cadres should be selected through a gradual process from outstanding people in the countryside; they should be able to "go up or down"
as the case may be, that is, if elected, they would devote themselves to
their jobs; if not, they should remain good farmers. Wages and benefits of
current full-time cadres, including those working in collective economic
organizations, will not be changed. Newly elected cadres should be given
suitable stipends or subsidies.

In the past, some commune members had been selected to work in commune offices in various localities. Those among them who are suitable to
continue working can stay on their jobs; those who are not should be transferred back to productive work.

Third, township people's governments, after their establishment, should exercise
rights and responsibilities as stipulated in "The Organizational Law of the People's
Republic of China Concerning Local People's Congresses and People's Governments at Every Level"; they should lead the area's economic and cultural development and socialist construction projects and do a good job in public security, civil
and judicial affairs, cultural, educational and health undertakings, and family planning. At present, their emphasis should be on consolidating social order, cracking
down on crime, mobilizing the masses to formulate township rules and regulations, launching activities to establish socialist spiritual civilization, and promoting
the fundamental improvement of social order and practices.

Fourth, after the separation of government administration and commune management, the reform of the economic system ought to proceed in accordance with
the Central Committee's 1983 Document 1.

Among existing enterprises belonging to the communes or production brigades, the responsibility system should continue to be implemented and
improved. Democratic management by the masses should be strengthened,
so that such enterprises become genuinely cooperative economic units. In
the course of reform, any damage to property or graft should be strictly
guarded against.

Ongoing reforms should be kept up in grassroots undertakings engaged
in technical dissemination, forestry, veterinary medicine, farm machine-
building, and economic management, as well as supply and marketing cooperatives and credit cooperatives. The scope of services should be widened
and quality raised; a service system embracing technology dispensation,

management, circulation, and finance should gradually be set up to facilitate development of diverse economic forms and commodity production.

Fifth, budget making, final accounting, and other financial systems should be set up at the township level after the establishment of township governments; the scope of revenues and expenditures should be defined. Concrete regulations pertaining to this area should be formulated by the Finance Ministry.

Villagers' committees are the grassroots organs of mass autonomy and should be established in accordance with the geographic distribution of villagers. These committees should actively promote public welfare and assist local governments in administrative work and leadership over production. Committee chairmen, vice-chairmen, and members are elected. Working regulations for these committees should be established separately according to local circumstances. After a period of implementation, experience should be summed up, from which unified organizational regulations should be formulated for the whole nation. Where economic units such as agricultural cooperatives existed in natural hamlets [instead of administratively divided villages—tr.], should the villagers wish to have only one leading body for both the economic organization and the villagers' committee, their wishes should be agreed to for trial implementation.

Sixth, separating of government administration and commune management and establishment of township governments is a matter of major importance over which Party committees at every level should strengthen leadership. The mass line should be followed and political and ideological work reinforced. Experiments could first be carried out in selected areas to gain experiences, after which work should expand to include all areas. The task must be performed well. Where reforms have already been carried out, the existing scope and structure should be tested out in practice and changes made where necessary.

To do this work well, civil affairs departments should take charge of relevant day-to-day work. The Rural Policy Research Department under the Party Central Committee and the Civil Affairs Ministry should be contacted for problems pertaining to economic and government structure. Major issues should be reported to the Central Committee and State Council as soon as possible.

NOTES

PROLOGUE

1. Xi Jinping, "Uphold and Develop Socialism with Chinese Characteristics," speech given on January 5, 2013, in Xi Jinping, *The Governance of China* (Beijing: Foreign Languages Press, 2014), 24–25. Chinese available at http://news.xinhuanet.com /english/bilingual/2013-01/06/c_132083883.htm.
2. Images from within the Xiaogang Museum, including the contract on display can be viewed at http://bbs1.people.com.cn/post/2/1/2/141694563.html. The heading reads: "We agreed to divide up the land among the households. The head of each household will sign and seal this contract with his fingerprint or family chop. If it works, every household will promise to give its production quota of grain to the collective and will no longer ask the state for money or food. If it doesn't work, we cadres are willing to be put into prison or executed, and the remaining commune members would raise our children until age 18."
3. "The Xiaogang Village Story," *People's Daily*, November 11, 2008, http://en.people .cn/90002/95607/6531490.html. At least two additional versions of the "secret contract" can be found online; however, only the two presented here have been identified as "authentic" by the Chinese authorities.
4. Office of National People's Congress Financial and Economic Affairs Committee, Department of Development Planning, National Development and Reform Commission, ed., "1976–1985 nian fazhan guomin jingji shinian guihua gangyao (caoan)" [Ten-Year Plan for the Development of National Economy as of 1976–1985], in *Jianguo yilai guomin jingji he shehui fazhan wunian jihua zhongyao wenjian huibian* [Selected Important Documents of the Five-Year Plans for National Economy and Societal Development since the Founding of PRC] (Beijing: China Democracy and Legal Press, 2008); Hua Guofeng, "1978 State Council's Governmental Report," presented at the First Plenary Session of the Fifth National

People's Congress, February 26, 1978), February 16, 2006, http://www.gov.cn /test/2006-02/16/content_200704.htm.
5. Justin Lin Yifu, "The Household Responsibility Reform and the option of Hybrid Rice in China," *Journal of Developmental Economics* 36, no. 2 (1991): 359.
6. Paul Robbins, *Political Ecology: A Critical Introduction* (West Sussex: Wiley-Blackwell, 2012), 59.

1. INTRODUCTION

1. John McMillan, John Whalley, and Zhu Li Jing attribute about 78 percent of productivity gains between 1978 and 1984 to economic reforms associated with decollectivization. See McMillan, Whalley, and Zhu, "The Impact of China's Economic Reforms on Agricultural Productivity Growth," *Journal of Political Economy* 97, no. 4 (1989): 781–807. For additional works that argue the commune was not productive, see Justin Yifu Lin, "Rural Reforms and Agricultural Growth in China," *American Economic Review* 82, no. 1 (1992): 34–51; Kate Xiao Zhou, *How the Farmers Changed China: Power of the People* (Boulder, CO: Westview Press, 1996); Fei Hsiao-tung, *Rural Development in China: Prospect and Retrospect* (Chicago: University of Chicago Press, 1989); Tony Saich, *Governance and Politics of China* (London: Palgrave Macmillan, 2001); Anne Thurston, *Muddling Toward Democracy: Political Change in Grassroots China* (Washington, DC: U.S. Institute of Peace, 1998); He Hongguang, *Governance, Social Organisation and Reform in Rural China: Case Studies from Anhui Province* (New York: Palgrave Macmillan, 2015); John K. Fairbank and Merle Goldman, *China: A New History* (Cambridge, MA: Harvard University Press, 2006); Kenneth Lieberthal, *Governing China: From Revolution Through Reform* (New York: W.W. Norton, 2004); Zhang Yulin, "Readjustment and Reform in Agriculture," in *China Economic Reforms*, eds. Lin Wei and Arnold Chao (Philadelphia: University of Pennsylvania Press, 1982); Carl Riskin, *China's Political Economy: The Quest for Development since 1949* (Oxford: Oxford University Press, 1987); Zhao Ziyang, *Prisoner of the State: The Secret Journal of Premier Zhao Ziyang* (New York: Simon & Schuster, 2009); Erza Vogel, *Deng Xiaoping and the Transformation of China* (Cambridge, MA: Harvard University Press, 2011).
2. Numerous scholarly works that argue the commune increased agricultural productivity. Publications that support this contention in one way or another include Fan Shenggen and Philip Pardey, "Research, Productivity, and Output Growth in Chinese Agriculture," *Journal of Development Economics* 53, no. 1 (1997): 115–37; Arthur Galston, *Daily Life in People's China* (New York: Simon & Schuster, 1973); Li Huaiyin, *Village China Under Socialism and Reform: A Micro-History, 1948–2008* (Stanford CA: Stanford University Press, 2009); Mobo C. F. Gao, *Gao Village: Rural Life in Modern China* (Honolulu: University of Hawaii Press, 1999); Leslie T. C. Kuo, *Agriculture in the People's Republic of China: Structural Changes and Technical Transformation* (New York: Praeger Publishers, 1976); Han Dongping, *The Unknown Cultural Revolution: Life and Change in a Chinese Village* (New York: Monthly Review Press, 2008); John Wong, "Some Aspects of China's Agricultural Development Experience: Implications for Developing Countries in Asia," *World*

Development 4, no. 6 (June 1976): 488. Wong's additional contributions to the literature include "Agriculture in the People's Republic of China," in *China: Cultural and Political Perspective*, ed. D. Bing (London: Longman Paul, 1975); "Communication of Peasant Agriculture: China's Organizational Strategy for Agricultural Development," in *Cooperative and Commune: Group Farming in the Economic Development of Agriculture*, ed. Peter Dorner (Madison: University of Wisconsin Press, 1977); *An Economic Overview of Agriculture in the People's Republic of China* (New York: Agricultural Development Council, 1973); "Grain Output in China: Some Statistical Implications," *Current Scene* 9, no. 2 (1973); Marc Blecher, *China Against the Tides: Restructuring through Revolution, Radicalism and Reform* (New York: Continuum, 2010); Steven Butler, *Agricultural Mechanization in China: The Administrative Impact* (New York: Columbia University Press, 1978); Gordon Bennett, *Huadong: The Story of a People's Commune* (Boulder, CO: Westview Press, 1978); Nicholas Lardy, *Agriculture in China's Modern Economic Development* (Cambridge, MA: Cambridge University Press, 1983); Dwight Perkins and Shahid Yusuf, *Rural Development in China* (Baltimore, MD: Johns Hopkins University Press, 1984); On Kit Tam, *China's Agricultural Modernization: The Socialist Mechanization Scheme* (London: Croom Helm, 1985); Peggy Printz and Paul Steinle, *Commune* (New York: Dodd, Mead, 1977); Dwight Perkins, *Rural Small-Scale Industry in the people's Republic of China* (Berkeley: University of California Press, 1977); Chris Bramall, *The Industrialization of Rural China* (New York: Oxford University Press, 2007); Chris Bramall, *Chinese Economic Development* (Hoboken, NJ: Taylor & Francis, 2008); Philip C. Huang, *The Peasant Family and Rural Development in the Yangzi Delta, 1350–1988* (Stanford, CA: Stanford University Press, 1990).

3. Decollectivization, which took place between 1977 and 1983, was a gradual and uneven process that began in different time in different provinces.
4. "Luoshi jingji zhengce, shougou gengduo de tufu chanpin" [Implement Economic Policy, Purchase More Agricultural Products], *People's Daily*, December 12, 1971; "Jianchi shehui zhuyi daolu, xianzhi jichan jieji faquan" [Maintain the Socialist Road, Restrict Bourgeois Rights], *Red Flag* [Hongqi] 20, no. 8 (August 1975): 26.
5. Yang Kuisong and Stephen A. Smith, "Communism in China, 1900–2010," in *The Oxford Handbook of the History of the Communism*, ed. S.A. Smith (Oxford: Oxford University Press, 2014), 227.
6. Lin Chen, "The Agricultural Plight of the Chinese Communists," *Issues and Studies* 5, no. 5 (1970): 41–42.
7. David Zweig, *Agrarian Radicalism in China, 1968–1981* (Cambridge, MA: Harvard University Press, 1989), 61, 226.
8. Zweig, *Agrarian Radicalism*, 61, 227.
9. Fairbank and Goldman, *China*, 405.
10. Lieberthal, *Governing China*, 124.
11. Luo Hanxian, *Economic Changes in Rural China* (Beijing: New World Press, 1985), 89. Also see Zhang, "Readjustment and Reform," 128. As deputy chief of *Hunan Nongmin Bao* (Hunan Peasants' Daily) Zhang's arguments closely reflect the official line at that time. The official condemnation and rectification of the communes "Left errors" came in June 1981. See "Resolution on Certain Questions in the History of Our Party since the Founding of the People's Republic of China (June 27, 1981)," *Peking Review* 24, no. 27 (July 1981): 20–26. "At a work conference

called by the Central Committee in April 1979, the Party formulated the principle of 'readjusting, restructuring, consolidating and improving' the economy as a whole in a decisive effort to correct the shortcomings and mistakes of the previous two years in our economic work and eliminate the influence of 'Left' errors that had persisted in this field. . . . The Party has worked conscientiously to remedy the errors in rural work since the later stage of the movement for agricultural cooperation, with the result that the purchase prices of farm and sideline products have been raised, various forms of production responsibility introduced whereby remuneration is determined by farm output, family plots have been restored and appropriately extended, village fairs have been revived, and sideline occupations and diverse undertakings have been developed. All these have greatly enhanced the peasants' enthusiasm. Grain output in the last two years reached an all-time high, and at the same time industrial crops and other farm and sideline products registered a big increase. Thanks to the development of agriculture and the economy as a whole, the living standards of the people have improved."

12. Luo, *Economic Changes*, 90, 94–95.
13. Fairbank and Goldman, *China*, 398.
14. Riskin, *China's Political Economy*, 288.
15. Zhou, *How the Farmers*, 2–3.
16. "The Xiaogang Village Story," *People's Daily*, November 11, 2008. Accessed January 1, 2018. http://en.people.cn/90002/95607/6531490.html.
17. He, *Governance, Social Organisation and Reform*, 42. His work includes almost no discussion of Xiaogang between 1962 and 1976.
18. "The Xiaogang Village Story."
19. Thurston, *Muddling Toward Democracy*, 7.
20. "The Xiaogang Village Story."
21. Saich, *Governance and Politics*, 61.
22. Zhao, *Prisoner of the State*, 142.
23. Saich, *Governance and Politics*, 61.
24. Vogel, *Deng Xiaoping*, 443.
25. Jonathan Unger, *The Transformation of Rural China* (Armonk: M.E. Sharpe, 2002), 97.
26. Fei, *Rural Development in China*, 232–33.
27. Fairbank and Goldman, *China*, 411–12.
28. Hu Yaobang, "Zai qingzhu zhongguo gongchandang chengli liushi zhounian dahui shang de jianghua (1981nian 7yue 1ri)" [Speech at the meeting in celebration of the sixtieth anniversary of the founding of the Communist Party of China (July 1, 1981)], in *Sanzhong quanhui yilai zhongyao wenxian xuanbian xia* [Selected Important Documents since Third Plenary Session of the Eleventh Central Committee], ed. Zhonggong zhongyang wenxian yanjiu shi [Central Chinese Communist Party Literature Research Office] (Beijing: Zhonggong zhongyang dangxiao chubanshe, 1981); see the English version at https://www.marxists.org/subject/china/documents/cpc/history/02.htm.
29. Zhou, *How the Farmers*, 1.
30. See "Resolution on Certain Questions."
31. Huang Yasheng, *Capitalism with Chinese Characteristics* (New York: Cambridge University Press, 2008), xiv.

32. The term "Reform and Opening Up" also has been used to include China's experimental foreign trade and investment policies introduced in select special economic zones along the coastline beginning in the early 1980s. For the purposes of this study, however, this term refers only to the policy changes Deng Xiaoping and his reform faction pursued in the agricultural sector. Rural reforms happened first, and were the most important from both an economic and a political perspective.

33. In 1984, American poet and scholar Willis Barnstone, who had visited China in 1972, was denied a visa for his Fulbright teaching fellowship. On a subsequent visit, the vice president of the Foreign Studies University told him: "Willis, do you remember when you were going to come to China, but we didn't give you a visa? We were afraid you were a Maoist. The last thing we wanted was a Maoist!" See Ian Johnson, "Q. and A.: Willis Barnstone on Translating Mao and Touring Beijing with Allen Ginsberg," *New York Times*, April 17, 2015.

34. Luo, *Economic Changes*, 90.

35. In March 2016, a group of former Henan officials, wrote to China's Supreme Court demanding the rehabilitation of more than 1 million people whom they said were wrongfully arrested after Deng's victorious "reformers" rounded up numerous people whose only crime, they argue, was belonging to the wrong faction. "Unlikely Hero: A Local Leader Jailed for Extremism During the Cultural Revolution Has Many Devoted Followers," *Economist*, August 6, 2016.

36. Although the phrase "to get rich is glorious" often is attributed to Deng Xiaoping, there is no proof he actually said it. See Evelyn Iritani, "Great Idea but Don't Quote Him," *Los Angeles Times*, September 9, 2004.

37. Bramall, *Industrialization*, 145.

38. The term "green revolution" was coined in 1968 by the director of the U.S. Agency for International Development (USAID) William Gaud. Gaud juxtaposed the term with the Soviet's "violent Red Revolution," arguing that agricultural productivity growth was a political as well as economic imperative. William Gaud, "AID Supports the Green Revolution," Address before the Society for International Development, Washington, DC, March 8, 1968. Sigrid Schmalzer observes that "contrary to common perception . . . the green revolution in red China looked strikingly similar to the green revolution as Gaud had imagined it." Sigrid Schmalzer, *Red Revolution, Green Revolution: Scientific Farming in Socialist China* (Chicago: University of Chicago Press, 2016), 3. Accounts of the green revolution are too numerous to list here. For one particularly noteworthy contribution see Raj Patel, "The Long Green Revolution," *Journal of Peasant Studies* 40, no. 1 (2013): 1–63.

39. Schmalzer, *Red* Revolution, 9.

40. Wong, "Some Aspects," 492.

41. White's book won the 1999 Association for Asian Studies Joseph Levenson Book Prize for Outstanding Nonfiction Scholarly Book on China. Lynn T. White III, *Unstately Power: Volume I Local Causes of China's Economic Reforms* (Armonk, NY: M.E. Sharpe, 1998), 93.

42. White, *Unstately Power*, 85.

43. Bramall, *Industrialization*, 145.

44. Barry Naughton, *The Chinese Economy: Transitions and Growth* (Cambridge, MA: MIT Press, 2007), 253.

45. Louis Putterman, *Continuity and Change in China's Rural Development: Collective and Reform Eras in Perspective* (Oxford: Oxford University Press, 1993), 15.

46. Putterman, *Continuity and Change*, 15.
47. Examples of these publications include: G. F. Sprague, "Agriculture in China," *Science* 188, no. 4188 (May 1975): 549–55. Merle Esmay and Roy Harrington, *Glimpses of Agricultural Mechanization in the PRC: A Delegation of 15 Members report on their technical inspection in China Aug. 18–Sept. 8, 1979* (St. Joseph, MI: American Society of Agricultural Engineers, 1979); American Plant Studies Delegation, *Plant Studies in the People's Republic of China: A Trip Report of the American Plant Studies Delegation* (Washington, DC: National Academy of Sciences, 1975); Jacob A. Hoefer and Patricia J. Tsuchitani, *Animal Agriculture in China: A Report of the Visit of the Committee on Scholarly Communication with the People's Republic of China Animal Sciences Delegation* (Washington, DC: National Academy of Sciences, 1980); Per Brinck, *Insect Pest Management in China: A Delegation Report* (Stockholm: Royal Swedish Academy of Engineering Sciences, 1979).
48. Three excellent examples of such publications, which are too numerous to recount here, include Roderick MacFarquhar and Michael Schoenhals, *Mao's Last Revolution* (Cambridge, MA: Harvard University Press, 2006); Joseph Esherick, Paul Pickowicz, and Andrew Walder, *The Cultural Revolution as History* (Stanford, CA: Stanford University Press, 2006); Elizabeth Perry and Li Xun, *Proletarian Power: Shanghai in the Cultural Revolution* (Boulder, CO: Westview Press, 1997). For the late 1970s and early 1980s, see Richard Baum, *Burying Mao: Chinese Politics in the Age of Deng Xiaoping* (Princeton, NJ: Princeton University Press, 1994).
49. American Plant Studies Delegation.
50. Sprague, "Agriculture in China," 549.
51. Esmay and Harrington, *Glimpses of Agricultural Mechanization*, 2.
52. Esmay and Harrington, *Glimpses of Agricultural Mechanization*, 1, 9.
53. Bruce Stone, "The Basis for Chinese Agricultural Growth in the 1980s and 1990s: A Comment on Document No. 1, 1984," *The China Quarterly* 101 (1985): 114. Also see Naughton, *Chinese Economy*, 253.
54. Bruce Stone, "Developments in Agricultural Technology," *The China Quarterly* 116 (1988): 767.
55. Anthony M. Tang and Bruce Stone, *Food Production in the People's Republic of China* (Washington, DC: International Food Policy Research Institute, 1980), 6, 117, 123.
56. In addition to his book, *The Politics of Agricultural Mechanization in China* (Ithaca, NY: Cornell University Press, 1978), Benedict Stavis also published *Making Green Revolution: The Politics of Agricultural Development in China* (Ithaca, NY: Rural Development Committee of Cornell University, 1974); *People's Communes and Rural Development in China* (Ithaca, NY: Rural Development Committee of Cornell University, 1974); "Agricultural Research and Extension Services in China," *World Development* 6, no. 5 (1978): 631–45.
57. Stavis, *The Politics of Agricultural Mechanization*, 15.
58. *The Politics of Agricultural Mechanization*, which traces the political process associated with agricultural mechanization and its relationship to yield output, has its weak points. Stavis's work suffers, argues Vivienne Shue in her review for the *American Political Science Review*, because he fails to adopt any particular theory or model to assist in explaining policy change over time. The discussion leaps from the consequences of technological insufficiencies, to the vagaries of Politburo

infighting, to the machinations of middle-level bureaucratic politics. Shue writes, "All are treated more or less equally as 'constraints' on the process of China's agricultural mechanization, providing the reader almost no help in weighting the import of these various factors, and no clues for the construction of predictive hypotheses." The book is, she concludes, more a chronicle than an analysis that "touches only the high points." Shue was not alone in suggesting Stavis was painting an overly rosy picture of Chinese agricultural development. Audrey Donnithorne's review in the *Journal of Asian Studies* notes that Stavis's last chapter "is devoted to an advocacy of the Chinese system." See Vivienne Shue, "Book Review: The Politics of Agricultural Mechanization in China, by Benedict Stavis," *American Political Science Review* 73, no. 3 (1979): 926–927. Also see Donnithorne, "The Politics of Agricultural Mechanization in China by Benedict Stavis," *Journal of Asian Studies* 38, no. 4 (1979): 760.

59. Stavis, "Agricultural Research and Extension," 631.

60. Stavis, *Politics of Agricultural Mechanization*, 261.

61. Stavis, *Politics of Agricultural Mechanization*, 18.

62. For additional works that help explain the sources of commune productivity, see Marc Blecher and Vivienne Shue, *Tethered Deer: Government and Economy in a Chinese County* (Stanford, CA: Stanford University Press, 1996); Steven Butler, *Agricultural Mechanization in China: The Administrative Impact* (New York: Columbia University Press, 1978); Jean Oi, *Rural China takes Off* (Berkeley: University of California Press, 1999); Zweig, *Agrarian Radicalism*; Edward Friedman, Paul Pickowicz and Mark Selden, *Revolution, Resistance and Reform in Village China* (New Haven, CT: Yale University Press, 2007); Edward Friedman, Paul Pickowicz and Mark Selden, *Chinese Village, Socialist State* (New Haven, CT: Yale University Press, 1993); Richard Madsen, *Morality and Power in a Chinese Village* (Berkeley: University of California Press, 1984); Anita Chan, Richard Madsen, and Jonathan Unger, *Chen Village: The Recent History of a Peasant Community in Mao's China* (Berkeley: University of California Press, 1992); William Parish and Martin King Whyte, *Village and Family in Contemporary China* (Chicago: University of Chicago Press, 1978).

63. These conclusions were supported by interviews with agricultural historians and rural residents in Jiangxi, Henan, Jiangsu, Jilin, Hubei, Guangdong, and Shandong.

64. Luo, *Economic Changes*, 92.

65. Arthur Conan Doyle, *Sherlock Holmes: A Scandal in Bohemia* (London: The Strand Magazine, 1891).

66. Bramall and White III provide especially valuable provincial and sub-provincial-level data.

67. Research trips to acquire agricultural data were made, in chronological order, to Henan Agricultural University (2011), Jiangxi Agricultural University (2011), Nanjing Agricultural University (2012), Nanjing University (2012), Huazhong Agricultural University (2012), Wuhan University (2012), Jilin Agricultural University (2012), Jilin University (2012), Dalian University of Technology (2013), Liaoning Normal University (2013), Sichuan University (2013), Sun Yatsen University (2013), Zhejiang University (2014), and Henan University (2015).

68. This approach was informed by Naughton, who also uses grain, meat, and edible oil production to measure China's national agricultural productivity. That study, however, is missing data from 1958 to 1963 and from 1967 to 1976. See Naughton, *Chinese Economy*, 253.

69. China's 1978 Ten-Year Plan and its accompanying State Council report both called for the expanded production of cash crops, including oil-yielding plants. Although the former document was later forsworn, the latter was not and remains available on the Chinese government's official website. Office of National People's Congress Financial and Economic Affairs Committee, Department of Development Planning, National Development and Reform Commission, ed., "1976–1985 nian fazhan guomin jingji shinian guihua gangyao (caoan)" [Ten-Year Plan for the Development of National Economy as of 1976–1985 (draft)], in *Jianguo yilai guomin jingji he shehui fazhan wunian jihua zhongyao wenjian huibian* [Selected Important Documents of the Five-Year Plans for National Economy and Societal Development since the Founding of PRC] (Beijing: China Democracy and Legal Press, 2008). Hua Guofeng, "1978 State Council's Governmental Report," presented at the First Plenary Session of the Fifth National People's Congress, February 26, 1978, February 16, 2006, http://www.gov.cn/test/2006-02/16/content_200704.htm.

70. In 1980 China had 99,305,333 hectares of arable land, compared with the United States, which had 188,755,333 hectares. See *Agricultural Economic Statistics, 1949–1983* [Nongye jingji ziliao, 1949–1983] (Beijing: Ministry of Agriculture Planning Bureau, 1983), 590.

71. After visiting Chinese facilities in 1974, Sprague observed that U.S. pigs generally reached approximately 100 kg in six months or less, whereas their Chinese counterparts were about half that weight in eight months to a year. Sprague, "Agriculture in China," 555.

72. "China's Economic Policy and Performance," in *Cambridge History of China*, vol. 15, *The People's Republic, Part 2: Revolutions within the Chinese Revolution, 1966–1982*, ed. John K. Fairbank and Roderick MacFarquhar (Cambridge, MA: Cambridge University Press, 1991), 517. Also see Tang and Stone, *Food Production*, 6; Fan and Pardey, "Research, Productivity, and Output," 127; and On Kit Tam, *China's Agricultural Modernization*, 64.

73. I have long maintained that official Chinese economic data can be used to reveal macroeconomic trends. See Joshua Eisenman, Eric Heginbotham, and Derek Mitchell, *China and the Developing World: Beijing's Strategy for the Twenty-First Century* (Armonk, NY: M.E. Sharpe, 2007), 41.

74. Jonathan Spence, *The Search for Modern China*, 3rd ed. (New York: W.W. Norton and Company, 2013), 531.

75. Interview with Li Yankun, associate director of the Central Party School of the CPC Central Committee, Tonglu County, Zhejiang Province, November 7, 2015.

76. Fairbank and Goldman, *China*, 356.

77. Bramall, *Industrialization*, 145.

2. INSTITUTIONAL ORIGINS AND EVOLUTION

1. Mao Zedong, "On Contradiction," in *Selected Works of Mao Tse-tung*, vol. 1 (Peking, China: Foreign Languages Press, 1965), 322.

2. Dwight Perkins and Shahid Yusuf, *Rural Development in China* (Baltimore, MD: Johns Hopkins University Press, 1984), 74. Also see John Wong, "Some Aspects of

China's Agricultural Development Experience: Implications for Developing Countries in Asia," *World Development* 4, no. 6 (1976): 493.

3. Perkins and Yusuf, *Rural Development*, 75.

4. Benedict Stavis, *People's Communes and Rural Development in China* (Ithaca, NY: Cornell University Rural Development Committee, 1974), 43.

5. Stavis, *People's Communes*, 44.

6. Stavis, *People's Communes*, 44.

7. Perkins and Yusuf, *Rural Development*, 75.

8. Mao Zedong, *On the Question of Agricultural Co-operation* (Beijing, China: Foreign Languages Press, 1956), 33–34.

9. Perkins and Yusuf, *Rural Development*, 75–76.

10. Richard Baum, "Lecture 14: The Chinese People Have Stood Up," in *The Fall and Rise of China* (Chantilly, VA: The Teaching Company, 2010), 24 audio discs.

11. Stavis, *People's Communes*, 44.

12. Stavis, *People's Communes*, 44.

13. Stavis, *People's Communes*, 44.

14. Perkins and Yusuf, *Rural Development*, 76.

15. Nicholas Lardy, *Agriculture in China's Modern Economic Development* (Cambridge: Cambridge University Press, 1983), 39–40.

16. Perkins and Yusuf, *Rural Development*, 77.

17. Stavis, *People's Communes*, 35.

18. Stavis, *People's Communes*, 44.

19. William Skinner, "Marketing and Social Structure in Rural China: Part III," *Journal of Asian Studies* 24, no. 3 (1965): 385.

20. Stavis, *People's Communes*, 44.

21. Comment on article "Mobilize Women to Take Part in Production to Solve the Difficulties of the Insufficiency of Labor Power," cited in Pang Xianzhi, *Upsurge of Socialism in China's Countryside: Document of Historical Significance in the Party's Leadership of the Socialist Revolution in the Rural Areas* (Peking, China: Xuexi, 1956), 27; also available in *Socialist of Socialism in the China's Countryside* (Beijing, China: Foreign Languages Press, 1957), 286.

22. "History of Struggle Between the Two Lines (on China's Farm Machinery Front)," *Nongye Jixie Jishu* [Agricultural Machinery Technique], no. 9 (1968) in *Selections from China Mainland Magazines* (hereinafter referred to as SCMM), no. 633 (November 1968): 10.

23. "History of Struggle," *SCMM* 633, 10.

24. Huang Jing, "The Problem of Farm Mechanization in China," *People's Daily*, October 24–25, 1957.

25. "The Research Work in Agricultural Machinery Should Be Ahead of Agricultural Mechanization," *Zhongguo Nongye Jixie* [China Agricultural Machinery], no. 9 (September 1962): 2–4.

26. Mao Zedong, "Intraparty Correspondence (April 29, 1959)," in *Miscellany of Mao Tsetung Thought: 1949–1968*, vol. 1 (Washington, DC: Joint Publication Research Service, 1978), 171; also see Mao Zedong, *Mao Papers, Anthology and Bibliography*, ed. Jerome Chen (Oxford: Oxford University Press, 1970), 7. Chen dates the letter as November 29, 1959.

27. Mao Zedong, "Speech at the Lushan Conference (July 23, 1959)," in *Chairman Mao Talks to the People: Talks and Letters: 1956–1971*, ed. S. Schram (New York: Pantheon Press, 1975), 144; "Resolution of the Standing Committee of the National People's Congress on Adjusting the Main Indicators of the National Economic Plan of 1959 and Carrying out the Movement of Increasing Output and Conservation," *People's Daily*, August 28, 1959.

28. Editorial, "Nongcun gongzu gaige de xinfazhan" [The New Development of Farm Tool Reform], *People's Daily*, January 13, 1960; Editorial, "Kaizhan yige shougong caozuo jixiehua banjixiehua de quanmin yundong" [Carry Out a National Movement of Manual Operation for Mechanization and Semi-Mechanization], *People's Daily*, February 25, 1960.

29. Niu Zhonghuang, "On the Technical Transformation of China's Agriculture," *People's Daily*, August 26, 1969.

30. Mao Zedong, "Communes are Better," in *Selected Works of Mao Tse-tung*, August 9, 1958, extracted from the account of Mao's inspection tour in Shandong as reported in *People's Daily*, August 13, 1958.

31. Lardy, *Agriculture in China*, 41.

32. Richard Baum, "Lecture 18: The Great Leap Forward (1958–60)," in *The Fall and Rise of China* (Chantilly, VA: The Teaching Company, 2010), 24 audio discs.

33. Baum, "Lecture 18."

34. Shui Fu, "A Profile of Dams in China," in *The River Dragon Has Come*, ed. Dai Qing (New York: Routledge, 2015).

35. *Agricultural Economic Statistics, 1949–1983* [Nongye jingji ziliao, 1949–83] (Beijing, China: Ministry of Agriculture Planning Bureau, 1983), 47, 80.

36. Perkins and Yusuf, *Rural Development*, 77.

37. Baum, "Lecture 18."

38. Phyllis Andors, *The Unfinished Liberation of Chinese Women, 1949–1980* (Bloomington: Indiana University Press, 1983).

39. Carl Riskin, *China's Political Economy: The Quest for Development since 1949* (Oxford: Oxford University Press, 1987), 138.

40. Stephan Uhalley, *A History of the Chinese Communist Party* (Stanford, CA: Hoover Institution Press, 1988), 131.

41. Uhalley, *A History*, 131.

42. Victor Lippit, "The Commune in Chinese Development," *Modern China* 3, no. 2 (April 1977): 232.

43. Perkins and Yusuf, *Rural Development*, 78–79; Y.Y. Kueh, *Agricultural Instability in China, 1931–1991: Weather, Technology and Institutions* (Oxford: Clarendon Press, 1995), 155.

44. Jonathan Unger, *The Transformation of Rural China* (Armonk, NY: M.E. Sharpe, 2002), 75.

45. Parris H. Chang, "Struggle Between the Two Roads in China's Countryside," *Current Scene* 6 (1968); also see Parris H. Chang, *Patterns and Processes of Policy Making in Communist China, 1955–1962: Three Case Studies* (Ann Arbor, MI: University Microfilms, 1973), chap. 5.

46. Perkins and Yusuf, *Rural Development*, 78.

47. Richard Baum, *Prelude to Revolution: Mao the Party, and the Peasant Question* (New York: Columbia University Press, 1975), 162–64; also see Lardy, *Agriculture in China*, 44; Uhalley, *A History*, 128, 131.

48. Zhao Ziyang, *Prisoner of the State: The Secret Journal of Zhao Ziyang* (New York: Simon & Schuster, 2009), 139; also see Unger, *The Transformation*, 75; Baum, *Prelude to Revolution*, 164.
49. Unger, *The Transformation*, 75.
50. Stavis, *People's Communes*, 57–58.
51. Lardy, *Agriculture in China*, 43–44.
52. Dick Wilson, "The China After Next," *Far Eastern Economic Review* (1968): 193.
53. Stavis, *People's Communes*, 58.
54. A.Z.M. Obaidullah Khan, ed., "Class Struggle in Yellow Sandhill Commune," *The China Quarterly* 51 (1972): 536–37.
55. The canonical text on the rural household's willingness to sacrifice some measure of profit maximization in favor of a baseline food security is James C. Scott, *The Moral Economy of the Peasant: Rebellion and Subsistence in Southeast Asia* (New Haven, CT: Yale University Press, 1976). This position was challenged by Samuel Popkin. See Samuel L. Popkin, *The Rational Peasant: The Political Economy of Rural Society in Vietnam* (Berkeley: University of California Press, 1979).
56. Unger, *The Transformation*, 76.
57. "Communiqué of the Tenth Plenary Session of the Eighth Committee of the CPC," *Xinhua*, September 28, 1962.
58. *Xinhua*, January 14, 1963, cited in Zheng Zhuyuan, *Scientific and Engineering Manpower in Communist China, 1949–1963* (Washington, DC: U.S. National Science Foundation, 1965), 281–82.
59. Liu Rixin, "Exploration of a Few Problems Concerning Mechanization of Our Agriculture," *People's Daily*, June 20, 1963.
60. Editorial, "'Demonstration Farms' Are Main Centers through Which Agricultural Science May Serve Production," *People's Daily*, October 25, 1964.
61. Chao Kang, *Agricultural Production in Communist China, 1949–1965* (Madison: University of Wisconsin Press, 1970), 111.
62. "Tian Chenlin's Crime of Sabotage," *SCMM* 624, 3.
63. Benedict Stavis, *The Politics of Agricultural Mechanization in China* (Ithaca, NY: Cornell University Press, 1978), 183 and 195.
64. "Completely Settle the Heinous Crimes," *SCMM* 610, 30.
65. "Reactionary Nature of China's Khrushchev," *SCMM* 613, 22.
66. "Reactionary Nature of China's Khrushchev," *SCMM* 613, 20–21.
67. In the course of Mao's talk at Enlarged Meeting of the Political Bureau, March 20, 1966, see Mao, *Miscellany*, 379.
68. Perkins and Yusuf, *Rural Development*, 76.
69. Stavis, *Politics of Agricultural Mechanization*, 202–203.
70. Xiang Nan, "Stable and High Yields and Agricultural Mechanization," *People's Daily*, March 22, 1965; and Xiang Nan, "Agricultural Mechanization Can Be Achieved with Good and Fast Results," *People's Daily*, July 6, 1965. The *People's Daily* series was culled from Xiang's article "An Inspection Report on the Mechanization of Our Agriculture," *Zhongguo Nongye Jixie*, May 1965, 11–20.
71. Xiang, "Stable."
72. Xiang, "Stable."

73. Work team of Central-South Bureau of the CPC Central Committee, "Where Should Revolutionary Zeal be Exerted? Second Question Concerning Organization of a High Tide in Agricultural Production," *Nanfang Ribao*, March 28, 1965.

74. "Wipe Out State Monopoly and Promote Mechanization on the Basis of Self-Reliance in a Big Way," *Nongye Jixie Jishu*, no. 6 (September 1967) in *SCMM* 610 (January 1968): 14.

75. "Shanxi Held Provincial People's Congress and Elected Representatives for Third National People's Congress," *People's Daily*, October 16, 1964.

76. *China Pictorial*, no. 1 (January 1968): 27; Chen Yonggui, "Tachai Goes Ahead in the Struggle Against China's Khrushchov," *Peking Review* 10, no. 50 (December 1, 1967): 22.

77. Baum, *Prelude to Revolution*, 119–20.

78. Chen Yonggui, "Dazhai zai Mao Zedong sixiang de guanghui zhaoyao xia qianjin" [Dazhai Moves Forward in the Brilliant Shine of Mao Zedong Thoughts], *Red Flag* [Hongqi] no. 5 (March 10, 1967): 49–50.

79. Mao Zedong, "Talk on the Four Cleanups Moments (January 3, 1965)," in *Long Live Mao Tse-tung Thought* (n.p.: Red Guard Publication, n.d.); see English translation at https://www.marxists.org/reference/archive/mao/selected-works/volume-9/mswv9_38.htm.

80. Mao, "Talk on the Four Cleanups Movement."

81. Luo Hanxian, *Economic Changes in Rural China* (Beijing, China: New World Press, 1985), 97.

82. "Chairman Mao with Representatives of National People's Congress," *People's Daily*, December 30, 1964.

83. "Postulation by the CPC Hubei Provincial Committee Concerning Gradual Realization of Agricultural Mechanization," *Canton Evening News*, April 4, 1966; also see "Editor's Note on Postulation by the CPC Hubei Provincial Committee Concerning Gradual Realization of Agricultural Mechanization," *People's Daily*, April 9, 1966.

84. Benedict Stavis, *The Politics of Agricultural Mechanization in China* (Ithaca, NY: Cornell University Press, 1978), 224.

85. Mao, "Instructions on Agricultural Mechanization," in *Miscellany*, 373; also available in "Last-Ditch Struggle," *SCMM* 613, 26; On Kit Tam, *China's Agricultural Modernization: The Socialist Mechanization Scheme* (Kent, England: Croom Helm), 37.

86. Mao Zedong, "A Letter on Farm Mechanization (March 12, 1966)," *Peking Review* 20, no. 52 (December 26, 1977): 7–9.

87. See "Postulation by the CPC Hubei Provincial Committee," and "Editor's Note on Postulation."

88. "May 7 Directive," *The History of the People's Republic of China*, http://www.hprc.org.cn/gsgl/dsnb/zdsj/200908/t20090820_28344.html. "May 7 Directive" refers to Mao's letter to Lin Biao, see http://en.people.cn/dengxp/vol2/note/B0070.html.

89. "Woguo nongye jixie gongye jinnian huode zuida fazhan" [China's Agricultural Mechanization Has Realized the Maximum Development This Year], *People's Daily*, October 18, 1966.

90. "Running Enterprises in Line with Mao Tse-tung's Thinking (April 3, 1966)," *People's Daily* editorial, *Peking Review* 9, no. 16 (April 15, 1966): 11.

91. Stavis, *Politics of Agricultural Mechanization*, 238–40.

92. Revolutionary Committee for Jincheng County, Shanxi, "Use Mao Tse-tung's Thought to Direct the Work of Sending down the Farm Machines and Tools of State Stations," *Nongye Jixie Jishu*, no. 11 (November 8, 1968) in *SCMM* 643, 4.

93. "It Is Good for Tractors to Revert to Chairman Mao's Revolutionary Line—Report on Investigation of Change in Management of Tractors by the Collective in Lankao County, Henan," *Nongye Jiexie Jishu*, no. 10 (October 8, 1968) in *SCMM* 643, 17.

94. On Kit Tam, *China's Agricultural Modernization*, 40–41.

95. Production Brigade no. 2, Hsukuang Commune, O-ch'eng County, Hubei, "The Question of Mechanization by the Collective," *Nongye Jiexie Jishu*, no. 9 (September 1968) in *SCMM* 644, 15.

96. "Communiqué of the Eleventh Plenary Session of the Eighth Central Committee of the Communist Party of China (August 12, 1966)," *Peking Review* 9, no. 34 (August 19, 1966): 4–8.

97. Stavis, *Politics of Agricultural Mechanization*, 226–27.

98. Lin Chen, "The Agricultural Plight of the Chinese Communists," *Issues and Studies* 5, no. 5 (1970): 41–42; Stavis, *Politics of Agricultural Mechanization*, 228.

99. Writing group of the Peking Revolutionary Committee, "The Road to China's Socialist Industrialization," *Red Flag*, no. 10 (October 1969): 30.

100. Radio Shanghai, November 10, 1969, in *United States Foreign Broadcast Information Service China Report*, November 19, 1969.

101. Although some overzealous local leaders did infringe on the Three Small Freedoms, these decisions were taken contrary to the official policy as stated within the *Sixty Articles*.

102. The national ethos of life under conditions of resource scarcity had a powerful psychological influence on two generations of Chinese. Their waste-not-want-not approach to personal consumption and savings is comparable to that of the U.S. Great Depression generation.

3. CHINA'S GREEN REVOLUTION

1. The Dazhai Commune and Brigade, located in Xiyang County, Shanxi Province, began its rise to national prominence in 1964 and 1965 and became the model for the eponymous nationwide agricultural modernization program. For a description of the evolution of Dazhai during the 1960s, see Richard Baum, *Prelude to Revolution: Mao the Party, and the Peasant Question* (New York: Columbia University Press, 1975), 117–22.

2. The relevant official documents, which are located in appendix C, are *State Council Report on the 1970 Northern Regions Agricultural Conference*, December 11, 1970; and Hua Guofeng, "Report on the 1975 Dazhai Conference (Central Document no. 21) Mobilize the Whole Party, Make Greater Efforts to Develop Agriculture and Strive to Build Dachai-Type Counties," *Peking Review* 18, no. 44 (October 31, 1975): 7–10.

3. For the Nobel Prize–winning economic theory that best explains this development approach, see W. Arthur Lewis, "Economic Development with Unlimited Supplies of Labour," *The Manchester School* 22, no. 2 (May 1954): 139–91.

4. For a detailed analysis of China's 1970s agricultural research and extension system, see Sigrid Schmalzer, *Red Revolution, Green Revolution: Scientific Farming in Socialist China* (Chicago: University of Chicago Press, 2016); also see Benedict Stavis, "Agricultural Research and Extension Services in China," *World Development* 6, no. 5 (May 1978): 631–45; and Lynn T. White III, *Unstately Power*: Vol. 1, *Local Causes of China's Economic Reforms* (Armonk, NY: M.E. Sharpe, 1998), 85.

5. While conducting fieldwork between 2011 and 2015, I had the pleasure of exchanging views with numerous experts at provincial-level agricultural universities around China, who explained the agricultural modernization process in their provinces.

6. Data available at Zheng Jiaheng, *Zhongguo tongji nianjian* [Statistical Yearbook of China] (Beijing: China Statistics Press, 1992), 158. For an excellent explanation of how decollectivization precipitated this fall in agricultural investment, see Jean Oi, *Rural China Takes Off* (Berkeley: University of California Press, 1999), 19–23.

7. Louis Putterman, *Continuity and Change in China's Rural Development* (New York: Oxford University Press, 1993), 13.

8. David Bachman, *Chen Yun and the Chinese Political System* (Berkeley: University of California, Institute of East Asian Studies, 1985), 104–1055.

9. Edward Friedman, Paul G. Pickowicz, and Mark Selden, *Revolution, Resistance, and Reform in Village China*, (New Haven, CT: Yale University Press, 2005), 151.

10. Bachman, *Chen Yun*, 102–105.

11. Friedman et al., *Revolution, Resistance*, 155.

12. Friedman et al., *Revolution, Resistance*, 155.

13. Friedman et al., *Revolution, Resistance*, 155.

14. Harry Harding, "Modernization and Mao: The Logic of the Cultural Revolution and the 1970s," conference paper presented to the Institute of World Affairs, San Diego State University, August 1970, 11.

15. Benedict Stavis, *The Politics of Agricultural Mechanization in China* (Ithaca: Cornell University Press, 1978), 229. For instance, see "Jiaxing diqu jianchi liangtiao luxian douzheng, fazhan nongye jidian shiye" [Adhere to Two-line Struggle, Develop Agricultural Electronics and Mechanization in Jiaxiang (Zhejiang Province)]; "Xinzhouxian jiasu fazhan nongye jixiehua" [Speed up the Development of Agricultural Mechanization in Xinzhou County (Hubei Province)]; "Shuangchengxian zili gengsheng ban nongye jiexie" [Self-reliance and Undertake Agricultural Machinery in Shuangcheng County (Heilongjiang Province)], *People's Daily*, October 19, 1970.

16. Harding, "Modernization and Mao," 19.

17. Stavis, "Agricultural Research," 634.

18. Fan Shenggen and Philip Pardey, "Research, Productivity, and Output Growth in Chinese Agriculture," *Journal of Development Economics* 53, no. 1 (June 1997): 126–27.

19. "Ba puji xiandai nongye kexue jishu jianli zai qunzhong de jichu shang" [Build Dissemination of Modern Agricultural Science and Technology on the Foundation of the Masses], *People's Daily*, May 21, 1964. Dangdai Zhongguo congshu bianji weiyuanhui, ed., *Dangdai Zhongguo de Nongye* [Agriculture of Contemporary China] (Beijing: Zhongguo shehui kexue chubanshe, 1992), 571.

20. "Banhao sanjiehe de yangbantian, cujin nongke kexue shiyan yundong" [Organizing three-in-one demonstration fields and promoting the agricultural scientific experiment movement], *People's Daily*, March 28, 1965.

21. American Plant Studies Delegation, *Plant Studies in the People's Republic of China: A Trip Report of the American Plant Studies Delegation* (Washington, DC: National Academy of Sciences, 1975), 118, 120.

22. Xinhua tongxun she, ed., *Dagao kexue zhongtian, jiasu nongye fazhan: jieshao Hunan Huarong xian siji nongye kexue shiyan wang* [Greatly Undertake Scientific Farming, Accelerate Agricultural Development: Introducing Hunan Province, Huarong County's Four-Level Agricultural Scientific Experiment Network] (Beijing: Remin meishu chubanshe, 1975).

23. Xinhua tongxun she, *Dagao kexue zhongtian*.

24. Schmalzer, *Red Revolution*, 22, 40–41.

25. Stavis, "Agricultural Research," 633–34.

26. Stavis, "Agricultural Research," 633–35; also see Han Dongping, *The Unknown Cultural Revolution: Life and Change in a Chinese Village* (Boston, MA: Monthly Review Press, 2008), 136.

27. Han, *The Unknown*, 136.

28. Han, *The Unknown*, 136.

29. Stavis, "Agricultural Research," 634.

30. Schmalzer, *Red Revolution*, 137.

31. This idea can be traced back to Guanzi's "Quan xiu" in the spring and autumn periods (771 to 476 B.C.). In contemporary Chinese, the common phrase is "Shinian shumu, bainian shuren."

32. Shanxi sheng Xinxian diqu geweihui, Nonglin shuili ju keji xiaozu, eds. *Xinxian diqu nongye kexue shiyan* [Xin County region agricultural scientific experiment], n.p., 1971, 15.

33. Stavis, "Agricultural Research," 634.

34. Stavis, "Agricultural Research," 631–37; also see Schmalzer, *Red Revolution*, 40.

35. Stavis, "Agricultural Research," 636–37.

36. Justin Y. F. Lin, "The Household Responsibility Reform and the Option of Hybrid Rice in China," *Journal of Developmental Economics* 36, no. 2 (1991): 359.

37. Nicholas Lardy, "Prospects and Some Policy Problems of Agricultural Development in China," *Journal of Agricultural Economics* 68, no. 2 (1986): 452–53.

38. Leo Orleans, *China's Experience in Population Control: The Elusive Model*, prepared for the Committee on Foreign Affairs of the U.S. House of Representatives by the Congressional Research Service, Library of Congress (Washington, DC: U.S. Government Printing Office, 1974); also included in Neville Maxwell, *China's Road to Development* (New York: Pergamon Press, 1979), 101.

39. *Agricultural Economic Statistics*, 34–35.

40. *Agricultural Economic Statistics*, 46.

41. American Plant Studies Delegation, xiii.

42. Orleans, *China's Experience*, 102.

43. For a description of China's family planning policies, see Tyrene White, *China's Longest Campaign: Birth Planning in the People's Republic, 1949–2005* (Ithaca, NY: Cornell University Press, 2006).

44. "Chinese Observer on Population Question," *Peking Review* 49 (December 7, 1973): 10–11.
45. *Agricultural Economic Statistics*, 35.
46. Michelangelo Antonioni, dir. *Chung Kuo, Cina*, RAI Radiotelevisione Italiana, 1972, film. At 1 hour, 1 minute, 16 seconds, Antonioni films an illegal urban settlement, with voiceover dialogue stating, "There is also a new growing Beijing. Although the government does not favor urban expansion, the natural growth cannot be stopped."
47. Orleans, *China's Experience*, 106.
48. Suzanne Paine, "Balanced Development: Maoist Conception and Chinese Practice," *World Development* 4, no. 4 (April 1976): 290.
49. Orleans, *China's Experience*, 106.
50. Speech by Wang Renzhong to U.S. delegation in China, quoted in Merle Esmay and Roy Harrington, *Glimpses of Agricultural Mechanization in the PRC* (St. Joseph, MI: American Society of Agricultural Engineers, 1979), 7; also see John Wong, "Some Aspects of China's Agricultural Development Experience: Implications for Developing Countries in Asia," *World Development* 4, no. 6 (1976): 493.
51. Dwight Perkins, *Rural Small-Scale Industry in the People's Republic of China* (Berkeley: University of California Press, 1977), 255.
52. Arthur Galston, *Daily Life in People's China* (New York: Washington Square Press, 1973), 111.
53. Keith Griffin and Ashwani Saith, *Growth and Equality in Rural China* (Geneva: Asian Employment Programme, 1981), 151.
54. Harding, "Modernization and Mao," 16.
55. Orleans, *China's Experience*, 106.
56. Griffin and Saith, *Growth and Equality*, 151.
57. Benedict Stavis, *People's Communes and Rural Development in China* (Ithaca, NY: Rural Development Committee of Cornell University, 1974), 111.
58. Steven Butler, *Agricultural Mechanization in China: The Administrative Impact* (New York: Columbia University Press, 1978), 22.
59. Stavis, *People's Communes and Rural Development*, 111.
60. Butler, *Agricultural Mechanization*, 33.
61. Butler, *Agricultural Mechanization*, 22; Stavis, *The Politics of Agricultural Mechanization*, 79.
62. Wu Chou, *Report from Tungting: A People's Commune on Taihu Lake* (Beijing: Foreign Languages Press, 1975) 14.
63. Guan Shengtang, interview, Yuhai County, Jiangxi Province, December 26, 2011.
64. Griffin and Saith, *Growth and Equality*, 150.
65. Peggy Printz and Paul Steinle, *Commune: Life in Rural China* (New York: Dodd, Mead, 1977), 68–69.
66. Galston, *Daily Life*, 107–109.
67. Butler, *Agricultural Mechanization*, 22.
68. Chris Bramall, *The Industrialization of Rural China* (Oxford: Oxford University Press, 2007), 23.
69. Butler, *Agricultural Mechanization*, 22.
70. Bramall, *Industrialization*, 23.
71. Butler, *Agricultural Mechanization*, 22.

72. Griffin and Saith, *Growth and Equality*, 150.

73. Griffin and Saith, *Growth and Equality*, 150.

74. Butler, *Agricultural Mechanization*, 22.

75. "Twelve Million School Graduates Settle in the Countryside," *Peking Review* 19, no. 2 (January 9, 1976): 11–13.

76. Thomas Bernstein, *Up to the Mountains and Down to the Villages: The Transfer of Youth from Urban to Rural China* (New Haven, CT: Yale University Press, 1977), 33.

77. Bernstein, *Up to the Mountains*, 39–40.

78. Bernstein, *Up to the Mountains*, 38.

79. Bernstein, *Up to the Mountains*, 40.

80. *Zhongguo qingnian bao* [China Youth Daily] (September 8, 1964), in *Communist China Digest*, no. 132, *Joint Publications Research Service* (JPRS) no. 27303, November 10, 1964.

81. Bernstein, *Up to the Mountains*, 222–24.

82. Radio Nanchang, December 29, 1975; Zhi Jian, "Gunggu he fazhan shangshan xiaxiang de chengguo" [Consolidate and develop the effectiveness of up to the mountains and down to the countryside], *Red Flag* [Hongqi], no. 7 (July 1, 1975): 6–9.

83. Stavis, "Agricultural Research," 634.

84. Works on the relationship between Sent-Down urbanites and their rural hosts include Shi Tiesheng, "Wode yaoyuan de qingpingwan" [My Faraway Qingpingwan], *Qingnian wenxue* [Youth Literacy] 1 (1983); Liang Xiaosheng, *Jinye you baofengxue* [The Snowstorm Tonight] (Shanghai: Wenhui Publishing House, 2009); Liu Yaqiu, "Zhiqing kunan yu xiangcun chengshi jian guanxi yanjiu" [A Study on the Relationship between the Hardship of Educated Youth and Rural Cities], *Qinghua daxue xuebao* [Journal of Tsinghua University] 23, no. 2 (2008): 135–48.

85. China's National Bureau of Statistics, *Chinese Population Census 2000*,

86. Han, *The Unknown*, 127.

87. Robert J. Lifton, "Thought Reform of Chinese Intellectuals: A Psychiatric Evaluation," *Journal of Asian Studies* 16, no. 1 (November 1956): 75–88; Theodore Hsi-en Chen, "The New Socialist Man," *Comparative Education Review* 13, no. 1 (February 1969): 88–95.

88. Friedman et al., *Revolution, Resistance*, 132.

89. Sun Guihua, interview, December 10, 2011.

90. Galston, *Daily Life*, 188.

91. Stavis, "Agricultural Research," 634.

92. Galston, *Daily Life*, 189.

93. Galston, *Daily Life*, 191.

94. *Agricultural Economic Statistics*, 120.

95. Bruce Stone, "Developments in Agricultural Technology," *The China Quarterly* 116 (December 1988): 767.

96. Yuan-li Wu and Robert Sheeks, *The Organization and Development of Scientific Research and Development in Mainland China* (New York: Praeger, 1970), 355–57.

97. Galston, *Daily Life*, 51, 77.

98. American Plant Studies Delegation, 118, 120.

99. Wong, "Some Aspects," 493.

100. Han, *The Unknown*, 133. See also description of "5406" at "Prospects for the Technical Development of Bio-fertilizer," State Intellectual Property Office of the PRC website.

101. Bruce Stone, *Evolution and Diffusion of Agricultural Technology in China* (Washington, DC: International Food Policy Research Institute, 1990), 51–52.

102. Per Brinck, *Insect Pest Management in China: A Swedish Delegation Report* (Stockholm: Ingenjorsvetenskapsakademien, 1979), 10–11.

103. Stavis, "Agricultural Research," 639.

104. Wu and Sheeks, *The Organization and Development*, 355.

105. Brinck, 10–11.

106. Han, *The Unknown*, 133; also see Richard Hoyt, "Gibberellic Acid in Plant Growth," eHow.com, undated.

107. Stavis, "Agricultural Research," 639.

108. Wu and Sheeks, *The Organization and Development*, 359–360.

109. Wu and Sheeks, *The Organization and Development*, 355. See also Stavis, "Agricultural Research," 639.

110. Stavis, "Agricultural Research," 638–40.

111. Scott Rozelle, "Annex I: China's Corn Economy, A Brief Introduction," n.d., posted on University of California, Davis website.

112. Wu and Sheeks, *The Organization and Development*, 352.

113. Stone, *Evolution and Diffusion*, 44.

114. Stavis, "Agricultural Research," 638–40.

115. Schmalzer, *Red Revolution*, 73–100.

116. See Lin, "Household Responsibility Reform," 355; also Stavis, "Agricultural Research," 633 and 638; and Wu and Sheeks, *The Organization and Development*, 353.

117. Lin, "Household Responsibility Reform," 354–56.

118. Mobo Gao, *The Battle for China's Past: Mao and the Cultural Revolution* (Ann Arbor, MI: Pluto Press, 2008), 147; and "Li Zhensheng breeds wheat to help feed the nation," *People's Daily*, February 28, 2007.

119. Valerie Karplus and Xing Wang Deng, *Agricultural Biotechnology in China: Origins and Prospects* (New York: Spring, 2008), 40; also Stavis, "Agricultural Research," 638.

120. Karplus and Deng, *Agricultural Biotechnology*, 40.

121. *Agricultural Economic Statistics*, 296–97.

122. Jae Ho Chung, "The Politics of Agricultural Mechanization in the Post-Mao Era, 1977–87," *The China Quarterly*, no. 134 (June 1993), 264–90.

123. *Agricultural Economic Statistics*, 298.

124. *Agricultural Economic Statistics*, 299.

125. Chu Li and Tien Chieh-yun, *Inside a People's Commune: Report from Chiliying* (Beijing: Foreign Languages Press, 1974), 135.

126. *Agricultural Economic Statistics*, 296.

127. Han, *The Unknown*, 130–31; also see Marc Blecher and Vivian Shue, *Tethered Deer: Government and Economy in a Chinese County* (Stanford, CA: Stanford University Press, 1996).

128. Wu and Sheeks, *The Organization and Development*, 359.

129. *Agricultural Economic Statistics*, 297.

130. *Agricultural Economic Statistics*, 296–97.

131. Perkins, *Rural Small-Scale Industry*, 121.

132. *Agricultural Economic Statistics*, 296–99.

133. Wu and Sheeks, *The Organization and Development*, 358.

134. Richard Baum, "Lecture 18: The Great Leap Forward (1958–60)," *The Fall and Rise of China* (Chantilly, VA: The Teaching Company, 2010), 24 audio discs.

135. Stavis, "Agricultural Research," 635.

136. Wu and Sheeks, *The Organization and Development*, 360.

137. Baum, "Lecture 18."

138. Anthony Tang and Bruce Stone, *Food Production in the People's Republic of China* (Washington, DC: International Food Policy Research Institute, 1980), 6, 123; also see Harding, "Modernization and Mao," 19.

139. Han, *The Unknown*, 129.

140. *Agricultural Economic Statistics*, 288.

141. *Agricultural Economic Statistics*, 291.

142. Bruce Stone, "The Basis for Chinese Agricultural Growth in the 1980s and 1990s: A Comment on Document No. 1, 1984," *The China Quarterly* 101 (March 1985): 114; see also Barry Naughton, *The Chinese Economy: Transitions and Growth* (Cambridge, MA: MIT Press, 2007), 253.

143. Harding, "Modernization and Mao," 16.

144. *Agricultural Economic Statistics*, 290.

145. *Agricultural Economic Statistics*, 286–87.

146. *Agricultural Economic Statistics*, 286–87, 290.

147. Han, *The Unknown*, 131.

148. *Agricultural Economic Statistics*, 286–87.

149. *Agricultural Economic Statistics*, 288–89.

150. *Agricultural Economic Statistics*, 294–95.

151. *Agricultural Economic Statistics*, 295.

152. Lardy, "Prospects," 453.

153. *Agricultural Economic Statistics*, 286–89.

154. Putterman, *Continuity and Change*, 13. For two more authoritative account of rural industrialization, see Bramall, *Industrialization*; and American Rural Small-Scale Industry Delegation, *Rural Small-Scale Industry in the People's Republic of China* (Berkeley: University of California Press, 1977).

4. ECONOMICS

1. E. L. Jones, *Agriculture and the Industrial Revolution* (Oxford: Blackwell, 1974), 67.

2. Barry Naughton, "Rural Saving and Credit Supply Before and After Collectives," paper presented to UCLA Seminar on Economic and Historical Perspectives on China's Collectives, February 21, 1987, 6.

3. I assume a Cobb-Douglas production function given by $Y = AK^{\alpha}L^{1-\alpha}$ ($0 < \alpha < 1$), and, which expressed in per capita form becomes $y = Ak^{\alpha}$.

4. The official policy documents detailing the reforms that produced China's 1970s green revolution available in appendix C are the "State Council Report on the 1970 Northern Regions Agricultural Conference," dated December 11, 1970; and Central

Document No. 82, "Central Committee Instructions on Distribution within Communes," December 26, 1971.

5. Philippe Aghion and Peter Howitt, *Endogenous Growth Theory* (Cambridge, MA: MIT Press, 1997), 11.

6. Robert Barro and Xavier Sala-i-Martin, *Economic Growth* (Cambridge, MA: MIT Press, 1999), 15.

7. Jasper Becker, *Hungry Ghosts: Mao's Secret Famine* (New York: Henry Holt, 1998), 103, 111, 118, 138.

8. For an excellent description of this fall in agricultural investment, see Jean C. Oi, *Rural China Takes Off: Institutional Foundations of Economic Reform* (Berkeley: University of California Press, 1999), 10–23.

9. Oi, *Rural China*, 20.

10. W. Arthur Lewis, "Economic Development with Unlimited Supplies of Labour," *The Manchester School of Economic and Social Studies* 22, no. 2 (1954).

11. Lewis, "Economic Development," 401–402.

12. Lewis, "Economic Development," 412.

13. Lewis, "Economic Development," 412–13.

14. Nicholas Kaldor, *Causes of Growth and Stagnation in the World Economy* (Cambridge: Cambridge University Press, 1996), 43.

15. Lewis, "Economic Development," 419.

16. Lewis, "Economic Development," 415.

17. Kaldor, *Causes of Growth*, 43.

18. Lewis, "Economic Development," 415.

19. Kaldor, *Causes of Growth*, 44–45.

20. Bruce Stone, "Developments in Agricultural Technology," *The China Quarterly* 116 (1988): 767.

21. Kaldor, *Causes of Growth*, 47.

22. Lewis, "Economic Development," 416–17.

23. *Agricultural Economic Statistics, 1949–1983* [nongye jingji ziliao, 1949–1983] (Beijing: Ministry of Agriculture Planning Bureau, 1983), 514.

24. *Agricultural Economic Statistics*, 516–17.

25. *Agricultural Economic Statistics*, 516–17.

26. Traditionally, rural China suffered from overconsumption. Although this problem is often blamed on gluttonous elites, in some areas, the extensive number of traditional Chinese traditional festivals also played a role. Jonathan Spence notes that although "heat and hunger, dampness and diseases are never far away," in nineteenth-century Hua County, Guangdong rural residents used precious resources on rites. To placate the grain spirits, villagers might sacrifice a pig, "eat dried fish in bulk," "burn model houses of bamboo and stay awake all night," or hang strings of oranges from their doors. Jonathan Spence, *God's Chinese Son: The Taiping Heavenly Kingdom of Hong Xiuquan* (New York: W.W. Norton, 1996), 34–37.

27. Lau Siu-kai, "The People's Commune and the Diffusion of Agri-Technology in China," paper presented at Communication and Cultural Change in China, East-West Center, Honolulu, Hawaii, January 1978, 39.

28. Barro and Sala-i-Martin, *Economic Growth*, 21.

29. Leslie T. C. Kuo, *Agriculture in the People's Republic of China: Structural Changes and Technical Transformation* (New York: Praeger, 1976), 45.

30. Jonathan Unger, *The Transformation of Rural China* (Armonk, NY: M.E. Sharpe, 2002), 88–89.
31. Unger, *The Transformation*, 87–89.
32. Steven Butler, "Price Scissors and Commune Administration in Post-Mao China," in *Chinese Rural Development*, ed. William Parrish (Armonk, NY: M.E. Sharpe, 1985), 104–105.
33. Butler, "Price Scissors," 105.
34. Gordon Bennett, Ken Kieke, and Ken Yoffy, *Huadong: The Story of a People's Commune* (Boulder, CO: Westview Press, 1978), 98.
35. Unger, *The Transformation*, 78–79. In Weihai, Shandong, for instance, the job of drying corn was considerably easier than shucking, although the workpoints awarded were the same and women did both jobs. There was a good deal of jockeying among members at team meetings to determine who would be assigned which job. Sun Guihua, interview, Los Angeles, July 30, 2013.
36. Unger, *The Transformation*, 76–77.
37. Li Huaiyin, "Institutions and Work Incentives in Collective Farming in Maoist China," *Journal of Agrarian Change* 17, no. 4 (2016): 4.
38. Bennett et al., *Huadong*, 98. Unger, *The Transformation*, 88–89.
39. Butler, "Price Scissors," 104.
40. Li, "Institutions," 4.
41. Peggy Printz and Paul Steinle, *Commune Life in Rural China* (New York: Dodd, Mead, 1973), 84–85.
42. Sun Guihua, interview, Los Angeles, August 29, 2013.
43. Bennett et al., *Huadong*, 98.
44. Li Huaiyin, *Village China under Socialism and Reform: A Micro-History, 1948–2008* (Stanford, CA: Stanford University Press, 2010), 131–32.
45. Li, *Village China*, 10–11. For depictions of local cadres as "native emperors" (*tuhuangdi*) see Daniel Kelliher, *Peasant Power in China: The End of the Reform Era* (New Haven, CT: Yale University Press, 1992), 19–25; J. Sachs and W.T. Woo, "Structural Factors in the Economic Reforms of China, Eastern Europe, and the Former Soviet Union," *Economic Policy* 18 (1994): 114–15; Kate Xiao Zhou, *How the Farmers Changed China: Power of the People* (Boulder: Westview Press, 1996), 30–33.
46. Li, *Village China*, 11.
47. Peter Nolan and Gordon White, "Distribution and Development in China," *Bulletin of Concerned Asia Scholars* 13, no. 3 (1981): 13–14.
48. Nolan and White, "Distribution and Development," 11–12.
49. Shanxi Datong City Farm Machine Station of Changtang Commune, "Rely on the Masses to Run the Farm Machine Station Democratically," *Nongye Jixie Jishu* [Agricultural Machinery Techniques], no. 9 (September 1968) in *Selections from China Mainland Magazines*, no. 644: 10.
50. Nolan and White, "Distribution and Development," 11–12.
51. Naughton, "Rural Saving," 1–2.
52. Naughton, "Rural Saving," 5.
53. Naughton, "Rural Saving," 6.
54. Naughton, "Rural Saving," 5, 10–11.
55. Harry Harding, "Modernization and Mao: The Logic of the Cultural Revolution and the 1970s," conference paper presented to the Institute of World Affairs, San Diego State University, August 1970, 19.

56. Zhou, *How the Farmers*, 2.
57. Benedict Stavis, *People's Commune and Rural Development in China* (Ithaca, NY: Cornell University Press, 1974), 53–54; also see William L. Parish, Jr., "Socialism and the Chinese Peasant Family," *Journal of Asian Studies* 34 (1975): 619.
58. Dali Yang, *Calamity and Reform in China: State, Rural Society, and Institutional Change since the Great Leap Famine* (Stanford, CA: Stanford University Press, 1996), 144–45.
59. John Pelzel, "Economic Management of a Production Brigade in Post-Leap China," in *Economic Organization in Chinese Society*, ed. W.E. Willmott (Stanford, CA: Stanford University Press, 1972), 393.
60. Steven Butler, *Agricultural Mechanization in China: The Administrative Impact* (New York: East Asian Institute of Columbia University, 1978), 9.
61. Keith Griffin and Ashwani Saith, *Growth and Equality in Rural China* (Geneva: Asian Employment Programme, 1981), 127.
62. The private sector was a touchy ideological subject in 1970s China, and Antonioni was excoriated in the official Chinese press because of his depiction. Andrea Barbato, *Chung Kuo—Cina*, dir. Michelangelo Antonioni (Italy: RAI Radiotelevisione Italiana, 1973), film.
63. Guan Shengtang, interview, December 26, 2011.
64. Li Huaiyin, interview, March 21, 2015.
65. Interviews in Gansu and Jiangxi, November and December 2011.
66. "Jianchi shehui zhuyi daolu, xianzhi zichan jieji faquan" [Maintain the Socialist Road, Restrict Bourgeois Rights], *Red Flag* [Hongqi], no. 8 (August 1975): 26.
67. Virgil Mays, "Swine Production," in *China: A Report of the Visit of the CSCPRC Animal Science Delegation*, ed. Jacob Hoefer and Patrica Tsuchitani (Washington, DC: National Academy Press, 1980), 48–50.
68. Mays, "Swine Production," 41.
69. By 1979, all Chinese pigs were immunized against hog cholera and swine erysipelas; see Mays, "Swine Production," 51.
70. Mays, "Swine Production," 49.
71. G. F. Sprague, "Agriculture in China," *Science* 188, no. 4188 (1975): 555.
72. "Jianchi," 26.
73. Ding Shaosheng, "Duzu ziben zhuyi daolu, maikai shehui zhuyi dabu" [Block the Capitalist Road, Take Big Steps for Socialism], *Shehui yu pipan* [Society and Critiques] (November 1975): 8–9.
74. Butler, *Agricultural Mechanization in China*, 11.
75. "Buduan gonggu nongcun shehui zhuyi zhendi" [Continue to Consolidate the Position of Socialism in the Villages], *Lishi renzhi* [Understandings of the History] 2 (1975): 37.

5. POLITICS

1. Lewis Mumford, *The Story of Utopias* (New York: Boni and Liveright, 1962).
2. Rosabeth Moss Kanter, *Communes: Creating and Managing the Collective Life* (New York: Harper & Row, 1973), 5.

3. "Shakers," *New World Encyclopedia*, undated, http://www.newworldencyclopedia
   .org/entry/Shakers.
4. Kanter, *Communes*, 7.
5. Kathleen M. Hogan, "Robert Owen and New Harmony," University of Virginia
   American Studies Project Website. Accessed January 18, 2017. http://xroads
   .virginia.edu/~hyper/HNS/Cities/newharmony.html.
6. See George B. Lockwood, *Labor Note*, 1905, The New Harmony Movement,
   D. Appleton and Company, New York, https://jewettc.wikispaces.com/MWF+11.15
   +-+Roberty+Owen.Harmony+Soc.
7. Kanter, *Communes*, 3–4.
8. Cited in Kanter, *Communes*, 3, 7.
9. Plato, "The Republic," in *The Republic of Plato: with Studies for Teachers*, ed.,
   William L. Bryan and Charlotte L. Bryan (New York: Charles Scribner's Sons,
   1898), 120.
10. James C. Scott, *Seeing Like a State: How Certain Schemes to Improve the Human
    Condition Have Failed* (New Haven, CT: Yale University Press, 1999), 184.
11. Scott, *Seeing Like a State*, 189.
12. Scott, *Seeing Like a State*, 183.
13. Scott, *Seeing Like a State*, 184.
14. Michael Gold, "Is the Small Farmer Dying?" *New Republic*, October 7, 1931, 211.
15. Scott, *Seeing Like a State*, 190–91.
16. Deborah Fitzgerald, *Yeoman No More: The Industrialization of American Agricul-
    ture* (New Haven, CT: Yale University Press, 2009), 31.
17. Scott, *Seeing Like a State*, 189.
18. Scott, *Seeing Like a State*, 203.
19. Scott, *Seeing Like a State*, 191.
20. Katherine Verdery, *The Vanishing Hectare: Property and Value in Postsocialist
    Transylvania* (Ithaca, NY: Cornell University Press, 2003), 46.
21. Verdery, *The Vanishing Hectare*, 46.
22. Kanter, *Communes*, 5.
23. Kanter, *Communes*, 6–7.
24. Ran Abramitzky, "On the (lack of) Stability of Communes: An Economic Per-
    spective," in *Oxford Handbook of the Economics of Religion*, ed. Rachel McCleary
    (Oxford: Oxford University Press, 2011), 1.
25. Abramitzky, "On the (lack of) Stability," 1. Also see Edward Lazear, "Salaries and
    Piece Rates," *Journal of Business* 59, no. 3 (1986): 405–31; Edward Lazear, "Perfor-
    mance Pay and Productivity," *American Economic Review* 90, no. 5 (2000): 1346–
    61; Edward Lazear, "The Power of Incentives," *American Economic Review* 90, no. 2
    (2000): 410–14; Bengt Holmstrom, "Moral Hazard in Teams," *The Bell Journal of
    Economics* 13, no. 2 (1982): 324–40. For a survey on the literature on incentives
    in firms, see Canice Prendergast, "The Provision of Incentives in Firms," *Journal
    of Economic Literature* 37, no. 1 (1999): 7–63; Canice Prendergast, "The Tenuous
    Trade-off between Risk and Incentives," *Journal of Political Economy* 110, no. 5
    (2002): 1071–102. For the results of laboratory experiments on free-riding, see Ernst
    Fehr and Simon Gächter, "Cooperation and Punishment in Public Goods Experi-
    ments," *American Economic Review* 90, no. 4 (2000): 980–94. For a review of the
    selection and incentive effects of increased income equality within communes, see

Ran Abramitzky, "The Effect of Redistribution on Migration: Evidence from the Israeli Kibbutz," *Journal of Public Economics* 93, no. 3 (2009): 498–511.

26. Illiterate individuals were more likely to enter Shaker communes, see John Murray, "Human Capital in Religious Communes: Literacy and Selection of Nineteenth Century Shakers," *Explorations in Economic History* 32, no. 2 (1995): 217–35. Individuals who earned lower wages were more likely to enter kibbutzim, see Ran Abramitzky, "The Limits of Equality: Insights from the Israeli Kibbutz," *Quarterly Journal of Economics* 123, no. 3 (2008): 1111–59.

27. More educated and skilled members were more likely to leave Israel's kibbutzim as the outside economy began to offer greater returns to skills in the 1980s and 1990s. See Ran Abramitzky, "The Effect of Redistribution on Migration." At the end of the nineteenth century, Equality, a socialist commune in Washington State, lost its more talented members when they were lured by new outside opportunities. Similarly, the decline of members at Sunrise, a commune in Michigan, was attributed to its proximity to Detroit, which experienced an economic boom at the end of the Great Depression; see Iaácov Oved, *Two Hundred Years of American Communes* (New Brunswick, Canada: Transaction Books, 1993). Literate members of Shaker communes in nineteenth-century America were more likely to exit; see Murray, "Human Capital." Those leaving Bishop Hill, a Swedish religious commune, were primarily members with a greater chance of success outside; see Donald Pitzer. *America's Communal Utopias* (Chapel Hill: University of North Carolina Press, 1997).

28. Amia Lieblich, *Kibbutz Makom: Report from an Israeli Kibbutz* (New York: Pantheon Books, 1981); Haim Barkai, *Kibbutz Efficiency and the Incentive Conundrum* (Jerusalem: Maurice Falk Institute for Economic Research in Israel, 1987); Laurence Iannaccone, *Sacrifice and Stigma: Reducing Free-riding in Cults, Communes, and Other Collectives* (Palo Alto, CA: Hoover Institution, Stanford University, 1992); Eli Berman, *Sect, Subsidy, and Sacrifice: An Economist's View of Ultra-orthodox Jews* (Cambridge, MA: National Bureau of Economic Research, 1998); Richard Sosis, "Religion and Intragroup Cooperation: Preliminary Results of a Comparative Analysis of Utopian Communities," *Cross-Cultural Research* 34, no. 1 (2000): 70–87; Levhari Keren and Michael Byalsky, "On the Stability and Viability of Co-operatives: The Kibbutz as an Example," *Acta Oeconomica* 56, no. 3 (2006): 301–21.

29. Abramitsky, "On the (lack of) Stability," 18.

30. Abramitsky, "On the (lack of) Stability," 18.

31. Among nineteenth-century American communes, religious communes tended to be the longest lasting type; see Sosis, "Religion and Intragroup Cooperation. In Israel, religious kibbutzim have been more successful than their secular counterparts; see Aryei Fishman, *Judaism and Modernization on the Religious Kibbutz* (Cambridge: Cambridge University Press, 1992); Aryei Fishman, "Religious Socialism and Economic Success on the Orthodox Kibbutz," *Journal of Institutional and Theoretical Economics* 150, no. 4 (1994): 763–68. Members of religious kibbutzim tend to cooperate more with other members than members of secular kibbutzim; see Richard Sosis and Bradley Ruffle, "Religious Ritual and Cooperation: Testing for a Relationship on Israeli Religious and Secular Kibbutzim," *Current Anthropology* 44, no. 5 (December 2003): 713–22.

32. Abramitsky, "On the (lack of) Stability," 18.

33. Kanter, *Communes*, 3, 7. From 1787 to 1796, Shaker communities were under the strict leadership of Father Joseph Meacham. Edward Andrews, *The Gift to Be Simple Songs Dances and Rituals of the American Shakers* (New York: J. J. Augustin, 1940), 5.

34. Hogan, "Robert Owen."

35. Andrews, *The Gift to Be Simple*, 5.

36. Laurence Iannaccone, "Sacrifice and Stigma: Reducing Free-Riding in Cults, Communes, and Other Collectives," *Journal of Political Economy* 100, no. 2 (1992): 271–91.

37. Andrews, *The Gift to Be Simple*, 5.

38. Kanter, *Communes*, 10.

39. Oved, *Two Hundred Years*, 185. Also see Donald Pitzer, *America's Communal Utopias* (Chapel Hill: University of North Carolina Press, 1997).

40. Menachem Rosner, Itzhak Ben David, Alexander Avnat, Neni Cohen, and Uri Leviatan, *The Second Generation: Continuity and Change in the Kibbutz* (New York: Greenwood Press, 1990).

41. Abramitsky, "On the (lack of) Stability," 18.

42. Andrews, *The Gift to Be Simple*, 5.

43. Abramitsky, "On the (lack of) Stability," 3–4.

44. A religion, according to Emile Durkheim, is "a unified system of beliefs and practices relative to sacred things, that is to say, things set apart and forbidden—beliefs and practices which unite into one single moral community called a Church, all those who adhere to them"; see Emile Durkheim, *The Elementary Forms of the Religious* Life, trans. Joseph Ward Swain (New York: Free Press, 1965), 62.

45. David Zweig, *Agrarian Radicalism in China* (Cambridge, MA: Harvard University Press, 1989), 7.

46. Zweig, *Agrarian Radicalism*, 7.

47. Tuo Wang, *The Cultural Revolution and Overacting: Dynamics Between Politics and Performance* (Lanham, MD: Lexington Books, 2014), 10; also see Richard Baum, *China Watcher: Confessions of a Peking Tom* (Seattle: University of Washington Press, 2010), 113.

48. Richard Madsen, *Morality and Power in a Chinese Village* (Berkeley: University of California Press, 1985), 136–37.

49. Madsen, *Morality and Power*, 136–37.

50. Madsen, *Morality and Power*, 136–37.

51. Marc Blecher, *China Against the Tides: Restructuring Through Revolution, Radicalism and Reform*, 3rd ed. (New York: Bloomsbury Academic, 2009), 98.

52. Martin K. Whyte, *Small Groups and Political Rituals in China* (Berkeley: University of California Press, 1974), 13–14, 211–12.

53. Whyte, 13–14, 211–12.

54. Abramitsky, "On the (lack of) Stability," 21.

55. Wang, *The Cultural Revolution*, 12. Also see Whyte, *Small Groups*, 212–13.

56. Madsen, *Morality and Power*, 131.

57. Wang, *The Cultural Revolution*, 12.

58. Abramitsky, "On the (lack of) Stability," 21.

59. Wang, *The Cultural Revolution*, 20.

60. Madsen, *Morality and Power* 133.

61. Wang, *The Cultural Revolution*, 20.

62. Chen Ruoxi, *The Execution of Mayor Yin and Other Stories from the Great Proletarian Cultural Revolution* (Bloomington: Indiana University Press, 2009), 44.

63. *The East Is Red*, http://people.cas.sc.edu/moskowitz/Lyrics/red/red.htm.

64. Zweig, *Agrarian Radicalism*, 7.

65. "Ba qiye bancheng Mao Zedong sixiang daxuexiao" [Change Businesses into Universities of Mao Zedong Thought], *People's Daily*, August 28, 1966.

66. Wang, *The Cultural Revolution*, 11 and 15.

67. Wang, *The Cultural Revolution*, 13.

68. See Fr. Tony Kadavil, "Solemnity of Christ the King," *Vatican Radio*, November 22, 2015, http://en.radiovaticana.va/news/2015/11/17/solemnity_of_christ_the_king_%E2%80%93_nov_22,_2015/1187444.

69. Wang, *The Cultural Revolution*, 27.

70. Sun Guihua, interview, March 1, 2013.

71. Jin Chunming, Huang Yuchong, and Chang Huimin, *"Wen Ge" Shiqi Guaishi, Guaiyu* [Strange Events and Strange Language During the "Cultural Revolution"] (Peking: Qiushi chubanshe, 1989), 189.

72. Zhang Dong, *Boji Yishu Rensheng: Tian Hua Zhuan* [A Biography of Tian Hua] (Beijing: Zhongguo Dianying Chubanshe, 2006), 218.

73. Madsen, *Morality and Power*, 134.

74. Madsen, *Morality and Power*, 134.

75. Madsen, *Morality and Power*, 136.

76. Tania Branigan, "Red Songs Ring Out in Chinese City's New Cultural Revolution." *The Guardian*. April 22, 2011, https://www.theguardian.com/world/2011/apr/22/red-songs-chinese-cultural-revolution.

77. Madsen, *Morality and Power*, 135.

78. Wang, *The Cultural Revolution*, 21.

79. Wang, *The Cultural Revolution*, 22.

80. Alexander Cook, *Mao's Little Red Book: A Global History* (Cambridge: Cambridge University Press, 2014), 23.

81. Fang Houshu, "Stories Behind the Publication of the *Little Red Book*," *Xinhua*, July 13, 2004.

82. For detailed descriptions of how rituals help define group membership, see Iannaccone, "Sacrifice and Stigma"; Berman, *Sect, Subsidy, and Sacrifice*; Sosis, "Religion and Intragroup Cooperation."

83. Wang, *The Cultural Revolution*, 27.

84. Yu Juan, "Wenge qijian guwu yaobei maozhuixi yulu" [The Required Quotation Exchange while Shopping during the Cultural Revolution], October 6, 2012, www.xici.net/d121565728.htm.

85. Li Huaiyin, e-mail correspondence, December 8, 2015.

86. Madsen, *Morality and Power*, 136.

87. Tang Ying, interview, December 4, 2015.

88. Whyte, *Small Groups*, 216. Whyte described "pockets of privacy and de-politicization" and observed that "in the wake of the Cultural Revolution, some efforts are being made to cover the existing 'dead spot' in the politicization of society." It is noteworthy that as he was writing in 1974, Whyte considered the Cultural Revolution was already over.

89. Lu Lian, *Yangtian Changxiao: Yige Danjian Shiyinian De Hongweibing Yuzhong Yutianlu* [A Long Sigh: A Memoir of a Red Guard Imprisoned for Eleven Years] (Hong Kong: Hong Kong Chinese University Press, 2005), 286.

90. Wang, *The Cultural Revolution*, 20.

91. Edward Friedman, Paul Pickowicz, and Mark Selden, *Revolution, Resistance, and Reform in Village China* (New Haven, CT: Yale University Press, 2005), 146.

92. Ralph L. Powell, "Everyone a Soldier: The Communist Chinese Militia," *Foreign Affairs* (October 1960): 3.

93. Richard Thornton, *China: The Struggle for Power, 1917–1972* (Bloomington: Indiana University Press, 1973), 245.

94. Whyte, *Small Groups*,143.

95. "Quanguo douyao xue jiefangjun" [Learn from the PLA across the Country], *People's Daily*, February 1, 1964. "An Mao Zedong sixiang ban qiye" [Establish enterprises based on Mao Zedong Thought], *People's Daily*, April 3, 1966.

96. Zheng Keming, "Report to Jiangxi's Militia Work Conference," *Jiangxi Ribao* [Jiangxi Daily], December 13, 1959.

97. Freidman et al., *Revolution, Resistance*, 139–41.

98. Friedman et al., *Revolution, Resistance*, 140–41.

99. "Hold the Great Red Banner of Mao Tse-tung's Thought Still Higher, Bring the Mass Movement of Creatively Studying and Applying Chairman Mao's Works to a New Stage and Turn the PLA Into a Truly Great School of Mao Tse-tung's Thought," *Peking Review* 10, no. 3 (January 13, 1967): 8–13.

100. Chu Li and Tien Chieh-yun, *Inside a People's Commune* (Beijing: Foreign Languages Press, 1974), 128.

101. Madsen, *Morality and Power*, 133.

102. Freidman et al., *Revolution, Resistance,* 140

103. Madsen, *Morality and Power*, 138.

104. Tang Ying, interview.

105. Abramitsky, "On the (lack of) Stability," 15.

106. Sun Guihua, interview, November 10, 2014.

107. Blecher, *China Against the Tides* 98.

108. More social interaction among neighbors leads households to become more collectively oriented, see Thomas Macias and Kristin Williams "Know Your Neighbors, Save the Planet Social Capital and the Widening Wedge of Pro-Environmental Outcomes," *Environment and Behavior* 48, no. 3 (2016): 391.

109. Madsen, *Morality and Power*, 139.

110. William T. Liu, "Family Change and Family Planning in the People's Republic of China," paper presented at the annual meeting of the Population Association of America, New York, April 19, 1974; see Leo Orleans, "China's Experience in Population Control: The Elusive Model," in *China's Road to Development*, ed. Neville Maxwell (New York: Pergamon Press, 1979), 121.

111. Peggy Printz and Paul Steinle, *Commune: Life in Rural China* (New York: Dodd, Mead, 1977), 71.

112. Madsen, *Morality and Power*, 139.

113. Madsen, *Morality and Power*, 138, 140.

114. Madsen, *Morality and Power*, 141.

115. Sun Guihua, interview, March 1, 2013.

116. Arthur Galston and Jean Savage, *Daily Life in People's China* (New York: Crowell, 1973), 115.
117. Orleans, "China's Experience in Population Control," 107.
118. Galston and Savage, *Daily Life*, 119.
119. Chen, *The Execution*, 43.
120. Fei Xiaotong, *China's Gentry: Essays in Rural-Urban Relations* (Chicago: University of Chicago Press, 1958), 116.
121. Tang Ying, interview.
122. Stan Alcorn, "Ethics in Finance: Stuck at Mediocre" *NPR's Marketplace*, May 19, 2015, http://www.marketplace.org/2015/05/19/business/ethics-finance-stuck-mediocre.
123. Blecher, *China Against the Tides* 144.
124. Printz and Steinle, *Commune*, 85.
125. Madsen, *Morality and Power*, 142.
126. Jonathan Unger, *The Transformation of Rural China* (Armonk, NY: M.E. Sharpe, 2002), 78.
127. Madsen, *Morality and Power*, 124.
128. Unger, *The Transformation*, 79.
129. Unger, *The Transformation*, 77–78.
130. Unger, *The Transformation*, 79.
131. Madsen, *Morality and Power*, 143,
132. Unger, *The Transformation*, 79.
133. Madsen *Morality and Power*, 144.
134. Unger, *The Transformation*, 88–89.
135. Han Dongping, *The Unknown Cultural Revolution: Life and China in a Chinese Village* (New York: Monthly Review Press, 2008), 17–19, 70–71.
136. Unger, *The Transformation*, 79, 83–84.
137. Madsen, *Morality and Power*, 143.
138. Unger, *The Transformation*, 76–77.
139. Gordon Bennett, *Huadong: The Story of a Chinese People's Commune* (Boulder, CO: Westview Press, 1978), 98.
140. Bennett, *Huadong*, 98; Steven Butler, "Price Scissors and Commune Administration in Post-Mao China," in *Chinese Rural Development*, ed. William Parrish (Armonk, NY: ME Sharpe, 1985), 106; Li Huaiyin, *Village China Under Socialism and Reform: A Micro-History, 1948–2008* (Stanford, CA: Stanford University Press, 2009), 131–32.
141. Li, *The Transformation*, 131–32.
142. Rebecca McInroy, "Two Guys on Your Head: Egocentric Bias: Why You Think You Invented the Internet, and Why You're Kinda Right," *KUT National Public* Radio, October 15, 2015.
143. For a discussion of the selection and incentive effects of equal sharing see Abramitzky, "On the (lack of) Stability of Communes," 18. In the context of Israeli kibbutzim, see Bradley Ruffle and Richard Sosis, "Cooperation and the In-Group-Out-Group Bias: A Field Test on Israeli Kibbutz Members and City Residents," *Journal of Economic Behavior and Organization* 60, no. 2 (2006): 147–63; Ran Abramitzky, "Lessons from the Kibbutz on the Equality—Incentives Trade-off," *Journal of Economic Perspectives* 25, no. 1 (2011): 185–208.

6. ORGANIZATION

1. For a review of the dynamics of Chinese agricultural collectivization, see Ying Bai and James Kai-sing Kung, "The Shaping of an Institutional Choice: Weather Shocks, the Great Leap Famine, and Agricultural Decollectivization in China," *Explorations in Economic History* 54 (October 2014): 1–26.

2. *Henan Agricultural Statistics, 1949–1979 [Jianguo sanshinian Henan sheng nongye tongji ziliao]* (Zhengzhou: Henan Provincial Bureau of Statistics Agriculture Department, 1981).

3. Rosabeth Moss Kanter, *Communes: Creating and Managing the Collective Life* (New York: Harper & Row, 1973), 3.

4. James C. Scott, *Seeing Like a State: How Certain Schemes to Improve the Human Condition Have Failed* (New Haven, CT: Yale University Press, 1999), 221.

5. Ran Abramitzky "On the (lack of) Stability of Communes: An Economic Perspective," in *Oxford Handbook the Economics of Religion*, ed. Rachel McCleary (Oxford: Oxford University Press, 2011), 3–4.

6. *Agricultural Economic Statistics, 1949–1983* [Nongye jingji ziliao, 1949–1983] (Beijing: Ministry of Agriculture Planning Bureau, 1983), 80–81.

7. Kanter, *Communes*, 3 7.

8. Edward Andrews, *The Gift to be Simple Songs Dances and Rituals of the American Shakers* (New York: J.J. Augustin, 1940), 5.

9. Andrews, *The Gift to be Simple*, 5.

10. The assumption that commune cadres adjusted subunit size in responsive to economic stimuli is not universally accepted. Kate Xiao Zhou argues that "cadres organized farming on a commune, brigade, or team basis, regardless of the implications for productivity." See Kate Xiao Zhou, *How the Farmers Changed China: Power of the People* (Boulder, CO: Westview Press, 1996), 3.

11. Studies that examine the Great Leap Forward agricultural crisis include Jasper Becker, *Hungry Ghosts: Mao's Secret Famine* (New York: Holt, 1998); Frank Dikötter, *Mao's Great Famine: The History of China's Most Devastating Catastrophe, 1958–1962* (New York: Walker & Co, 2010); Justin Yifu Lin, "Collectivization and China's Agricultural Crisis in 1959–1961," *Journal of Political Economy* 98, no. 6 (December 1990): 1228–52; James Kai-sing Kung and Shuo Chen, "The Tragedy of the *Nomenklatura*: Career Incentives and Political Radicalism During China's Great Leap famine," *American Political Science Review* 105, no. 1 (February 2011): 27–45.

12. Liu Fangying, trans., *Issues and Studies* (Taipei: Institute of International Relations, 1979), 94.

13. For a summary of the different roles of the commune and its subunits, see Benedict Stavis, *People's Commune and Rural Development in China* (Ithaca, NY: Cornell University Rural Development Committee, 1974).

14. Frederick T. Evers, Joe M. Bohlen, and Richard D. Warren, "The Relationships of Selected Size and Structure Indicators in Economic Organizations," *Administrative Science Quarterly* 21, no. 2 (June 1976): 326–42; Nan Weiner and Thomas A. Mahoney, "A Model of Corporate Performance as a Function of Environmental, Organizational, and Leadership Influences," *Academy of Management Journal* 24, no. 3 (September 1981): 453–70.

15. Howard E. Aldrich, *Organizations and Environments* (Englewood Cliffs, NJ: Prentice-Hall, 1979); Daniel Katz and Robert L. Kahn, *The Social Psychology of Organizations*, 2nd ed. (New York: Wiley, 1978); Henry Mintzberg, *The Structuring of Organizations* (Englewood Cliffs, NJ: Prentice-Hall, 1979); Malcolm C. Sawyer, *The Economics of Industries and Firms: Theories, Evidence, and Policy* (New York: St. Martin's Press, 1981); William G. Shepherd, *The Economics of Industrial Organization* (Englewood Cliffs, NJ: Prentice-Hall, 1979); Kenneth D. George and Caroline Joll, *Industrial Organisation: Competition, Growth, and Structural Change*, 3rd ed., vol. 5 (London: Allen & Unwin, 1981).

16. Katz and Kahn, *The Social Psychology*; Ephraim Yuchtman, and Stanley E. Seashore, "A System Resource Approach to Organizational Effectiveness," *American Sociological Review* 32, no. 6 (December 1967): 891–903.

17. Richard Z. Gooding and John A. Wagner III, "A Meta-Analytic Review of the Relationship Between Size and Performance: The Productivity and Efficiency of Organizations and Their Subunits," *Administrative Science Quarterly* 30, no. 4 (December 1985): 462–63.

18. Gooding and Wagner, "A Meta-Analytic Review," 477.

19. Gooding and Wagner, "A Meta-Analytic Review," 478.

20. Dan R. Dalton, William D. Todor, Michael J. Spendolini, Gordon J. Fielding, and Lyman W. Porter, "Organization Structure and Performance: A Critical Review," *Academy of Management Review* 5, no. 1 (January 1980): 49–64; P.G. Herbst, "Measurement of Behavior Structure by Means of Input-Output Data," *Human Relations* 10 (1957): 335–46; R. W. Revans, "Human Relations, Management, and Size," in *Human Relations and Modern Management*, eds. Hugh-Jones and Edward Maurice (Amsterdam: North-Holland, 1958), 77–120.

21. James H. Davis, *Group Performance* (Reading, MA: Addison-Wesley, 1969); John Fleishman, "Collective Action as Helping Behavior: Effects of Responsibility Diffusion on Contributions to a Public Good," *Journal of Personality and Social Psychology* 38, no. 4 (April 1980): 629–37; Bernard P. Indik and Stanley F. Seashore, *Effects of Organization Size on Member Attitudes and Behavior* (Ann Arbor: University of Michigan, 1961); Raymond A. Katzell, Richard S. Barrett, and Treadway C. Parker, "Job Satisfaction, Job Performance and Situational Characteristics," *Journal of Applied Psychology* 45, no. 2 (April 1961): 65–72; R. Marriott, "Size of Working Group and Output," *Occupational Psychology* 23 (1949): 47–57; Ivan D. Steiner, "Models for Inferring Relationships Between Group Size and Potential Group Productivity," *Behavioral Science* 11, no. 4 (July 1966): 273–83; Ivan D. Steiner, *Group Processes and Productivity* (New York: Academic Press, 1972).

22. Phoebe M. Carillo and Richard E. Koeplman, "Organization Structure and Productivity: Effects of Subunits Size, Vertical Complexity, and Administrative Intensity on Operating Efficiency," *Group and Organization Studies* 16, no. 1 (March 1991): 55.

23. Carillo and Kopelman, "Organization Structure," 44–59.

24. Carillo and Kopelman, "Organization Structure," 57.

25. Gooding and Wagner III, "A Meta-Analytic Review," 475; also see James M. Buchanan, *The Demand and Supply of Public Goods* (Chicago: Rand McNally, 1968); Gareth R. Jones, "Task Visibility, Freeriding, and Shirking: Explaining the Effect of Structure and Technology on Employee Behavior," *Academy of Management*

Review 9, no. 4 (October 1984): 684–95; Bibb Latane, "The Psychology of Social Impact," *American Psychologist* 36, no. 4 (April 1981): 343–56; James W. McKie, "Changing Views," in *Social Responsibility and the Business Predicament,* eds. James W. McKie (Washington, DC: Brookings Institution, 1974), 17–40; Mancur Olson, *The Logic of Collective Action* (Cambridge, MA: Harvard University Press, 1971); Oliver E. Williamson, *Markets and Hierarchies: Analysis and Antitrust Implications* (New York: Free Press, 1975).

26. For example, see Indik and Seashore, *Effects of Organization Size*; Revans, "Human Relations."
27. Richard Albanese and David D. Van Fleet, "Rational Behavior in Groups: The Free-Riding Tendency," *Academy of Management Review* 10, no. 2 (April 1985): 244–55.
28. Fleishman, "Collective Action."
29. Olson, *The Logic.*
30. For example, see Buchanan, *The Demand and Supply*; Olson, *The Logic.*
31. Gooding and Wagner III, "A Meta-Analytic Review," 476.
32. Dalton et al., "Organization Structure," 53.
33. John R. Kimberly, "Organizational Size and the Structuralist Perspective: A Review, Critique, and Proposal," *Administrative Science Quarterly* 21, no. 4 (December 1976): 571–97.
34. Gooding and Wagner III, "A Meta-Analytic Review," 484.
35. Gooding and Wagner III, "A Meta-Analytic Review," 462–81. Studies that use the number of employees include Marriott, "Size of Working Group and Output" and Charles A. Glisson and Patricia Yancy Martin, "Productivity and Efficiency in Human Service Organizations as Related to Structure, Size, and Age," *Academy of Management Journal,* 23, no. 1 (March 1980): 21–37; Evers et al., "The Relationships of Selected Size," use the log number of employees.
36. Dalton et al., "Organization Structure," 49–64.
37. Victor D. Lippit, "The Commune in Chinese Development," *Modern China* 3, no. 2 (April 1977): 248.
38. Bai and Kung, "The Shaping," 1–26; Lippit, "The Commune," 229–55; Greg O'Leary and Andrew Watson, "The Role of the People's Commune in Rural Development in China," *Pacific Affairs* 55, no. 4 (Winter 1982): 593–612.
39. Steven Butler, *Agricultural Mechanization in China: The Administrative Impact* (New York: East Asian Institute, Columbia University, 1978), 33–34.
40. Butler, *Agricultural Mechanization,* 18.
41. The income and accounting tasks have been shifted downward to brigades in 1959 and to production teams in 1961; see Lippit, "The Commune," 229–55.
42. Justin Yifu Lin, "The Household Responsibility System in China's Agricultural Reform: A Theoretical and Empirical Study," *Economic Development and Cultural Change* 36, no. 3 (April 1988): 199–224; Peter Nolan, "De-Collectivisation of Agriculture in China, 1979–82: A Long-Term Perspective," *Cambridge Journal of Economics* 7, no. 3/4 (September/December 1983): 381–403; Peter Nolan, *The Political Economy of Collective Farms: An Analysis of China's Post-Mao Rural* Reforms (Cambridge: Polity Press, 1988).
43. By 1984, 99 percent of production teams had adopted the HRS; see Justin Yifu Lin, "Rural Reforms and Agricultural Growth in China," *The American Economic Review* 82, no. 1 (March 1992): 38.

44. James Kai-sing Kung, "Transaction Costs and Peasants' Choice of Institutions: Did the Right to Exit Really Solve the Free Rider Problem in Chinese Collective Agriculture?" *Journal of Comparative Economics* 17, no. 2 (June 1993): 486. Kung's suggestion that teams could not use piece rates is, generally speaking, incorrect after 1970.

45. The number of teams in Henan remained relatively stable from 364,628 in 1962 to 333,657 in 1978. Between 1963 and 1979, the within-year standard deviation of the average number of households per team across counties ranged from 5.1 to 11.5. This observation was made anecdotally by Lippit, "The Commune."

46. Zhang Letian, *Gaobie Lixiang: Renmin Gongshe Zhidu Yanjiu* [Farewell to Dreams: A Study on the Commune System] (Shanghai: Shanghai People's Press, 1998), 260.

47. The ten prefectures are Anyang (安阳), Xinxiang (新乡), Shangqiu (商丘), Kaifeng (开封), Luoyang (洛阳), Xuchang (许昌), Zhoukou (周口), Zhu Madian (驻马店), Nanyang (南阳), and Xinyang (信阳).

48. Dali L. Yang, *Calamity and Reform in China: State, Rural Society, and Institutional Change since the Great Leap Famine* (Stanford, CA: Stanford University Press, 1998).

49. "Zhonggong zhongyang guanyu zai nongcun jianli renmin gongshe wenti de jueyi (August 29, 1958)" [CPC Central Committee's Resolution on the Establishment of People's Communes in Rural Area] in *Jianguo yilai zhongyao wenxian xuanbian* [Selected Important Documents since the Founding of the People's Republic of China], vol. 11 (Beijing: Zhongyang wenxian chubanshe, 1997).

50. When interaction is not included, the commune absolute size is negatively associated with per capita crop production with a p-value of 0.05; neither brigade size nor team size has statistically significant coefficients. When the three-way interactions between commune, brigade, and team sizes are included, none of the variables per se or the interactions are statistically significant.

51. The correlation between commune and brigade absolute size is 0.43 (p-value=0.000), the correlation between commune absolute size and team size is −0.29 (p-value=0.000), and the correlation between brigade absolute size and team size is −0.36 (p-value=0.000).

52. Mean centering does not change the coefficient of the interaction term between commune relative size and team size.

53. Rather than estimating the black line using year fixed effects, I instead estimate annual commune organizational structure's contribution to agricultural production based on the two size variables and their interaction of each observation, and the regression coefficients of the three values in table 6.1, column 4.

54. Data from 1958 were dropped from this analysis because of lagging independent variables.

7. BURYING THE COMMUNE

1. Zhao Ziyang, *Prisoner of the State* (New York: Simon and Schuster, 2009), 141.

2. Daniel Kelliher, *Peasant Power: The Era of Reform, 1979–1989* (New Haven, CT: Yale University Press, 1993), 30–31.

3. Frederick Teiwes, "A Critique of Western Studies of CCP Elite Politics," *IIAS Newsletter*, 1996.

4. Susan Shirk, *The Political Logic of Economic Reform in China* (Berkeley: University of California Press, 1993), 38. For works on rural residents' actual views and responses to decollectivization see Jonathan Unger, "The Decollectivization of the Chinese Countryside: A Survey of Twenty-Eight Villages," *Pacific Affairs* 58, no. 4 (1985): 585–606; Jonathan Unger, "Remuneration, Ideology, and Personal Interests in a Chinese Village, 1960–1980," in William L. Parish, ed., *Chinese Rural Development: The Great Transformation* (Armonk, NY: M.E. Sharpe, 1985); Anita Chan, Richard Madsen, and Jonathan Unger, *Chen Village: The Recent History of a Peasant in Mao's China* (Berkeley: University of California Press, 1984); William Hinton, *The Great Reversal: the Privatization of China, 1979–1989* (New York: Monthly Review Press, 1990).

5. Ren Xiangqin, interview, January 2016. Ren is from Lingbao County, Henan. She was a member of the Sixth Production Team, Yanxie Brigade, Chuankou Commune.

6. Tong Huaiping and Li Chengguan, *Deng Xiaoping baci nanxun jishi* [Record of Deng Xiaoping's Eight Southern Journeys] (Beijing: Jiefangjun wenyi chubanshe, 2002), 81.

7. Wang Shaoguang and Hu Angang, *The Chinese Economy in Crisis: State Capacity and Tax Reform* (Armonk, NY: M.E. Sharpe, 2001), 111.

8. Richard Baum, *Burying Mao: Chinese Politics in the Age of Deng Xiaoping* (Princeton, NJ: Princeton University Press, 1996), 9.

9. Ezra F. Vogel, *Deng Xiaoping and the Transformation of China* (Cambridge, MA: Harvard University Press, 2011), 439.

10. Baum, *Burying Mao*, 27.

11. Baum, *Burying Mao*, 27.

12. Avery Goldstein, *From Bandwagon to Balance-of-Power Politics: Structural Constraints and Politics in China, 1949–1978* (Stanford: Stanford University Press, 1991), 211–24; Lucian W. Pye, *The Dynamics of Chinese Politics* (Cambridge: Oelgeschlager, Gunn & Hain, 1981), 22–27.

13. Frederick Teiwes and Warren Sun, *The End of the Maoist Era: Chinese Politics During the Twilight of the Cultural Revolution, 1972–1976* (Armonk, NY: M.E. Sharpe, 2007), 351.

14. "Learn from Dazhai in Agriculture," *People's Daily*, September 23, 1970.

15. Zhang Hua, "1975 nian nongye xue dazhai huiyi yu nongye zhengdun de yaoqiu" [The 1975 Conference on Learning Agriculture from Dazhai and the Demand to Rectify Agriculture], *Dang de wenxian* [Documents of CPC] 6 (1999): 16–21, http://cpc.people.com.cn/BIG5/218984/218997/219022/14818432.html.

16. Richard Thornton, *China: A Political History, 1917–1980* (New York: Westview Press), 377.

17. Merle Goldman, *From Comrade to Citizen: The Struggle for Political Rights in China* (Cambridge, MA: Harvard University Press, 2005), 49.

18. David Zweig, *Agrarian Radicalism in China, 1968–1981* (Cambridge, MA: Harvard University Press, 1989), 65.

19. These articles appeared in the *People's Daily* on February 3, 4, 10, and 27, 1975. "Jianchi duli zizhu zili gengsheng de fangzhen" [Adhere to the Principle of Independence and Self-reliance], *People's Daily*, February 3, 1975; "Luxian duilletou, liangmian shuangfengshou" [Right Route Leads to Harvest of Grain and Cotton], *People's Daily*, February 4, 1975; "Jianchi jixu geming, pipan ziben zhuyi

qingxiang" [Insist on Continuing the Revolution, Criticize the Capitalist Tendencies], *People's Daily*, February 10, 1975; "Wei geming duo gaochan, wei guojia duozuo gongxian" [Achieve High Yields for the Sake of Revolution, Make More Contributions for the Country], *People's Daily*, February 27, 1975; "Gonggu wuchan jieji zhuanzheng shi changqi de zhandou renwu" [To Consolidate the Dictatorship of Proletariats Is a Long-Term Combat Task], *People's Daily*, February 27, 1975.

20. Ji Yan, "Xianzhi zican jieji faquan de sixiang wuqi" [Ideological Weapon for Restricting Bourgeois Right], *Red Flag* [Hongqi], no. 4 (April 1975): 30–36; Jiang Weiqing, "Jinyibu jiaqiang nongcun de wuchan jiejie zhuanzheng" [Further Consolidate the Dictatorship of Proletariats in Rural Areas], *Red Flag*, no. 5 (May 1975): 14–19; Cheng Yue, "Xuehao lilun zhixing zhengce" [Understand the Theory, Implement the Policy], *Red Flag*, no. 6 (June 1975): 10–12.

21. Jiang Qing, "Jiang Qing's Letter to the Delegates Attending to the CCP-CC All-China Conference on Professional Work in Agriculture (July 2, 1975)," *Issues and Studies* (October 1975): 86–87. Teiwes and Sun dispute the authenticity of the document, but not its representation of the radicals' views. See Teiwes and Sun, *The End of the Maoist Era*, 349.

22. Zhang, "1975 nian nongye xue dazhai"; also see Teiwes and Sun, *The End of the Maoist Era*, 358, 363.

23. Wu Jicheng, "Jiang Qing and the Dazhai Agricultural Conference," [Jiang Qing yu nongye xue dazhai huiyi] in *Witnessing History: China 1975–1976* [Jianzheng lishi: Zhongguo, 1975–1976], ed. Zhang Shujun (Changsha: Hunan People's Press, 2008), 30.

24. Teiwes and Sun, *The End of the Maoist Era*, 354.

25. Zweig, *Agrarian Radicalism*, 67.

26. Wu, "Jiang Qing," 28–29.

27. "Comrade Chen Yung-kuei's Report at the Second National Conference on Learning from Dazhai in Agriculture," *Peking Review* 20, no. 2 (January 7, 1977), 9.

28. The September issue of *Red Flag* contained Five Articles condemning the ancient popular novel *The Water Margin*; see "Lu Xun ping shui hui" [Lu Xun's Reviews of *The Water Margin*], *Red Flag*, no. 9 (1975): 5; "Duanping: zhongshi dui shuiwu de pinglun" [Attach Importance to Comments on *The Water Margin*], *Red Flag*, no. 9 (1975): 6–7; Fang Yanliang, "Shi renmin dou zhidao touxiangpai, xuexi Lu Xun dui Shuihui de lunshu" [Let All People Know About Yielders, Learn Lu Xun's Critiques of *The Water Margin*], *Red Flag*, no. 9 (1975): 8–12; "Yibu xuanyang touxiang zhuyi de fanmian jiaocai, ping Shuihu" [A Negative Example Advocating Capitulationism, the Review of *The Water Margin*], *Red Flag*, no. 9 (1975): 13–17; Zhong Gu, "Ping Shuihu de touxiang zhuyi luxian" [Discussions about the Capitulationism Courses in *The Water Margin*], *Red Flag*, no. 9 (1975): 18–25. On September 4 the *People's Daily* published an editorial condemning the novel buttressed with commentary from Mao; see "Carry out the Discussions About the Water Margin," *People's Daily*, September 4, 1975. According to Thornton, the campaign was intended to undermine Deng; see Thornton, *China*, 377.

29. Jiang Qing, "Jiejian Dazhai dagui ganbu he sheyuan shide jianghua" [Speech to Dazhai brigade cadre and commune members], *Chinese Cultural Revolution Database*, September 12, 1975, http://ccradb.appspot.com/post/3182. Both Chinese and

Western researchers generally agree that this version of Jiang's speech is either fake or a summary of her remarks. Whether precise or not, this quote captures the essence of Jiang's remarks as revealed in other official accounts and the memoirs of those who attended the 1975 Dazhai Conference. Attempts to acquire the speech from the Central Party School of the Central Committee of the CPC proved unsuccessful.

30. Jiang Qing, "Address at the National Conference on Learning from Dachai in Agriculture (September 15, 1975)," in *Classified Chinese Communist Documents: A Selection* (Taipei: Institute of International Relations, National Chengchi University, 1978), 639–43; see the English translation at https://www.marxists.org/archive/jiang-qing/1975/september/15.htm; see the Chinese at http://ccradb.appspot.com/post/3184.

31. Jiang, "Address at the National Conference."

32. "Comrade Chen," 7.

33. Teiwes and Sun, *The End of the Maoist Era*, 359. Similarly, in 1974, Mao had called on Deng to present his Three Worlds Theory to the United Nations General Assembly in New York. Once in power, however, Deng quickly disavowed that Maoist theory and moved toward reconciliation, first with the United States and then with the Soviet Union.

34. Zhongguo zhongyang wenxian yanjiu shi [Central Chinese Communist Party Literature Research Office] ed., *Deng Xiaoping nianpu (1975–1997)* [A Chronology of Deng Xiaoping, 1975–1997] (Beijing: Zhongyang wenxian chubanshe, 2004), 18.

35. Wu Jicheng, "Jiang Qing and the Dazhai Agricultural Conference," 30.

36. "Comrade Chen," 7.

37. "Conference on Learning Agriculture from Dazhai and Agricultural Rectification," people.com, August 14, 2014, http://history.people.com.cn/n/2014/0814/c387654-25468491.html. For excepts from Deng's September 15, 1975, speech in Chinese, see Deng Xiaoping, "Excerpts of Speech at the Opening Ceremony of National Conference on Learning from Dazhai in Agriculture," *Chinese Cultural Revolution Database*, September 15, 1975, http://ccradb.appspot.com/post/3183.

38. Given Deng's previous efforts to undermine Dazhai in the mid-1960s, it is plausible that Mao had enlisted Jiang to try to provoke Deng to make an unscripted anti-Dazhai comment, and then after the ploy failed, quickly disavowed her statements. There is, however, no proof this occurred.

39. Teiwes and Sun, *The End of the Maoist Era*, 354.

40. Deng Liqun, *Deng Liqun guoshi jiangtanlu* [Record of Deng Liqun's Lectures on National History] (Beijing: Zhonghua renmin gongheguo shigao bianweihui, 2000), vol. 3, 102.

41. Deng Xiaoping, "Things Must Be Put in Order in All Fields," in *The Selected Works of Deng Xiaoping: Modern Day Contributions to Marxism-Leninsim*. September 15 and October 4 1975; see the English translation at https://dengxiaopingworks.wordpress.com/2013/02/25/things-must-be-put-in-order-in-all-fields/; see the Chinese at http://www.jhwsw.com/zzdzb/ShowArticle.asp?ArticleID=868.

42. Deng Xiaoping, "Things Must Be Put in Order in All Fields."

43. Mao Mao [Deng Rong], *Wode fuqin Deng Xiaoping: "Wenge" suiyue* [My Father Deng Xiaoping: The "Cultural Revolution" Years] (Beijing: Zhongyang wenxian

chubanshe, 2000), trans. *Deng Xiaoping and the Cultural Revolution: A Daughter Recalls the Critical Years* (New York: Bertelsmann, 2005), 398–99; Chen Dabin, Jie yinfa de biange: yige zishen jizhe de qinshen jingli yu sikao [The Revolution Sparked by Famine: The Personal Experiences and Reflections of a Senior Journalist] (Beijing: Zhonggong dangshi chubanshe, 1998), 40–41.

44. Hua Guofeng, "Report on the 1975 Dazhai Conference (Central Document No. 21) Mobilize the Whole Party, Make Greater Efforts to Develop Agriculture and Strive to Build Dachai-type Counties," *Peking Review* 18, no. 44 (October 31, 1975): 7–10.

45. *Xinhua Press Release*, March 12, 1976.

46. Hua, "Report on the 1975 Dazhai Conference," 10.

47. Hua, "Report on the 1975 Dazhai Conference," 9.

48. Hua, "Report on the 1975 Dazhai Conference," 10.

49. Hua, "Report on the 1975 Dazhai Conference," 10.

50. Hua, "Report on the 1975 Dazhai Conference," 10.

51. Hua, "Report on the 1975 Dazhai Conference," 10.

52. Hua, "Report on the 1975 Dazhai Conference," 8.

53. "Comrade Chen," 8.

54. Chen Yonggui, "Chedi pipan 'sirenbang', xianqi puji dazhaixian yundong de xin-gaochao" [Thoroughly Expose and Criticize the "Gang of Four," Set off a New Upsurge in Popularizing Dazhai Movement], *People's Daily*, December 24, 1976; *Chedi jiefang pipan "sirenbang" cuandang duoquan de taotian zuixing* [Thoroughly Expose and Criticize the Monstrous Crimes of the "Gang of Four" in Overthrowing the Party and Seizing Power] (Beijing: Renmin chubanshe, 1977), 189; "Comrade Chen," 9.

55. Ministry of Agriculture and Forestry Mass Criticism Group, "Two Line Struggle around the First National Conference on Learning from Dazhai in Agriculture," *Red Flag*, no. 1 (January 1977).

56. "Comrade Chen," 9.

57. *Issues and Studies*, October 1977.

58. "Ministry Mass Criticism Group Exposes Crimes of 'Gang of Four' in Undermining Agriculture," *Xinhua News Agency*, no. 6817 (November 1976): 406; also see "Comrade Chen," 9.

59. Zweig, *Agrarian Radicalism*, 68.

60. Guo Jian and Yongyi Song, *Historical Dictionary of the Chinese Cultural Revolution* (Lanham, MD: Scarecrow Press, 2006), xxxvii.

61. "Yaohai shi fupi ziben zhuyi" [The Critical Issue Is the Restoration of Capitalism], *People's Daily*, February 17, 1976.

62. Chi Heng, "Cong zichan jieji minzhupai dao zouzipai" [From the Bourgeois Democrats to the Capitalists], *People's Daily*, March 2, 1976.

63. "Fan'an bude renxin" [The Overturn Cannot Win Popular Support], *People's Daily*, March 10, 1976.

64. Baum, *Burying Mao*, 37.

65. "Resolution of CPC Central Committee On Dismissing Teng Hsiao-ping From All Posts Both Inside and Outside Party," *Peking Review* 19, no.15 (April 9, 1976): 3.

66. Thornton, *China*, 383.

67. Zweig, *Agrarian Radicalism*, 68.

68. Zweig, *Agrarian Radicalism*, 68–69; also see Thornton, *China*, 387–88, and Baum, *Burying Mao*, 39–40.

69. Baum, *Burying Mao*, 43.

70. Hua Guofeng, "Memorial Speech by Hua Kuo-Feng, First Chairman of Central Committee of Communist Party of China and Premier of State Council, at Mass Memorial Meeting for Great Leader and Teacher Chairman Mao Tsetung," *Peking Review* 19, no. 39 (September 24, 1976): 15.

71. Baum, *Burying Mao*, 39.

72. "Comrade Wu De's Speech at the Celebration Rally in the Capital," *Peking Review* 19, no. 44 (October 29, 1976): 13.

73. "Third Session of Standing Committee of Fourth National People's Congress Convened in Peking," *Peking Review* 19, no. 50 (December 10, 1976): 11.

74. Mao Zedong, "On the Ten Great Relationships (April 25, 1956)," in *Selected Works of Mao Tse-tung* (Peking: Foreign Languages Press, 1977), vol. 5.

75. Thornton, *China*, 392–93.

76. Chen, "Thoroughly Expose and Criticize," 14–15.

77. Chen, "Thoroughly Expose and Criticize," 15.

78. Fang Weizhong, ed., *Zhonghua renmin gongheguo jingji dashiji, 1949–1980* [Major Economic Events of the PRC, 1949–1980] (Beijing: Beijing chubanshe, 1985), 582; Zweig, *Agrarian Radicalism*, 70–71.

79. "Jiakuai nongye fazhan sudu shi quandang de zhandou renwu" [Accelerating the Pace of Agricultural Development Is the Combat Task of the Whole Party], *People's Daily*, December 11, 1977.

80. Ministry of Agriculture and Forestry, *Puji Dazhai Xian Gongzuo zuotanhui taolun de ruogan wenti* [Outline Report for the Politburo on the Working Forum for Popularizing Dazhai Counties], 21 *Shiji xiangzhen gongzuo quanshu* [Town Work Book of 21st Century] (Beijing: Zhongguo nongye chubanshe, 1999); also see Zhang Quanyou, *Hongyawan de mimi: 1978 nian longxi shuaixian shixing baochan daohu shilu* [The Secret of Hongyawan: Record of Longxi that Firstly Conducted Households Production Contract in 1978] (Lanzhou Shi: Gansu renmin chubanshe, 2010), 219.

81. Zweig, *Agrarian Radicalism*, 71.

82. Baum, *Burying Mao*, 5.

83. Maurice Meisner, *Mao's China and After: A History of the People's Republic* (New York: Free Press, 1999), 437.

84. Baum, *Burying Mao*, 14.

85. Baum, *Burying Mao*, 46.

86. Thornton, *China*, 395–96.

87. Zweig, *Agrarian Radicalism*, 169.

88. Thornton, *China*, 395; also see Wang Hsiao-hsien, "The Turmoil in Yunnan," *Issues and Studies* 13, no. 12 (December 1977): 41–52.

89. Wu Xiang et al., "Wan Li tan shiyijie sanzhong quanhui qianhou de nongcun gaige" [Wan Li on Agricultural Reform Before and After the Third Plenum of the Eleventh Central Committee], in *Gaibian Zhongguo mingyun de 41 tian* [The 41 Days That Changed the Destiny of China], eds. Yu Guangyuan et al. (Shenzhen: Haitian Publishing House, 1998), 281–89.

90. Vogel, *Deng Xiaoping*, 437–38.

91. Vogel, *Deng Xiaoping*, 437–38; also see Liu Changgen and Ji Fei, *Wan Li zai Anhui* [Wan Li in Anhui] (Beijing: Xinhua chubanshe, 2002), 83.

92. Jilin Provincial Radio, November 14, 1977, cited in Peter Nolan and Gordon White, "Distribution and Development in China," *The Bulletin of Concerned Asian Scholars* 13, no. 3 (1981): 14.

93. "Zhuahao shouyi fenpei, shixian zengchan zengshou" [Refine Income Distribution, To Achieve an Increased Production], *People's Daily*, December 20, 1977.

94. Sichuan Provincial Radio, December 22, 1977, cited in Nolan and White, "Distribution and Development," 14.

95. Du Xianyuna, "Minyi ruchao, lishi jubian" [Waves of Historic Changes in Public Opinions] in *Gaibian Zhongguo mingyun de 41 tian* [The 41 Days That Changed the Destiny of China], eds. Yu Guangyuan et al. (Shenzhen: Haitian Publishing House, 1998), 218–23; Liu and Ji, *Wan Li zai Anhui*, 83.

96. Zweig, *Agrarian Radicalism*, 171–72.

97. Zweig, *Agrarian Radicalism*, 171–72.

98. Dong Tai, "Nongcun jishi maoyi shi ziben zhuyi de ziyou shichang ma?" [Is the Rural Market a Free Trade Market for Capitalism?] *People's Daily*, January 31, 1978; Wei Jianyi, "Luoshi zhengce shi zuohao beigeng gongzuo de zhongyao huanjie" [Implementing the Policy is an Important Piece in Preparation for Farming], *People's Daily*, February 22, 1978.

99. "Jianjue jiuzheng pingdiao shengchandui zicai de waifeng" [Correct the Unhealthy Trend of Leveling the Wealth of the Production Team], *People's Daily*, April 2, 1978.

100. Zweig, *Agrarian Radicalism*, 171.

101. Wan Li, "Diligently Carry out the Party's Agricultural Policy," *Red Flag*, no. 3 (March 1978): 92–97.

102. Nolan and White, "Distribution and Development," 15.

103. "'Sanji suoyou, duiwei jichu' yingai wending" ["The System of Three Level Ownership with the Production Team as the Basic Ownership Unit" Should Be Maintained], *People's Daily*, March 15, 1979.

104. Vogel, *Deng Xiaoping*, 438.

105. Vogel, *Deng Xiaoping*, 439.

106. Liu and Ji, *Wan Li zai Anhui*, 163.

107. Hua's Ten-Year Plan and its accompanying State Council report in February 1978 both called on communes to "not only focus on grain production, but also on cash crops including cotton, oil-yielding and sugar-yielding plants." See Office of National People's Congress Financial and Economic Affairs Committee, Department of Development Planning, National Development and Reform Commission, ed., "1976–1985 nian fazhan guomin jingji shinian guihua gangyao (caoan)" [Ten-year Plan for the Development of National Economy as of 1976–1985 (draft)], in *Jianguo yilai guomin jingji he shehui fazhan wunian jihua zhongyao wenjian huibian* [Selected Important Documents of the Five-Year Plans for National Economy and Societal Development since the Founding of PRC] (Beijing: China Democracy and Legal Press, 2008); Hua Guofeng, "1978 State Council's Governmental Report," presented at the First Plenary Session of the Fifth National People's Congress, February 26, 1978), February 16, 2006, http://www.gov.cn/test/2006-02/16/content_200704.htm.

108. Office of National People's Congress Financial and Economic Affairs Committee, Department of Development Planning, National Development and Reform Commission, "1976–1985 nian fazhan guomin jingji shinian guihua gangyao (caoan)" [Ten-Year Plan for the Development of National Economy as of 1976–1985 (draft)].

109. Baum, *Burying Mao*, 96.

110. "Luoshi dangde zhengce, jianqing nongmin fudan" [Implement the Party's Policy, Lighten the Peasants' Burden], *People's Daily*, July, 5, 1978.

111. Zweig, *Agrarian Radicalism*, 171.

112. Zweig, *Agrarian Radicalism*, 71.

113. Zweig, *Agrarian Radicalism*, 73.

114. Zweig, *Agrarian Radicalism*, 71, 73, 171.

115. Meisner, *Mao's China*, 435–36.

116. Goldman, *From Comrade*, 31.

117. Goldman, *From Comrade*, 31–32.

118. Goldman, *From Comrade*, 43.

119. Deng Xiaoping, "Uphold the Four Cardinal Principles" in *Selected Works of Deng Xiaoping 1975–82* (Beijing: Foreign Languages Press, 1995), 182, 183.

120. Ye Jianying, "Speech at the Closing of Ceremony of the Central Work Conference of the CPC Central Committee (December 13, 1978)," in *Ye Jianying xuanji* [Selected Works of Ye Jianying] (Beijing: People's Publishing House, 1996), 494.

121. Goldman, *From Comrade*, 49.

122. Meisner, *Mao's China*, 437.

123. Chen Yonggui and Ji Dengkui lost control over agricultural policy, which was placed under the newly appointed reformist Vice-Premier Wang Renzhong; Zweig, *Agrarian Radicalism*, 173.

124. Zweig, *Agrarian Radicalism*, 174.

125. Zweig, *Agrarian Radicalism*, 175; also see Vogel, *Deng Xiaoping*, 441.

126. Meisner, *Mao's China*, 438.

127. Zweig, *Agrarian Radicalism*, 175.

128. Vogel, *Deng Xiaoping*, 441.

129. Vogel, *Deng Xiaoping*, 440; also see Wu Xiang et al., "Wan Li," 288.

130. Deng Xiaoping, *Selected Works of Deng Xiaoping, 1982–1992* (Beijing: Foreign Languages Press, 1994), 314–316; Zhongguo zhongyang wenxian yanjiu shi, *Deng Xiaoping nianpu*, May 31, 1980.

131. Zweig, *Agrarian Radicalism*, 175.

132. Deng Xiaoping, "Guanche tiaozheng fangzhen, baozheng anding tuanjie (1980nian 12yue 25ri)" [Implement the Policy of Adjustment, Ensure Stability and Unity], *CCTV*, September 16, 2002, http://www.cctv.com/special/756/1/50172.html.

133. Wu Xiang et al., "Wan Li," 289; Liu and Ji, *Wan Li zai Anhui*, 178–79; Yang Jisheng, *Deng Xiaoping shidai: Zhongguo gaige kaifang ershinian jishi* [The Age of Deng Xiaoping: A Record of Twenty Years of China's Reform and Openings] (Beijing: Zhongyang bianyi chubanshe, 1998), vol. 1, 187–88; Vogel, *Deng Xiaoping*, 442.

134. *Yang Yichen huiyilu* [Memoirs of Yang Yichen] (Beijing: Zhongyang wenxian chubanshe, 1996), 316; Li Haiwen and Liu Ronggang, "Guizhou shixian lianchan chengbaozhi de qianqian houhou: Fang Chi Biqing" [The Story of the Implementation of the Output-Linked Contract System in Guizhou: An Interview with Chi Biqing], *Zhonggong dangshi ziliao* [CCP History Materials], no. 68 (1998): 90;

Wang Weiqun, "Weida de diyibu: Zhongguo nongcun gaige qidian shilu" [The First Step: The True Account of the Starting Point of China's Rural Reform], December 17, 2008, http://news.qq.com/a/20081217/001228.htm; Wu Xiang, "E duzi shi tuidong gaige de zuichu liliang" [Hungry Stomachs Are the Earliest Force Driving Reform], January 20, 2013, http://www.reformdata.org/content/20130120/15430.html; Zhongguo shehui kexuyuan jingji yanjiusuo [Economics Institute of the Chinese Academy of Social Science], *Xue Muqiao gongzuo biji, xiace* (1963–1982) [Xue Muqiao's Work Notes (1963–1982)], internal materials, 416–18; Dali L. Yang, *Calamity and Reform in China: State, Rural Society, and Institutional Change since the Great Leap Famine* (Stanford, CA: Stanford University Press, 1996), 170.

135. Frederick Teiwes and Warren Sun, *Paradoxes of Post-Mao Rural Reform: Initial Steps Toward a New Chinese Countryside* (London: Routledge, 2015), 184.

136. Teiwes and Sun, *Paradoxes of Post-Mao Rural Reform*, 184.

137. Teiwes and Sun, *Paradoxes of Post-Mao Rural Reform*, 185, 187.

138. For Chinese materials documenting the policy process associated with decollectivization see "Guanyu jinyibu jiaqiang he wanshan nongye shengchan zerenzhi de jige wenti" [On Several Issues in Further Strengthening and Perfecting the Agricultural Responsibility System] (September 27, 1980) in *Nongye jitihua zhongyao wenjian huibian* (1958–1981) [Selected Important Documents of Agricultural Responsibility System], 411; Zhang Wanshu, "Dabaogan neimu" [The Inside Story of All-round Contracting], *Zhongguo zuojia* [Chinese writers], no. 11 (2007): 35; Ma Guochuan, "Weida de chuangzao: Du Rensheng fangtanlu" [(Household Farming Is) A Great Innovation (of the Peasants): Record of an Interview with Du Runsheng], December 17, 2008, http://www.aisixiang.com/data/23385-2.html; Ren Bo, "Ziyuan bingfu renduo dishao maodun guidingle Zhongguo nongdi zhidu: Zhuanfang yuan zhongyang nongcun zhengce yanjiushi zhuren Du Runsheng" [The Natural Resource Endowment Contradiction of a Large Population and Limited Land Determines China's Rural Land System: A Special Visit to Former Central Rural Policy Research Office Director Du Runsheng], October 5, 2002, http://magazine.caixin.com/2002-10-5/100079968.html. Lin Shanshan and Du Qiang, "Jiuhaoyuan de nianqingren" [The Young People of Compound No. 9], *Nanfang renwu zhoukan* [Southern People Weekly], no. 28 (2013), August 26, 2013; "Nongcun gaige zuotanhui tanhua jilu" [Record of Talks at the Seminar on Rural Reform], July 18, 2003, 4.

139. Teiwes and Sun, *Paradoxes of Post-Mao Rural Reform*, 187.

140. Teiwes and Sun, *Paradoxes of Post-Mao Rural Reform*, 187.

141. Teiwes and Sun, *Paradoxes of Post-Mao Rural Reform*, 187, 190–91.

142. Lu Mai, "Zhongguo nongcun gaige de juece guocheng" [The Policy-making Process of China's Rural Reform], http://gongfa.com/nongcungaigejuece.htm; Zhang Jingdong, Du Runsheng tamen [Du Runsheng and Those Sharing His Views] (Hong Kong: Zhongguo guoji wenhua chuban youxian gongsi, 2011), 27; Zhou Qiren, "Shencai feiyang Du Ruizhi" [The Ebullient Du Ruizhi], March 18, 2003, http://www.eeo.com.cn/2013/0318/241351.shtml; *Xi zhongxun zhuan* [Biography of Xi Zhongxun] (Beijing: Zhongyang wenxian chubanshe, 2013), vol. 2, 439.

143. Zweig, *Agrarian Radicalism*, 169–70.

144. Zhao, *Prisoner of the State*, 141.

145. Zhao, *Prisoner of the State*, 141.

146. Li Lanqing, *Breaking Through: The Birth of China's Opening-Up Policy* (Oxford: Oxford University Press, 2009), 31.

147. Meisner, *Mao's China*, 428.

148. Baum, *Burying Mao*, 37–38.

149. Baum, *Burying Mao*, 51.

150. Meisner, *Mao's China*, 433.

151. Li, *Breaking Through*, 31–32.

152. Baum, *Burying Mao*, 46–47.

153. Deng Xiaoping, "Closing Address at the Eleventh CCP Congress," *Peking Review* (September 2, 1977): 38–40.

154. Zweig, *Agrarian Radicalism*, 172.

155. Zweig, *Agrarian Radicalism*, 174.

156. Robert L. Worden, Andrea Matles Savada, and Ronald E. Dolan, eds. *China: A Country Study* (Washington, DC: Government Printing Office for the Library of Congress, 1987).

157. Wang Shuguang and Hu Angang, *The Chinese Economy*, 111.

158. Meisner, *Mao's China*, 441–43.

159. Baum, *Burying Mao*, 65.

160. "Unlikely Hero: A Local Leader Jailed for Extremism During the Cultural Revolution Has Many Devoted Followers," *Economist*, August 6, 2016.

161. Meisner, *Mao's China*, 443.

162. Yong Zhou, ed. "Jiang Qing: 'Without Law, Without Heaven,'" in *Great Trial in Chinese History: The Trial of the Lin Biao and Jiang Qing Counter-Revolutionary Cliques, Nov. 1980–Jan. 1981* (Beijing: New World Press, 1981), 105.

163. Deng Xiaoping, "Resolution on Certain Questions in the History of Our Party since the Founding of the People's Republic of China," speech during the preparatory meeting for the Sixth Plenary Session of the Eleventh Central Committee, June 22, 1981; see Deng, *Selected Works of Deng Xiaoping*, 51, 287.

164. Meisner, *Mao's China*, 446.

165. Wu Li ed., *Zhonghua renmin gongheguo jingjishi, 1949–1999* [An Economic History of the PRC, 1949–1999] (Beijing: Zhongguo jingji chubanshe, 1999), vol. 2, 838–40.

166. "CPC Central Committee announcement on Realizing the Separation of Government from the Commune and Establishing Village Governments (October 12, 1983)," in *Xinshiqi nongcun he nongye gongzuo zhongyao wenxian xuanbian* [Selected Important Documents of Rural Areas and Agricultural Work in the New Era] (Beijing: Zhongyang Wenxian chubanshe, 1992), http://cpc.people.com.cn /GB/64184/64186/66701/4495412.html.

167. Richard Baum, *China Watcher: Confessions of a Peking Tom* (Seattle: University of Washington Press, 2010), 213.

168. Baum, *Burying Mao*, 10.

169. Zhao, *Prisoner of the State*, 141.

8. CONCLUSION

1. Lin Biao, "Comrade Lin Biao's Speech at Peking Rally Commemorating the Fiftieth Anniversary of the October Revolution (November 6, 1967)," in *Advance Along the Road Opened up by the October Socialist Revolution* (Peking: Foreign Languages Press, 1967), 1–10.

2. *Agricultural Economic Statistics, 1949–1983* [Nongye jingji ziliao, 1949–1983] (Beijing: Ministry of Agriculture Planning Bureau, 1983), 80–81.
3. W. Arthur Lewis, "Economic Development with Unlimited Supplies of Labour," *The Manchester School of Economic and Social Studies* 22, no. 2 (1954): 155–56.
4. Interviews with former commune members, Tonglu County, Zhejiang, November 7, 2015.
5. Ran Abramitzky "On the (lack of) Stability of Communes: An Economic Perspective," in *Oxford Handbook of the Economics of Religion*, ed. Rachel McCleary (Oxford: Oxford University Press, 2011), 170–71.
6. Richard Madsen, *Morality and Power in a Chinese Village* (Berkeley: University of California Press, 1985), 136–37.
7. Abramitzky, "On the (lack of) Stability," 1.
8. Office of National People's Congress Financial and Economic Affairs Committee, Department of Development Planning, National Development and Reform Commission, "1976–1985 nian fazhan guomin jingji shinian guihua gangyao (caoan)" [Ten-Year Plan for the Development of National Economy as of 1976–1985 (draft)], in *Jianguo yilai guomin jingji he shehui fazhan wunian jihua zhongyao wenjian huibian* [A Selection of Important Documents Regarding the Five-Year Plan for National Economy and Societal Development since the Founding of PRC] (Beijing: China Democracy and Legal Press, 2008).
9. "'Sanji suoyou, duiwei jichu' yingai wending" ["The System of Three Level Ownership with the Production Team as the Basic Ownership Unit" Should Be Maintained], *People's Daily*, March 15, 1979.
10. Daniel Leese, "A Single Spark: Origins and Spread of the Little Red Book in China," in *Mao's Little Book: A Global History*, ed. Alexander C. Cook (Cambridge: Cambridge University Press, 2014), 24.
11. Huang Yasheng, *Capitalism with Chinese Characteristics* (New York: Cambridge University Press, 2008), 36.
12. *Zhongguo tongji nianjian* [China Statistical Yearbook] (Beijing: Zhongguo tongji chubanshe, 1994), 31, 215, 218; Wang Shaoguang and Hu Angang, *The Chinese Economy in Crisis: State Capacity and Tax Reform* (Armonk, NY: M.E. Sharpe, 2001), 111.
13. Pei Minxin, *China's Trapped Transition: The Limits of Developmental Autocracy* (Cambridge, MA: Harvard University Press, 2008), 26; Zhao Ziyang, *Prisoner of the State: The Secret Journal of Premier Zhao Ziyang* (New York: Simon & Schuster, 2009), 142.

APPENDIX C: ESSENTIAL OFFICIAL AGRICULTURAL POLICY STATEMENTS ON THE COMMUNE, 1958-1983

1. *People's Daily*, September 10, 1958, translated in *Peking Review* 1, no. 29 (September 16, 1958): 21–23.
2. Mark Selden and Patti Eggleston, *The People's Republic of China: A Documentary History of Revolutionary Change* (New York: Monthly Review Press, 1979), 516–17.
3. Liu Fangying, trans., *Issues and Studies* 15, no. 10 (Taipei: Institute of International Relations, 1979): 93–111; 15, no. 12 (Taipei: Institute of International Relations, 1979): 106–115.

4. The "Strike" refers to a crackdown on the activities of "counterrevolutionary" elements in China, and the "Three Antis" were "graft and embezzlement," "profiteering," and "extravagance and waste."

5. The "Program" refers to the National Program for Agricultural Development.

6. The "three freedoms and one contract" policy refers to more sideline plots for private use, more free markets, more enterprises with sole responsibility for their own profit or loss, and fixing output quotas on a household basis.

7. The "four big freedoms" refers to freedom of usury, of hiring labor, land sale, and private enterprise.

8. The grain yield targets set by the National Program for Agricultural Development for different areas of the country are 200 kilograms per mu (one-fifteenth of a hectare) for areas north of the Yellow River, the Qinling Mountains, and the Bailong River; 250 kilograms per mu for areas south of the Yellow River and north of the Huai River; and 400 kilograms per mu for areas south of the Huai River, the Qinling Mountains, and the Bailong River. To surpass the 200-kilogram target is described as "crossing the Yellow River" and to exceed the 400-kilogram target as "crossing the Yangtze River."

9. The "five excesses" were excessive assigned tasks, meetings and assembles, paper works, organizations, and side jobs for activists.

10. *Issues and Studies* 9, no. 6 (March 1973).

11. "Four category elements" refers to landlords, rich peasants, counterrevolutionaries, and bad elements.

12. "Barefoot doctors" refers to medical officials in the rural areas. Because of the shortage of qualified physicians, Chinese Communists provided several months of medical training to elementary school and middle school graduates and then assigned them to rural areas to practice medicine. These "doctors" also had to perform farming work as ordinary commune members. According to *Red Flag* no. 3 (September 10, 1968), the barefoot doctors made "an outstanding achievement" in the suburbs of Shanghai.

13. "Three nondisengaged" refers to (1) not disengaged from reality; (2) not disengaged from productive labor; and (3) not disengaged from the masses.

14. The *Sixty Articles* refers to "The Statute Governing the Work of Rural People's Communes" published in 1960, which is composed of sixty articles.

15. "Production grading and sending up" refers to arbitrary grading of production results and sending the products to higher levels.

16. Guofeng Hua, "Report on the 1975 Dazhai Conference (Central Document No. 21) Mobilize the Whole Party, Make Greater Efforts to Develop Agriculture and Strive to Build Dachai-Type Counties," *Peking Review* 18, no. 44 (October 31, 1975): 7–10, 18.

17. The grain yield targets set by the National Program for Agricultural Development for different areas of the country are 200 kilograms per mu (one-fifteenth of a hectare) for areas north of the Yellow River, the Qinling Mountains, and the Bailong River; 250 kilograms per mu for areas south of the Yellow River and north of the Huai River; 400 kilograms per mu for areas south of the Huai River, the Qinling Mountains, and the Bailong River. To surpass the 200-kilogram target is described as "crossing the Yellow River" and to exceed the 400-kilogram target as "crossing the Yangtze River."

18. The Eight-Point Charter for agriculture includes soil improvement, rational application of fertilizer, water conservancy, improved seed strains, rational close-planting, plant protection, field management, and innovation of farm implements.
19. Deng Xiaoping, *Selected Works of Deng Xiaoping, 1975–1982* (Beijing: Foreign Languages Press, 1994), https://dengxiaopingworks.wordpress.com/2013/02/25/on-questions-of-rural-policy/.
20. The "five guarantees" refers to "childless and infirm old persons who are guaranteed food, clothing, medical care, housing and burial expenses by the people's commune."
21. *Chinese Law and Government* 19, no. 4 (1986): 34–37.
22. The originally translated transcript does not include this paragraph.

BIBLIOGRAPHY

Abramitzky, Ran. "The Limits of Equality: Insights from the Israeli Kibbutz." *Quarterly Journal of Economics* 123, no. 3 (2008): 1111–59.

——. "The Effect of Redistribution on Migration: Evidence from the Israeli Kibbutz." *Journal of Public Economics* 93, no. 3 (2009): 498–511.

——. "On the (lack of) Stability of Communes: An Economic Perspective." In *Oxford Handbook of the Economics of Religion*, edited by Rachel M. McCleary, 169–89. Oxford: Oxford University Press, 2011.

——. "Lessons from the Kibbutz on the Equality—Incentives Trade-off." *Journal of Economic Perspectives* 25, no. 1 (2011): 185–208.

Achievements of the Thirty-Five-Year Socialist Construction in Jilin Province [Jilinsheng sanshiwunian shehui zhuyi jianshe guanghui chengjiu]. Changchun: Statistical Bureau of Jilin Province, 1984.

Aghion, Philippe, and Peter Howitt. *Endogenous Growth Theory*. Cambridge, MA: MIT Press, 1997.

Agricultural Statistics of Jiangxi Province, 1949–1979 [Jiangxisheng nongye tongji ziliao, 1949–1979]. Nanchang: Agricultural Department of Jiangxi Province, 1996.

Albanese, Richard, and David D. Van Fleet. "Rational Behavior in Groups: The Free-Riding Tendency." *Academy of Management Review* 10, no. 2 (April 1985): 244–55.

Alcorn, Stan. "Ethics in Finance: Stuck at Mediocre." *NPR's Marketplace*. May 19, 2015. http://www.marketplace.org/2015/05/19/business/ethics-finance-stuck-mediocre.

Aldrich, Howard E. *Organizations and Environments*. Englewood Cliffs, NJ: Prentice-Hall, 1979.

American Plant Studies Delegation. *Plant Studies in the People's Republic of China: A Trip Report of the American Plant Studies Delegation*. Washington, DC: National Academy of Sciences, 1975.

Andors, Phyllis. *The Unfinished Liberation of Chinese Women, 1949–1980*. Bloomington: Indiana University Press, 1983.

Andrews, Edward. *The Gift to Be Simple Songs Dances and Rituals of the American Shakers*. New York: J. J. Augustin, 1940.

Bachman, David. *Chen Yun and the Chinese Political System*. Berkeley: University of California, Institute of East Asian Studies, 1985.

Bai, Ying, and James Kai-sing Kung. "The Shaping of an Institutional Choice: Weather Shocks, the Great Leap Famine, and Agricultural Decollectivization in China." *Explorations in Economic History* 54 (October 2014): 1–26.

Barbato, Andrea. *Chung Kuo—Cina*. Directed by Michelangelo Antonioni. Italy: RAI Radiotelevisione Italiana, 1973. Film.

Barkai, Haim. *Kibbutz Efficiency and the Incentive Conundrum*. Jerusalem: Maurice Falk Institute for Economic Research in Israel, 1987.

Barro, Robert, and Xavier Sala-i-Martin. *Economic Growth*. Cambridge, MA: MIT Press, 1999.

Baum, Richard. *Prelude to Revolution: Mao the Party, and the Peasant Question*. New York: Columbia University Press, 1975.

——. *Burying Mao: Chinese Politics in the Age of Deng Xiaoping*. Princeton, NJ: Princeton University Press, 1994.

——. "Lecture 14: The Chinese People Have Stood Up." In *The Fall and Rise of China*. Chantilly, VA: The Teaching Company, 2010, 24 audio discs.

——. "Lecture 18: The Great Leap Forward (1958–60)." In *The Fall and Rise of China*. Chantilly, VA: The Teaching Company, 2010, 24 audio discs.

——. *China Watcher: Confessions of a Peking Tom*. Seattle: University of Washington Press, 2010.

Becker, Jasper. *Hungry Ghosts: Mao's Secret Famine*. New York: Holt, 1998.

Beijing shi geming weiyuanhui xiezuo xiaozu 北京市革命委员会写作小组 [Writing group of the Peking Revolutionary Committee]. "Zhongguo shehui zhuyi gongyehua de daolu" 中国社会主义工业化的道路 [The Road to China's Socialist Industrialization]. *Red Flag* 红旗 [Hongqi], no. 10 (October 1969): 22–31.

Bennett, Gordon, Ken Kieke, and Ken Yoffy. *Huadong: The Story of a Chinese People's Commune*. Boulder, CO: Westview Press, 1978.

Berman, Eli. *Sect, Subsidy, and Sacrifice: An Economist's View of Ultra-orthodox Jews*. Cambridge, MA: National Bureau of Economic Research, 1998.

Bernstein, Thomas. *Up to the Mountains and Down to the Villages: The Transfer of Youth from Urban to Rural China*. New Haven, CT: Yale University Press, 1977.

Blecher, Marc. *China Against the Tides: Restructuring through Revolution, Radicalism and Reform*. 3rd ed. New York: Continuum, 2010.

Blecher, Marc, and Vivienne Shue. *Tethered Deer: Government and Economy in a Chinese County*. Stanford, CA: Stanford University Press, 1996.

Bramall, Chris. *The Industrialization of Rural China*. Oxford: Oxford University Press, 2007.

Branigan, Tania. "Red Songs Ring Out in Chinese City's New Cultural Revolution." *The Guardian*, April 22, 2011. https://www.theguardian.com/world/2011/apr/22/red-songs-chinese-cultural-revolution.

Brinck, Per. *Insect Pest Management in China: A Delegation Report*. Stockholm: Royal Swedish Academy of Engineering Sciences, 1979.

Buchanan, James M. *The Demand and Supply of Public Goods*. Chicago: Rand McNally, 1968.

"Buduan gonggu nongcun shehui zhuyi zhendi" 不断巩固农村社会主义阵地 [Continue to Consolidate the Position of Socialism in the Villages]. *Lishi renzhi* 历史认知 [Understandings of the History] 2 (1975): 37.

Butler, Steven. *Agricultural Mechanization in China: The Administrative Impact*. New York: Columbia University Press, 1978.

——. "Price Scissors and Commune Administration in Post-Mao China." In *Chinese Rural Development: The Great Transformation*, edited by William L. Parrish, 95–114. Armonk, NY: M. E. Sharpe, 1985.

Canton Evening News. "Postulation by the CPC Hubei Provincial Committee Concerning Gradual Realization of Agricultural Mechanization." April 4, 1966.

Carillo, Phoebe M., and Richard E. Koeplman. "Organization Structure and Productivity: Effects of Subunits Size, Vertical Complexity, and Administrative Intensity on Operating Efficiency." *Group and Organization Studies* 16, no. 1 (March 1991): 44–59.

Chan, Anita, Richard Madsen, and Jonathan Unger. *Chen Village: The Recent History of a Peasant Community in Mao's China*. Berkeley: University of California Press, 1992.

Chang, Parris H. "Struggle Between the Two Roads in China's Countryside." *Current Scene* 6, no. 3 (February 15, 1968): 3–13.

——. *Patterns and Processes of Policy Making in Communist China, 1955–1962: Three Case Studies*. Ann Arbor, MI: University Microfilms, 1973.

Chao, Kang. *Agricultural Production in Communist China, 1949–1965*. Madison: University of Wisconsin Press, 1970.

Chedi jiefang pipan "sirenbang" cuandang duoquan de taotian zuixing [Thoroughly Expose and Criticize the Monstrous Crimes of the "Gang of Four" in Overthrowing the Party and Seizing Power]. Beijing: Renmin chubanshe, 1977.

Chen, Dabin. *Ji'e yinfa de biange: yige zishen jizhe de qinshen jingli yu sikao* 饥饿引发的变革：一个资深记者的亲身经历与思考 [The Revolution Sparked by Famine: The Personal Experiences and Reflections of a Senior Journalist]. Beijing: Zhonggong dangshi chubanshe, 1998.

Chen, Ruoxi. *The Execution of Mayor Yin and Other Stories from the Great Proletarian Cultural Revolution*. Bloomington: Indiana University Press, 2009.

Chen, Theodore Hsi-en. "The New Socialist Man." *Comparative Education Review* 13, no. 1 (February 1969): 88–95.

Chen, Yonggui. "Dazhai zai Mao Zedong sixiang de guanghui zhaoyao xia qianjin" 大寨在毛泽东思想的光辉照耀下前进 [Dazhai Moves Forward in the Brilliant Shine of Mao Zedong Thoughts]. *Red Flag* 红旗 [Hongqi] no. 5 (March 10, 1967): 48–51.

——. "Tachai Goes Ahead in the Struggle Against China's Khrushchov." *Peking Review* 10, no. 50 (December 1, 1967): 19–22.

——. "Chedi pipan 'sirenbang', xianqi puji dazhaixian yundong de xingaochao" 彻底批判四人帮，掀起普及大寨县的新高潮 [Thoroughly Expose and Criticize the "Gang of Four," Set off a New Upsurge in Popularizing Dazhai Movement]. *People's Daily*, December 24, 1976.

——. "Report at the Second National Conference on Learning from Dazhai in Agriculture." *Peking Review* 20, no. 2 (January 7, 1977): 5–17.

Cheng, Yue. "Xuehao lilun zhixing zhengce" 学好理论执行政策 [Understand the Theory, Implement the Policy]. *Red Flag* 红旗 [Hongqi], no. 6 (June 1975): 10–12.

Chi, Heng. "Cong zichan jieji minzhupai dao zouzipai" 从资产阶级民主派到走资派 [From the Bourgeois Democrats to the Capitalists]. *People's Daily*, March 2, 1976.

China Pictorial, no. 1 (January 1968): 27–29.

China's New Footprint: Impact of the 1970s [Xin zhongguo jiaoyin: Qishiniandai yingxiang]. 1967. AFP/Getty Images. http://chenmodemaque.blog.163.com/blog /static/16389212920129174522870/.

Chinese Law and Government 19, no. 4 (1986): 34–37.

"Chinese Observer on Population Question." *Peking Review* 16, no. 49 (December 7, 1973): 10–11.

Chu, Li, and Tien Chieh-yun. *Inside a People's Commune.* Beijing: Foreign Languages Press, 1974.

Chung, Jae Ho. "The Politics of Agricultural Mechanization in the Post-Mao Era, 1977–87." *The China Quarterly*, no. 134 (June 1993): 264–90.

"Communiqué of the Eleventh Plenary Session of the Eighth Central Committee of the Communist Party of China (August 12, 1966)." *Peking Review* 9, no. 34 (August 19, 1966): 4–8.

"Completely Settle the Heinous Crimes." *Selections from China Mainland Magazines*, no. 610. Hong Kong: U.S. Consulate General, 1968.

Cook, Alexander. *Mao's Little Red Book: A Global History.* Cambridge: Cambridge University Press, 2014.

"CPC Central Committee announcement on Realizing the Separation of Government from the Commune and Establishing Village Governments (October 12, 1983)." In *Xinshiqi nongcun he nongye gongzuo zhongyao wenxian xuanbian* 新世纪农村和农业工作重要文献汇编 [Selected Important Documents of Rural Areas and Agricultural Work in the New Era]. Beijing: Zhongyang Wenxian chubanshe, 1992. http:// cpc.people.com.cn/GB/64184/64186/66701/4495412.html.

Dalton, Dan R., William D. Todor, Michael J. Spendolini, Gordon J. Fielding, and Lyman W. Porter. "Organization Structure and Performance: A Critical Review." *Academy of Management Review* 5, no. 1 (January 1980): 49–64.

Dangdai Zhongguo congshu bianji weiyuanhui, ed. 当代中国丛书编辑委员会 [Editorial Board of Chinese Contemporary Books]. *Dangdai Zhongguo de nongye* 当代中国的农业 [Agriculture of Contemporary China]. Beijing: Zhongguo shehui kexue chubanshe, 1992.

Davis, James H. *Group Performance.* Reading, MA: Addison-Wesley, 1969.

Dikötter, Frank. *Mao's Great Famine: The History of China's Most Devastating Catastrophe, 1958–1962.* New York: Walker & Co, 2010.

Ding, Shaosheng. "Duzu ziben zhuyi daolu, maikai shehui zhuyi dabu" 堵住资本主义道路, 迈开社会主义大步 [Block the Capitalist Road, Take Big Steps for Socialism]. *Shehui yu pipan* 社会与批判 [Society and Critiques] (November 1975): 8–9.

Deng, Liqun. *Deng Liqun guoshi jiangtanlu, vol. 3* 邓力群国史讲谈录 [Record of Deng Liqun's Lectures on National History]. Beijing: Zhonghua renmin gongheguo shigao bianweihui, 2000.

Deng, Xiaoping. "Excerpts of Speech at the Opening Ceremony of National Conference on Learning from Dazhai in Agriculture." Chinese Cultural Revolution Database. September 15, 1975. http://ccradb.appspot.com/post/3183.

——. "Closing Address at the Eleventh National Congress of the Communist Party of China (August 19, 1977)." *Peking Review* 20, no. 36 (September 2, 1977): 38–40.

——. "Resolution on Certain Questions in the History of Our Party since the Founding of the People's Republic of China." Speech during the preparatory meeting for the Sixth Plenary Session of the Eleventh Central Committee, June 22, 1981. *People's Daily* online. http://en.people.cn/dengxp/vol2/text/b1420.html.

——. "Things Must Be Put in Order in All Fields." In *Selected Works of Deng Xiaoping, 1975–1982*. Beijing: Foreign Languages Press, 1984. https://dengxiaopingworks.wordpress.com/2013/02/25/things-must-be-put-in-order-in-all-fields/.

——. "Uphold the Four Cardinal Principles." In *Selected Works of Deng Xiaoping, 1975–1982*. Beijing: Foreign Languages Press, 1984.

——. *Selected Works of Deng Xiaoping, 1982–1992*. Beijing: Foreign Languages Press, 1994.

——. "Guanche tiaozheng fangzhen, baozheng anding tuanjie (1980nian 12yue 25ri)" 贯彻调整方针，保证安定团结 [Implement the Policy of Adjustment, Ensure Stability and Unity]. *CCTV*. September 16, 2002. http://www.cctv.com/special/756/1/50172.html.

Destroy the Old World; Forge a New World [dasui jiu shijie, chuangli xin shijie]. 1967. Beijing, Creature and Creator. http://creatureandcreator.ca/wp-content/uploads/2014/10/destroy-the-old.jpg.

Dong, Tai. "Nongcun jishi maoyi shi ziben zhuyi de ziyou shichang ma?" 农村集市贸易是资本主义的自由市场吗？ [Is the Rural Market a Free Trade Market for Capitalism?]. *People's Daily*, January 31, 1978.

Donnithorne, Audrey. "The Politics of Agricultural Mechanization in China by Benedict Stavis." *Journal of Asian Studies* 38, no. 4 (1979): 758–60.

Doyle, Arthur Conan. *Sherlock Holmes: A Scandal in Bohemia*. London: The Strand Magazine, 1891.

Du, Xianyuan. "Minyi ruchao, lishi jubian" 民意如潮历史巨变 [Waves of Historic Changes in Public Opinions]. In *Gaibian Zhongguo mingyun de 41 tian* 改变中国命运的41天 [The 41 Days that Changed the Destiny of China], edited by Yu Guangyuan, 218–223. Shenzhen: Haitian Publishing House, 1998.

"Duanping: zhongshi dui shuihu de pinglun" 短评：重视对水浒的评论 [Attach Importance to Comments on The Water Margin]. *Red Flag* 红旗 [Hongqi], no. 9 (1975): 6–7.

Durkheim, Emile. *The Elementary Forms of the Religious Life*. Translated by Joseph Ward Swain. New York: Free Press, 1965.

Economist. "Unlikely Hero: A Local Leader Jailed for Extremism During the Cultural Revolution Has Many Devoted Followers." August 6, 2016. http://www.economist.com/news/china/21703365-local-leader-jailed-extremism-during-cultural-revolution-has-many-devoted.

Eisenman, Joshua. *A Home in Rural Weihai, Shandong*. June 29, 2016. Weihai, Shandong.

——. A Label Pin with Mao Zedong. December 7, 2016. Guangzhou, Guangdong.

Eisenman, Joshua, Eric Heginbotham, and Derek Mitchell, eds. *China and the Developing World: Beijing's Strategy for the 21st Century*. Armonk, NY: M. E. Sharpe, 2007.

Esherick, Joseph, Paul Pickowicz, and Andrew Walder. *The Cultural Revolution as History*. Stanford, CA: Stanford University Press, 2006.

Esmay, Merle, and Roy Harrington. *Glimpses of Agricultural Mechanization in the PRC: A Delegation of 15 Members Report on Their Technical Inspection in China Aug. 18–Sept. 8, 1979*. St. Joseph, MI: American Society of Agricultural Engineers, 1979.

Evers, Frederick T., Joe M. Bohlen, and Richard D. Warren. "The Relationships of Selected Size and Structure Indicators in Economic Organizations." *Administrative Science Quarterly* 21, no. 2 (June 1976): 326–42.

Fairbank, John K. and Merle Goldman. *China: A New History*. Cambridge, MA: Harvard University Press, 2006.

Fan, Shenggen, and Philip Pardey. "Research, Productivity, and Output Growth in Chinese Agriculture." *Journal of Development Economics* 53, no. 1 (1997): 115–37.

Fang, Houshu. "Stories Behind the Publication of the *Little Red Book*." *Xinhua*. July 13, 2004.

Fang, Weizhong. *Zhonghua renmin gongheguo jingji dashiji, 1949–1980* 中华人民共和国经济大事记, 1949–1980 [Major Economic Events of the PRC, 1949–1980]. Beijing: Beijing chubanshe, 1985.

Fang, Yanliang. "Shi renmin dou zhidao touxiangpai, xuexi Lu Xun dui shuihu de lun-shu" 使人民都知道投降派, 学习鲁迅对水浒的论述 [Let All People Know About Yielders, Learn Lu Xun's Critiques of *The Water Margin*]. *Red Flag* [Hongqi], no. 9 (1975): 8–12.

Fehr, Ernst, and Simon Gächter. "Cooperation and Punishment in Public Goods Experiments." *American Economic Review* 90, no. 4 (2000): 980–94.

Fei, Xiaotong. *China's Gentry: Essays in Rural-Urban Relations*. Chicago: University of Chicago Press, 1958.

——. *Rural Development in China: Prospect and Retrospect*. Chicago: University of Chicago Press, 1989.

Fishman, Aryei. *Judaism and Modernization on the Religious Kibbutz*. Cambridge: Cambridge University Press, 1992.

——. "Religious Socialism and Economic Success on the Orthodox Kibbutz." *Journal of Institutional and Theoretical Economics* 150, no. 4 (1994): 763–68.

Fitzgerald, Deborah. *Yeoman No More: The Industrialization of American Agriculture*. New Haven, CT: Yale University Press, 2009.

Fleishman, John. "Collective Action as Helping Behavior: Effects of Responsibility Diffusion on Contributions to a Public Good." *Journal of Personality and Social Psychology* 38, no. 4 (April 1980): 629–37.

Friedman, Edward, Paul G. Pickowicz, and Mark Selden. *Chinese Village, Socialist State*. New Haven, CT: Yale University Press, 1993.

——. *Revolution, Resistance and Reform in Village China*. New Haven, CT: Yale University Press, 2005.

Galston, Arthur W., and Jean S. Savage. *Daily Life in People's China*. New York: Crowell, 1973.

Gao, Mobo C. F. *Gao Village: Rural Life in Modern China*. Honolulu: University of Hawaii Press, 1999.

——. *The Battle for China's Past: Mao and the Cultural Revolution*. Ann Arbor, MI: Pluto Press, 2008.

Gaud, William. "AID Supports the Green Revolution." Address Before the Society for International Development, Washington, DC, March 8, 1968.

General Office of the Central Committee of the Communist Party of China. *Socialist Upsurge in China's Countryside*. Beijing: Foreign Languages Press, 1957.

George, Kenneth D., and Caroline Joll. *Industrial Organisation: Competition, Growth, and Structural Change*. 3rd ed. Vol. 5. London: Allen and Unwin, 1981.

Glisson, Charles A., and Patricia Yancy Martin. "Productivity and Efficiency in Human Service Organizations as Related to Structure, Size, and Age." *Academy of Management Journal* 23, no. 1 (March 1980): 21–37.

Gold, Michael, and Malcolm Cowley. "Is the Small Farmer Dying?" *New Republic* 68 (October 7, 1931): 211–3.

Goldman, Merle. *From Comrade to Citizen: The Struggle for Political Rights in China*. Cambridge, MA: Harvard University Press, 2005.

Goldstein, Avery. *From Bandwagon to Balance-of-Power Politics: Structural Constraints and Politics in China, 1949–1978*. Stanford, CA: Stanford University Press, 1991.

Gooding, Richard Z., and John A. Wagner III. "A Meta-Analytic Review of the Relationship Between Size and Performance: The Productivity and Efficiency of Organizations and Their Subunits." *Administrative Science Quarterly* 30, no. 4 (December 1985): 462–81.

Griffin, Keith, and Ashwani Saith. *Growth and Equality in Rural China*. Geneva: Asian Employment Programme, 1981.

Guan, Shengtang. Interview by author. December 26, 2011.

"Guanyu jinyibu jiaqiang he wanshan nongye shengchan zerenzhi de jige wenti (1980 nian 9 yue 27 ri)" 关于进一步加强和完善农业生产责任制的几个问题 [On Several Issues in Further Strengthening and Perfecting the Agricultural Responsibility System (September 27, 1980)]. In *Nongye jitihua zhongyao wenjian huibian (1958–1981)* 农业集体化重要文件汇编 [Selected Important Documents of Agricultural Responsibility System (1958–1981)].

Guo, Jian, and Yongyi Song. *Historical Dictionary of the Chinese Cultural Revolution*. Lanham, MD: Scarecrow Press, 2006.

Han, Dongping. *The Unknown Cultural Revolution: Life and Change in a Chinese Village*. New York: Monthly Review Press, 2008.

Harding, Harry. "Modernization and Mao: The Logic of the Cultural Revolution and the 1970s." Conference Paper presented to the Institute of World Affairs, San Diego State University. August 1970.

He, Hongguang. *Governance, Social Organisation and Reform in Rural China: Case Studies from Anhui Province*. New York: Palgrave Macmillan, 2015.

Henan sheng tongjiju, Henan sheng nongyeting, ed. 河南省统计局，河南省农业厅 [Henan Statistical Bureau and Agricultural Department]. *Jianguo sanshinian Henan sheng nongye tongji ziliao* 建国三十年河南省农业统计资料 [Henan Agricultural Statistics, 1949–1979]. Zhengzhou: Henan Statistical Bureau, 1981.

Herbst, P. G. "Measurement of Behavior Structure by Means of Input-Output Data." *Human Relations* 10 (1957): 335–46.

"History of Struggle Between the Two Lines (on China's Farm Machinery Front)." *Nongye jixie jishu* 农业机械技术 [Agricultural Machinery Technique], no. 9 (1968). In *Selections from China Mainland Magazines*, no. 633 (November 1968): 1–35.

The History of the People's Republic of China. "Wuqi zhishi" 五七指示 [May 7 Directive]. July 1, 2015. http://www.hprc.org.cn/gsgl/dsnb/zdsj/200908/t20090820_28344.html.

Hoefer, Jacob A., and Patricia J. Tsuchitani. *Animal Agriculture in China: A Report of the Visit of the Committee on Scholarly Communication with the People's Republic of China Animal Sciences Delegation*. Washington, DC: National Academy of Sciences, 1980.

Hogan, Kathleen M. "Robert Owen and New Harmony." University of Virginia American Studies Project Website. Accessed January 18, 2017. http://xroads.virginia.edu/~hyper/HNS/Cities/newharmony.html.

"Hold the Great Red Banner of Mao Tse-tung's Thought Still Higher, Bring the Mass Movement of Creatively Studying and Applying Chairman Mao's Works to a New Stage and Turn the PLA Into a Truly Great School of Mao Tse-tung's Thought." *Peking Review* 10, no. 3 (January 13, 1967): 8–13.

Holmstrom, Bengt. "Moral Hazard in Teams." *Bell Journal of Economics* 13, no. 2 (1982): 324–40.

Hoyt, Richard. "Gibberellic Acid in Plant Growth." eHow.com.

Hu, Yaobang. "Zai qingzhu zhongguo gongchandang chengli liushi zhounian dahui shang de jianghua (1981 nian 7 yue 1 ri)" 在庆祝中国共产党成立六十周年大会上的讲话（1981年7月1日）[Speech at the Meeting in Celebration of the Sixtieth Anniversary of the Founding of the Communist Party of China (July 1, 1981)]. In *Sanzhong quanhui yilai zhongyao wenxian xuanbian xia* 三中全会以来重要文献汇编下 [Selected Important Documents since Third Plenary Session of the Eleventh Central Committee], edited by Zhonggong zhongyang wenxian yanjiu shi 中共中央文献研究室 [Central Chinese Communist Party Literature Research Office]. Beijing: Zhonggong zhongyang dangxiao chubanshe, 1981.

Hua, Guofeng. "Report on the 1975 Dazhai Conference (Central Document No. 21) Mobilize the Whole Party, Make Greater Efforts to Develop Agriculture and Strive to Build Dachai-Type Counties." *Peking Review* 18, no. 44 (October 31, 1975): 7–10, 18.

——. "Memorial Speech by Hua Kuo-Feng, First Chairman of Central Committee of Communist Party of China and Premier of State Council, at Mass Memorial Meeting for Great Leader and Teacher Chairman Mao Tsetung." *Peking Review* 19, no. 39 (September 24, 1976): 12–16.

——. "1978 State Council's Governmental Report." Presented at the First Plenary Session of the Fifth National People's Congress, February 26, 1978. February 16, 2006. http://www.gov.cn/test/2006-02/16/content_200704.htm.

Huang, Jing. "The Problem of Farm Mechanization in China." *People's Daily*, October 24–25, 1957.

Huang, Yasheng. *Capitalism with Chinese Characteristics*. New York: Cambridge University Press, 2008.

Hubei sheng nongye ju, ed. 湖北省农业局 [Hubei Agricultural Bureau]. *Hubei sheng nongye tongji ziliao 1949–1978* 湖北省农业统计资料 1949–1978 [Agricultural Statistics of Hubei Province, 1949–1978]. Wuhan: Hubei Agricultural Bureau, 1980.

Hunan sheng geming weiyuanhui, ed. 湖南省革命委员会 [Hunan Revolutionary Committee, Administration Bureau of Agricultural Mechanics], *Hunan sheng nongye jixiehua tongji ziliao 1967–1978* 湖南省农业机械化统计资料1967–1978 [Statistical Materials of Agricultural Mechanization in Hunan Province, 1967–1978]. Changsha: Hunan Revolutionary Committee, 1979.

Iannaccone, Laurence. *Sacrifice and Stigma: Reducing Free-riding in Cults, Communes, and Other Collectives*. Palo Alto, CA: Hoover Institution, Stanford University, 1992.

——. "Sacrifice and Stigma: Reducing Free-Riding in Cults, Communes, and Other Collectives." *Journal of Political Economy* 100, no. 2 (1992): 271–91.

In Following the Revolutionary Road, Strive for an Even Greater Victory. 1970. Shanghai: Shanghai Publishing System Revolutionary Publishing Group.

Indik, Bernard P., and Stanley F. Seashore. *Effects of Organization Size on Member Attitudes and Behavior*. Ann Arbor: University of Michigan, 1961.

Interviews in Gansu and Jiangxi. November and December 2011.

Interviews in Qinzhou. June 2012.

Interviews with former commune members. Tonglu County, Zhejiang. November 7, 2015.

Iritani, Evelyn. "Great Idea but Don't Quote Him." *Los Angeles Times*, September 9, 2004.

Issues and Studies 9, no. 6 (March 1973).

Issues and Studies. October 1977.

"It Is Good for Tractors to Revert to Chairman Mao's Revolutionary Line—Report on Investigation of Change in Management of Tractors by the Collective in Lankao County, Henan." *Nongye jiexie jishu* 农业机械技术 [Agricultural Machinery Technique], no. 10 (October 8, 1968). In *Selections from China Mainland Magazines*, no. 643. Hong Kong: U.S. Consulate General, 1969.

Ji Yan, "Xianzhi zican jieji faquan de sixiang wuqi" 限制资产阶级法权的思想武器 [Ideological Weapon for Restricting Bourgeois Right]. *Red Flag* 红旗 [Hongqi], no. 4 (April 1975): 30–36.

"Jianchi shehui zhuyi daolu, xianzhi zichan jieji faquan" 坚持社会主义道路，限制资产阶级法权 [Maintain the Socialist Road, Restrict Bourgeois Rights]. *Red Flag* 红旗 [Hongqi] 20, no. 8 (August 1975): 25–28.

Jiang, Qing. "Jiejian Dazhai dahui ganbu he sheyuan shide jianghua" 接见大寨大会干部和社员时的讲话 [Speech to Dazhai brigade cadre and commune members]. Chinese Cultural Revolution Database. September 12, 1975. http://ccradb.appspot.com/post/3182.

——. "Jiang Qing's Letter to the Delegates Attending to the CCP-CC All-China Conference on Professional Work in Agriculture (July 2, 1975)." *Issues and Studies* (October 1975): 86–87.

——. "Address at the National Conference on Learning from Dachai in Agriculture (September 15, 1975)." In *Classified Chinese Communist Documents: A Selection*, 639–643. Taipei: Institute of International Relations, National Chengchi University, 1978.

——. "Without Law, Without Heaven." In *Great Trial in Chinese History: The Trial of the Lin Biao and Jiang Qing Counter-Revolutionary Cliques*, edited by Yong Zhou. Beijing: New World Press, 1981.

Jiangsu sheng geming weiyuanhui nongyeju, ed. 江苏省革命委员会农业局 [Jiangsu Revolutionary Committee, Agricultural Bureau]. *Jiangsu sheng nongye tongji ziliao, 1949–1980* 江苏省农业统计资料1949–1980 [Agricultural Statistics of Jiangsu Province, 1949–1980]. Nanjing: Jiangsu Revolutionary Committee, 1982.

Jiangxi sheng nongye ting, ed. 江西省农业厅 [Agricultural Department of Jiangxi]. *Jiangxi sheng nongye tongji ziliao 1949–1979* 江西省农业统计资料1949–1979 [Agricultural Statistics of Jiangxi Province, 1949–1979]. Nanchang: Agricultural Department of Jiangxi Province, 1980.

Jilin sheng nongye ting, ed. 吉林省农业厅 [Agricultural Department of Jilin]. *Jilin sheng nongye jingji tongji ziliao, 1949–1985* 吉林省农业经济统计资料1949–1985 [Agricultural Economic Statistics of Jilin Province, 1949–1985]. Changchun: Agricultural Department of Jilin Province, 1986.

Jin, Chunming, Huang Yuchong, and Chang Huimin. *"Wen Ge" Shiqi Guaishi Guaiyu* "文革"时期怪事怪语 [Strange Events and Strange Language During the "Cultural Revolution"]. Beijing: Qiushi chubanshe, 1989.

"Jinyibu jiaqiang nongcun de wuchan jieji zhuanzheng" 进一步加强农村的无产阶级专政 [Further Consolidate the Dictatorship of Proletariats in Rural Areas]. *Red Flag* 红旗 [Hongqi], no. 5 (May 1975): 7–11.

Johnson, Ian. "Q and A: Willis Barnstone on Translating Mao and Touring Beijing with Allen Ginsberg." *New York Times*, April 17, 2015.

Jones, E. L. *Agriculture and the Industrial Revolution*. Oxford: Blackwell, 1974.

Jones, Gareth R. "Task Visibility, Freeriding, and Shirking: Explaining the Effect of Structure and Technology on Employee Behavior." *Academy of Management Review* 9, no. 4 (October 1984): 684–95.

Kadavil, Fr. Tony. "Solemnity of Christ the King." *Vatican Radio*. November 22, 2015. http://en.radiovaticana.va/news/2015/11/17/solemnity_of_christ_the_king_%E2%80%93_nov_22,_2015/1187444.

Kaldor, Nicholas. *Causes of Growth and Stagnation in the World Economy*. Cambridge: Cambridge University Press, 1996.

Kanter, Rosabeth Moss. *Communes: Creating and Managing the Collective Life*. New York: Harper and Row, 1973.

Karplus, Valerie J., and Deng Xingwang. *Agricultural Biotechnology in China: Origins and Prospects*. New York: Springer, 2008.

Katz, Daniel, and Robert L. Kahn. *The Social Psychology of Organizations*. 2nd ed. New York: Wiley, 1978.

Katzell, Raymond A., Richard S. Barrett, and Treadway C. Parker. "Job Satisfaction, Job Performance and Situational Characteristics." *Journal of Applied Psychology* 45, no. 2 (April 1961): 65–72.

Kelliher, Daniel. *Peasant Power in China: The End of the Reform Era, 1979–1989*. New Haven, CT: Yale University Press, 1992.

Keren, Levhari, and Michael Byalsky. "On the Stability and Viability of Co-operatives: The Kibbutz as an Example." *Acta Oeconomica* 56, no. 3 (2006): 301–21.

Khan, A. Z. M. Obaidullah, ed. "Class Struggle in Yellow Sandhill Commune." *The China Quarterly*, no. 51 (1972): 535–46.

Kimberly, John R. "Organizational Size and the Structuralist Perspective: A Review, Critique, and Proposal." *Administrative Science Quarterly* 21, no. 4 (December 1976): 571–97.

Kraus, Willy. *Economic Development and Social Change in the People's Republic of China*. New York: Springer-Verlag.

Kueh, Y. Y. *Agricultural Instability in China, 1931–1991: Weather, Technology and Institutions*. Oxford: Clarendon Press, 1995.

Kung, James Kai-sing. "Transaction Costs and Peasants' Choice of Institutions: Did the Right to Exit Really Solve the Free Rider Problem in Chinese Collective Agriculture?" *Journal of Comparative Economics* 17, no. 2 (June 1993): 485–503.

Kuo, Leslie T. C. *Agriculture in the People's Republic of China: Structural Changes and Technical Transformation*. New York: Praeger, 1976.

Lardy, Nicholas. *Agriculture in China's Modern Economic Development*. Cambridge: Cambridge University Press, 1983.

——. "Prospects and Some Policy Problems of Agricultural Development in China." *Journal of Agricultural Economics* 68, no. 2 (1986): 451–7.

"Last-Ditch Struggle." *Selections from China Mainland Magazines*, no. 613. Hong Kong: U.S. Consulate General, 1968.

Latane, Bibb. "The Psychology of Social Impact." *American Psychologist* 36, no. 4 (April 1981): 343–56.

Lau, Siu-kai. "The People's Commune and the Diffusion of Agri-Technology in China." Paper presented at Communication and Cultural Change in China, East-West Center, Honolulu, Hawaii. January 1978.

Lazear, Edward. "Salaries and Piece Rates." *Journal of Business* 59, no. 3 (1986): 405–31.

——. "The Power of Incentives." *American Economic Review* 90, no. 2 (2000): 410–14.

——. "Performance Pay and Productivity." *American Economic Review* 90, no. 5 (2000): 1346–61.

Leese, Daniel. "A Single Spark: Origins and Spread of the *Little Red Book* in China." In *Mao's Little Book: A Global History*, edited by Alexander C. Cook, 23–42. Cambridge: Cambridge University Press, 2014.

Lewis, W. Arthur. "Economic Development with Unlimited Supplies of Labour." *Manchester School of Economic and Social Studies* 22, no. 2 (May 1954): 139–91.

Li, Chu, and Tien Chieh-yun. *Inside a People's Commune: Report from Chiliying*. Beijing: Foreign Languages Press, 1974.

Li, Haiwen, and Liu Ronggang. "Guizhou shixing lianchan chengbao zerenzhi de qianqian houhou: fang Chi Biqing" 贵州实行联产承包责任制的前前后后：访迟必卿 [The Story of the Implementation of the Output-Linked Contract System in Guizhou: An Interview with Chi Biqing]. *Zhonggong dangshi ziliao* 中共党史资料 [CCP Historical Materials], no. 68 (1998): 90.

Li, Huaiyin. *Village China Under Socialism and Reform: A Micro-History, 1948-2008*. Stanford, CA: Stanford University Press, 2009.

——. "Institutions and Work Incentives in Collective Farming in Maoist China." *Journal of Agrarian Change* 17, no. 4 (2016): 1–20.

——. Interview by author. March 21, 2015.

——. E-mail correspondence. December 8, 2015.

Li, Yankun (associate director of the Central Party School of the CPC Central Committee, Tonglu County, Zhejiang province). Interview by author. November 7, 2015.

Liang, Xiaosheng. *Jinye you baofengxue* 今夜有暴风雪 [The Snowstorm Tonight]. Shanghai: Wenhui Publishing House, 2009.

Liaoning sheng nongye ting, ed. 辽宁省农业厅 [Liaoning Agricultural Department]. *Liaoning sheng nongcun renmin gongshe sanji jingji qingkuang tongji ziliao, 1957-1979* 辽宁省农村人民公社三级经济情况统计资料 [Statistical Data of Three-level Economic Information in Liaoning Province Rural People's Commune, 1957-1979]. Shenyang: Agricultural Department of Liaoning Province, 1980.

Liaoning sheng tongji ju, ed. 辽宁省统计局 [Liaoning Statistical Bureau]. *Liaoning sheng renkou tongji ziliao, 1949-1984* 辽宁省人口统计资料1949-1984 [Population Statistics of Liaoning Province, 1949-1984]. Shenyang: Statistical Bureau of Liaoning Province, 1985.

Lieberthal, Kenneth. *Governing China: From Revolution Through Reform*. New York: W.W. Norton, 2004.

Lieblich, Amia. *Kibbutz Makom: Report from an Israeli Kibbutz*. New York: Pantheon Books, 1981.

Lifton, Robert J. "Thought Reform of Chinese Intellectuals: A Psychiatric Evaluation." *Journal of Asian Studies* 16, no. 1 (November 1956): 75–88.

Lin, Biao. "Comrade Lin Biao's Speech at Peking Rally Commemorating the Fiftieth Anniversary of the October Revolution (November 6, 1967)." In *Advance Along the Road Opened Up by the October Socialist Revolution*, 1–10. Peking: Foreign Languages Press, 1967.

Lin, Chen. "The Agricultural Plight of the Chinese Communists." *Issues and Studies* 5, no. 5 (1970): 41–42.

Lin, Justin Yifu. "The Household Responsibility System in China's Agricultural Reform: A Theoretical and Empirical Study." *Economic Development and Cultural Change* 36, no. 3 (April 1988): 199–224.

——. "Collectivization and China's Agricultural Crisis in 1959–1961." *Journal of Political Economy* 98, no. 6 (December 1990): 1228–52.

——. "The Household Responsibility System Reform and the Adoption of Hybrid Rice in China." *Journal of Developmental Economics* 36, no. 2 (1991): 353–72.

——. "Rural Reforms and Agricultural Growth in China." *American Economic Review* 82, no. 1 (1992): 34–51.

Lin, Justin Yifu, James Kai-sing Kung, and Shuo Chen. "The Tragedy of the Nomenklatura: Career Incentives and Political Radicalism During China's Great Leap Famine." *American Political Science Review* 105, no. 1 (February 2011): 27–45.

Lin, Shanshan, and Du Qiang. "Jiuhaoyuan de nianqingren" [The Young People of Compound No. 9]. *Nanfang renwu zhoukan* [Southern People Weekly], August 26, 2013.

Lippit, Victor D. "The Commune in Chinese Development." *Modern China* 3, no. 2 (April 1977): 229–55.

Liu, Changgen, and Ji Fei. *Wan Li zai Anhui* 万里在安徽 [Wan Li in Anhui]. Beijing: Xinhua chubanshe, 2002.

Liu, Fangying, trans. *Issues and Studies*. Taipei: Institute of International Relations, 1979.

Liu, Rixin. "Guanyu woguo shixian nongye xiandaihua de jige wenti de tantao" 关于我国实现农业现代化的几个问题的探讨 [Discussion on a Few Problems of Agricultural Mechanization in China]. *People's Daily*, June 20, 1963.

Liu, William T. "Family Change and Family Planning in the People's Republic of China." Paper presented at the Annual Meeting of the Population Association of America, New York. April 19, 1974.

Liu, Yaqiu. "Zhiqing kunan yu xiangcun chengshi jian guanxi yanjiu" 知青苦难与乡村城市间关系研究 [A Study on the Relationship Between the Hardship of Educated Youth and Rural Cities]. *Qinghua daxue xuebao* 清华大学学报 [Journal of Tsinghua University] 23, no. 2 (2008): 135–48.

Lockwood, George B. *Labor Note*. The New Harmony Movement. New York: D. Appleton, 1905. https://jewettc.wikispaces.com/MWF+11.15+-+Roberty+Owen. Harmony+Soc.

Lu, Li'an. *Yangtian changxiao: yige danjian shiyinian de hongweibing yuzhong yutianlu* 仰天长啸：一个单监十一年的红卫兵狱中吁天录 [Outcry from a Red Guard Imprisoned for Eleven Years], edited by Wang Shaoguang. Hong Kong: Chinese University of Hong Kong Press, 2005.

Lu, Mai. "Zhongguo nongcun gaige de juece guocheng" 中国农村改革决策过程 [The Policy-making Process of China's Rural Reform]. http://gongfa.com/nongcungaigejuece.htm.

"Lu Xun ping shuihu" 鲁迅评水浒 [Lu Xun's Reviews of The Water Margin]. *Red Flag* 红旗 [Hongqi], no. 9 (1975): 5.

Luo, Hanxian. *Economic Changes in Rural China*. Beijing: New World Press, 1985.

Ma, Guochuan. "Weida de chuangzao: Du Runsheng fangtanlu" 伟大的创造：杜润生访谈录 [(Household Farming Is) A Great Innovation (of the Peasants): Record of an Interview with Du Runsheng]. *Economic Observer*, December 17, 2008. http://www.aisixiang.com/data/23385-2.html.

MacFarquhar, Roderick, and Michael Schoenhals. *Mao's Last Revolution*. Cambridge, MA: Harvard University Press, 2006.

Macias, Thomas, and Kristin Williams. "Know Your Neighbors, Save the Planet Social Capital and the Widening Wedge of Pro-Environmental Outcomes." *Environment and Behavior* 48, no. 3 (2016): 391–420.

Madsen, Richard. *Morality and Power in a Chinese Village*. Berkeley: University of California Press, 1984.

Mao, Mao (Deng Rong). *Deng Xiaoping and the Cultural Revolution: A Daughter Recalls the Critical Years*, translated by Sidney Shapiro. New York: Bertelsmann, 2005. Originally published in *Wode fuqin Deng Xiaoping: "Wenge" suiyue* [My Father Deng Xiaoping: The "Cultural Revolution" Years]. Beijing: Zhongyang wenxian chubanshe, 2000.

Mao, Zedong. "Communes Are Better." In *Selected Works of Mao Tse-tung*, vol. 8. Originally published in "Mao zhuxing shichan Shandong cunnong" 毛主席视察山东农村 [Mao's inspection tour in Shandong rural areas]. *People's Daily*, August 13, 1958.

——. "On Contradiction." In *Selected Works of Mao Tse-tung*, vol. 2, 311–345. Peking: Foreign Languages Press, 1965.

——. "Talk on the Four Cleanups Moments (January 3, 1965)." In *Long Live Mao Tse-tung Thought*. N.p.: Red Guard Publication, 1969.

——. "Talk at the Enlarged Meeting of the Political Bureau (March 20, 1966)." In *Long Live Mao Tse-tung Thought*. N.p.: Red Guard Publication, 1969.

——. *Mao Papers, Anthology and Bibliography*, edited by Jerome Chen. Oxford: Oxford University Press, 1970.

——. "Intraparty Correspondence (April 29, 1959)." In *Miscellany of Mao Tsetung Thought: 1949–1968*. Arlington, VA: Joint Publication Research Service, 1974.

——. "Instructions on Agricultural Mechanization." In *Miscellany of Mao Tsetung Thought: 1949–1968*. Arlington, VA: Joint Publication Research Service, 1974.

——. "Speech at the Lushan Conference (July 23, 1959)." In *Chairman Mao Talks to the People: Talks and Letters: 1956–1971*, edited by S. Schram. New York: Pantheon Press, 1975.

——. "On the Ten Great Relationships (April 25, 1956)." In *Selected Works of Mao Tsetung*, vol. 5, 284–307. Peking: Foreign Languages Press, 1977.

——. "A Letter on Farm Mechanization (March 12, 1966)." *Peking Review* 20, no. 52 (December 26, 1977): 7–9.

——. "The Question of Agricultural Cooperation (July 31, 1955)." In *Sources of Chinese Tradition: From 1600 Through the Twentieth Century*, compiled by Wm. Theodore de Bary and Richard Lufrano, 2nd ed., vol. 2, 458–9. New York: Columbia University Press, 2000.

Marriott, R. "Size of Working Group and Output." *Occupational Psychology* 23 (1949): 47–57.

Maxwell, Neville. *China's Road to Development*. New York: Pergamon Press, 1979.

Mays, Virgil. "Swine Production." In *China: A Report of the Visit of the CSCPRC Animal Science Delegation*, edited by Jacob Hoefer and Patrica Tsuchitani, 41–51. Washington, DC: National Academy Press, 1980.

McInroy, Rebecca. "Egocentric Bias: Why You Think You Invented the Internet, and Why You're Kinda Right." *KUT National Public Radio*. October 15, 2015. http://kut .org/post/egocentric-bias-why-you-think-you-invented-internet-and-why-youre -kinda-right-0.

McKie, James W. "Changing Views." In *Social Responsibility and the Business Predicament*, edited by James W. McKie, 17–40. Washington, DC: Brookings Institution, 1974.

McMillan, John, John Whalley, and Zhu Lijing. "The Impact of China's Economic Reforms on Agricultural Productivity Growth." *Journal of Political Economy* 97, no. 4 (1989): 781–807.

Meisner, Maurice. *Mao's China and After: A History of the People's Republic*. New York: Free Press, 1999.

Militia in the Red Era [Hongse shidai de minbing]. 1967. Shanghai People's Fine Arts Publishing House. http://chenmodemaque.blog.163.com/blog/static/1638921292012927985398/.

Ministry of Agriculture and Forestry Mass Criticism Group. "Two Line Struggle Around the First National Conference on Learning from Dazhai in Agriculture." *Red Flag* 红旗 [Hongqi], no. 1 (January 1977): 96–101.

Mintzberg, Henry. *The Structuring of Organizations*. Englewood Cliffs, NJ: Prentice-Hall, 1979.

Mumford, Lewis. *The Story of Utopias*. New York: Boni and Liveright, 1962.

Murray, John. "Human Capital in Religious Communes: Literacy and Selection of Nineteenth Century Shakers." *Explorations in Economic History* 32, no. 2 (1995): 217–35.

Naughton, Barry. "Rural Saving and Credit Supply Before and After Collectives." Paper presented to UCLA Seminar on Economic and Historical Perspectives on China's Collectives. February 21, 1987.

——. *The Chinese Economy: Transitions and Growth*. Cambridge, MA: MIT Press, 2007.

Niu, Zhonghuang. "On the Technical Transformation of China's Agriculture." *People's Daily*, August 26, 1969.

Nolan, Peter. "De-Collectivisation of Agriculture in China, 1979–82: A Long-Term Perspective." *Cambridge Journal of Economics* 7, no. 3/4 (September/December 1983): 381–403.

——. *The Political Economy of Collective Farms: An Analysis of China's Post-Mao Rural Reforms*. Cambridge: Polity Press, 1988.

Nolan, Peter and Gordon White. "Distribution and Development in China." *Bulletin of Concerned Asia Scholars* 13, no. 3 (1981): 2–18.

"Nongcun gaige zuotanhui tanhua jilu" 农村改革座谈会谈话记录 [Record of Talks at the Seminar on Rural Reform]. Internet Document. July 18, 2003.

Nongye jingji ziliao, 1949–1983 农业经济资料 [Agricultural Economic Statistics, 1949–1983]. Beijing: Ministry of Agriculture Planning Bureau, 1983.

Office of National People's Congress Financial and Economic Affairs Committee, Department of Development Planning, National Development and Reform Commission, ed. "1976–1985 nian fazhan guomin jingji shinian guihua gangyao (caoan)" 1976-1985年发展国民经济十年规划纲要（草案）[Ten-Year Plan for the

Development of National Economy as of 1976–1985 (draft)]. In *Jianguo yilai guomin jingji he shehui fazhan wunian jihua zhongyao wenjian huibian* 建国以来国民经济和社会发展五年计划重要文件汇编 [Selected Important Documents of the Five-Year Plans for National Economy and Societal Development since the Founding of PRC]. Beijing: China Democracy and Legal Press, 2008.

Oi, Jean C. *Rural China takes Off: Institutional Foundations of Economic Reform*. Berkeley: University of California Press, 1999.

O'Leary, Greg, and Andrew Watson. "The Role of the People's Commune in Rural Development in China." *Pacific Affairs* 55, no. 4 (Winter 1982): 593–612.

Olson, Mancur. *The Logic of Collective Action*. Cambridge, MA: Harvard University Press, 1971.

Orleans, Leo. *China's Experience in Population Control: The Elusive Model*. Prepared for the Committee on Foreign Affairs of the U.S. House of Representatives by the Congressional Research Service, Library of Congress. Washington, DC: U.S. Government Printing Office, 1974.

——. "China's Experience in Population Control: The Elusive Model." In *China's Road to Development*, edited by Neville Maxwell, 97–135. New York: Pergamon Press, 1979.

Oved, Iaácov. *Two Hundred Years of American Communes*. New Brunswick, Canada: Transaction Books, 1993.

Paine, Suzanne. "Balanced Development: Maoist Conception and Chinese Practice." *World Development* 4, no. 4 (April 1976): 277–304.

Pang, Xianzhi. *Upsurge of Socialism in China's Countryside: Document of Historical Significance in the Party's Leadership of the Socialist Revolution in the Rural Areas*. Peking: Xuexi, 1956.

Parish, William L. "Socialism and the Chinese Peasant Family." *Journal of Asian Studies* 34, no. 3 (1975): 613–30.

Parish, William L., and Martin King Whyte. *Village and Family in Contemporary China*. Chicago: University of Chicago Press, 1978.

Patel, Raj. "The Long Green Revolution." *Journal of Peasant Studies* 40, no. 1 (2013): 1–63.

Pei, Minxin. *China's Trapped Transition: The Limits of Developmental Autocracy*. Cambridge, MA: Harvard University Press, 2008.

Pelzel, John. "Economic Management of a Production Brigade in Post-Leap China." In *Economic Organization in Chinese Society*, edited by William E. Willmott, 387–416. Stanford, CA: Stanford University Press, 1972.

People's Daily. "Resolution of the Standing Committee of the National People's Congress on Adjusting the Main Indicators of the National Economic Plan of 1959 and Carrying out the Movement of Increasing Output and Conservation." August 28, 1959.

——. "Nongcun gongju gaige de xinfazhan" 农村工具改革的新发展 [The New Development of Farm Tool Reform]. January 13, 1960.

——. "Kaizhan yige shougong caozuo jixiehua banjixiehua de quanmin yundong" 开展一个手工操作机械化半机械化的全民运动 [Carry Out a National Movement of Manual Operation for Mechanization and Semi-Mechanization]. February 25, 1960.

——. "Quanguo douyao xue jiefangjun" 全国都要学解放军 [Learn from PLA Across the Country]. February 1, 1964.

——. "Ba puji xiandai nongye kexue jishu jianli zai qunzhong de jichu shang" 把普及现代农业科学技术建立在群众的基础上 [Build Dissemination of Modern Agricultural Science and Technology on the Foundation of the Masses]. May 21, 1964.

——. "Shanxi juxing shengrendai dahui, Bo Yibo tongzhi deng dangxuanwei sanjie quanguo renda daibiao" 山西举行省人代大会，薄一波同志等当选为三届全国人大代表 [Shanxi Held Provincial People's Congress and Elected Representatives Including Comrade Bo Yibo for Third National People's Congress]. October 16, 1964.

——. "'Yangbantian' shi nongye kexue wei shengchan fuwu de zhuyao zhendi" "样板田"是农业科学为生产服务的主要阵地 ["Demonstration Farms" Are Main Centers Through Which Agricultural Science May Serve Production"]. October 25, 1964.

——. "Mao zhuxi he renda daibiao zaiyiqi" 毛主席和人大代表在一起 [Chairman Mao with Representatives of National People's Congress]. December 30, 1964.

——. "Banhao sanjiehe de yangbantian, cujin nongke kexue shiyan yundong" 办好三结合的样板田，促进农科学实验运动 [Organizing three-in-one demonstration fields and promoting the agricultural scientific experiment movement]. March 28, 1965.

——. "An Mao Zedong sixiang ban qiye" 按毛泽东思想办企业 [Do Business Based on Maoist]. April 3, 1966.

——. "Hubei shengwei guanyu zhubu shixian nongye jixiehua de shexiang" 湖北省委关于逐步实现农业机械化的设想 [Editor's Note on Postulation by the CPC Hubei Provincial Committee Concerning Gradual Realization of Agricultural Mechanization]. April 9, 1966.

——. "Ba qiye bancheng Mao Zedong sixiang daxuexiao" 把企业办成毛泽东思想大学校 [Change Businesses into Universities of Mao Zedong Thought]. August 28, 1966.

——. "Woguo nongye jixie gongye jinnian huode zuida fazhan" 我国农业机械工业今年获得最大发展 [China's Agricultural Mechanization Has Realized the Maximum Development This Year]. October 18, 1966.

——. "Nongye xue Dazhai." 农业学大寨 [Learn from Dazhai in Agriculture]. September 23, 1970.

——. "Jiaxing diqu jianchi liangtiao luxian douzheng, fazhan nongye jidian shiye" 嘉兴地区坚持两条路线斗争，发展农业机电事业 [Adhere to Two-line Struggle, Develop Agricultural Electronics and Mechanization in Jiaxiang (Zhejiang Province)]. October 19, 1970.

——. "Xinzhouxian jiasu fazhan nongye jixiehua" 新州县加速发展农业机械化 [Speed Up the Development of Agricultural Mechanization in Xinzhou County (Hubei Province)]. October 19, 1970.

——. "Shuangchengxian ziligengsheng ban nongye jixie" 双城县自立更生办农业机械 [Self-reliance and Undertake Agricultural Machinery in Shuangcheng County (Heilongjiang Province)]. October 19, 1970.

——. "Luoshi jingji zhengce, shougou gengduo de nongfu chanpin" 落实经济政策，收购更多的农副产品 [Implement Economic Policy, Purchase More Agricultural Products]. December 12, 1971.

——. "Jianchi dulizizhu ziligengsheng de fangzhen" 坚持独立自主自立更生的发展 [Adhere to the Principle of Independence and Self-reliance]. February 3, 1975.

——. "Luxian duilletou, liangmian shuangfengshou" 路线对了头，粮棉双丰收 [Right Route Leads to Harvest of Grain and Cotton]. February 4, 1975.

——. "Jianchi jixu geming, pipan ziben zhuyi qingxiang" 坚持继续革命，批判资本主义倾向 [Insist on Continuing the Revolution, Criticize the Tendency of Capitalist]. February 10, 1975.

——. "Wei geming duo gaochan, wei guojia duozuo gongxian" 为革命多高产，为国家多做贡献 [Achieve High Yields for the Sake of Revolution, Make More Contributions for the Country]. February 27, 1975.

——. "Gonggu wuchan jieji zhuanzheng shi changqi de zhandou renwu" 巩固无产阶级转正后是长期的战斗任务 [To Consolidate the Dictatorship of Proletariats Is a Long-Term Combat Task]. February 27, 1975.

——. "Carry Out the Discussions About the Water Margin." September 4, 1975.

——. "Yaohai shi fupi ziben zhuyi" [The Critical Issue Is the Restoration of Capitalism]. February 17, 1976.

——. "Fan'an bude renxin" [The Overturn Cannot Win Popular Support]. March 10, 1976.

——. "Jiakuai nongye fazhan sudu shi quandang de zhandou renwu" [Accelerating the Pace of Agricultural Development Is the Combat Task of the Whole Party]. December 11, 1977.

——. "Zhuahao shouyi fenpei, shixian zengchan zengshou" 抓好收益分配，实现增产增收 [Refine Income Distribution, To Achieve an Increased Production]. December 20, 1977.

——. "Jianjue jiuzheng pingdiao shengchandui zicai de waifeng" [Correct the Unhealthy Trend of Leveling the Wealth of the Production Team]. April 2, 1978.

——. "Luoshi dangde zhengce, jianqing nongmin fudan" [Implement the Party's Policy, Lighten the Peasants' Burden]. July 5, 1978.

——. "'Sanji suoyou, duiwei jichu' yingai wending" ["The System of Three Level Ownership with the Production Team as the Basic Ownership Unit" Should Be Maintained]. March 15, 1979.

——. "Li Zhensheng Breeds Wheat to Help Feed the Nation." February 28, 2007. http://en.people.cn/200702/28/eng20070228_352897.html.

——. "The Xiaogang Village Story." *People's Daily*, November 11, 2008. http://en.people.cn/90002/95607/6531490.html.

Perkins, Dwight. *Rural Small-Scale Industry in the People's Republic of China.* Berkeley: University of California Press, 1977.

——. "China's Economic Policy and Performance." In *Cambridge History of China.* Vol. 15, *The People's Republic, Part 2: Revolutions within the Chinese Revolution, 1966–1982,* edited by John K. Fairbank and Roderick MacFarquhar, 475–539. Cambridge: Cambridge University Press, 1991.

Perkins, Dwight, and Shahid Yusuf. *Rural Development in China.* Baltimore, MD: Johns Hopkins University Press, 1984.

Perry, Elizabeth and Li Xun. *Proletarian Power: Shanghai in the Cultural Revolution.* Boulder, CO: Westview Press, 1997.

Pitzer, Donald. *America's Communal Utopias.* Chapel Hill: University of North Carolina Press, 1997.

Plato. "The Republic." In *The Republic of Plato: with Studies for Teachers,* edited by William L. Bryan and Charlotte L. Bryan, 55–298. New York: Charles Scribner's Sons, 1898.

Popkin, Samuel L. *The Rational Peasant: The Political Economy of Rural Society in Vietnam.* Berkeley: University of California Press, 1979.

Powell, Ralph L. "Everyone a Soldier: The Communist Chinese Militia." *Foreign Affairs* (October 1960): 3.

Prendergast, Canice. "The Provision of Incentives in Firms." *Journal of Economic Literature* 37, no. 1 (1999): 7–63.

——. "The Tenuous Trade-off Between Risk and Incentives," *Journal of Political Economy* 110, no. 5 (2002): 1071–102.

Printz, Peggy, and Paul Steinle. *Commune: Life in Rural China*. New York: Dodd, Mead, 1977.

Production Brigade No. 2, Hsukuang Commune, O-ch'eng County, Hubei. "The Question of Mechanization by the Collective." *Nongye jixie jishu*农业机械技术 [Agricultural Machinery Technique], no. 9 (September 1968). In *Selections from China Mainland Magazines*, no. 644. Hong Kong: U.S. Consulate General, 1969.

Putterman, Louis. *Continuity and Change in China's Rural Development: Collective and Reform Eras in Perspective*. Oxford: Oxford University Press, 1993.

Pye, Lucian W. *The Dynamics of Chinese Politics*. Cambridge: Oelgeschlager, Gunn & Hain, 1981.

Radio Nanchang. December 29, 1975.

Radio Shanghai. November 10, 1969. In *United States Foreign Broadcast Information Service China Report*. November 19, 1969.

"Reactionary Nature of China's Khrushchev." *Selections from China Mainland Magazines*, no. 613. Hong Kong: U.S. Consulate General, 1968.

Ren, Bo. "Ziyuan bingfu renduo dishao maodun guidingle Zhongguo nongdi zhidu: Zhuanfang yuan zhongyang nongcun zhengce yanjiushi zhuren Du Runsheng" 资源禀赋人多地少矛盾规定了中国农地制度: 专访原中央农村政策研究室主任杜润生 [The Natural Resource Endowment Contradiction of a Large Population and Limited Land Determines China's Rural Land System: A Special Visit to Former Central Rural Policy Research Office Director Du Runsheng]. *Caixin*. October 5, 2002. http://magazine.caixin.com/2002-10-5/100079968.html.

Ren, Xiangqin. Interview by author. January 2016.

Renmin wang [People's Daily Online]. "Notes." Accessed January 20, 2017. http://en.people.cn/dengxp/vol2/note/B0070.html.

——. "Conference on Learning Agriculture from Dazhai and Agricultural Rectification." August 14, 2014. http://history.people.com.cn/n/2014/0814/c387654-25468491.html.

"Research Work in Agricultural Machinery Should Be Ahead of Agricultural Mechanization." *Zhongguo nongye jixie*中国农业机械 [Chinese Agricultural Machinery], no. 9 (September 1962): 2–4.

"Resolution of CPC Central Committee On Dismissing Teng Hsiao-ping From All Posts Both Inside and Outside Party." *Peking Review* 19, no. 15 (April 9, 1976): 3.

"Resolution on Certain Questions in the History of Our Party since the Founding of the People's Republic of China (June 27, 1981)." *Peking Review* 24, no. 27 (July 1981): 10–39.

Revans, R. W. "Human Relations, Management, and Size." In *Human Relations and Modern Management*, edited by Hugh-Jones and Edward Maurice, 177–220. Amsterdam: North-Holland, 1958.

Revolutionary Committee for Jincheng County, Shanxi. "Use Mao Tse-tung's Thought to Direct the Work of Sending Down the Farm Machines and Tools of State Stations." *Nongye jixie jishu*农业机械技术 [Agricultural Machinery Technique], no. 11 (November 8, 1968). In *Selections from China Mainland Magazines*, no. 643. Hong Kong: U.S. Consulate General, 1969.

Riskin, Carl. *China's Political Economy: The Quest for Development since 1949*. Oxford: Oxford University Press, 1987.

Robbins, Paul. *Political Ecology: A Critical Introduction*. West Sussex: Wiley-Blackwell, 2012.

Rosner, Menachem, Itzhak Ben David, Alexander Avnat, Neni Cohen, and Uri Leviatan. *The Second Generation: Continuity and Change in the Kibbutz*. New York: Greenwood Press, 1990.

Rozelle, Scott. "Annex I: China's Corn Economy, A Brief Introduction." University of California, Davis website.

Ruffle, Bradley, and Richard Sosis. "Cooperation and the In-Group-Out-Group Bias: A Field Test on Israeli Kibbutz Members and City Residents." *Journal of Economic Behavior and Organization* 60, no. 2 (2006): 147–63.

"Running Enterprises in Line with Mao Tse-tung's Thinking (April 3, 1966)." *People's Daily* editorial. *Peking Review* 9, no. 16 (April 15, 1966): 11–15.

Sachs, J., W. T. Woo, S. Fischer, and G. Hughes. "Structural Factors in the Economic Reforms of China, Eastern Europe, and the Former Soviet Union." *Economic Policy* 9, no. 18 (1994): 102–45.

Saich, Tony. *Governance and Politics of China*. London: Palgrave Macmillan, 2001.

Sawyer, Malcolm C. *The Economics of Industries and Firms: Theories, Evidence, and Policy*. New York: St. Martin's Press, 1981.

Schmalzer, Sigrid. *Red Revolution, Green Revolution: Scientific Farming in Socialist China*. Chicago: University of Chicago Press, 2016.

Scott, James C. *The Moral Economy of the Peasant: Rebellion and Subsistence in Southeast Asia*. New Haven, CT: Yale University Press, 1976.

——. *Seeing Like a State: How Certain Schemes to Improve the Human Condition Have Failed*. New Haven, CT: Yale University Press, 1999.

Selden, Mark, and Patti Eggleston. *The People's Republic of China: A Documentary History of Revolutionary Change*. New York: Monthly Review Press, 1979.

Skinner, G. William. "Marketing and Social Structure in Rural China, Part III." *Journal of Asian Studies* 24, no. 3 (1965): 363–99.

"Shakers." *New World Encyclopedia*. Last modified September 10, 2015. http://www.newworldencyclopedia.org/entry/Shakers.

Shakers Near Lebanon State of N. York, Their Mode of Worship. 1830. The Library of Congress, California. https://www.loc.gov/item/00650589/.

Shanxi Datong City Farm Machine Station of Changtang Commune. "Rely on the Masses to Run the Farm Machine Station Democratically." *Nongye jixie jishu*农业机械技术 [Agricultural Machinery Technique], no. 9 (September 1968). In *Selections from China Mainland Magazines*, no. 644. Hong Kong: U.S. Consulate General, 1968.

Shanxi sheng Xinxian diqu geweihui, nonglin shuili ju keji xiaozu 山西省新县地区革委会农林水利局科技小组 [Science and Technology Group of Agriculture, Forestry and Water Conservancy Bureau, Revolutionary Committee of Xin County, Shanxi Province]. *Xinxian diqu nongye kexue shiyan* 新县地区农业科学实验 [Xin County Region Agricultural Scientific Experiment]. 1971.

Shepherd, William G. *The Economics of Industrial Organization*. Englewood Cliffs, NJ: Prentice-Hall, 1979.

Shi, Tiesheng. "Wode yaoyuan de qingpingwan" 我的遥远的清平湾 [My Faraway Qingpingwan]. *Qingnian wenxue* 青年文学 [Youth Literature] 1 (1983).

Shirk, Susan. *The Political Logic of Economic Reform in China*. Berkeley: University of California Press, 1993.

Shue, Vivienne. "Book Review: The Politics of Agricultural Mechanization in China, by Benedict Stavis." *American Political Science Review* 73, no. 3 (1979): 926–27.

Sosis, Richard. "Religion and Intragroup Cooperation: Preliminary Results of a Comparative Analysis of Utopian Communities." *Cross-Cultural Research* 34, no. 1 (2000): 70–87.

Sosis, Richard, and Bradley Ruffle. "Religious Ritual and Cooperation: Testing for a Relationship on Israeli Religious and Secular Kibbutzim." *Current Anthropology* 44, no. 5 (December 2003): 713–22.

Spence, Jonathan D. *God's Chinese Son: The Taiping Heavenly Kingdom of Hong Xiuquan*. New York: W.W. Norton, 1996.

——. *The Search for Modern China*. 3rd ed. New York: W.W. Norton, 2013.

Sprague, G. F. "Agriculture in China." *Science* 188, no. 4188 (May 1975): 549–55.

State Intellectual Property Office of the PRC. "Prospects for the Technical Development of Bio-fertilizer." Official website.

Statistical Bureau of Ningxia Hui Autonomous Region, ed. *Collection of Statistical Materials on Ningxia's Rural Areas* [Ningxia nongcun tongji ziliao huibian]. Beijing: China Statistics Press, 1998.

Stavis, Benedict. *Making Green Revolution: The Politics of Agricultural Development in China*. Ithaca, NY: Rural Development Committee of Cornell University, 1974.

——. *People's Communes and Rural Development in China*. Ithaca, NY: Rural Development Committee of Cornell University, 1974.

——. "Agricultural Research and Extension Services in China." *World Development* 6, no. 5 (1978): 631–45.

——. *The Politics of Agricultural Mechanization in China*. Ithaca, NY: Cornell University Press, 1978.

Steiner, Ivan D. "Models for Inferring Relationships Between Group Size and Potential Group Productivity." *Behavioral Science* 11, no. 4 (July 1966): 273–83.

——. *Group Processes and Productivity*. New York: Academic Press, 1972.

Stone, Bruce. "The Basis for Chinese Agricultural Growth in the 1980s and 1990s: A Comment on Document No. 1, 1984." *The China Quarterly* 101 (1985): 114–21.

——. "Developments in Agricultural Technology." *The China Quarterly* 116 (1988): 767–822.

——. *Evolution and Diffusion of Agricultural Technology in China*. Washington, DC: International Food Policy Research Institute, 1990.

Sun, Guihua. Interview by author. December 10, 2011.

——. Interview by author. March 1, 2013.

——. Interview by author in Los Angeles. July 30, 2013.

——. Interview by author in Los Angeles. August 29, 2013.

——. Interview by author. November 10, 2014.

Tam, On Kit. *China's Agricultural Modernization: The Socialist Mechanization Scheme*. London: Croom Helm, 1985.

Tang, Anthony M., and Bruce Stone. *Food Production in the People's Republic of China*. Washington, DC: International Food Policy Research Institute, 1980.

Tang, Ying. Interview by author. December 4, 2015.

Teiwes, Frederick. "A Critique of Western Studies of CCP Elite Politics." *IIAS Newsletter*. 1996.

Teiwes, Frederick, and Warren Sun. *The End of the Maoist Era: Chinese Politics During the Twilight of the Cultural Revolution, 1972–1976*. Armonk, NY: M. E. Sharpe, 2007.

——. *Paradoxes of Post-Mao Rural Reform: Initial Steps toward a New Chinese Countryside*. London: Routledge, 2015.

"Third Session of Standing Committee of Fourth National People's Congress Convened in Peking." *Peking Review* 19, no. 50 (December 10, 1976): 8–12.

Thirty Years Since the Founding of the People's Republic of China: Agricultural Statistics of Henan Province, 1949–1979 [Jianguo sanshinian: henansheng nongye tongji ziliao, 1949–1979]. Zhengzhou: Statistical Bureau of Henan Province, 1981.

Thornton, Richard C. *China: The Struggle for Power, 1917–1972*. Bloomington: Indiana University Press, 1973.

——. *China: A Political History, 1917–1980*. New York: Westview Press, 1982.

Thurston, Anne. *Muddling Toward Democracy: Political Change in Grassroots China*. Washington, DC: U.S. Institute of Peace, 1998.

"Tian Chenlin's Crime of Sabotage." *Selections from China Mainland Magazines*, no. 624. Hong Kong: U.S. Consulate General, 1968.

Tong, Huaiping, and Li Chengguan. *Deng Xiaoping baci nanxun jishi* 邓小平八次南巡纪实 [Record of Deng Xiaoping's Eight Southern Journeys]. Beijing: Jiefangjun wenyi chubanshe, 2002.

"Twelve Million School Graduates Settle in the Countryside." *Peking Review* 19, no. 2 (January 9, 1976): 11–13.

Uhalley, Stephan. *A History of the Chinese Communist Party*. Stanford, CA: Hoover Institution Press, 1988.

Unger, Jonathan. *The Transformation of Rural China*. Armonk, NY: M. E. Sharpe, 2002.

Verdery, Katherine. *The Vanishing Hectare: Property and Value in Postsocialist Transylvania*. Ithaca, NY: Cornell University Press, 2003.

Vogel, Erza F. *Deng Xiaoping and the Transformation of China*. Cambridge, MA: Harvard University Press, 2011.

Wan, Li. "Diligently Carry Out the Party's Agricultural Policy." *Red Flag* [Hongqi], no. 3 (March 1978): 92–7.

Wang, Hsiao-hsien. "The Turmoil in Yunnan." *Issues and Studies* 13, no. 12 (December 1977): 41–52.

Wang, Shaoguang, and Hu Angang. *The Chinese Economy in Crisis: State Capacity and Tax Reform*. Armonk, NY: M. E. Sharpe, 2001.

Wang, Tuo. *The Cultural Revolution and Overacting: Dynamics Between Politics and Performance*. Lanham, MD: Lexington Books, 2014.

Wang, Weiqun. "Weida de diyibu: Zhongguo nongcun gaige qidian shilu" 伟大的第一步：中国农村改革起点实录 [The First Step: The True Account of the Starting Point of China's Rural Reform]. Youth.com. December 17, 2008. http://news.qq.com/a/20081217/001228.htm.

Wang, Zhaoda. *Mao Zedong Thought Is the Peak of Contemporary Marxism and Leninism*. 1968. Zhejiang People's Fine Art Publishing House.

Wei, Jianyi. "Luoshi zhengce shi zuohao beigeng gongzuo de zhongyao huanjie" 落实政策是做好备耕工作的重要环节 [Implementing the Policy Is An Important Piece in Preparation for Farming]. *People's Daily*, February 22, 1978.

Weiner, Nan, and Thomas A. Mahoney. "A Model of Corporate Performance as a Function of Environmental, Organizational, and Leadership Influences." *Academy of Management Journal* 24, no. 3 (September 1981): 453–70.

White, Lynn T. *Unstately Power: Volume I Local Causes of China's Economic Reforms.* Armonk, NY: M. E. Sharpe, 1998.

White, Tyrene. *China's Longest Campaign: Birth Planning in the People's Republic, 1949–2005.* Ithaca, NY: Cornell University Press, 2006.

Whyte, Martin K. *Small Groups and Political Rituals in China.* Berkeley: University of California Press, 1974.

Williamson, Oliver E. *Markets and Hierarchies: Analysis and Antitrust Implications.* New York: Free Press, 1975.

Wilson, Dick. "The China After Next." *Far Eastern Economic Review* (1968): 189–95.

"Wipe Out State Monopoly and Promote Mechanization on the Basis of Self-Reliance in a Big Way." *Nongye jixie jishu* 农业机械技术 [Agricultural Machinery Technique], no. 6 (September 1967) in *Selections from China Mainland Magazines*, no. 610 (January 1968): 10–16.

Wong, John. *An Economic Overview of Agriculture in the People's Republic of China.* New York: Agricultural Development Council, 1973.

——. "Grain Output in China: Some Statistical Implications." *Current Scene* 11, no. 2 (1973).

——. "Agriculture in the People's Republic of China." In *China: Cultural and Political Perspective*, edited by D. Bing. Auckland, New Zealand: Longman Paul, 1975.

——. "Some Aspects of China's Agricultural Development Experience: Implications for Developing Countries in Asia." *World Development* 4, no. 6 (June 1976): 485–97.

——. "Communication of Peasant Agriculture: China's Organizational Strategy for Agricultural Development." In *Cooperative and Commune: Group Farming in the Economic Development of Agriculture*, edited by Peter Dorner. Madison: University of Wisconsin Press, 1977.

Worden, Robert L., Andrea Matles Savada, and Ronald E. Dolan, eds. *China: A Country Study.* Washington, DC: U.S. Government Printing Office for the Library of Congress, 1987.

Work Team of Central-South Bureau of the CPC Central Committee. "Where Should Revolutionary Zeal Be Exerted? Second Question Concerning Organization of a High Tide in Agricultural Production." *Nanfang Ribao* 南方日报 [Southern Daily], March 28, 1965.

World Bank. *World Development Indicators 2015.* Washington, DC: World Bank, 2015.

Wu, De. "Speech at the Celebration Rally in the Capital." *Peking Review* 19, no. 44 (October 29, 1976): 12–14.

Wu, Jicheng. "Jiang Qing yu nongye xue dazhai huiyi" 江青与农业学大寨会议 [Jiang Qing and the Dazhai Agricultural Conference]. In *Jianzheng lishi: Zhongguo, 1975–1976* 见证历史：中国1975–1976 [Witnessing History: China 1975–1976], edited by Zhang Shujun. Changsha: Hunan People's Press, 2008.

Wu, Li, ed. *Zhonghua renmin gongheguo jingjishi, 1949–1999, vol. 2* 中华人民共和国经济史，1949–1999 [An Economic History of the PRC, 1949–1999]. Beijing: Zhongguo jingji chubanshe, 1999.

Wu, Xiang. "Wan Li tan shiyijie sanzhong quanhui qianhou de nongcun gaige" 万里谈十一届三中全会前后的农村改革 [Wan Li on Agricultural Reform Before and

After the Third Plenum of the Eleventh Central Committee]. In *Gaibian Zhongguo mingyun de 41 tian* 改变中国命运的41天 [The 41 Days That Changed the Destiny of China], edited by Yu Guangyuan, 281–89. Shenzhen: Haitian Publishing House, 1998.

——. "E duzi shi tuidong gaige de zuichu liliang" 饿肚子是推动改革的最初力量 [Hunger Is the Initial Power to Promote Reform]. *Reform Data*. January 20, 2013. http://www.reformdata.org/content/20130120/15430.html.

Wu, Yuan-li, and Robert Sheeks. *The Organization and Development of Scientific Research and Development in Mainland China*. New York: Praeger, 1970.

Xi Zhongxun editorial board. *Xi Zhongxun zhuan, vol. 2* 习仲勋传 [Biography of Xi Zhongxun]. Beijing: Zhongyang wenxian chubanshe, 2013.

Xiang, Nan. "Wending gaochan he nongye jiexiehua" 稳产高产和农业机械化 [Stable and High Yields and Agricultural Mechanization]. *People's Daily*, March 22, 1965.

——. "Nongye jiexiehua keyi bande youhaoyoukuai" 农业机械化可以办得又好又快 [Agricultural Mechanization Can Be Achieved with Good and Fast Results]. *People's Daily*, July 6, 1965.

——. "An Inspection Report on the Mechanization of Our Agriculture." *Zhongguo nongye jixie* 中国农业机械 [Chinese Agricultural Machinery] (May 1965): 11–20.

Xi, Jinping. *The Governance of China*. Beijing: Foreign Languages Press, 2014.

Xinhua. "Communiqué of the Tenth Plenary Session of the Eighth Committee of the CPC." September 28, 1962.

——. Press Release. March 12, 1976.

——. "Ministry Mass Criticism Group Exposes Crimes of 'Gang of Four' in Undermining Agriculture." Xinhua News Agency, no. 6817 (November 1976): 4–6.

Xinhua tongxun she 新华通讯社 [Xinhua News Agency]. *Dagao kexue zhongtian, jiasu nongye fazhan: jieshao Hunan Huarong xian siji nongye kexue shiyan wang* 大搞科学种田，加速农业发展：介绍湖南华容县四级农业科学实验网 [Greatly Undertake Scientific Farming, Accelerate Agricultural Development: Introducing Hunan Province, Huarong County's Four-Level Agricultural Scientific Experiment Network]. Beijing: Remin meishu chubanshe, 1975.

Yang, Dali L. *Calamity and Reform in China: State, Rural Society, and Institutional Change since the Great Leap Famine*. Stanford, CA: Stanford University Press, 1996.

Yang, Jisheng. *Deng Xiaoping shidai: Zhongguo gaige kaifang ershinian jishi*, vol. 1 [The Age of Deng Xiaoping: A Record of Twenty Years of China's Reform and Openings]. Beijing: Zhongyang bianyi chubanshe, 1998.

Yang, Kuisong and Stephen A. Smith. "Communism in China, 1900–2010." In *The Oxford Handbook of the History of the Communism*, edited by S. A. Smith, 220–35. Oxford: Oxford University Press, 2014.

Yang, Yichen. *Yang Yichen huiyilu* [Memoirs of Yang Yichen]. Beijing: Zhongyang wenxian chubanshe, 1996.

Ye, Jianying. "Speech at the Closing of Ceremony of the Central Work Conference of the CPC Central Committee (December 13, 1978)." In *Ye Jianying xuanji* 叶剑英选集 [Selected Works of Ye Jianying], 493–502. Beijing: People's Publishing House, 1996.

"Yibu xuanyang touxiang zhuyi de fanmian jiaocai, ping shuihu" [A Negative Example Advocating Capitulationism, the Review of *The Water Margin*]. *Red Flag* 红旗 [Hongqi], no. 9 (1975): 13–17.

Yu, Juan. "Wenge qijian gouwu yaobei Maozhuixi yulu" 文革期间购物要背毛主席语录 [The Required Quotation Exchange While Shopping During the Cultural Revolution]. October 6, 2012. http://www.xici.net/d121565728.htm.

Yuchtman, Ephraim, and Stanley E. Seashore. "A System Resource Approach to Organizational Effectiveness." *American Sociological Review* 32, no. 6 (December 1967): 891–903.

Zhang, Dong. *Boji yishu rensheng: Tian Hua zhuan* 搏击艺术人生：田华传 [Fighting in the Artistic Life: A Biography of Tian Hua]. Beijing: Zhongguo Dianying Chubanshe, 2006.

Zhang, Hua. "1975 nian nongye xue dazhai huiyi yu nongye zhengdun de yaoqiu" 1975年农业学大寨会议与农业整顿的要求 [The 1975 Conference on Learning Agriculture from Dazhai and the Demand to Rectify Agriculture]. *Dangde wenxian* 党的文献 [Documents of CPC] 6 (1999): 16–21.

Zhang, Jingdong. *Du Runsheng tamen* 杜润生他们 [Du Runsheng and Those Sharing His Views]. Hong Kong: Zhongguo guoji wenhua chuban youxian gongsi, 2011.

Zhang, Letian. *Gaobie lixiang: renmin gongshe zhidu yanjiu* 告别理想：人民公社制度研究 [Farewell to Dreams: A Study on the Commune System]. Shanghai: Shanghai People's Press, 1998.

Zhang, Wanshu. "Dabaogan neimu" 大包干内幕 [The Inside Story of All-Round Contracting]. *Zhongguo zuojia* 中国作家 [Chinese writers], no. 6 (2007): 4–39.

Zhang, Yulin. "Readjustment and Reform in Agriculture." In *China Economic Reforms*, edited by Lin Wei and Arnold Chao, 123–146. Philadelphia: University of Pennsylvania Press, 1982.

Zhao, Ziyang. *Prisoner of the State: The Secret Journal of Premier Zhao Ziyang*. Translated and edited by Bao Pu, Renee Chiang, and Adi Ignatius. New York: Simon and Schuster, 2009.

Zheng, Keming. "Report to Jiangxi's Militia Work Conference." *Jiangxi Ribao* 江西日报 [Jiangxi Daily], December 13, 1959.

Zheng, Zhuyuan. *Scientific and Engineering Manpower in Communist China, 1949–1963*. Washington, DC: U.S. National Science Foundation, 1965.

Zhejiang sheng tongji ju, ed. 浙江省统计局 [Zhejiang Statistical Bureau]. *Zhejiang sheng wushinian tongji ziliao huibian* 浙江省五十年统计资料汇编 [Statistical Materials Compilation of Zhejiang in the Past Fifty Years]. Beijing: China Statistics Press, 2000.

Zhi, Jian. "Gonggu he fazhan shangshanxiaxiang de chengguo" 巩固和发展上山下乡的成果 [Consolidate and develop the effectiveness of up to the mountains and down to the countryside]. *Red Flag* 红旗 [Hongqi], no. 7 (July 1, 1975): 6–9.

"Zhonggong zhongyang guanyu zai nongcun jianli renmin gongshe wenti de jueyi (1958nian 8yue 29ri)" 中共中央关于在农村建立人民公社问题的决议 [CPC Central Committee's Resolution on the Establishment of People's Communes in Rural Areas (August 29, 1958)]. In *Jianguo yilai zhongyao wenxian xuanbian, vol. 11* 建国以来重要文献汇编 [Selected Important Documents since the Founding of the People's Republic of China]. Beijing: Zhongyang wenxian chubanshe, 1997.

Zhong, Gu. "Ping shuihu de touxiang zhuyi luxian" [Discussions About the Capitulationism Courses in *The Water Margin*]. *Red Flag* 红旗 [Hongqi], no. 9 (1975): 18–25.

Zhonggong zhongyang wenxian yanjiu shi 中共中央文献研究室 [Central Chinese Communist Party Literature Research Office]. *Deng Xiaoping nianpu (1975–1997)*

邓小平年谱 (1975-1997) [A Chronology of Deng Xiaoping, (1975-1997)]. Beijing: Zhongyang wenxian chubanshe, 2004.

Zhongguo guojia tongjiju 中国国家统计局 [State Statistical Bureau]. *Zhongguo tongji nianjian* 中国统计年鉴 [Statistical Yearbook of China]. Beijing: Zhongguo tongji chubanshe, 1992.

——. *Zhongguo tongji nianjian* 中国统计年鉴 [Statistical Yearbook of China]. Beijing: Zhongguo tongji chubanshe, 1994.

——. Chinese Population Census 2000. Accessed December 16, 2016.

Zhongguo jiaoyu bu jihua caiwu si, ed. 中华人民共和国教育部计划财务司 [China's Ministry of Education, Planning and Finance Division]. *Zhongguo jiaoyu chengjiu tongji ziliao 1949-1983* 中国教育成就: 统计资料 1949-1983 [Achievement of Education in China, 1949-1983]. Beijing: Renmin jiaoyu chubanshe, 1984.

Zhongguo qingnian bao 中国青年报 [China Youth Daily], September 8, 1964. In *Joint Publications Research Service* (JPRS) no. 27303 (November 10, 1964).

Zhongguo shehui kexuyuan jingji yanjiusuo [Economics Institute of the Chinese Academy of Social Science]. *Xue Muqiao gongzuo biji, xiace* (1963-1982) [Xue Muqiao's Work Notes (1963-1982)], internal materials, 416-18.

Zhou, Kate Xiao. *How the Farmers Changed China: Power of the People*. Boulder, CO: Westview Press, 1996.

Zhou, Qiren. "Shencai feiyang Du Ruizhi" [The Ebullient Du Ruizhi]. *The Economic Observer*, March 18, 2013. http://www.eeo.com.cn/2013/0318/241351.shtml.

Zuo, Xiaoqin. *National Conference on Learning from Dazhai in Agriculture*. Voice of China. Accessed December 6, 2016. http://bbs.voc.com.cn/archiver/tid-2754371.html.

Zuo, Xiaoqin. *Deng Xiaoping at 1975 Dazhai Conference*. Voice of China. Accessed December 6, 2016. http://bbs.voc.com.cn/archiver/tid-2754371.html.

Zuo, Xiaoqin. *Hua Guofeng and Chen Yonggui at 1975 Dazhai Conference*. Voice of China. Accessed December 6, 2016. http://bbs.voc.com.cn/archiver/tid-2754371.html.

Zweig, David. *Agrarian Radicalism in China, 1968-1981*. Cambridge, MA: Harvard University Press, 1989.

INDEX

Page numbers in italics refer to figures and tables.